Development of Antisocial and Prosocial Behavior
Research, Theories, and Issues

D1545848

DEVELOPMENTAL PSYCHOLOGY SERIES

SERIES EDITOR
Harry Beilin

Developmental Psychology Program
City University of New York Graduate School
New York, New York

A complete list of titles in this series is available from the publisher.

Development of
Antisocial and Prosocial Behavior
Research, Theories, and Issues

Edited by

Dan Olweus
Department of Personality Psychology
University of Bergen
Bergen, Norway

Jack Block
Department of Psychology
University of California
Berkeley, California

Marian Radke-Yarrow
Laboratory of Developmental Psychology
National Institute of Mental Health
Bethesda, Maryland

1986

ACADEMIC PRESS, INC.
Harcourt Brace Jovanovich, Publishers

Orlando   San Diego   New York   Austin
London   Montreal   Sydney   Tokyo   Toronto

ACADEMIC PRESS, INC.
Orlando, Florida 32887

United Kingdom Edition published by
ACADEMIC PRESS INC. (LONDON) LTD.
24–28 Oval Road, London NW1 7DX

LIBRARY OF CONGRESS CATALOGING-IN-PUBLICATION DATA

Main entry under title:

Development of antisocial and prosocial behavior.

    Based on a conference on the development of
antisocial and prosocial behavior, held at Voss,
Norway, 7/4–10/82.
    Includes index.
    1. Deviant behavior—Congresses.   2. Social
adjustment—Congresses.   3. Aggressiveness (Psychology)
—Congresses.   4. Criminal behavior—Congresses.
I. Olweus, Dan, Date   II. Block, Jack, Date
III. Radke-Yarrow, Marian, Date
HM291.D4815   1985   302.5'42   85-9083
ISBN 0-12-525880-1 (alk. paper)
ISBN 0-12-525881-X (paperback)

PRINTED IN THE UNITED STATES OF AMERICA

86 87 88 89   9 8 7 6 5 4 3 2 1

Contents

PART IV

SOCIALIZATION IN THE FAMILY, CHILDHOOD GROUPS, AND SOCIETY

Contributors

Numbers in parentheses indicate the pages on which the authors' contributions begin.

Jack Block (1, 177), Department of Psychology, University of California, Berkeley, California 94720

Beverley D. Cairns (315), Department of Psychology, University of North Carolina at Chapel Hill, Chapel Hill, North Carolina 27514

Robert B. Cairns (315), Department of Psychology, University of North Carolina at Chapel Hill, Chapel Hill, North Carolina 27514

Gena N. Emery (75), Department of Psychology, University of North Carolina at Chapel Hill, Chapel Hill, North Carolina 27514

Leonard D. Eron (285), Department of Psychology, University of Illinois, Chicago, Illinois 60680

David P. Farrington (359), Institute of Criminology, University of Cambridge, Cambridge CB3 9DT, England

William Gabrielli Jr.[1] (33), Department of Psychiatry, University of Kansas Medical Center, Kansas City, Kansas 66103

Per F. Gjerde (177), Department of Psychology, University of California, Berkeley, California 94720

Dale F. Hay (97), State University of New York at Stony Brook, Stony Brook, New York 11794

Robert A. Hinde (13, 127), MRC Unit on the Development and Integration of Behaviour, Madingley, Cambridge CB3 8AA, England

L. Rowell Huesmann (285), Department of Psychology, University of Illinois, Chicago, Illinois 60680

Barry Hutchings (33), Institute of Clinical Psychology, University of Copenhagen, Copenhagen, Denmark

---

[1] Present address: Department of Psychiatry, University of Kansas College of Health Sciences and Hospital, Kansas City, Kansas 66103.

Eleanor E. Maccoby (263), Department of Psychology, Stanford University, Stanford, California 94305

Joan McCord (343), Drexel University, Philadelphia, Pennsylvania 19104

Sarnoff A. Mednick (33), Social Science Research Institute, University of Southern California, Los Angeles, California 90089-1111

Terrie Moffitt[2] (33), Social Science Research Institute, University of Southern California, Los Angeles, California 90089-1111

Dan Olweus (1, 51), University of Bergen, Department of Personality Psychology, N-5000 Bergen, Norway

G. R. Patterson (235), Oregon Social Learning Center, Eugene, Oregon 97401

Lea Pulkkinen (149), Department of Psychology, University of Jyvaskyla, 40100 Jyvaskyla 10, Finland

Marian Radke-Yarrow (1, 207), Laboratory of Developmental Psychology, National Institute of Mental Health, Bethesda, Maryland 20205

Harriet L. Rheingold (75), Department of Psychology, University of North Carolina at Chapel Hill, Chapel Hill, North Carolina 27514

John E. Richters (97), Department of Psychology, State University of New York at Stony Brook, Stony Brook, New York 11794

Lee N. Robins (385), Department of Psychiatry, Washington University, School of Medicine, St. Louis, Missouri 63110

Anne E. Simpson (127), Medical Research Council, MRC Unit on the Development and Integration of Behaviour, Cambridge University, Madingley, Cambridge CB3 8AA, England

Joan Stevenson-Hinde (127), Medical Research Council, MRC Unit on the Development and Integration of Behaviour, Cambridge University, Madingley, Cambridge CB3 8AA, England

Everett Waters (97), Department of Psychology, State University of New York at Stony Brook, Stony Brook, New York 11794

Carolyn Zahn-Waxler (207), Laboratory of Developmental Psychology, National Institute of Mental Health, Bethesda, Maryland 20205

[2] Present address: Health and Development Research Unit, Medical School, Dunedin, New Zealand.

Acknowledgments

This book is based on a conference on the Development of Antisocial and Prosocial Behavior, held at Voss, Norway, July 4–10, 1982. We want to express our thanks to the Swedish Tercentenary Fund and the Norwegian Research Council for Social Science and the Humanities (NAVF) for the grants that made the conference possible.

We are also grateful to Irene Kashani, who contributed in many ways to the preparation and carrying through of the conference.

1

Introduction

DAN OLWEUS, JACK BLOCK, and MARIAN RADKE-YARROW

Antisocial and prosocial behaviors have been, and continue to be, insistent issues in the sciences of human behavior. Conceptually they are very much opposites and very much one in the sense of representing the "moral" behavioral domains. In this book we examine their many sides in ways that allow us to understand their development and their coexistence in human personality.

There is an immodesty in the title of this book. It poses the problem of human nature, the good and the bad, and appears to span discourse from philosophy to biology. The objective is much more confined, of course. With each generation of scientists, there are renewed and new efforts to better understand the characteristics of antisocial and prosocial behaviors, their etiologies, how they are maintained, and how they change in the life course of the individual. The aim of this book is to capture some of the current work and thinking about these issues. What are some of the present perspectives? Do they represent basic changes? And, how do research findings in the two domains relate to one another?

The study of antisocial behavior has a lineage dating back a long time in empirical research in psychology and sociology; prosocial behavior, on the other hand, has a much shorter history. The antisocial problems of human behavior have dominated research. The prosocial systems and the attachments or social bonds among individuals remain less thoroughly studied. Moreover, research in the two domains has proceeded differently and separately. The literature on antisocial behavior, particularly its exemplar, aggression, extends throughout the repertoire of research strategies and methods in behavioral science. Surveys, case studies, institutional public records, epidemiological designs, family studies, peer studies, longitudinal research, intervention studies, laboratory experiments—all of these have been used extensively. In contrast, the investigation of prosocial behavior has been much more limited; laboratory experiments, some naturalistic observations, and interviews have been the main research avenues. Longitudinal data are virtually nonexistent, although a few retrospective case histories provide accounts of individual continuities. There are no population statistics on prosocial behaviors. Research on antisocial behavior has not encountered arguments as to the authenticity or identity of the concepts; prosocial behavior, especially if conceived of as altruism, has.

Before we proceed further to bring into focus the themes that are dealt with in this book, the concepts of antisocial and prosocial behavior deserve some examination. Many kinds of actions are subsumed under each label. *Antisocial behavior* can be viewed as a violation of a formal or informal social rule, including serious criminal acts or flagrant disregard for conventional standards of approved behavior, as well as more private and momentary oppositional and hurtful acts. If we proceed to inventory specific kinds of acts that are antisocial, we become caught in an endless and fruitless catalogue that is of little help scientifically. For specific research purposes, one always sets up criteria relevant to the populations and questions under study.

Much the same can be said regarding *prosocial behavior*. Under this rubric, too, fall quite diverse behaviors; the concept is more vague than the concept of antisocial. It is generally reserved for a band of behaviors narrower than all positive social acts. Sociability, for example, would not seem to fall within the boundaries; friendliness might or might not. Simply *not* aggressing or not fighting certainly does not qualify as prosocial behavior. A core of the concept is the idea of benefiting another by helping, providing, or improving the lot of another. The forms of benefit, like the forms of violation, vary on many dimensions. Again, it is wise to resist compiling an index.

We have described prosocial and antisocial behaviors in terms of acts; however, inquiry often focuses on the intentions of the individual, or on the personality or character of individual children, such as the acting-out child, the hostile–aggressive youth, the altruistic, and so on, with the implicit assumption of generality or consistency within the person's behavior. The research reported in this book has utilized these varied objectives and approaches in the investigation of antisocial and prosocial behaviors.

ORGANIZATION OF THE BOOK

Development is the organizing framework for the essays in this book. They deal with the following broad themes: (1) biosocial approaches to antisocial and prosocial development; (2) early developmental patterns; (3) impulse control; (4) socialization in the family, childhood groups, and society; and (5) continuities into adulthood. These topics bring different emphases and perspectives to the study of antisocial and prosocial behavior. Dispositional factors of the individual and of the species, individual developmental courses, and social environmental influences on these behaviors are considered. The essays are not chapters in a text book in which each topic is comprehensively reviewed. Rather, they represent what the authors have "read into" the topics in terms of their own research and experience. The sampling reflects their individual interests and biases, and often their current activities. Conceptualizations, methods, and empirical findings receive variable emphasis.

BIOSOCIAL APPROACHES TO ANTISOCIAL AND PROSOCIAL BEHAVIOR

Robert Hinde's essay (Chapter 2) provides a kind of ground work for all of the following chapters. He discusses the development of human prosocial and antisocial behavior in the light of modern evolutionary theory, summarizing some essential acknowledgments and comparative data bearing on altruism, cooperation, and aggression. For instance, he shows that parent–offspring conflict is inevitable: In evolutionary terms the costs of parental care will outweigh the benefits to the parent before it is in the interests of the infant to become independent. Which of the parental styles is optimal will to some extent vary with circumstances. Functional considerations only permit some speculations about the determinants of behavior. Nevertheless, the biological viewpoint can be valuable to the developmental psychologist in that it considers the circumstances for which different styles of behavior could have been selected. As Hinde observes, however, a sociobiological perspective is more valuable for integrating diverse facts than for predicting behavior.

Authors Mednick, Moffitt, Gabrielli, and Hutchings (Chapter 3) deal with the possible role of genetic factors and genetic–environmental interactions in the development of deviant, criminal behavior. They base their conclusions on a large-scale adoption study, which comprises some 14,000 Danish adoptees. Their results suggest that individual differences in genetic endowment may have some impact on the development of antisocial behavior. Such effects are likely to be more marked in the case of relatively serious deviations, such as persistent criminal behavior.

These findings emphasize the importance of taking individual and sex-linked biological predispositions into account to achieve a fuller understanding of antisocial phenomena. It should be underscored, however, that the knowledge of genetic effects obtained so far has little specificity; which of the inherited mechanisms are involved in the predisposition toward criminality is still very much a matter for speculation.

Olweus (Chapter 4) discusses at a more specific level the relation between aspects of aggressive behavior and two biological variables, testosterone and adrenaline (epinephrine). His empirical analyses suggest that testosterone, or a closely related variable, may affect an adolescent male's readiness to respond vigorously and assertively to provocations and threats—producing a kind of defensive aggressiveness. With regard to adrenaline level, a fairly strong and inverse relation was obtained with aggressive behavior of a negative, destructive character. In the context of an elaborate model, an individual's level of adrenaline was interpreted as an indicator of cortical arousal, and some implications of this view for the development of aggressive behavior are discussed. Generally, these analyses, too, point to the importance of taking biological variables into account.

EARLY DEVELOPMENTAL PATTERNS

A subject of study by which the authors evidence their strong interest in prosocial dispositions is the early developmental patterns in the human child. This is in contrast, as we shall see, to other chapters dealing with subjects of older ages and questions of life-course development, wherein the authors' study of pervasive and socially deviant behavior is emphasized.

Rheingold and Emery's chapter (Chapter 5) focuses attention on the very young of the human species with an examination of the appearance of caregiving behaviors in $1\frac{1}{2}$- to $2\frac{1}{2}$-year-old children. Their data are observations of children in simple and standard circumstances that combine experimental and natural qualities. The authors make a case for "the overwhelmingly more common prosocial behaviors" of young children (as opposed to their aggressive and disturbed behaviors); they document the forms of child prosocial behaviors and discuss their emergence in terms of, and in relation to, the developmental acquisitions and processes of this age period.

Inquiry into origins and early patterns of prosocial and antisocial behavior leads inevitably to examination of the role of early experience. In the chapter by Waters, Hay, and Richters (Chapter 6), the infant–mother attachment relationship is the focus of such an examination. Their presentation of the major theoretical perspectives—ethology, psychoanalysis, and learning theory—concerning the child's early relationship provides context for their discussion of the research literature that links the quality of early attachment and later prosocial and antisocial behaviors of children. These findings are, in the authors' words, "data in search of explanation." Several models are offered to identify possible paths of influence that may explain the associations of various child behaviors with early attachment. Their discussion of theoretical issues and empirical data suggests an array of research undertakings that could contribute to an understanding of underlying processes.

The chapter by Stevenson-Hinde, Hinde, and Simpson (Chapter 7) is a serious search, conceptually and empirically, for an understanding of links between home influences and children's behavior in preschool. Simple direct effects are neither assumed nor sought. Rather, patterns of home variables are discussed in relation to children's immediate and sometimes temporary responses and their long-term predispositions. The variables include the child's own characteristics, which are seen as influencing, as well as being influenced by, relationships and events in the family. The authors stress the necessity of a conjunction of critical variables for the production of given behavioral outcomes.

IMPULSE CONTROL

Impulse control is a trans-age variable and core personality quality relevant to both prosocial and antisocial behavior. The Pulkkinen chapter (Chapter 8) brings together a diverse literature bearing on the many ways of conceptualizing impulse control and the many ways differences in impulse control are manifest in behavior. Psychoanalytic, trait, temperament, and cognitive approaches to impulse control in social development are considered. Pulkkinen then brings forward her own integrative theoretical approach, developed and refined over many years in a longitudinal study. She leaves the reader with a recognition of the complexities of the concept, and the ways it bears on prosocial and antisocial behavior. As she observes, both prosocial and antisocial behavior can be impulsive or deliberate.

Block and Gjerde (Chapter 9) attempt to demonstrate the value of delineating differences between the conceptually related constructs of undercontrol and antisocial behavior. Personality characteristics conceptually associated with antisocial behavior were specified by seven psychologists using the California Child Q-sort (CCQ) to describe independently a prototypically antisocial adolescent. Next, CCQ descriptions of adolescents in a longitudinal study were correlated with the prototype. The degree of congruence between an actual CCQ description and the prototype was used as an index of antisocial behavior. Undercontrol was operationalized similarly. The results support the utility of this methodology for establishing the discriminant validity of the two constructs. Numerous indices of substance use, adolescent self-image, and parental socialization discriminated between antisocial behavior and undercontrol. The findings should prove useful in furthering developmental understanding of these two domains.

SOCIALIZATION IN THE FAMILY, CHILDHOOD GROUPS, AND SOCIETY

This is an enormous and complex topic that lends itself to analyses at the level of the individual and family, as well as at the levels of events and culture. The predominant consideration in these chapters is how prosocial and antisocial behaviors are learned by the individual. The reader can carry into these discussions the perspectives of the preceding essays on biological, developmental, and dispositional contributors to the socialization processes.

The chapter by Radke-Yarrow and Zahn-Waxler (Chapter 10) is about familial influences on the development of children's prosocial behavior. Prosocial behavior has been narrowed for purposes of an integrative review of those behaviors that are positively responsive to the needs and welfare of others, that is, the humaneness of human behavior. The authors disabuse the reader of expectations of simple and direct links between familial variables and the child's prosocial development; they instead point to the multiple routes of development. In addition to integrating existing research evidence, the authors are critically evaluative regarding research questions and designs that have characterized this field of research, and they suggest other perspectives and strategies.

Patterson's chapter (Chapter 11) likewise deals in detail with processes in the family. It is assumed that factors that disrupt family management practices can set the stage for subtle changes in interactional patterns involving the "target" child and the caretaker. These disruptions in family management, in turn, permit a rapid increase in the rate, duration, and intensity of coercive exchanges between child and siblings. Irritable exchanges with siblings are thought to provide a major contribution to training the child how, when, where, and whom to hit. It is further assumed that this advanced training enhances the likelihood that the child will engage in physical fighting both within the home and in settings outside the home. The results based on correlational analyses of both normal and clinical samples are consistent with the idea that siblings make a contribution to fight training.

The perspective that Maccoby (Chapter 12) brings to children's prosocial and antisocial behavior comes from her long-standing interests and investigations concerning sex differences in the behavior of young children. She points out that the groups in which children play and participate, from an early age, are same-sex clusters. This segregation is likely to be partly determined by sex-linked differences in activity level, impulsivity, and similar characteristics. It is clearly documented that these social groupings are characteristically different in setting and content. Finally, Maccoby explores the implications of these sex-typed social groupings for aggressive and prosocial behaviors and makes a case for the contributions of peer group to both positive and negative individual behavior.

Socialization by television is examined by Eron and Huesmann (Chapter 13). From the abundant research literature and their own recent longitudinal study, they provide an integration of findings relevant to the issue of how television (TV) affects the antisocial and prosocial behavior of children. The emphasis in their analysis is on the boundary and mediating variables that influence the relation between TV and behavior. Among the variables discussed are age, sex, social class, viewing intensity, and psychological characteristics of the child. Psychological mechanisms that help explain how effects of TV viewing are produced include arousal, observational learning, norm-setting, and behavioral rehearsal. The authors conclude by suggesting that, in the case of aggressive behavior, the processes involved are bidirectional, especially for girls, with more aggressive children selecting more violent TV and TV violence increasing their aggression. Bidirectional effects have not been noted for prosocial behaviors.

CONTINUITIES INTO ADULTHOOD

This topic takes us to the studies in which individuals have been followed from points in childhood to adulthood. These ventures focus on antisocial beginnings and outcomes. To our knowledge, there has not been a comprehensive longitudinal study of prosocial dispositions.

The chapter by Cairns and Cairns (Chapter 14) is a methodological essay and analysis that, although not longitudinal, addresses issues of measurement and scaling relevant to findings and interpretations of consistency and continuity in behavior. These authors present a "develop-mental–interactional" analysis of continuities and changes in aggressive behavior of preadolescents. They elaborate a theoretical and a method-ological perspective, using their own studies as referents. They make use of multiple types of assessments of the child's aggression, each of which is interpreted as indexing meaningful facets of the aggression component in the children's evaluations of self and in their relationships with their peers. Gender differences in aggression are examined in detail and viewed developmentally.

Joan McCord (Chapter 15) presents results showing how the family in adolescence (and presumably in childhood) affects a male's probability of later committing serious crime. Information on 232 adolescent boys and their families was related to an independent classification of the subjects as criminals and noncriminals. The latter categorization was based on the individuals' court records for a period of approximately 30 years. The results show that a number of familial variables, such as degree of paren-tal conflict and hostility, maternal affection, and maternal permissiveness, to a considerable extent predict later criminality. These findings, com-bined with the results from several other studies in this area, attest to the pervasive and enduring effects of the family environment on antisocial development.

Farrington (Chapter 16) presents findings from a prospective, longitudi-nal study of 411 boys from a working class area of London. The boys were interviewed and tested a number of times from age 8 to 24, and data were also collected from their parents and teachers. In addition, conviction records were obtained for the boys from age 10–25. Farrington finds appreciable continuity in norm-breaking and criminal behavior from child-hood to young adulthood; the best predictors of convictions and self-reported delinquency at any age are convictions and self-reported delin-quency at an earlier age. Other independent predictors of delinquent and criminal behavior include family criminality, economic deprivation, poor parental child rearing, scholastic failure, and delinquent friends. Far-rington offers a tentative theory that is intrinsically psychological, stress-ing the importance of motivational factors and belief systems, but also sociological, recognizing the directing and constraining influence of the social context.

The Robins' chapter (Chapter 17) presents a focused effort to cast light on conduct discorders in girls and their long-term implications. Using interview data from an epidemiological catchment area study of mental health in the general population, Robins goes well beyond the established finding that boys manifest conduct disorders more frequently than girls. Her analyses suggest that conduct disorders have over the years increased in frequency in both boys and girls. Furthermore, her data reveal a major difference between the sexes with regard to the adult consequences of conduct disorder: For males, early conduct disorder predicts later antisocial tendencies; for females, early conduct disorder predicts antisocial tendencies, but also a variety of other pathological outcomes involving "internalizing" symptoms. Thus, when the adult outcome studied is general adjustment, rather than solely antisocial problems, the consequences of conduct disorders in girls can be seen to have as great implications (but broader in range) for adult behavior as has been observed in boys.

PART I

Biosocial Approaches to Antisocial and Prosocial Development

2

Some Implications of Evolutionary Theory and Comparative Data for the Study of Human Prosocial and Aggressive Behaviour

ROBERT A. HINDE

SELECTION AND BEHAVIOUR

Tits and chickadees have a repertoire of movements which enables them to peel bark off trees to find insects, open seeds, and so on. In searching for food they are attracted to white objects, and to places where other tits are feeding.

In Great Britain milk is usually left in bottles on the doorstep. The tits have learned to open the bottles and drink the milk. They are attracted to bottles when they see other tits near them and use the same movements to open the bottles as they use when feeding on natural objects. Casual observation suggests that, in some areas, milk may be an important addition to the diet of some individuals (Hinde & Fisher, 1951).

Tits also sometimes enter houses and use similar movements to tear wallpaper, peck lampshades, and so on, without apparently obtaining any benefits. Indeed entering houses is dangerous, and they are sometimes trapped indoors. Thus propensities useful in the natural context have given rise to a useful cultural habit of bottle opening and to a dysgenic one of tearing wallpaper (Logan Home, 1953; Hinde, 1953).

In this essay I discuss the ontogeny of prosocial and antisocial behaviour in humans in the light of modern evolutionary theory. I take the view that it does not make sense to search for evolutionary explanations of every human action any more than it makes sense to seek for the adaptive advantage to a bird of entering a house and tearing paper. However, a new perspective is added to the understanding of paper tearing and milk bottle opening if we see them as respectively useless and useful applications of propensities evolved for other contexts. In the same way, we can gain a new perspective on certain aspects of prosocial and antisocial behaviour if we reflect on the probable adaptiveness in other contexts of the propensities displayed.

Human behavioural propensities have been shaped by evolutionary forces. Like other species humans have a repertoire of species-characteristic behaviour: by their nature they respond to some stimulus situations more readily than to others, and they have predispositions to learn some things and are constrained from learning others (e.g., Hinde & Stevenson-Hinde, 1973; Seligman & Hager, 1972). At some point in the past, when living in an "environment of evolutionary adaptedness" (Bowlby, 1969), human behaviour became suited to the social and environmental conditions then prevailing. We do not know precisely what those conditions were, but they are generally presumed to have much in common with some of the remaining hunter–gatherer societies (Lee & De Vore, 1968). Since the behaviour and structure of every species form a coadapted complex, we can infer something about early humans' behaviour from our current structure. For instance, the sexual dimorphism in body size and build, considered against the background of comparable differences in other species, suggests a difference in fighting ability, with men competing for women. The large penis, breast development, and concealment of ovulation suggest that sex had a secondary nonreproductive function, presumably promoting continued association between individual men and women. Together, these facts suggest a serially polygynous mating system with some paternal investment in the offspring (Alexander & Noonan, 1979; Hinde, 1984; Short, 1979). Because the environment of humans has changed more rapidly than our behavioural propensities, we retain behavioural predispositions that may not precisely fit the desiderata of the modern world. However, the flexibility of human behaviour has enabled the species to flourish. This concept of an environment of evolutionary adaptedness, though admittedly loose, is heuristically valuable; its fertility is shown, for instance, by the manner in which the so-called "irrational fears of childhood" can be seen as an essential protection against the dangers that then prevailed (Bowlby, 1969).

In what follows, I generalize broadly about aggressive and antisocial behaviour on the one hand, and prosocial and altruistic behaviour on the other. In applying evolutionary principles to humans the paucity of the evidence does not yet justify finer distinctions (see though Lumsden & Wilson, 1981). Even so, a good deal of speculation of a type familiar to some sociobiologists is necessary; that the proposals about the adaptiveness of some aspects of human behaviour are only speculations should be borne constantly in mind. I also take it for granted that the ontogeny of prosocial and antisocial propensities is subject to influences both from within and from outside the family: while it is the responsibility of the other contributions to this volume to consider those influences in detail, I speculate about the manner in which they may have been shaped by evolutionary forces.

GROUP VERSUS INDIVIDUAL SELECTION

It is first necessary to summarize modern views on how natural selection acts. In the first place natural selection can operate only on genetically influenced differences in behaviour. This does not of course mean that the behaviour is genetically determined; the development of behaviour depends on long sequences of events into which environmental influences enter, and natural selection may, for instance, be concerned with a predisposition to learn one pattern of behaviour rather than another.

Darwin's theory of evolution by natural selection laid emphasis on individual success: those individuals most fitted to survive and reproduce are better represented in the next generation. However, some facts seem not to fit. How could selection for individual success give rise to the specialized worker and soldier castes of social insects when the individuals themselves are completely sterile? Why should a bird utter an alarm call if doing so increases its own vulnerability to the predator? Why should some sea birds refrain from breeding for one or more seasons after maturity?

A possible answer lay in some sort of group selection. The sterile workers and the bird's alarm call benefit other members of the species, so perhaps selection operates for the benefit of the group or species and not the individual. Perhaps some seabirds refrain from breeding to prevent the overfishing of food supplies. Such a view, advanced by some after careful appraisal of the evidence (Wynne Edwards, 1962) and merely implied by others as an off-the-cuff explanation of observed phenomena, has proved inadequate. Group selection is unlikely to be important in most circumstances, because its consequences would usually be susceptible to invasion by an individual who "cheated." For example, if most recently mature seabirds postponed their breeding, an individual who did not would be at an advantage (e.g., Lack, 1954, 1966; Maynard Smith, 1976b; Williams, 1966). Thus, it is now generally agreed that selection acts primarily, though not invariably (see e.g., D. S. Wilson, 1979), at the level of the individual.

KIN SELECTION: ALTRUISM AND COOPERATION

How then is the evolution of behaviour that benefits others at the expense of the individual concerned to be explained? In a seminal paper Hamilton (1964) pointed out that a genetic change disadvantageous to one individual might yet be selected for if it benefitted sufficiently others who were genetically closely related to it ("Kin selection"). In bees, wasps, and ants the males develop from unfertilized eggs and are therefore haploid, while the workers are diploid. If the queen mates only once, the workers will be more closely related to each other (on average they share 75% of their rare genes) than they would be to their own offspring (fertilised by a different male). Their genes are thus propagated better if they help the queen to rear their own sisters than they would be if they were to breed themselves. Such cases suggest an emphasis not on groups or even individuals seeking to perpetuate their genes, but on the genes themselves: Dawkins (1976) takes the view that the genes are the essential replicators, using the bodies of their hosts to perpetuate themselves.

Ants and bees are a long way from humans, and conclusions from them could be irrelevant to higher animals. However, Hamilton's ideas provide a possible explanation for many examples of apparently altruistic behaviour along the following lines. The individuals in any population are on the whole genetically similar to each other, but differ in certain relatively rare genes or gene combinations. On the average, parent, child, and full siblings share half their rare genes; grandparents and grandchildren (assuming no inbreeding) share one quarter; cousins (in a monogamous species) one eighth; and so on. A gene for altruistic behaviour will be selected if its costs to the possessor are less than half its benefit to a sibling, or one eighth its benefit to a cousin, and so on. For example, suppose a gene programmed an individual to sacrifice its life in circumstances that would save those of others. If the gene bearer died, one copy of that gene would disappear, but if the act saved the life of more than two offspring, two siblings, four grandchildren, or eight cousins, the gene would still increase in frequency in the population. Death is of course an extreme case, but the principle applies equally to acts that decrease the actor's chances of reproduction, but augment the chances of relatives. In general a gene for behaviour will be selected not just through the consequences of the behaviour for the individual showing it, but through the consequences of that behaviour for all other individuals carrying the gene.[1] Thus we should expect relatives to show prosocial behaviour to each other more than to unrelated individuals: considerable evidence from animals supports this view (e.g., Sherman, 1977).

RECIPROCAL ALTRUISM

However not all examples of apparent altruism are to be understood in terms of inclusive fitness. In some cases a good turn is worthwhile because it is likely to be reciprocated (Trivers, 1971). For example, a male baboon who helps another in an encounter with a third male may be helped by his former ally on a subsequent occasion (Packer, 1977).

Whilst this seems good sense in every day terms, it is not immediately obvious how cooperation could arise through natural selection acting on individuals. Consider a situation, occurring from time to time in the life of a species, in which an individual could behave either altruistically, incurring immediate costs itself but benefitting others who could later benefit it, or selfishly, gaining benefits itself at others' costs. If all individuals behaved altruistically, a mutation producing individuals who behaved selfishly would clearly be at a selective advantage. And if all individuals behaved selfishly, a mutation producing an altruist could never spread in the absence of kin selection, because the altruism would never be reciprocated. Selfish behaviour would thus seem to be "evolutionarily stable," that is, under the specified conditions a population of individuals using that strategy could not be invaded by a rare mutant using a different

---

[1] Hamilton thus referred to natural selection as maximising the "inclusive fitness" of the gene. Less accurately, the concept of inclusive fitness is often applied to individuals so that the older view that individuals are selected to behave in such a way that they maximize their individual fitness (measured in terms of their own survival and reproduction) is replaced by the view that they are selected to maximize their inclusive fitness (measured in terms of their own survival and reproduction and that of their relatives, though devalued in the latter case according to the degree of relatedness). Discussion in terms of the inclusive fitness of individuals is often a convenient shorthand, but can lead to confusion in quantitative studies.

strategy. However in a population in which individuals are likely to meet each other frequently and recognise each other as individuals, selfishness is not the only possible evolutionarily stable strategy (Trivers, 1974). Axelrod and Hamilton (1981), using a model based on the Prisoners' Dilemma, have shown that other options are possible, including especially the strategy of Tit for Tat, that is, of behaving cooperatively with an individual the first time you meet him or her, and then on subsequent encounters behaving as the other had done (cooperatively or selfishly) on the previous encounter. Such a strategy, they argue, is stable if individuals have a sufficiently large probability of meeting again after each encounter. Axelrod and Hamilton meet the problem of how such a strategy could arise in the first instance by proposing that genes for cooperation first enter the population through kin selection. Thereafter, they suggest, selection will favour the use of correlates of relatedness to cue cooperative behaviour. One such cue could be simply the reciprocation of cooperation. In that way cooperation could be favoured with progressively less and less related individuals.

Two points about this analysis require comment. First, the model advanced by Axelrod and Hamilton involves behaving cooperatively at first encounter with another individual, and thus seems to be at odds with the suspiciousness of strangers shown by animals and humans. This particular model is perhaps more applicable to altruism in a very broad sense than to acts of prosocial behaviour. Second, any model involving reciprocation can apply only to situations in which the altruist has a high chance of meeting the recipient again. It is thus not immediately obvious how to explain the occurrence of human altruism to strangers who are unlikely to be met again. Even in that case, however, we can speculate about possible evolutionary explanations. One is that altruism was originally selected for in small groups in which every nonhostile individual encountered was likely both to be related and to be met again, so that selection limiting altruism on the basis of reencounter probability would not operate. Another possibility is that under certain circumstances it is advantageous to behave altruistically to strangers in case the opportunity for reciprocation should arise.

To summarize the considerations about prosocial behaviour, the evolutionary argument is that (1) selection operates to cause individuals to behave in ways that further the propagation of their own genes; and (2) it can nevertheless operate to provide individuals with a propensity to act to their own disadvantage provided either (a) the act promotes the survival of genes identical with their own that are currently residing in the bodies of relatives or (b) the act, though temporarily to their disadvantage, is likely later to bring reciprocation.

DIRECTION OF PROSOCIAL BEHAVIOUR

We have discussed two principles which together go a long way toward explaining how prosocial behaviour in animals is selected for—kin selection and reciprocal altruism. In nature, their effects may be closely interwoven. For example, studies of grooming behaviour in monkeys show that females tend to direct their grooming behaviour preferentially to near-kin, and an explanation in terms of kin selection seems plausible. However Cheney (1978) found that the dominance status of adult females groomed by adolescent baboons varies with the sex of the latter. Adolescent females groom primarily dominant females, whilst adolescent males groom primarily subordinate ones. Cheney explains this in terms of the appropriateness of the investment in each case. The young females will stay in the troop for life, so the dominant females may later prove powerful allies. The adolescent males, who will later emigrate from the troop and thus have little interest in forming very long-term relationships, groom the only females they are likely to be able to mount without interference from dominant males.

It is worth emphasizing that such explanations in terms of kin selection or reciprocal altruism refer only to the selective forces operating and say nothing about mechanism.

PARENTAL CARE AND PARENT–CHILD CONFLICT

Now we take it for granted that parents should, to some degree, sacrifice their own interests for the sake of their offspring. In biological terms, however, this is the most general case of kin selection. Since individuals obtain genes from each parent, the parent is securing the survival of his or her own genes by looking after the young.

However, in considering the effects of natural selection on parental care, we must consider the effects of parental care not only on the offspring to which it is directed, but also on the mother's subsequent reproductive potential (Trivers, 1972). The principle is illustrated in a simplified form in Figure 1.1. Consider a female cat rearing its first litter. The chances of survival of the kittens may be enhanced the later they are weaned. However the longer the first litter is suckled, the lower the chances of survival for the second litter. The point in the development of the first litter at which the mother's total reproductive success is greatest precedes the point at which the survival of the first litter is maximal (Bateson, 1981). Thus there will be a period in which it will be in the mother's interests to wean the first litter, and in the kittens' interests to continue to suckle.

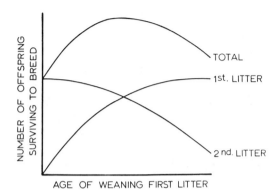

Figure 2.1. The effects of natural selection on parental care. The hypothetical numbers of offspring surviving to breed in the first and second litters of a cat are plotted against the time of weaning of the first litter.

More generally, the argument can be stated as follows. Each offspring carries only half the (rare) genes of each parent, so the parent should give benefits to the offspring only so long as the costs to himself or herself (in terms of the effect on his or her chances of survival and further reproduction) are less than half the benefit (similarly measured) to the offspring. More precisely, the parent will profit (in evolutionary terms) from giving parental care through the eventual reproductive success of the offspring, but incur costs through any reduction in the probable reproductive success of possible future offspring consequent upon investment in the current ones. (We may for brevity ignore effects on other related individuals). Benefit to the infant lies through increments to its own reproductive success, cost in decrements to the reproductive success of its (perhaps unborn) siblings. In the case of a mammalian litter of one, the infant may at first be absolutely dependent on its mother; the benefits to it may be large, but the costs to the mother small. However, as the infant grows, its milk consumption increases, and thus the costs to the mother also increase. At the same time it becomes increasingly able to fend for itself, and so the benefit it derives from maternal care decreases. If cost and benefit are measured in the same terms, the costs to the mother will come to exceed the benefit to the young. However, the infant will continue to benefit from maternal care in its own right, and the cost to the mother will affect its inclusive fitness only half as much as it affects the mother's, since only half their (rare) genes are shared. Thus the infant will continue to profit until the cost to the mother is more than twice the benefit to the infant. From the time when maternal costs and benefits are equal, until the costs become twice the benefits, maternal care will reduce the mother's inclusive fitness and enhance the infant's. During this period natural selection will favour the mother's halting maternal care and the infant's eliciting it (Trivers, 1972). It is apparent that the length of the intervening period will depend on a variety of factors, including the paternity of the mother's future offspring and the rates of change of cost and benefit to mother and infant. However, on all reasonable assumptions the infant must be selected to elicit more parental investment than the parent is selected to give.

Data on the mother–infant relationship in monkeys support this view. The rate at which the infant becomes independent of the mother seems at first sight to be determined by the infant's increasing physical capacities and exploratory tendencies, but analysis shows that it is controlled more by changes in the mother than by changes in the infant (Hinde, 1969, 1979). The weaning conflict is thus firmly based in the processes of evolution. In general, parents incur costs in benefitting their offspring, but only up to a point. Reflection suggests that many human mothers do likewise push the baby from breast to solid food, from cot to bed, or from home to school faster than the child, if allowed to decide for itself, would proceed.

If the difference between the interests of parent and offspring result in the parent rejecting the infant before it is otherwise ready to leave, natural selection will act to adapt infants to that situation. Thus, whilst infants may be adapted to get as much parental care as they reasonably can, their development may be optimal when they do not get as much as they would "like," or if their parents treat them as more mature than they actually are. Indeed, there is evidence that cognitive development depends in part on parents treating children as if their capacities slightly exceeded those currently developed (Bruner, 1978). In modern society with planned families, extended maternal protection of one infant may have no effect on the mother's prospects for rearing more, but unlimited maternal solicitude can have effects that we should consider as detrimental on the child. Biological considerations emphasize the importance both of parental sensitivity and of parental encouragement of independence.

ALTERNATIVE STRATEGIES

At this point it is necessary to emphasize that the parental, filial, aggressive, and other types of behaviour of a species do not consist of set sequences of response, but of behaviour that is variable within wide limits to meet the requirements of the situations in which individuals find themselves. Consider the familiar dominance hierarchy. It is usually best to be at the top, because this brings better access to food, mates, and other resources. But animals that find themselves to be subordinate do not spend all their time striving to be at the top in the face of impossible odds. Instead they bide their time, awaiting their opportunity, and in the meanwhile avoid provoking their superiors. Individuals are constructed so that they will strive to be or remain dominant given one set of circumstances, but will behave as subordinates, or in some intermediate manner, in another (Lack, 1954, 1966). Such issues are often referred to as *conditional strategies,* though there is no necessary implication that they are to be thought of as abstract plans or indeed as discreet entities.

IS THERE A BEST MATERNAL STYLE?

A similar issue arises with regard to maternal styles, because mothers must adapt their behaviour to circumstances. Thus Altmann (1980) has contrasted "restrictive" with "laissez-faire" baboon mothers: *restrictive mothering* protects babies from accidents, predation, and kidnapping in their early months, but leads to slower independence, and thus to infants less able to survive if orphaned, than *laissez-faire mothering.* The relative merits of these strategies might change with the dominance status of the mother: the infants of high-status females are less susceptible to mishap, so for them restrictive mothering might be less important than for low-status mothers, and the balance could swing in the direction of laissez-faire. The parental style optimal for the survival of the infant thus varies with the mother's social status.

Furthermore, we have just seen that the parents' interests may not be the same as those of the infant: in attempting to specify an optimal maternal style, we should have to specify whether it was optimal for mother, for infant, or for the dyad. In general, the behaviour that is optimal for either party varies with many factors, including the sex of the infant, its ordinal position in the family, the mother's social status, the state of physical resources, caregiving contributions from other family members, and so on.

Consider another example. In general, the variance in reproductive success of males is higher than that of females. Thus a female whose offspring were likely to have high reproductive success would have more descendents in the second generation if she had mostly male offspring, but a female whose offspring were likely to be of poor quality might do better to make sure of having a few descendents by having mostly female (Alexander, 1974; Trivers & Willard, 1973). Some evidence in favour of this view is found from studies of female infanticide in human societies

(Dickemann, 1979). However, such considerations depend on assumptions about the social structure: for instance, if males emigrate but daughters remain, acquiring and/or augmenting the mother's status and thus augmenting their mutual reproductive success, a mother's investment might have less influence on the reproductive success of sons than on that of daughters. This may occur in monkeys (Altmann, 1980; Simpson & Simpson, 1982).

Differences in the linkage of maternal effort to reproductive success between sons and daughters might underlie a whole host of differences in the relationships between mother–son and mother–daughter relationships. Furthermore, insofar as reproductive success depends on different behavioural characteristics in males and females, one must expect parents to behave differently to sons and to daughters, and to encourage different traits within them. For instance, mothers should encourage aggressive behaviour more in sons than in daughters.

The biologist, judging success in terms of reproductive fitness, would thus expect parents to adjust their style according to a host of conditions in ways that have been shaped by natural selection. But two limitations of the biologists' position must be made clear. First, their analysis concerns breeding success or inclusive fitness, whilst the desiderata of the man-in-the-street, the psychologist, and the psychiatrist are much more likely to concern the happiness, adjustment, and intelligence of the child, with perhaps some reference to the child's capacity to adhere to cultural norms. The sociobiologist might argue that, in our environment of evolutionary adaptedness, all these goals would have been reached in the same way. Clearly, this is not true today; in our society happiness and reproductive success are not necessarily to be equated. Thus the style most acceptable to the evolutionary biologist is not necessarily that we would most want to encourage.

Second, a biological view is not necessarily a wholly biologically deterministic one. Parents may be predisposed to behave in ways that favour perpetuation of their genes, but whether they necessarily follow their predispositions is another matter. Many human parents, and even more human nonparents, clearly do not.

However, these two points only partially lessen the impact of the biological considerations. If we wish to understand the factors that determine parental style, or the further problem of how parental style affects the individual characteristics of the offspring, it would surely be helpful to understand the sort of selective forces that have shaped the susceptibility of parental style to environmental or experiential factors, and the responsiveness of offspring to different parental styles.

SOME SOCIOBIOLOGICAL SPECULATIONS

The developmental psychologist thus has at least two sets of questions for the sociobiologist. First, in what sort of circumstances would natural selection have put a premium on this or that parental style? And second, what behavioural characteristics would it be advantageous for the young to develop, given the parents and other circumstances with which it finds itself? In general, it is easier for the sociobiologist to argue post hoc that a given response pattern is optimal than it is to predict in advance which would be best, but speculation is possible.

With regard to maternal styles, we might suspect that parents would be ready to promote the independence of a first-born so that they could concentrate their energies on the greater needs of a younger baby. We would expect them to invest most in a child who they saw as a last born. We might expect maternal rejection to be favoured by limitations of resources that made it difficult for the mother to sustain herself and her infant; but we might expect her to be the more willing to drain her own resources to save her infant, the smaller her own further reproductive expectations. However, if the infant were advanced toward independence, an increase in maternal vulnerability might make further promotion of that independence even more evolutionarily desirable. We might expect the mother to favour sons or daughters according to her circumstances as stated above. Such speculations do not take us far beyond what we already know, but perhaps suggest a framework which integrates otherwise isolated facts.

Turning to the effects of selective forces acting on the infant, these would operate in the first place to make the infant cope as best it could with the sort of mother it found itself to have. An interesting example is provided by the behaviour of babies in the Ainsworth "Strange situation" (see Ainsworth, Blehar, Waters, & Wall, 1978). The Strange situation is a technique for assessing the nature of the mother–child relationship in a laboratory playroom by a series of episodes, in some of which the mother temporarily leaves the room. When she returns, many children go to her immediately, and then continue with their play or exploration, using her as a secure base. However some children avoid their mothers on reunion, looking away and making no attempt to achieve close contact. The mothers of such children tend to be restricted in their emotional expression. Faced with a nonwelcoming mother on reunion, we might have expected exaggerated attempts to gain the mother's attention, for avoidance seems maladaptive. However, in a penetrating analysis, Main (1981) has suggested that the "avoidant infants" are behaving in a more subtle way: by not challenging the potentially rejecting mother they are managing to maintain proximity to her, averting the behavioural disorganisation that could follow outright rejection.

In the longer term, we might expect natural selection to have shaped offspring to use parental styles as cues to the environmental conditions they will have to face in their turn. For example, if maternal rejection is induced by a competitive social situation, those of her offspring who develop aggressive, nonaltruistic temperaments may do better than those who do not. On the other hand, infants brought up in an equable sociable environment might do better to develop propensities for reciprocal altruism and cooperation. In a very general sense, the modelling of one's parent's example could be the behaviour selected for.

Now it is known that reasonable maturity demands by the parent seem to promote prosocial tendencies in children (Baumrind, 1971). Whilst such a finding should be interpreted with caution by sociobiologists, for maturity is to some extent relative to cultural norms, it is compatible with the views that, in our environment of evolutionary adaptedness, prosocial behaviour was selected for and that infants are adapted to having their independence promoted by their mothers (see above). (Nothing that is said here so far should be taken as implying that propensities toward prosocial or antisocial behaviour depend solely on family influences. Similar considerations apply to the peer group, which we return to shortly).

Finally, does this perspective enable us to predict how individuals will direct their social behaviour? Clearly the kin-selection hypothesis would lead us to expect prosocial behaviour to be directed especially toward kin and could provide a basis for some examples of family loyalty. Other factors likely to promote prosocial behaviour (as discussed by Mussen & Eisenberg-Berg, 1977) are understandable in terms of reciprocal altruism. For instance, individuals are more likely to behave altruistically to particular individuals than to abstract classes of individuals (e.g., old people), to known individuals rather than strangers, to liked individuals (especially to others known to show prosocial behaviour often) rather than to disliked individuals, and to others seen as competent rather than their less competent peers.

It is less clear why individuals should be prone to show prosocial behaviour to others seen as victims of circumstance, helpless, or dependent—though the sociobiologist could no doubt produce an explanation in terms of the greater benefits conferred to such a recipient for given costs to the actor, or even by extending the principle of reciprocity to embrace the sentiment, "There but for the grace of god go I." And the finding that children may give less to generous friends than to those seen as less generous, if due to a view that there is no need to be generous to those who can already be counted on to provide benefits, illustrates the manner in which complexity of cognitive functioning produces behaviour which is explicable, but not predictable, in terms of functional considerations.

AGGRESSIVE BEHAVIOUR

We may now turn to aggressive and other antisocial behaviour. Within many species, competition for necessary resources is direct and involves aggressive encounters between individuals. These encounters may involve actual combat, but are often limited to an exchange of threat signals. Ethologists have shown that the threat signals can be interpreted as depending on conflicting tendencies to attack and flee from the rival, and are given when the two tendencies are more or less in balance (Baerends, 1975). In the course of evolution the postures have become elaborated or "ritualised" to make them effective as signals. At the same time, selection has modified the responsiveness of other individuals to the signals. The selection pressures on the actor and those on the reactor are of course distinct—the former promoting behaviour and structure in the actor that will influence the reactor's behaviour to the actor's advantage and the latter promoting responsiveness in the reactor to his own advantage (Blest, 1961; Caryl, 1979; Dawkins & Krebs, 1978). An individual who was definitely going either to attack or to flee would best do so quickly, without signalling his or her intentions; threatening occurs when the two tendencies are more or less in balance and the actor is perhaps uncertain of his or her next move, and/or that move depends in part on the behaviour of the reactor (Hinde, 1972, 1981). Threat can be seen as a process of negotiation with the rival about what to do next.

Now let us suppose that all individuals in a population used conventional threat signals, retreating from a context if there was any real danger. A new mutant who fought vigorously in every encounter would then clearly be at an advantage, because he or she would be likely to win every encounter. However if the mutant spread, vicious fighters would often meet vicious fighters. In such encounters someone would be liable to get hurt; if the gains of winning were less than the costs of losing (in terms of inclusive fitness, as discussed above), it might be better not to be a vicious fighter. Maynard Smith (i.e., Maynard Smith, 1976a; Maynard Smith & Price 1973) has shown that, given certain assumptions, a stable situation would arise when there were particular proportions of conventional and vicious fighters, or when each individual adopted each strategy for a particular proportion of the time. This is another example of an "evolutionarily stable state."

POSSIBLE APPLICATIONS TO HUMAN AGGRESSION

What relevance has this to agonistic behaviour in humans? In the first place, it has some relevance to the nature of threat. It suggests that the title of Darwin's (1872) book, *The Expression of the Emotions,* has led to a biassed emphasis in the study of threat signals (and indeed other expressive movements) (Hinde, 1985). Threat signals are to be seen not only as a (usually vague) expression of internal state, but also as part of a process of negotiation between two rivals in which the behaviour to be shown by one depends in part on the expected next response of the other. Thus, since it cannot be in the direct interests of a threatening individual to reveal his or her precise intentions, and since what he or she does depends in part on the rival, we must expect an individual's gestures and other signals to give an imprecise indication of what he or she will do next. Some looseness in the relation between signal and ensuing behaviour is present in birds (Stokes, 1962a, 1962b), more marked in apes (Lawick-Goodall, 1971; Menzel, 1971), and profound in humans (Ekman, 1981). This in turn suggests that if the relation between internal state and expressive movement is modified by learning, that modification may be situation specific—a view in keeping with Patterson's (1977) finding that modifying the aggressive behaviour of boys at home does not necessarily carry over to other situations. It also suggests that modification of the situation-specific relation between internal state and action is likely to involve processes different from those necessary for modifying the propensity to aggression itself.

In the longer term these considerations indicate that the advantages accruing to an individual from being a vicious fighter depend both on the benefits of winning encounters (and thus on the scarcity of the resources over which the encounters take place) and on the costs of engaging in them—benefits and costs being reckoned ultimately in evolutionary terms. The benefits will vary between individuals and between classes of individuals. One issue here concerns the differences between the sexes. As we saw earlier, human sex differences, interpreted in the light of comparative data on other species, suggest that in our environment of evolutionary adaptedness males competed for females (see Short, 1979). Selection would then have enhanced aggressiveness in males more than in females. (This in itself says nothing about the way in which this would come about: for instance, selection could operate to make males inherently more aggressive than females, or to make parents encourage aggressiveness in boys more than in girls, or both, or in some other manner.)

Considerations of costs and benefits (in either evolutionary or more immediate terms) should also warn us against expecting any simple relations between exposure, either at home or in the peer group, to aggression in development and aggressiveness in adulthood, for the costs and benefits of aggressiveness vary with the probability of meeting other aggressive individuals and with the scarcity of resources. In a population containing few vicious fighters and plentiful resources the advantages to individuals of cooperating in group living may detract from the advantages of being an egotistical vicious fighter. In a population containing a moderate number of vicious fighters and in which resources are scarce, it may be necessary to be a vicious fighter or succumb. But if nearly everyone is a vicious fighter, so that the costs of encounters are certain to be great, it may be better to contract out and seek another means of access to the resources. These speculations about crude caracatures of "cooperators" and "vicious fighters" must not of course be taken too seriously, but they do sound a warning against expectations of simple monotonic relations between childhood experiences and later characteristics.

RECIPROCALLY ALTRUISTIC AGGRESSION

So far the functional determinants of aggression and prosocial behaviour have been discussed as though they were separate issues. However, the issues merge in the study of aiding and coalitions in aggressive interactions. It is now well established that many aggressive interactions in monkeys are triadic, with one individual aiding another against a third. In the complexly structured society of female macaques, such interactions appear to be largely explicable in terms of kin selection (see Datta, 1981). In other cases, as amongst male baboons, one male may aid another to obtain a desired resource (e.g., an oestrous female) and subsequently receive aid reciprocally (Packer, 1977).

CULTURAL DIFFERENCES

A final issue concerns the great cultural differences existing in the human case. This affects these arguments in a number of ways. First, parents feel obligated to try to create parent–child relationships of a type regarded as desirable in their particular culture, and also have expectations with regard to this and to their relationships with each other and with outsiders. Such obligations and expectations may conflict, so that neither are fully realised. This may have repercussions on the offspring.

Second, differences in mothering styles may be related to cultural desiderata for the personality of offspring on the one hand and for other aspects of parental life style on the other (e.g., Mead, 1935; Whiting & Whiting, 1975). How far these desiderata are related to the inclusive fitness of individuals is a further issue. Some biologists argue that the cultural differences are "generated and shaped by biological imperatives while biological traits are simultaneously altered by genetic evolution in response to cultural innovation" (Lumsden & Wilson, 1981). For example, to return to the tits and milk bottles, not only is the development of the habit consequent upon genetically influenced species–characteristic patterns, but it is at least possible that the success of the habit is resulting in selection that will further predispose individuals to develop it. Or, in a small human group, each individual may be better off if all individuals are predisposed to act prosocially rather than antisocially. Social constraints on antisocial behaviour are thus likely to arise, and these social constraints could come (or have come) to have a genetic basis. However, whilst some cultural differences, such as the low priority set on salt by Australian aborigines in comparison with other cultures, can apparently be related to physiological differences (e.g., the low salt content of their perspiration), it must be acknowledged that there is as yet little hard evidence for genetic bases for cultural differences.

Third, just as the tits' propensities to tear loose bark can lead them into dangerous cultural practices, human culture may place a premium on propensities—selfish egoism, self-sacrifice, cooperativeness, aggressiveness—that, in our original environment of evolutionary adaptedness, were in the appropriate circumstances conducive to inclusive fitness, but are so no longer. Culture produces celibate priests and barren heroines.

CONCLUSION

Two points relevant to the conduct of studies of the development of prosocial and antisocial behaviour in children are worth making. Whilst both are implicit in some recent studies in the child development literature, they receive additional emphasis from these evolutionary considerations. First, the circumstances in which it is adaptive to show, or to develop a propensity for, prosocial behaviour are not necessarily the opposite to those for aggression. Natural selection is likely to have shaped individuals' development so that the two have different, and not merely complementary, determinants. Thus studies of factors that promote prosocial behaviour could lead us to different conclusions about social desiderata from studies of factors that minimize antisocial behaviour. It would seem to be wise to conduct at least some studies concerned simultaneously with both. Second, natural selection will operate not (or not only) to affect behavioural propensities, but to affect the expression of those propensities towards particular individuals. It may pay to be kind to A but not to B, to be hostile to X but not Y. This suggests that studies of supposedly global propensities may be misleading: the children who show hostile behaviour to peers may not do so to teachers, and children behave differently to friends from the way in which they behave to other peers (Hinde, Easton, Meller & Tamplin, 1983). Thus it may be wise, in studies of prosocial and antisocial behaviour, to specify the nature of the target.

Finally, I would not want to leave the impression that sociobiology, at the present stage in its development, has a very great deal to offer the developmental psychologist. The message, I suggest, is that reflection on the circumstances in which various kinds of prosocial or antisocial behaviour might have augmented individuals' reproductive success may help us to understand why (in a functional sense) they are accentuated more in some individuals and societies than in others, and why some parents and cultures create situations in which they are augmented more than do others. Such considerations also provide a conceptual framework for linking apparently independent facts about human behaviour, and perhaps also for linking apparently independent areas of human knowledge. They are less valuable for prediction.

ACKNOWLEDGMENTS

I am grateful to Drs. P. Bateson and Joan Stevenson-Hinde for their comments on the manuscript. The work was supported by the Royal Society and the Medical Research Council.

REFERENCES

Ainsworth, M. D. S., Blehar, M. C., Waters, E., & Wall, S. *Patterns of attachment*. Hillsdale, NJ: Erlbaum, 1978.
Alexander, R. D. The evolution of social behavior. *Annual Review of Ecology and Systematics*, 1974, *5*, 325–383.
Alexander, R. D., & Noonan, K. M. Concealment of ovulation, parental care and human social evolution. In N. A. Chagnon & W. Irons (Eds.), *Evolutionary biology and human social behaviour: an anthropoligical perspective*. North Scituate, MA: Duxbury Press, 1979.
Altmann, J. *Baboon mothers and infants*. Cambridge, MA: Harvard University Press, 1980.
Axelrod, R., & Hamilton, W. D. The evolution of cooperation. *Science*, 1981, *211*, 1390–1396.
Baerends, G. P. An evaluation of the conflict hypothesis as an explanatory principle for the evolution of displays. In G. P. Baerends, C. Beer & A. Manning (Eds.), *Function and evolution in behaviour*. Oxford: Oxford University Press, 1975.
Bateson, P. Discontinuties in development and changes in the organization of play in cats. In

K. Immelmann, G. W. Barlow, L. Petrinovich & M. Main (Eds.), *Behavioral development*. The Bielefeld Interdisciplinary Project. Cambridge: Cambridge University Press, 1981.

Baumrind, D. Current patterns of parental authority. *Developmental Psychology Monographs,* 1971, *1,* 1–103.

Blest, A. D. The concept of ritualization. In W. H. Thorpe & O. L. Zangwill (Eds.), *Current problems in animal behaviour.* Cambridge: Cambridge University Press, 1961.

Bowlby, J. Attachment and loss (Vol. 1 Attachment). London: Hogarth, 1969.

Bruner, J. Learning how to do things with words. In J. S. Bruner & A. Gartlan (Eds.), *Human growth and development.* Oxford: Clarendon Press, 1978.

Caryl, P. G. Communication by agonisitic displays: What can games theory contribute to ethology? *Behaviour,* 1979, *68,* 136–169.

Cheney, D. Interactions of immature male and female baboons with adult females. *Animal Behaviour,* 1978, *26,* 389–408.

Darwin, C. *The expression of emotions in man and the animals.* London: Murray, 1872.

Datta, S. B. *Dynamics of dominance among free ranging rhesus females.* Ph.D. Thesis, Cambridge, 1981.

Dawkins, R. *The selfish gene.* Oxford: Oxford University Press, 1976.

Dawkins, R., & Krebs, J. R. Animal signals: Information or manipulation? In J. R. Krebs & N. B. Davies (Eds.), *Behavioural ecology: An evolutionary approach.* Oxford: Blackwell, 1978.

Dickemann, M. Female infanticide, reproductive strategies and social stratification: A preliminary model. In N. A. Chagnon & W. Irons (Eds.), *Evolutionary biology and human social behaviour: An anthropological perspective.* North Scituate, MA: Duxbury Press, 1979.

Ekman, P. Mistakes when deceiving. *Annals of the New York Academy of Sciences,* 1981, *364,* 269–278.

Hamilton, W. D. The genetical theory of social behaviour. *Journal of Theoretical Biology,* 1964, *7,* 1–52.

Hinde, R. A. A possible explanation of paper-tearing behaviour in birds. *British Birds,* 1953,*46,* 16–23.

Hinde, R. A. Analyzing the roles of the partners in a behavioral interaction: Mother-infant relations in rhesus macaques. *Annals of the New York Academy of Sciences,* 1969, *159,* 651–667.

Hinde, R. A. Social behavior and its development in subhuman primates. *Condon Lectures.* Eugene: Oregon Press, 1972.

Hinde, R. A. *Towards understanding relationships.* London: Academic Press, 1979.

Hinde, R. A. Animal signals: Ethological and games-theory approaches are not incompatible. *Animal Behaviour,* 1981, *29,* 535–542.

Hinde, R. A. Was 'The expression of emotions' a misleading phrase? *Animal Behaviour,* 1985. (in press)

Hinde, R. A., & Fisher, J. Further observations on the opening of milk bottles by birds. *British Birds,* 1951, *44,* 393–396.

Hinde, R. A., Easton, D. F., Meller, R. E., & Tamplin, A. Nature and determinants of preschoolers' differential behaviour to adults and peers. *British Journal of Developmental Psychology,* 1983, *1,* 3–19.

Hinde, R. A., & Stevenson-Hinde, J. *Constraints on Learning.* London: Academic Press, 1973.

Lack, D. *The natural regulation of animal numbers.* Oxford: Clarendon, 1954.

Lack, D. *Population studies of birds.* Oxford: Clarendon, 1966.

Lawick-Goodall, J. van. *In the shadow of man.* Boston: Houghton, Mifflin, 1971.

Lee, R. B., & De Vore, I. *Man the hunter.* Chicago: Aldine-Atherton, 1968.

Logan Home, W. M. Paper-tearing by birds. *British Birds,* 1953, *46,* 16–20.

Lumsden, C., & Wilson, E. O. *Genes, mind and culture: The co-evolutionary process.* Cambridge, MA: Harvard University Press, 1981.

Main, M. Avoidance in the service of attachment: A working paper. In K. Immelmann, G. W. Barlow, L. Petrinovich, & M. Main (Eds.), *Behavioral development.* The Bielefeld Interdisciplinary Project. Cambridge: Cambridge University Press, 1981.

Maynard Smith, J., & Price, G. R. The logic of animal conflict. *Nature,* 1973, *246,* 15–18.

Maynard Smith, J. Evolution and the theory of games. *American Scientist,* 1976, *64,* 41–45. (a)

Maynard Smith, J. Group selection. *Quarterly Review of Biology,* 1976 *51,* 277–283. (b)

Mead, M. *Sex and temperament in three primitive societies.* New York: William Morrow, 1935.

Menzel, E. W. Communication about the environment in a group of young chimpanzees. *Folia Primatology,* 1971, *15,* 220–232.

Mussen, P., & Eisenberg-Berg, N. *Roots of caring, sharing and helping.* San Francisco: Freeman, 1977.

Packer, C. Reciprocal altruism in Papio anubis. *Nature,* 1977, *265,* 441–442.

Patterson, G. R. A performance theory for coercive family interaction. In R. Cairns (Ed.), *Social interaction: Methods, analysis, and illustration.* Society for Research in Child Development-sponsored publication. Chicago: Chicago University Press, 1977.

Seligman, M. E. P., & Hager, J. L. *Biological boundaries of learning.* New York: Appleton-Century-Crofts, 1972.

Sherman, P. W. Nepotism and the evolution of alarm calls. *Science,* 1977, *197,* 1246–1253.

Short, R. Sexual selection and its component parts, somatic and genital In J. S. Rosenblatt, R. A. Hinde, C. Beer, & M-C. Busnel (Eds.), *Selection, as illustrated by man and the great apes: Advances in the Study of Behaviour,* (Vol. 9), 1979.

Simpson, A. E., & Simpson, M. J. A. Birth sex ratios and social rank in rhesus mothers. *Nature,* 1982. Vol. 300, No. 5891, 440–441.

Stokes, A. W. Agonistic behaviour among blue tits at a winter feeding station. *Behaviour,* 1962, *19,* 118–138. (a)

Stokes, A. W. The comparative ethology of great, blue, marsh and coal tits at a winter feeding station. *Behaviour,* 1962, *19,* 208–218. (b)

Trivers, R. L. The evolution of reciprocal altruism. *Quarterly Review of Biology,* 1971, *46,* 35–57.

Trivers, R. L. Parental investment and sexual selection. In B. Campbell (Ed.), *Sexual selection and the descent of man.* Chicago: Aldine, 1972.

Trivers, R. L. Parent–offspring conflict. *American Zoologist,* 1974, *14,* 249–264.

Trivers, R. L. & Willard, D. E. Natural selection of parental ability to vary the sex ratio of offspring. *Science,* 1973, *179,* 90–92.

Whiting, B. B., & Whiting, J. W. M. *Children of six cultures: A psychocultural analysis.* Cambridge, MA: Harvard University Press, 1975.

Williams, G. C. *Adaptation and natural selection.* New Jersey: Princeton University Press, 1966.

Wilson, D. S. *Natural selection of populations and communities.* Menlo Park, CA: Benjamin/Cummings, 1979.

Wynne Edwards, V. C. *Animal dispersion in relation to social behaviour.* Edinburgh: Oliver & Boyd, 1962.

3

Genetic Factors in Criminal Behavior: A Review*

SARNOFF A. MEDNICK, TERRIE MOFFITT,
WILLIAM | GABRIELLI, Jr., and BARRY HUTCHINGS

INTRODUCTION

All human behavioral characteristics are products of an interaction between life experiences and a conglomerate of genetic factors. It is not unusual to consider the effects of genes as limiting normal development, as in rare states such as Down's syndrome, phenylketonuria (PKU), or Huntington's disease, in which single genes directly determine whether the disease will appear. But even in these cases, the environment helps shape the behavioral symptoms and the course of the illness.

Genes and environment also interact to produce behaviors that are not symptoms of disease states. One example is the genetic coding for eye structure and central nervous system (CNS) processing interacting with nutrition and visual environmental stimulation, which enables normal visual perceptual behaviors to take place. In actuality, without genetic coding, no behavior at all would exist.

If other behaviors are partially genetically determined, it does not seem unreasonable to test the hypothesis that gene–environment interactions

* This research was supported by USPHS grant No. 31353 from the Center for Studies of Crime and Delinquency. We wish to thank Professor Daniel Glaser for the critical reading of this manuscript.

33

also might influence deviant behaviors. In this essay we review the evidence for a genetic component in the etiology of the deviant state that is most troublesome to civilized society: criminal offending. We review the research in the field and describe some recent findings from our laboratory.

In our research review we relate results of studies from three approaches to genetic investigation. The first, family studies, provide valuable information about increased risk for deviance found among family members of affected individuals. However, family studies provide few conclusions about genetic etiology, because members of families share environments as well as genes. A second approach, the study of twins, offers a somewhat better separation of genetic and environmental effects. The twin studies compare monozygotic (MZ) twins, who are genetically identical, to fraternal, same-sex, dizygotic (DZ) twins who have no more genes in common than other siblings (50%). The research design assumes that the effect of hereditary factors is demonstrated if the MZ twins have more similar outcomes (concordance for deviance) than DZ twins. In almost all studies, the twins are reared together, and the method assumes that the environmental influences upon MZ twins are no different from those upon DZ twins. The possibility exists, however, that MZ pairs are reared more similarly than DZ pairs (Dalgaard & Kringlen, 1976).

A third approach, the adoption study, to a large extent overcomes the possibility of confounding genetic and environmental factors which limit inferences from the results of twin studies. In this method, the deviant outcomes of adopted children (separated early in life from their biological parents) are compared to the outcomes of their adoptive parents and their biological parents. Similarity in outcome between adoptees and biological parents indicates a genetic effect. In addition, with the application of cross-fostering analysis, relative contributions to deviance from genetic family and from family of rearing may be compared, and interactions between genetic and environmental factors may be examined.

The essay ends with a look at research efforts that are beginning to investigate some implications of the genetic findings reviewed.

SEX CHROMOSOME ANOMALIES

Men usually have 46 chromosomes. Two of these are the sex chromosomes, one X and one Y. The usual notation for this chromosomal configuration is XY. That there are men who have two Y chromosomes was first announced by Sandberg et al. (1961). This historic XYY man was *not* a

criminal. Surveys began to suggest, however, that XYY men are dispro-
portionately represented in maximum security hospitals. The descriptions
presented of the crimes perpetrated by some of these XYY men would
supply material for a series of horror films. An image quickly developed of
a huge, dangerous hulk of a "supermale" with super-aggressiveness spur-
red on by his extra male chromosome. Other hospital studies contradicted
these findings. The true facts would have some critical consequences
aside from their scientific interest. If the XYY–aggression relation were
reliably established, the legal implications would be of some importance
(see Georgetown Law Journal, 1969).

Sophisticated observers soon realized that the inconsistent findings resulted from the arbitrary, small samples being investigated (Kessler &
Moos, 1970). Other observers were politically opposed to the possibility
of any "internal causality" in "the causes of crime," referring to the
XYY research as "Demonism revisited" (e.g., Sarbin & Miller, 1970).
Sarbin and Miller called for a study that would "eliminate the sampling
bias by obtaining XYY subjects from the general population . . . . This in
itself would be an overwhelming project, requiring the chromosomal typing of possibly thousands of potential subjects."

Precisely such a study was undertaken at the Psykologisk Institut,
Kommunehospitalet, Copenhagen, Denmark. A cohort was identified
consisting of all the 31,436 men born in the municipality of Copenhagen
between 1944 and 1947. All those men who were 184 cm or above in
height ($n = 4,139$) were visited in their homes. Blood samples were taken
and karyotypes (systematically arranged photographs of their chromosomes) prepared. This process yielded 12 XYY men. The XYYs and their
controls were checked in the official Danish criminality records. There
was little or no recorded evidence of violent behavior by XYY men.
Although they did evidence significantly more criminal behavior than did
the XY men of their age, height, intelligence, and social class, the crimes
tended to be relatively trivial (Witkin, Mednick, Schulsinger, Bakkestrom, et al., 1977).

Note that this study selected all of the XYYs from a total birth cohort of
Danish, tall men. The results are reliable and generalizable to the population represented by the cohort. Careful investigation from this and other
laboratories helped to explode a disagreeable myth and tended to relieve a
class of men of a nasty label and perhaps of other unpleasant consequences.

But the XYY man is an exceedingly infrequent fellow. The critical
question is whether more commonly observed criminality and psychopathy are influenced by genetic factors.

GENETIC FAMILIAL TRANSMISSION OF CRIMINAL BEHAVIOR

Family Studies

It has long been observed that antisocial parents raise an excessive number of children who also become antisocial. In the classic study by Robins (1966), one of the best predictors of antisocial behavior in a child was the father's criminal behavior. In terms of genetics, however, very little can be concluded from such family data, because it is difficult to disentangle hereditary and environmental influences.

Twin Studies

In the first twin–criminality study, the German psychiatrist Lange (1929), found 77% concordance for criminality for his MZ twins and 12% concordance for his DZ twins. Lange concluded that "heredity plays a quite preponderant part among the causes of crime." Subsequently, studies of twins (until 1961 there were eight in all) have tended to confirm the direction of Lange's results. About 60% concordance has been reported for MZ and about 30% concordance for DZ twins (see Table 3.1). For a detailed discussion of these twin studies the reader may turn to Christiansen (1977a).

Some of these eight twin studies suffer from the fact that their sampling was rather haphazard. As mentioned above, many were carried out in Germany or Japan during a politically unfortunate period. They report too high a proportion of MZ twins. Concordant MZ pairs are more likely to be brought to the attention of the investigator. Twinship is usually easier to detect in the case of identical twins, especially if they end up in the same prison. All of these factors tend to inflate MZ concordance rates in non-systematic studies.

More recently, Christiansen (1977b) has reported on the criminality of a total population of 3586 twin pairs from a well-defined area of Denmark. He found 52% concordance for criminal behavior for (male–male) identical pairs and 22% concordance for (male–male) fraternal twin pairs. This result suggests that identical twins can inherit some biological characteristic (or characteristics) that increases their common risk of being registered for criminal behavior.

Adoption Studies

Limitations of the twin method in decisively separating genetic and environmental effects have led to hesitation in the full acceptance of the

Table 3.1

Twin Studies of Psychopathy and Criminality MZ and Same-Sexed DZ Twins Only

		Monozygotic			Dizogotic		
Study	Location	Total pairs	Concordant pairs	Concordant %	Total pairs	Concordant pairs	Concordant %
Lange 1929	Bavaria	13	10	77	17	2	12
Legras 1932	Holland	4	4	100	5	1	20
Rosanoff 1934	United States	37	25	68	28	5	18
Stumpfl 1936	Germany	18	11	61	19	7	37
Kranz 1936	Prussia	32	21	66	43	23	54
Borgstrom 1939	Finland	4	3	75	5	2	40
Slater 1953 (psychopathy)	England	2	1	50	10	3	30
Yoshimasu 1961	Japan	28	17	61	18	2	11
		138	92	67.2	145	45	31.0

genetic implications of twin research. The study of adoptions better sepa-
rates environment and genetics; if criminal adoptees have disproportion-
ately high numbers of criminal biological parents (given appropriate controls), this would suggest a genetic factor in criminality. This is especially
true since in almost all instances the adoptee has never seen the biological
father and does not know who he is; the adoptee may not even realize he
has been adopted.

Two United States adoption studies have reported highly suggestive
results. Crowe (1975) finds an increased rate of criminality in 18 Iowan
adoptees who have criminal biological mothers. Cadoret (1978) reports on
246 Iowans adopted at birth. Reports of antisocial behavior in these 246
adoptees are significantly related to antisocial behavior in the biological
parents.

A study of 1775 Swedish adoptions, originated by Bohman (Bohman,
Cloninger, Sigvardsson & von Knorring, 1982; Cloninger, Sigvardsson,
Bohman, & von Knorring 1982; Sigvardsson, Cloninger, Bohman, &
Knorring, 1982), found an increased rate of property crimes (nonviolent)
in adoptees with criminal biological parents.

We have reported earlier on a study of the criminal behavior of 1,145
adoptees from the County of Copenhagen (Hutchings & Mednick, 1974,
1975). In the following we describe the results with the complete sample
including adoptions from the entire Kingdom of Denmark.

New Results from Our Adoption Study

The present study is being conducted in the context of the cohort of
14,427 Danish adoptees (Kety, Rosenthal, Wender, & Schulsinger, 1974).
We hypothesized that registered criminality in the biological parents
would be associated with an increased risk of registered criminal behavior
in the adoptees.

Criminality Data   Court convictions were utilized as an index of criminal involvement. Court conviction information is maintained by the chief
of the police district in which an individual is born. The court records
contain information on the date of the conviction, the paragraphs of the
law violated, and the sanction.

In order to access these records it is necessary to know the place and
date of birth and, of course, the individual's name. When subjects were
lost to the investigation it was usually because of lack of information or
ambiguity regarding their place of birth. Incomplete identification of subjects occurred most frequently in the cases of biological fathers. In these
cases it was difficult to determine if the court conviction records we

Table 3.2

Conviction Rates of Completely Identified Members of the Adoptee Families

Family member	Number identified	Number not identified	Proportion with the following number of criminal law court convictions			
			None	One	Two	More than two
Male adoptee	6129	571	.841	.088	.029	.040
Female adoptee	7065	662	.972	.020	.005	.003
Adoptive fathers	13918	509	.938	.046	.008	.008
Adoptive mothers	14267	160	.981	.015	.002	.002
Biological fathers	10604	3823	.714	.129	.056	.102
Biological mothers	12300	2127	.911	.064	.012	.013

obtained were complete. Table 3.2 presents the numbers of adoptees, biological parents, and adopting parents for which we have complete information.

Results The levels of court convictions for each of the members of the "adoption family" are also given in Table 3.2. The biological fathers' and the male adoptees' conviction rates are considerably higher than the rates for the adoptive fathers. The adoptive father, in fact, is just about at the rate for men of this age group, in this time period, 8% (Hurwitz & Christiansen, 1971). Note also that most of the adoptive fathers' criminality is attributable to one-time offenders. The male adoptees and the biological fathers are relatively heavily recidivistic.

The rates of conviction for the women are considerably lower and there is considerably less recidivism. The biological mothers and female adoptees evidence higher levels of court conviction than the adoptive mothers. The adoptive mothers are at about the population average for women of this age range and time period: 2.2% (Wolf, Kaarsen, & Høgh, 1958). It seems that in this time period in Denmark, individuals who gave their children up for adoption and their adopted-out children, evidence higher rates of court convictions than the general population and the adoptive parents. One may be surprised by the adoptive parents' level of court convictions in view of the screening by the adoption agency. It should be recalled, however, that many of these adoptions took place during the Great Depression and the World War II years. It was more difficult to find acceptable adoptive homes in these periods, owing partly to the relative unavailability of adoptive parents and to the additional numbers of adoptees available. Adoptive parents were accepted if they had a 5-year crime-

Table 3.3

"Cross-Fostering" Analysis: Percentage of Adoptive
Sons Who Have Been Convicted of Criminal Law
Offenses[a]

	Are biological parents criminal?	
	Yes	No
Are adoptive parents criminal?		
Yes	24.5	14.7
	(143)	(204)
No	20.0	13.5
	(1226)	(2492)

[a] The numbers in parentheses are the total *N*s for
each cell.

free period before the adoption. Of course, no control was made for crime after the formal adoption.

Cross-Fostering Analysis Because of the size of the population it is possible to segregate subgroups of adoptees who have combinations of criminal and noncriminal biological and adoptive parents. Table 3.3 presents the four groups in a design that is analogous to the cross-fostering paradigm used in behavior genetics. As can be seen in the lower right-hand cell, if neither the biological nor adoptive parents are criminal, 13.5% of their sons are criminal. However, if the biological parents are not criminal, but the adoptive parents evidence criminality, this figure rises to 14.7%. In the lower left-hand cell of Table 3.3, note that 20.0% of the sons are criminal if the adoptive parents are *not* criminal and one of the biological parents *is* criminal. If at least one biological parent and at least one adoptive parent is criminal, we observe the highest level of criminality in the sons: 24.5%. The comparison analogous to the cross-fostering paradigm favors a partial genetic etiology assumption. We must caution, however, that simply knowing the adoptive father has been convicted of a crime does not tell us how criminogenic the adoptee's environment has been. On the other hand, at conception, the genetic influence of the biological father is already complete. Thus this analysis does not yield a fair comparison between environmental and genetic influences included in the Table. But this initial analysis does indicate that sons who have never seen their criminal, biological father have an elevated probability of becoming criminal. This suggests that some biological characteristic is

Table 3.4

Log-Linear Analysis: The Influence of Adoptive Parent and Biological Parent Criminality upon Male Adoptee Criminality[a]

Model	Model chi-square	df	p	Improvement chi-square	df	p
Baseline (S, AB)	32.91	3	.0001			
Adoptive parent (SA, AB)	30.71	2	.001	2.20	1	NS
Biological parent (SB, AB)	1.76	2	.415	31.15	1	.001
Combined influence (SB, SA, AB)	0.30	1	.585	32.61	2	.001
Biological parent given adoptive parent (SB/SA, AB)				30.41	1	.001
Adoptive parent given biological parent (SA/SB, AB)				1.46	1	NS

[a] S means adoptee son effect, A means adoptive parent effect, and B means biological parent effect.

transmitted from the criminal biological father to the son, which increases the son's risk of obtaining a court conviction for a criminal law offense.

A series of log-linear analyses of the frequencies observed in Table 3.3 is presented in Table 3.4. The adoptive parents' criminality is not associated with a significant increment in the son's criminality. The effect of the biological parents' criminality is marked. Study of the model presented in Table 3.4 reveals that the improvement in the chi square considering only the additive effect of the biological parent and adoptive parent leaves almost no room for improvement by any interaction effect. In view of the low frequency of court convictions in the adoptive parents, we report only on associations between biological parents' crime and adoptees' crime in cases wherein the adoptive parents are free of court conviction. This is done to facilitate interpretation. Analyses of biological parental influence upon adoptee crime rates, including the convicted adoptive parents, yield identical results.

Figure 3.1 presents the relationship between degree of recidivism in the biological parent and criminality in the sons. The relationship is positive. Note also that the relationship mainly affects property crimes in the adoptee. Log-linear analyses reveal that the relationship is highly significant for property crimes and not statistically significant for violent crimes. This may be due in part to the relatively low level of violent crime in Denmark (Wolf, Kaarsen, & Høgh, 1958).

The Chronic Offender　The chronic offender has been shown to commit a markedly disproportionate number of criminal offenses. The ex-

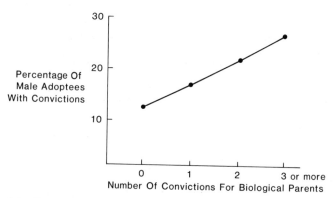

Figure 3.1. Percentage of adoptive male criminality by biological parent criminality (cases in which adoptive parents are non-criminal). Criminality is determined by criminal law convictions. This figure only includes cases in which the adoptive parents have no convictions. All convictions are for criminal law offenses.

tremely high rate of offenses for the chronic offender suggests that perhaps the environment plays a smaller role in the etiology of his or her offending. We examined the relationship between the chronic adoptee offenders and their biological parents.

In an important U.S. birth cohort study (Wolfgang, Figlio, & Sellin, 1972), the chronic offender was defined as one who had been arrested five or more times; these chronic offenders comprised 6% of the males and had committed 56% of the offenses. In our adoption cohort we have recorded court conviction rather than arrest data. If we select as chronic offenders those with three or more court convictions, this includes 4.09% of the male adoptees. This small group of recidivists accounts for 69.4% of all of the court convictions for all the male adoptees. This is a high concentration of crime in a very small fraction of the cohort.

Table 3.5 shows how the chronic offender, the other offenders (one or two convictions), and the non-offenders are distributed as a function of level of crime in the biological parents. As can be seen, the stated hypothesis is supported: The proportion of chronic adoptee offenders increases as a function of level of recidivism in the biological parents.

Another way of expressing this concentration of crime is to point out that the chronic adoptee offenders with chronic biological parent offenders number only 37 men. They comprise 1% of the 3,691 adoptees in Table 3.5; they are responsible, however, for *30%* of the male adoptee convictions. We should also note that the mean number of convictions for the adoptees increases sharply as a function of biological parent recidivism. The biological parents with 0,1,2, or 3 or more convictions have male adoptees with means of .30, .41, and .48 and .70 convictions, respectively.

Table 3.5

Proportion of Chronic Offenders, Other Offenders and Nonoffenders in Male Adoptees as a Function of Level of Crime in the Biological Parents[a]

Number of male adoptee convictions	Number of biological parent convictions			
	0	1	2	3 or more
Non-offenders (no convictions)	.87	.84	.80	.75
Other offenders (1 or 2 convictions)	.10	.12	.15	.17
Chronic offenders (3 or more convictions)	.03	.04	.05	.09
Number of adoptees	2492	547	233	419

[a] Table excludes cases in which adoptive parents have been convicted of criminal law violation.

We have presented evidence that there is an association between biological parent criminality and the criminality of their son given up for adoption. The relationship seems stronger for chronic offenders. The sons of chronic offenders account for a disproportionate amount of the convictions in the cohort.

Concordance in Siblings Raised Apart There are a number of instances in which a biological mother and/or a biological father contributed more than one of their children to this population. These offspring are, of course, full and half-siblings; they were sometimes placed in different adoptive homes. We would predict that the separated full siblings show more concordance for criminal convictions than the separated half-siblings. Both of these groups should show more concordance than two randomly selected, unrelated, separately reared male adoptees.

The probability of any one male adoptee being convicted is .159; the probability of any two unrelated, separated male adoptees being concordant for having at least one conviction is .025 (.159 × .159). There were 126 male–male half-sibling pairs placed in separate adoptive homes. Of these, 31 pairs had at least one member of the sibship convicted; of these 31 pairs, 4 pairs were concordant for convictions. This yields a concordance rate for half-siblings of 12.9%. There were 40 male–male full sibling pairs placed in different adoptive homes. Of these, 15 pairs had at least one member of the sibship convicted; of these 15 pairs, 3 pairs were concordant for convictions. This yields a concordance rate for full siblings of 20.0%. Note that as the degree of genetic relationship increases, the level of concordance increases (2.5%, 12.9%, and 20.0%). It is of interest also to note that if two genetically unrelated males are adopted

Table 3.6

Concordance for Criminal Law Convictions in Male
Siblings Placed in Separate Adoptive Homes

Degree of genetic relationship	Percentage pairwise concordance
Unrelated raised apart	2.5
Half siblings raised apart	12.9
Full siblings raised apart	20.0
Half and full siblings raised apart; criminal father	30.8
Unrelated "siblings" raised together in adoptive home	8.5

into the same home and raised together they evidence a concordance rate of 8.5%.

We also considered the level of concordance of the siblings pairs whose biological father was a criminal (he had at least one conviction). Of 98 fathers with at least one pair of male–male, separated, adopted siblings, 45 had received at least one conviction.[1]

We combined full-and-half sibling pairs (because of the small numbers and since the siblings shared criminal biological fathers). Of the 45 sibling pairs, 13 have at least one member with a conviction; of these 13, four pairs were concordant for convictions. This yields a concordance rate of 30.8%.[2] Complete data are presented in Table 3.6.

While these numbers are very small, they represent all of the cases, as defined, in a total cohort of adoptions. The results suggest that a number of these separated, adopted siblings inherited a characteristic that predisposed them both to criminal behavior. As would be expected, in those instances in which the biological father is criminal, the effect is enhanced.

Specificity of Genetic Relationship   Above, we mention a study of a small sample of adoptees. Crowe (1975) reports the impression that there was some similarity in the types of crimes of the biological mother and the adoptees. This suggests specific genetic predispositions for different types

---

[1] It should be noted that this is a significantly higher rate of convictions (45.9%) than the conviction rate (28.6%) for the total population of biological fathers (X^2 (1) = 14.6, p < 01).

[2] These pairwise concordance rates may be compared with the male–male rates for twins from a population twin study; Christiansen (1977) reports 36% pairwise concordance for identical twins and a 13% rate for fraternal twins. (For comparison it is important to note that the male–male twins have a conviction rate of 12.3%; the male adoptees have a conviction rate of 15.9%.)

of crimes. In order to explore this possibility, we examined the rates of violent crimes in the adoptees as a function of violent crime in the biological parents. We completed similar analyses for property crimes. We also examined more specific types of crimes (theft, fraud, assault, etc.) for similarity in the biological parent and the adoptee. If the genetic predisposition was specific for type of crime, these specificity analyses should have resulted in our observing a closer relationship between adoptee and biological parent levels of conviction for criminal law offenses. The best predictor of adoptee crimes, however, was the *number* of biological parent convictions rather than *type* of crime. This suggests that the biological predisposition the adoptee inherits must be of a general nature, helping to determine law abidance. It is also possible that detection of similarity would require careful coding of details of the criminal behavior. This was not possible in this study.

Sex of Biological Parent   Females who commit crimes must overcome more societal resistance to criminal behavior than do males. We explored the hypothesis that criminal behavior by the biological mother may be related more to her own personal characteristics and might therefore reflect factors which are heritable, whereas criminality in the father may be relatively more influenced by societal factors, which do not relate as strongly to heritable characteristics.

In every analysis we conducted, the relationship between biological mother crime and adoptee crime is stronger than the relationship between biological father criminal behavior and adoptee criminal behavior. The differences, however, are small and not statistically significant. In comparison to the biological fathers, crime in the biological mothers is more closely related to crime in the daughters. This result is statistically significant, but the low frequency of female criminality causes us to interpret these findings with caution.

CONTROLLING GENETIC INFLUENCE BETTER
TO EXAMINE ENVIRONMENTAL EFFECTS

In many social science investigations genetic variance is not considered. In some analyses, this may contribute error; in some cases, it may produce erroneous conclusions. Thus, separation from a father is associated with increased levels of delinquency in a son (Robins, 1966). This has been interpreted as a result of failure of identification or lack of consistent discipline. As we can see from Table 3.2, fathers who permit themselves to be separated from their children tend to have high levels of criminal

Table 3.7

Percentage Male Adoptees with Criminal Convictions as a
Function of Adoptive and Biological Parents' SES[a]

	Biological Parents' SES			
	High	Middle	Low	Total
High	9.30	11.52	12.98	11.58
	(441)	(903)	(775)	(2099)
Middle	13.44	15.29	16.86	15.62
	(320)	(870)	(795)	(1985)
Low	13.81	17.25	18.04	17.19
	(210)	(9568)	(787)	(1565)
	11.64	14.31	16.00	14.55
	(971)	(2341)	(2337)	(5649)

[a] Tabled values are the percentage of adoptees with criminal
convictions. Numbers in parentheses are cell total Ns.

conviction. The higher levels of delinquency found in "separation" studies might be partially due to genetic transmission of criminogenic predispositional characteristics. If one could account for this genetic variance, the environmental hypothesis could be more precisely tested. We have utilized such partial genetic control better to study an important criminogenic variable, social status. In a recent study by Van Dusen, Mednick, and Gabrielli (1983), we separated the variance ascribable to "genetic" social class and rearing social class. We examined adoptee crime as a joint function of biological parents' social class and adoptive parents' social class. The result for male adoptee crime may be seen in Table 3.7. It is clear from inspection of Table 3.7 that male adoptee crime varies both as a function of genetic and environmental social class; log-linear analyses reveal that both effects are statistically significant. Although the genetic effect is of interest, we wish to emphasize that, to our knowledge, this is the first controlled demonstration that *environmental* aspects of social class life influence the social class-crime relationship. This finding suggests that regardless of genetic background, improved social conditions are likely to lead to reductions in criminal behavior.

What Is Inherited in Criminal Behavior?

The preceding review has demonstrated that genetic factors can and do influence criminal behavior. What are the implications of this knowledge? To the list of environmental factors that are commonly acknowledged to contribute to crime, we must now add biological factors: It is through heritable biological structures and processes that the genes exert their influence. Identification of specific biological factors, which must be involved in the etiology of criminal behavior, is now a reasonable research goal; this goal suggests the kinds of research that might now be profitably undertaken. The remainder of this report describes current efforts to identify some of the biological factors involved in criminal offending.

Our work in Denmark suggests that one biological mechanism involved in a genetic predisposition toward criminal offending may be the responsiveness of the autonomic nervous system (ANS). Mednick (1977) has proposed a theory that includes relatively sluggish ANS responsiveness and slow ANS response recovery as critical components. There exists a literature supporting the notion that adult criminal offenders do exhibit lower arousal and slower recovery than non-offenders (Mednick & Volavka, 1981). Twin studies are available that have demonstrated the critical ANS components to be heritable (Bell, Mednick, Gottesman, & Sergeant, 1977). We have found that children of criminal offenders evidence the same patterns of ANS responding that we would have predicted their parents to have had (Mednick, 1977). Thus, we know that slow ANS responding is characteristic of adult criminal offenders and their children, and that ANS responsiveness is partially genetically determined.

Can ANS responsiveness, measured prospectively, predict to later antisocial behavior in the same individuals? Two of our studies provide evidence that ANS can predict behavior in this way. Low responsiveness has predicted delinquency and recidivism over a 10-year period in a Danish study (Loeb & Mednick, 1977). Also, in a study we are conducting on the island of Mauritius, an ANS half-recovery rate assessed in 3-year-olds is predictive over a 6-year period of behavioral precursors to delinquency such as fighting and bullying (Clark, 1982). These studies continue to reveal information useful in answering the question of what specific factors account for the results of family, twin, and adoption studies in criminal offending.

CONCLUSION

The argument is made from time to time that there is little use for genetic research into criminal behavior, because only the environmental influences are susceptible to alteration. The misconception is that a "genetic" problem is predetermined and unyielding to treatments applied after the genetic code is set; therefore, it is said, the information that criminal offending has heritable components is certainly interesting but not very useful. If genetic research ceased at the point of demonstrating heritability of deviance, this argument would be quite true. The real task is to identify the biological mechanisms through which heritable predispositions toward deviance are expressed. These mechanisms may suggest appropriate interventions, and most encouraging of all, *preventive* interventions.

PKU, a disease that causes mental retardation, was not identified as a heritable disease separate from other forms of retardation until 1934, when Folling conducted a study of sisters in Norway. Infants with PKU could then be identified, but identification was useless; the mechanism by which the genes produced PKU retardation was unknown. Not until 1958 was the mechanism, a deficient enzyme, discovered. Discovery of the specific biological mechanism opened the way for development of a diet intervention. Since that time, one of every 100 children genetically destined to suffer mental retardation has been spared this fate (Harsanyi & Hutton, 1981). Current research into the genetics of deviance is beginning to point to possible mechanisms of inheritance. Interventions are tentatively being suggested. The progress of this research will be exciting to watch.

REFERENCES

Bell, B., Mednick, S. A., Gottesmann, I. I., & Sergeant, J. Electrodermal parameters in young, normal male twins. In S. A. Mednick & K. O. Christiansen (Eds.), *Biosocial bases of criminal behavior*. New York: Gardner Press, 1977.

Bohman, M., Cloninger, C. R., Sigvardsson, S., & von Knorring, A. Predisposition to petty criminality in Swedish adoptees. I. Genetic and Environmental Heterogeneity. *Archives of General Psychiatry*, 1982, *39*, 11, 1233–1241.

Borgström, C. A. Eine Serie von Kriminellen Zwillingen. *Archiv für Rassenbiologie*, 1939.

Cadoret, R. J. Psychopathy in adopted away offspring of biological parents with anti-social behavior. *Archives of General Psychiatry*, 1978, *35*, 176–184.

Christiansen, K. O. A review of studies of criminality among twins. In S. A. Mednick & K. O. Christiansen (Eds.), *Biosocial bases of criminal behavior*. New York: Gardner Press, 1977. (a)

Christiansen, K. O. A preliminary study of criminality among twins. In S. A. Mednick & K. O. Christiansen (Eds.), *Biosocial bases of criminal behavior*. New York: Gardner Press, 1977. (b)

Clark, F. Relationship of electrodermal activity at age 3 to aggression at age 9: A study of a physiologic substrate of temperament. University of Southern California Library, 1982. (Dissertation)

Cloninger, C. R., Sigvardsson, S., Bohman, M., & von Knorring, A-L. Predisposition to petty criminality in Swedish adoptees: II. Cross-fostering analyses of gene-environment interaction. *Archives of General Psychiatry*, 1982, *39*, 11, 1242–1247.

Crowe, R. An adoptive study of psychopathy: Preliminary results from arrest records and psychiatric hospital records. In R. Fieve, D. Rosenthal & H. Brill (Eds.), *Genetic research in psychiatry*. Baltimore: Johns Hopkins University Press, 1975.

Dalgaard, O. S. and E. A. Kringlen. Norwegian twin study of criminality. *British Journal of Criminology*, 1976, *16*, 213–232.

Georgetown Law Journal. *Note: The XYY Chromosome defense*. 1969, *57*, 892–922.

Harsanyi, Z., & Hutton, R. *Genetic prophecy: Beyond the double helix*. New York: Rawson, Wade, 1981.

Hurwitz, S., & Christiansen, K. O. *Kriminologi*. Copenhagen: Glydendal, 1971.

Hutchings, B., & Mednick, S. A. Registered criminality in the adoptee and biological parents of registered criminal adoptees. In S. A. Mednick, et al. (Eds.), *Genetics, environment and psychopathology*. Amsterdam: North Holland/American Elsevier, 1974.

Hutchings, B., & Mednick, S. A. Registered criminality in the adoptive and biological parents of registered male criminal adoptees. In R. R. Fieve, D. Rosenthal, and H. Brill (Eds.), *Genetic Research in Psychiatry*. Baltimore: Johns Hopkins University, 1975.

Kessler, S., & Moos, R. H. The XYY Karotype and criminality: A review. *Journal of Psychiatric Research*, 1970, *7*, 153–170.

Kety, S. S., D. Rosenthal, P. H. Wender, & F. Schulsinger. The types and prevalence of mental illness in the biological and adoptive families of adopted schizophrenics. In S. A. Mednick, F. Schulsinger, J. Higgins and B. Bell (Eds.), *Genetics, Environment and Psychopathology*. Amsterdam: North Holland/Elsevier, 1974.

Kranz, H. *Lebensschicksale Kriminellen Zwillinge*. Berlin: Julius Springer, 1936.

Lange, J. *Verbrechen als Schicksal*. Leipzig: George Thieme, 1929. (English Edition, London: Unwin Brother, 1931.)

Legras, A. M. *Psychese en Criminalitet bij Twellingen*. Utrecht: Kemink en Zonn N. B., 1932. (A summary in German can be found in *Psychosen und Kriminalitatbei Zwillingen*: Zeitschrift für die gesamet Neurologie und Psychiatrie, 1933, 198–228.)

Loeb, J., & Mednick, S. A. A prospective study of predictors of criminality: Electrodermal response patterns. In S. A. Mednick and Christiansen, K. O. (Eds.), *Biosocial bases of criminal behavior*. New York: Gardner Press, 1977.

Mednick, S. A. A biosocial theory of the learning of law-abiding behavior. In S. A. Mednick and K. O. Christiansen (Eds.), *Biosocial bases of criminal behavior*. New York: Gardner Press, 1977.

Mednick, S. A., & Volavka, J. Biology and crime. In N. Morris and M. Tonry (Eds.), *Crime and Justice: An annual review of research* (Vol II). University of Chicago Press, 1980, Chicago.

Robins, L. N. *Deviant children grown up*. Baltimore: William and Wilkins, 1966.

Rosanoff, A. J., Handy L. M., & Rosanoff F. A. Criminality and delinquency in twins. *Journal of Criminal Law and Criminology*, 1934, *24*, 923–934.

Sandberg, A. A., Koepf, G. F., Ishihara, T., & Hauschka, J. S. An XYY human male. *Lancet*, 1961, 488–489.

Sarbin, T. R., & Miller, J. E. Demonism revisited: The XYY Chromosomal anomaly. *Issues in Criminology*, 1970, *5*, 195–207.

Sigvardsson, S., Cloninger, C. R., Bohman, M., & von Knorring, A-L. Presdiposition to petty criminality in Swedish adoptees: III. Sex differences and validation of the male typology. *Archives of General Psychiatry*, 1982, *39*, 11, 1248–1253.

Slater, E. The incidence of mental disorder. *Annals of Eugenics*, 1953, *6*, 172.

Stumpfl, F. *Die Ursprunge des Verberchens: Dargestellt am Lebenslauf von Zwillingen*. Leipzig: George Thieme, 1936.

Van Dusen Teilmann, K., Mednick, S. A., Gabrielli, W. F. & Hutchings, B. Social class and crime in an adoption cohort. *Journal of Criminal Law and Criminology*, 1983, *74*, 249–269.

Witkin, H. A., Mednick, S. A., Schulsinger, F., Bakkestrom, E. Christiansen, K. O.,

50

Goodenough D. R., Hirschhorn, K., Lundsteen, C., Ownen, D. R., Philip, J., Rubin, D. B., and Stocking, M. Criminality, aggression and intelligence among XYY and XXY men. In S. A. Mednick & K. O. Christiansen (Eds.), *Biosocial bases of criminal behavior.* New York: Gardner Press, 1977.

Wolf, P., Kaarsen, J., & Høgh E. Kriminalitetshyppigheden I Danmark. *Nordisk Tidsskrift for Kriminalvidenskab.* Copenhagen, 1958, *46,* 113–119.

Wolfgang, M. E., Figlio, R. M., & Sellin, T. *Delinquency in a birth cohort.* Chicago: University of Chicago Press, 1972.

Yoshimasu, S. The criminological significance of the family in the light of the studies of criminal twins. *Acta Criminologiae et Medicinae Legalis Japanica* 1961, *27.*

4

Aggression and Hormones: Behavioral Relationship with Testosterone and Adrenaline

DAN OLWEUS*

TESTOSTERONE

Recent studies of the relationship between plasma testosterone levels and aggressive and antisocial behavior in the human male have yielded somewhat conflicting results (see Olweus et al., 1980). However, when combined with findings from animal studies (e.g., Moyer, 1976; Rose, 1975), the studies with human males suggest that there may be a positive

* The research reported in this chapter was supported by grants from the Sweden Bank Tercentenary Foundation, the Swedish Delegation for Social Research (DSF), the Norwegian Research Council for Science and the Humanities, and the W. T. Grant Foundation (to A. Mattsson).

The present chapter consists of two relatively independent parts: One concerns the relationship of aggressive, antisocial behavior with testosterone; the other the relationship of the same or related behavior patterns with adrenaline. In many ways these relationships are quite different, but there is a common denominator in that both parts refer to an association of hormonal factors with aggressive, antisocial behavior. In addition, the empirical results are based on the same sample of healthy male adolescent subjects.

Basic information on the testosterone study can be found in other publications (e.g., Olweus, 1983; Olweus, Mattson, Schalling, & Löw. 1980). In this chapter, some new analyses of testosterone–behavior relationships are presented, using a causal analytic framework. The research on the adrenaline–behavior relationships has not been reported on before.

DEVELOPMENT OF ANTISOCIAL
AND PROSOCIAL BEHAVIOR

relationship between plasma testosterone levels and one or more aspects of aggressive, impulsive, and antisocial behavior patterns. For animals, the findings also indicate that testosterone may have a causal influence on some forms of aggressive behavior. This, of course, does not preclude the possibility of an individual's testosterone level being, at the same time, affected by environmental and experiential factors (including the individual's own behavior).

If a positive relationship is found between testosterone level and a particular aggressive or antisocial dimension (and if this relationship can be given a causal interpretation), it becomes essential to try to find the mechanisms mediating the relationship. The relative importance of the possible influence of testosterone on behavior is also of great interest. To highlight this issue, it is essential to have data on individual differences in the relevant behavior dimensions before the production of testosterone (in sizable quantites) is initiated and after it has continued for some time. Such information was available in the present project.

The issue of possible mechanisms (in a broad sense) in the testosterone–behavior relationship has been discussed in a previous publication (Olweus, 1983). However, that discussion was made in general terms, and in the present context the analyses are elaborated within a path-analytic framework. For such analyses to be reasonably complete and nonspurious, it is essential to include information on other, causally prior variables that may affect the individual's level of testosterone as well as his behavior patterns. Several data of this kind were also available in the present study.

Briefly on Procedure

The subjects were 58 healthy boys, 15–17 years old, with a median age of 16. They were selected from the public school districts of Solna, a suburb in the Stockholm metropolitan area in Sweden, to provide a roughly representative sample of the total male student population of the ninth grade (about 275 boys). The boys provided two sets of blood samples (separated by approximately 1 month) for plasma testosterone assays. The test–retest reliability or the stability of the individual differences, as expressed in the correlation between the two sets of measurements, was .63. The reliability of the individual average testosterone levels was .77 (Spearman–Brown corrected). The mean testosterone value for the whole group was 544 ± 141 ng/100 ml (range 197–901 ng/100 ml). Three of the boys were in Tanner Pubertal Stage 3; 9 in Stage 4; and 43 in Stage 5 (adult), according to pubic hair development. The correlation between pubertal stage and testosterone level was .44.

Approximately 1 month before the blood samples were drawn, the subjects completed a number of personality inventories (see Olweus et al., 1980). In addition, highly reliable peer ratings of habitual aggressive behavior and physical strength were available. Data on physical variables such as height, weight, chest circumference, and pubertal stage were collected in a physical examination.

Testosterone and Aggression

The basic finding of the study was a substantial correlation between testosterone and each of two scales of the Olweus Aggression Inventory, Verbal Aggression ($r = .38$) and Physical Aggression ($r = .36$). The simple composite of these two scales correlated .44 with testosterone.

Closer analysis of the individual items of the Verbal and Physical Aggression scales revealed an interesting pattern: It was primarily items involving a response to provocation, including threat or unfair treatment, that showed a clear correlation with testosterone levels (Table 4.1). The

Table 4.1

Correlation between Testosterone Levels and Individual Items from the Verbal and Physical Aggression Scales[a]

Item	Correlation coefficient, r
Verbal Aggression (5 items)	
1. When an adult is unfair to me, I get angry and protest.	.18
2. When an adult tries to take my place in a line, I firmly tell him it is my place.	.24
3. When a teacher criticizes me, I tend to answer back and protest.	.33
4. When a teacher has promised that we will have some fun but then changes his (her) mind, I protest.	.19
5. When an adult tries to boss me around, I resist strongly.	.33
Physical Aggression (5 items)	
6. When a boy starts fighting with me, I fight back.	.33
7. When a boy is nasty with me, I try to get even with him.	.37
8. When a boy teases me, I try to give him a good beating.	.15
9. I fight with other boys at school.[b]	.05
10. I really admire the fighters among the boys.[b]	.11

[a] $n = 58$.
[b] These items do not contain a clear element of provocative challenge.

first eight items of Table 4.1 all contain an element of provocation by adults or peers. The correlations with testosterone were quite high for several of these items, considering the fact that the reliability of individual items is generally rather low. Conversely, the correlations for the last two items, which do not imply provocation, were negligible.

In addition, the only peer-rating scale containing an element of provocation, Verbal Protest, showed the highest correlation ($r = .24$) with testosterone. The wording of this rating dimension was as follows: "When a teacher criticizes him, he tends to answer back and protest."

The correlation of testosterone with the composite of the three peer-rating dimensions, Start Fights, Verbal Protest, and Verbal Hurt, was .21. This composite has been used in several of my studies as a broad measure of aggressive, destructive behavior (e.g., Olweus, 1978, 1980, 1984).

In summarizing these findings, it was concluded that dimensions reflecting intensity and/or frequency of aggressive responses to provocation and threat appeared to be most clearly and directly related to testosterone. Other dimensions measuring aggressive attitude or impulses and unprovoked physical or verbal aggression also showed positive but weaker correlations with testosterone.

Testosterone and Frustration Tolerance

Another result of interest was the positive correlation ($r = .28$) between testosterone levels and a self-report scale called Lack of Frustration Tolerance. This scale contained only three items, all of them focusing on the individuals's habitual level of impatience and irritability: (1) "I become easily impatient and irritable if I have to wait," (2) "Others say that I easily lose patience," and (3) "I become easily impatient if I have to keep on with the same thing for a long time." The internal consistency (alpha) reliability of this short scale was .59. The above results suggested that adolescent boys with higher levels of testosterone tended to be habitually more impatient and irritable than boys with lower testosterone levels.

Causal Interpretations

A Few Methodological Comments The main findings of the present study were the positive associations of testosterone level with the self-report scales of verbal and physical aggression, mainly reflecting responsiveness to provocation and threat, and lack of frustration tolerance. In addition, lower positive correlations were obtained with peer ratings of aggressive behavior and a self-report scale of antisocial behavior (covering such behaviors as petty theft, truancy, and destruction of other's property; $r = .17$).

Theoretical considerations and preliminary statistical analyses of the available data suggested that testosterone in adolescent boys might have two chief effects on behavior: One was a mainly direct influence on what may be called Provoked Aggressive Behavior as measured by the self-report scales of Verbal and Physical Aggression; the other was a more indirect effect on Unprovoked (or destructive) Aggression, reflected in the peer-rating composite, and generally Antisocial Behavior (measured by the self-report scale of antisocial behavior) via the mediating variable (relative) Lack of Frustration Tolerance (called Low Frustration Tolerance in the following discussion). These and other possibilities are explored below using the technique of path analysis.

The above statements are based on the assumption that testosterone somehow acts as a causal variable that influences aggressive behavior. Such an assumption is not unreasonable in view of the findings from many experimental studies on animals. In addition, because data for the aggression and frustration tolerance variables were also available at an earlier time point, at Grade 6 (median age = 13 years), we were able to test the possibility of the individuals' level of testosterone being more or less "determined" by these same variables measured 3 years earlier. If such effects were found to be strong, it would very likely imply that what appeared to be causal effects of testosterone on aggressive behavior were, completely or partly, spurious relationships. Similarly, the inclusion of child-rearing variables (derived from parent interviews), which in previous analyses (Olweus, 1980) have been found to be important in the development of aggressive behavior (chiefly Unprovoked Aggressive Behavior), provided additional possibilities of detecting spuriousness in the testosterone–aggression relationships.

Details about path analysis and some relevant references to the literature on this topic can be found in Olweus (1980). Because the present sample was of limited size, the choice was made to retain path coefficients of variables that, in a stepwise regression, accounted for at least 1% of the variance in the relevant dependent variable. (The same procedure was followed in Olweus, 1980.)

Finally, it should be emphasized that the findings and interpretations presented here should be regarded as suggestive rather than conclusive: The results should be replicated on other samples before the offered lines of explanation can be considered reasonably tenable. Also, it must be kept in mind that the exact mechanisms by which testosterone—or closely related variables—may affect an individual's readiness to respond with aggressive behavior are not known at present.

Testosterone and Provoked Aggressive Behavior   The main results from the path analysis are presented in Figure 4.1. In this context, primary

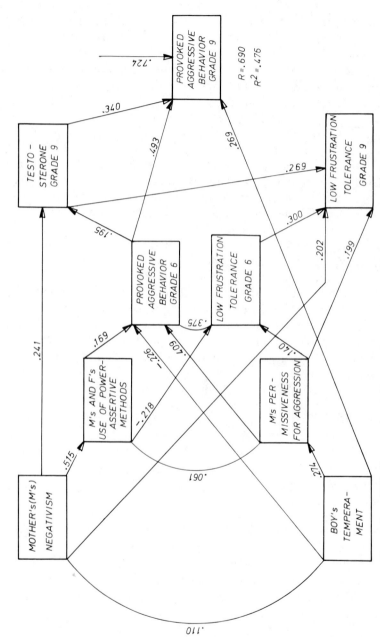

Figure 4.1. Path diagram of variables determining Provoked Agressive Behavior Grade 9 (*n* = 58).

attention is directed to the right part of the figure. The substantial coefficient (β = .340) for the path leading from Testosterone to Provoked Aggressive Behavior Grade 9 confirms the preliminary impression that testosterone exerts a direct causal influence on this aggression variable, reflecting responsiveness to provocation and threat. The original correlation of .44 was only moderately reduced when other, causally prior variables were controlled for. Given the causal ordering implied in the model, this result indicates that a higher level of testosterone leads to an increased readiness to respond vigorously and assertively to provocations and threats.

The figure also shows that testosterone resulted in a reduction in frustration tolerance at Grade 9 (β = .269). It should be noted, however, that Low Frustration Tolerance Grade 9 had no effect on the provoked aggression variable. This is in contrast with the results to be discussed below.

As could be expected, the largest path coefficient leading to Provoked Aggressive Behavior Grade 9 (β = .493) came from the variable itself, which had been measured 3 years earlier. This indicates a moderate degree of stability over time (r = .539) in this variable (see Olweus, 1979). However, the relative stability of the variable has not prevented testosterone from having a substantial effect on the Grade-9 behavior, as discussed above.

Testosterone and Unprovoked Aggressive Behavior   The pattern of findings is shown in Figure 4.2. It should be noted that testosterone had no direct effect on the ultimate dependent variable, Unprovoked Aggressive Behavior Grade 9. There was, however, a clear indirect effect (.269 × .337 = .091), with Low Frustration Tolerance Grade 9 as a mediating variable. The stability of the ultimate dependent variable was somewhat higher in this case (β = .582; r = .623) than in Figure 4.1.

I want to call attention to two additional points. First, there were no paths from Unprovoked Aggressive Behavior Grade 6 or Low Frustration Tolerance Grade 6 to the testosterone variable. Thus, the boys' levels of testosterone were not "determined" by these causally prior variables. Second, there was only a very weak correlation between Unprovoked Aggressive Behavior and Low Frustration Tolerance at Grade 6 (r = .053), whereas the correlation between them was considerably higher at Grade 9 (r = .408). Thus, an association had emerged in the period from Grade 6 to 9 and, according to the path-analytic results, testosterone was the major variable accounting for the association. This pattern of findings clearly supports the assumption that testosterone may act as a causal variable and exert an influence on some forms of aggressive behavior also in humans.

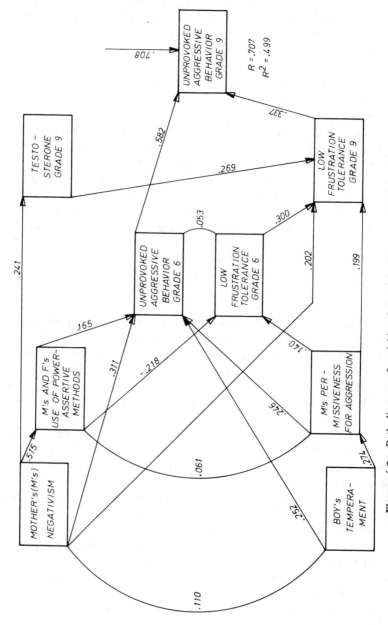

Figure 4.2. Path diagram of variables determining Unprovoked Aggressive Behavior Grade 9 ($n = 58$).

In sum, the path-analytic results indicate that a high level of testosterone in puberty made the boys more impatient and irritable, which increased their readiness to engage in aggressive behavior of the unprovoked and destructive kind (to start fights and say nasty things without being provoked). In contrast with the findings for Provoked Aggressive Behavior, the effects of testosterone were indirect in the present case.

Testosterone and Antisocial Behavior   The relationship of testosterone with the self-report scale of antisocial behavior (Grade 9) was positive but fairly weak ($r = .17$). A path analysis with the scale of antisocial behavior as the ultimate dependent variable (not shown here) gave results nearly parallel to those for Unprovoked Aggressive Behavior Grade 9. As could be expected, the correlation of these two variables was quite substantial, $r = .610$.

Thus, testosterone had no direct effect on Antisocial Behavior Grade 9 but only an indirect one, mediated by low frustration tolerance at Grade 9. The coefficient for the path from Low Frustration Tolerance Grade 9 to Antisocial Behavior Grade 9 was somewhat larger ($\beta = .460$) than that for the corresponding path in Figure 4.2.

The results of the path analysis suggest that a high testosterone level lowered the adolescent boys' tolerance of frustration, which lead to a heightened probability of engaging in antisocial behavior. This line of reasoning appears intuitively plausible and is consistent with the observation that many boys who behave in an antisocial way seem to do so out of a desire for excitement, change, and thrills (to avoid boredom).

The Possible Role of Pubertal Stage   In the present study, the best indicator of pubertal stage was a classification into Tanner stages on the basis of pubic hair development. If pubertal stage were included as a possible causal variable in the analyses, which may seem somewhat superfluous on theoretical grounds, it would be natural to place it after the Grade-6 variables but before testosterone and the other Grade-9 variables.

When the three path analyses were repeated with pubertal stage included, the path coefficients relevant to our discussion were practically unchanged. The effects of pubertal stage were totally indirect and mediated by the testosterone variable, as should be expected on theoretical grounds.

Strength of Relationships and Conclusion

To gain perspective on the previous discussion, it is essential also to consider the relative importance of testosterone in determining aggressive, antisocial behavior. With regard to Provoked Aggressive Behavior at Grade 9, the analyses indicated that the role of testosterone may be relatively marked. It may be added that the child-rearing factors found to be important in the development of Unprovoked Aggressive Behavior had weaker effects on the variable of the provoked kind.

Considering the boys' readiness to engage in aggressive–destructive and antisocial behavior patterns, it is obvious that testosterone was only one out of many possible causal factors and one with indirect and fairly weak effects. At the same time, it should be made clear that the reported coefficients, based on fallible variables, were underestimates of the true relations. All in all, it can be concluded that the role of testosterone in the development of aggressive and antisocial behavior patterns certainly merits further study.

ADRENALINE

Briefly on Procedure

In the same study as reported on in the section on testosterone, my colleagues (A. Mattsson, D. Schalling, L. Levi) and I also collected data on catecholamine excretion in the urine. On each of two mornings, separated by approximately 1 month, the subjects ($n = 59$) provided two samples of urine. The interval between the two samples on a day was about 2 hours. The first of the examination days can be generally considered more stressful than the second one, because it involved a venipuncture (for the determination of testosterone) and the majority of the boys (62%) had never before experienced venipuncture. In addition, the investigation took place in hospital localities that were unknown to the boys. On the second day, no blood samples were drawn and the boys delivered their two urine collections in a relatively familiar environment, the school nurse's office.

The urine samples were analyzed for free adrenaline and noradrenaline by a fluorimetric technique (Andersson, Hovmöller, Karlsson, & Svensson, 1974; von Euler & Lishajko, 1961). To take weight differences into account, the catecholamine variables were expressed in units of pico mole divided by body weight. However, the results would not change much if the analyses were made on weight-uncorrected values. Because the obtained relationships were weaker and less consistent with noradrenaline and with ratios of noradrenaline to adrenaline (NA/A), only findings with the adrenaline dimension are discussed here.

The average correlation of the four adrenaline samples was .45. If the average of the four measurements is used as a composite measure of adrenaline level, the reliability of this composite can be estimated to .762 (by the Spearman–Brown formula). The correlation of the first and the second sets of measurements was .48 (uncorrected for measurement errors), indicating a moderate stability over approximately 1 month.

These analyses of measurement characteristics suggest that use of a single adrenaline sample in a study may be of limited value, unless the relationships or effects investigated are quite strong.

The correlation between adrenaline level and testosterone level was weak and nonsignificant ($r = -.13$).

Some Results

From the perspective of the present book, the most interesting finding was the clear negative correlation of $-.44$ between adrenaline level and the peer rating composite of unprovoked aggressive–destructive behavior (Start Fights, Verbal Protest, and Verbal Hurt). If corrected for unreliability of measurement, this coefficient becomes $-.55$. Thus, the more aggressive boys had lower levels of adrenaline excretion as measured in these situations.

Similarly, a group of 14 highly aggressive bullies (see Olweus, 1978) chosen through teacher nominations (four of the bullies were included in the random sample of "normal" adolescents) had clearly lower levels of adrenaline than the remaining boys.

In another section I discuss this finding of a negative relationship between adrenaline level and Unprovoked Aggressive Behavior, but first I consider a few other results.

Some of the findings were that adrenaline level correlated negatively ($r = -.48$) with the Introversion–Extraversion scale from the Eysenck Personality Questionnaire (Eysenck & Eysenck, 1975) and positively with the Psychic Anxiety scale ($r = .42$), in particular, from the Multi-Component Anxiety Inventory (Schalling, Cronholm, & Åsberg, 1975) and the Situation-Oriented Questionnaire ($r = .39$). The latter measure (Situational Anxiety) was developed specifically to assess the subjects' degree of anxiety and worry in relation to the venipuncture and the investigative situation (see Olweus et al., 1980 for a brief description of this scale). The Psychic Anxiety scale, however, was designed to reflect more habitual anxiety reactions (trait anxiety). Their intercorrelation was .56, whereas the correlation of Unprovoked Aggressive Behavior with the Extraversion scale was .46.

The peer-rating dimension of Unprovoked Aggressive Behavior was largely independent of the two anxiety scales ($r = -.18$ with Psychic

62

Anxiety and $r = -.13$ with Situational Anxiety) whereas Extraversion showed higher correlations with them ($r = -.41$ and $-.38$, respectively).

Results along these lines, though somewhat weaker, were obtained also with other self-report scales: negative relationships of adrenaline level with scales measuring aggressive, impulsive, and acting-out behavior; and positive associations with measures of different aspects of anxiety, apprehension, and feelings of inadequacy.

Determination of an Individual's Adrenaline Level

These findings lead up to the question: What factors determine an individual's level of adrenaline excretion? Of course, this question cannot be dealt with here in a complete way. I only want to focus on a few central factors, of relevance from the present psychoendocrinological perspective.

It has been shown in extensive research programs (e.g., Frankenhaeuser, 1971, 1979; Levi, 1972) that situations characterized by novelty, uncertainty, change, effort, vigilance, and achievement demands tend to increase adrenaline excretion. Also, it has been found that emotionally stressful and threatening situations result in a higher adrenaline output. Sometimes the diffuse term *stress* has been used as a blanket term for situations that raise the individual's level of adrenaline excretion.

In an attempt to provide a possible integration of the somewhat disparate findings in the literature, a model of factors and processes involved in the determination of an individual's adrenaline output is presented. It should be noted, however, that only some of the main ideas can be outlined here and that the formulation is tentative; one or more aspects may need revision.

Going back to the empirical findings first, the boys' adrenaline levels seemed to be primarily related to two partly independent behavioral dimensions. One reflected aggressive, outgoing, and acting-out behavior and their opposite, well-controlled socialized, introverted, and nonaggressive behavior. This dimension is represented in the present study by the composite of Unprovoked Aggressive Behavior and Extraversion (given equal weight). The other dimension included anxious, insecure versus nonanxious, emotionally stable reaction patterns, here defined by the composite of Psychic Anxiety and Situational Anxiety (given equal weight).

The correlations of these composites with adrenaline level were $-.526$ and $.465$, respectively. When the two composites were combined in a multiple regression equation with adrenaline level as the dependent variable, R was $.601$. Addition of the interaction between the two composites

$(X_1 \cdot X_2)$ increased the multiple R to .641 ($p < .05$ for addition of the interaction term.) The interpretation of this interaction is that the negative relationship between aggressive, acting-out behavior and adrenaline level becomes increasingly stronger for higher levels of anxiety. Or, conversely, the positive relationship between anxiety and adrenaline becomes more marked the more well-controlled and socialized the boy.

If corrected for attenuation, this multiple R will be well above .70, which means that approximately 50% of the variance in average adrenaline levels can be accounted for by these two dimensions, measured without error.

A Tentative Model

A diagram of the proposed model is shown in Figure 4.3. In agreement with the representational system of structural modelling, rectangles are used to designate manifest, measured variables, whereas latent, unobserved variables or factors are portrayed by ellipses. The arrows show the direction of influence.

Though the basic elements of the model are somewhat different and certain additions have been made, the model is related to Eysenck's theorizing about cortical arousal (Eysenck, 1967, 1975). However, because there seem to be some differences of opinion as to the nature of the underlying neurophysiologic structures and processes, these aspects are not specified in the model. Instead, the general terms "Alertness Regulating System" and "Anxiety Regulating System" are used, thus leaving open the issue of the exact neurophysiologic mechanisms involved.

To my knowledge, an analysis along the lines developed here has not been made previously with reference to adrenaline excretion. However, the idea of two different arousal systems, as proposed by Eysenck, has also been put forth and documented by other researchers (e.g., Gellhorn & Longbourrow, 1963; Routtenberg, 1968). This conceptualization is central to Schalling's view of impulsiveness and anxiety proneness as two important personality dimensions (Schalling, 1977).

The basic idea of the model is that there are two partly independent, partly dependent pathways to cortical arousal. One is via the Alertness Regulating System (upper pathway), with little or no participation from the Anxiety Regulating System. The other is via the Anxiety Regulating System (lower pathway), in which case the Alertness Regulating System also becomes involved (see arrow connecting the lower and upper pathways).

Furthermore, it is assumed that the amount of adrenaline output is monotonically related to level of cortical arousal. However, because cor-

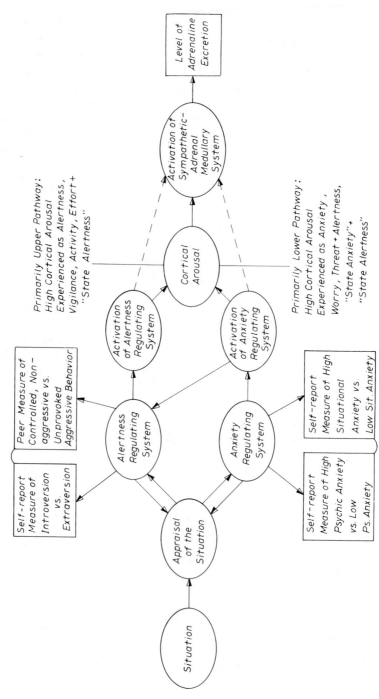

Figure 4.3. Tentative model of variables and processes involved in the determination of adrenaline excretion.

tical arousal can be produced via two different pathways, the processes involved should be reflected in the measure of adrenaline excretion. In the case of upper-pathway involvement, the adrenaline measure should correlate predominantly with indices of the Alertness Regulating System. On the other hand, when the Anxiety Regulating System is activated, adrenaline output should by related both to indices of this system and those of the Alertness Regulating System. Thus, under conditions of emotional involvement, adrenaline level should cover (at least) two different components (State Anxiety + State Alertness); whereas in cases of primarily cognitive alertness or involvement, output of adrenaline should mainly reflect the alertness component (State Alertness + possible other components not considered here).

Expanding somewhat on the previous formulation, it is assumed that situations involving demands on cognitive alertness and vigilance, on attention and effort but which are not threatening or emotionally disturbing, produce cortical arousal via the Alertness Regulating System (the upper pathway). This kind of stimulation thus has no or only weak effects on the Anxiety Regulating System. Higher levels of cortical arousal produced in this way are experienced as a state of alertness or cognitive involvement.

It is furthermore postulated that individuals differ markedly both in thresholds and habitual level of activation of the Alertness Regulating System. Well-controlled, nonaggressive individuals are assumed to have low thresholds and high habitual levels whereas the opposite is true of aggressive, acting-out individuals. The individual's predisposition to react to stimuli of varying intensity and with high or low levels (Trait Alertness) in the Alertness Regulating System and the ensuing state of cortical arousal (State Alertness) are indexed in the present study by the composite of Controlled, Nonaggressive vs. Unprovoked Aggressive Behavior and Introversion vs. Extraversion (the previously discussed composite with reversed scoring).

On the other hand, situations that are emotionally taxing ("stressful") will activate the Anxiety Regulating System. However, this activation is also assumed to affect the Alertness Regulating System. The basis for this assumption is behavioral and introspective observations as well as knowledge of the probable neurophysiological mechanisms involved in these processes (Eysenck, 1975; Gale, 1973). Thus, the cortical arousal produced in this way will contain two components related to the Anxiety Regulating System and to the Alertness Regulating System, respectively. The emotionally activated individual will be both anxious and alerted (State Anxiety + State Alertness).

Also with regard to the Anxiety Regulating System, individuals are assumed to differ substantially in thresholds and habitual levels. The individual's predisposition to react to stimuli of varying intensity and with high or low levels (Trait Anxiety) in the Anxiety Regulating System and the anxiety component of the ensuing state of cortical arousal (State Anxiety) are indexed in the present study by the composite of Psychic Anxiety vs. Low Psychic Anxiety and Situational Anxiety vs. Low Situational Anxiety. It can be assumed that a certain minimum level of stimulation is required for this composite or its component variables to reflect individual differences in the predisposition to alertness reactions. Accordingly, adrenaline levels under "resting conditions" may not be systematically related to individual differences in these indices.

Because an interaction was empirically found between the two composites in their relationship with adrenaline (p. 63), an interaction between the two arousal systems might be tentatively included as part of the model: The positive relationship between indices of the Alertness Regulating System and adrenaline is assumed to become increasingly stronger with higher levels of indices of the Anxiety Regulating System. It is understood that this interaction will be present only or mainly when the stimulus situation leads to an activation of the Anxiety Regulating System, i.e., is emotionally taxing.

Parenthetically, it may be mentioned that, in the two-arousal systems previously referred to (e.g., Eysenck, 1967, 1975; Routtenberg, 1968), what seems to correspond to the Alertness Regulating System and the upper pathway is chiefly identified with the brain stem reticular activation structures (ARAS). Similarly, the neurophysiological basis for the lower pathway and the Anxiety Regulating System is assumed to be some of the limbic structures, the hypothalamus, and the autonomic system. It should be noted, however, that the overlapping of the present model with previous two-arousal systems is not quite complete with regard to concepts used and operationalization of concepts.

Some Implications

Some correlational consequences of the preceding analyses have already been pointed out, for situations with or without emotional involvement (p. 65). In addition, it should follow that, in emotionally taxing situations, the individuals' adrenaline level should be more completely determined (R should be higher) than in (relatively) nonemotional situations. The rationale for this inference is that indices of the Anxiety Regulating System should have more predictive power in stressful as compared with nonstressful situations. In the present study, this prediction can be tested by contrasting the multiple Rs for adrenaline measures collected on the first (more taxing emotionally) and second examination days.

Furthermore, considering the suggestion of an interaction between the two arousal systems, one would expect a larger (more significant) contribution to R from the interaction term in emotionally activating situations. This could again be examined through a comparison of the results for the first and the second examination days.

Finally, a general consequence of the model is that an individual's adrenaline level cannot generally be construed as an indicator of the emotional impact or stressfulness of the stimulus situation. The previous analyses suggest that the adrenaline level reflects, depending upon the situation, either mainly an alertness component of cortical arousal (or adrenal–medullary activity) or a combination of alertness and anxiety ("stress") components. This view of adrenaline would seem to run counter to much current thinking in this area.

Some Empirical Tests

The previously reported empirical analyses (p. 62) showed that each of the composite indices of the Alertness Regulating System and the Anxiety Regulating System correlated substantially with the composite measure of adrenaline level. In addition, each composite index gave a significant contribution to explained variance over and above the contribution from the other composite. These composite indices were thus partly independent. To some extent, these findings constituted the starting point for the subsequent theoretical formulation.

However, these analyses can be carried further, taking the variation in stressfulness of the two examination days into account. In this context it is useful to report results separately for each of the two component variables making up the two composites (Figure 4.3).

First, looking at the zero-order correlations, it is obvious that the two alertness indices (Controlled, Nonaggressive Behavior and Introversion) correlated about as strongly with adrenaline level derived from the first and from the second examination days (average $r = .381$ for the first day and .406 for the second). This is in contrast with the results for the two anxiety indices, the average r being .388 for the first day and .260 for the second. A difference of this magnitude was obtained not only for the Situational Anxiety variable, which specifically referred to the first day but, more importantly, also for the Psychic Anxiety scale. This finding of a higher correlation between anxiety indices and adrenaline level for the first, emotionally more taxing day is certainly in agreement with the prediction derived from the theoretical model.

From a slightly different point of view, it was found that the multiple Rs for the four combinations of alertness and anxiety indices (one alertness index and one anxiety index) were consistently higher for adrenaline levels from the first as compared with the second examination day. Though the average difference was not very great ($\bar{R}$ = .482 and .436, respectively), the results showed that the anxiety indices had better predictive power for the adrenaline measure that referred to the emotionally more disturbing situation.

This was also evident from a comparison of the beta weights for the anxiety indices in the equations (each with two independent variables) predicting adrenaline level for the first and the second examination days. In three of four equations for the first day, the beta weights for the two anxiety indices were significant (and p was .06 for the beta weight in the fourth equation). This contrasts with the situation for the second day, where none of the four beta weights for the anxiety variables was significant. They were all positive ($\bar{r}$ = .260), however, thus indicating that the adrenaline measure for the second day also contained an anxiety component, though reduced in size, as expected. By comparison, the beta weights for the two alertness indices were all significant in these eight equations.

Considering possible interactions between alertness and anxiety indices, the results were clearly different for the two alertness variables. The peer measure of controlled, nonaggressive (versus unprovoked aggressive) behavior showed significant interactions with the Psychic Anxiety scale as well as the Situational Anxiety scale in predicting adrenaline level for the first examination day. This was in marked contrast with the Introversion vs. Extraversion scale, which did not even show a trend in that direction. For the adrenaline measure referring to the second day, there were no significant interactions whatsoever, as was expected on theoretical grounds.

On the basis of these results, it may be tentatively concluded that there was some support for the idea that the Alertness Regulating System and the Anxiety Regulating System interact (in the statistical sense, see Olweus, 1977) with each other in emotionally taxing situations. The present data suggested, however, that the two indices of the Alertness Regulating System functioned differently in this respect. This discrepancy merits further study.

Overall, the results presented were in general agreement with the predictions derived from the theoretical analyses. The results from the interaction analyses and the pattern of correlations between the alertness and anxiety indices may suggest that the peer measure of controlled, nonaggressive versus unprovoked aggressive behavior was the purer indicator of the Alertness Regulating System in this study.

Adrenaline and Unprovoked Aggressive Behavior

Up to now, the main focus has been on what factors and processes determine an individual's level of adrenaline excretion. It is now appropriate to change perspective and see if the previous analyses and findings can be of help in predicting aggressive behavior and in explaining its development.

With regard to prediction, it turned out that three of the four childhood factors (farthest to the left in Figure 4.2) that have been found to be important in determining Unprovoked Aggressive Behavior (Olweus, 1980), correlated very weakly with average adrenaline level ($r < \pm .100$). The exception was Mother's Permissiveness, which correlated $-.360$. Also the Grade-6 variables in Figure 4.2 correlated in the .30's with adrenaline level, but there remained a substantial negative relationship between adrenaline level and Unprovoked Aggressive Behavior Grade 9 also when the grade-6 variables and the four childhood variables were controlled for. Thus, it is very likely that adding adrenaline level to a regression equation with Unprovoked Aggressive Behavior (or similar dimensions) as the dependent variable will increase predictability in many situations.

In the previous analyses, an individual with a high level of habitual aggressive behavior and a low level of adrenaline as measured in nonstressful situations was assumed to have typically low cortical arousal. Partly following Eysenck (1967, 1975) and others, we can briefly pursue the reasoning along the following lines. A boy with a typically low level of cortical arousal will often experience a kind of stimulus hunger or craving. He becomes easily habituated and bored and has a desire for new and varied stimuli, for sensations and thrills. Strong stimuli are not experienced as aversive or disturbing as they would be for a boy with a typically high level of cortical arousal. Rather, they can be engaging and exciting.

In this way, a boy with a low level of cortical arousal who has been exposed to childhood conditions that predispose him to habitually aggressive behavior—conditions of the kind shown in the left part of Figure 4.2—may feel aroused and excited when he is provoked and engages in aggressive behavior and feels strong anger. Such behavior may thus be reinforcing to him. He can also be assumed to seek out situations in which there is a high probability of his behaving aggressively.

On the other hand, a boy with a typically low level of cortical arousal who has not experienced the above predisposing conditions (or fewer of them) can be assumed to show a good deal of outgoing, extraverted behavior patterns but he will himself initiate less aggressive behavior than the boy discussed in the preceding paragraph. However, when provoked, he will tend to respond with aggression.

Finally, a boy with a typically high level of cortical arousal will often experience aggressive behavior and strong anger of his own as aversive and unpleasant. Generally, he will not be inclined to seek out situations that easily lead to aggressive interactions. When provoked, he will try to use nonaggressive response modes of a submissive or a constructive nature.

It should be emphasized that the above formulations are not to be construed as precise predictions of behavior in particular situations. Rather, it is a question of broad predispositions that are assumed to increase or decrease the probability of certain behavior patterns in a range of situations. Thus, these behavioral tendencies are posited to affect the developmental course of an individual in a general way. For more specific predictions, however, other factors must be taken into account.

An analysis somewhat parallel to the above can be performed for antisocial behavior patterns. The self-report scale of Antisocial Behavior Grade 9 previously referred to correlated −.360 with average adrenaline level.

Some Related Findings

I close by briefly referring to two other, relatively recent studies that have found a negative relationship between adrenaline level and aggressive, acting-out behavior.

In a study by Johansson, Frankenhaeuser, and Magnusson (1973), a correlation of −.25 was found between teacher ratings of aggressiveness and level of adrenaline as measured during a 1-hour performance on arithmetic tests. The relationship of teacher-rated motor restlessness with adrenaline was −.34. The subjects in this study were 98 boys, aged 13, a largely representative sample of sixth-graders from a middle-sized Swedish town. The adrenaline values for this active period were based on only one urine sample. Adrenaline was also measured during a passive period when the subjects viewed a relaxing film. The correlation pattern for the latter adrenaline variable was similar to that for the active period but the relationships were generally weaker.

Also, Woodman and his associates in England have produced several different reports (e.g., Woodman, 1979; Woodman & Hinton, 1978) on a group of 58 maximum security hospital patients who were socially highly deviant. Among these patients, a subgroup was isolated with low adrenaline and high noradrenaline excretion in anticipation of a mildly stressing situation. Thus, their noradrenaline to adrenaline ratios were clearly higher than for the remaining group of patients. It was found that this subgroup was particularly characterized by a history of convictions for extreme physical violence.

Due to some procedural problems, it is difficult to know how reliable and generalizable the findings of this study are. Among other things, as many as two thirds of the patients were labelled "mentally ill" and it is unclear to what extent mental illness can have affected the patients' perception of the situation, and in that way, their catecholamine excretion. Nevertheless, these results, too, suggest a negative relationship between habitually aggressive, acting-out behavior and adrenaline level.

REFERENCES

Andersson, B., Hovmöller, S., Karlsson, C. -G., & Svensson, S. Analysis of urinary catecholamines: An improved auto-analyzer fluorescence method. *Clinica Chimica Acta*, 1974, *51*, 13–28.

Euler, U. S. von, & Lishajko, F. Improved technique for the fluorimetric estimation of catecholamines. *Acta Physiologica Scandinavica*, 1961, *51*, 348–355.

Eysenck, H. J. *The biological basis of personality*. Springfield, IL: Thomas, 1967

Eysenck, H. J. The measurement of emotion: Psychological parameters and methods. In L. Levi (Ed.), *Emotions: Their parameters and measurement*. New York: Raven Press, 1975.

Eysenck, H. J., & Eysenck, S. *Manual of the Eysenck Personality Questionnaire*. London: Hodder & Stoughton, 1975.

Frankenhaeuser, M. Behavior and circulating catecholamines. *Brain Research*, 1971, *31*, 241–262.

Frankenhaeuser, M. Psychoendocrine approaches to the study of emotion as related to stress and coping. In H. E. Howe & R. A. Dienstbier (Eds.), *Nebraska Symposium on Motivation 1978*. Lincoln: University of Nebraska Press, 1979.

Gale, A. The psychophysiology of individual differences: Studies of extraversion and the EEG. In P. Kline (Ed.), *New approaches in psychological measurement*. New York: Wiley, 1973.

Gellhorn, E., & Longbourrow, G. N. *Emotions and emotional disorders*. New York: Harper, 1963.

Johansson, G., Frankenhaeuser, M., & Magnusson, D. Catecholamine output in school children as related to performance and adjustment. *Scandinavian Journal of Psychology*, 1973, *14*, 20–28.

Levi, L. Stress and distress in response to psychosocial stimuli. Laboratory and real life studies on sympathoadrenomedullary and related reactions. *Acta Medica Scandinavica*, 1972, (Suppl. 528), *191*, pp. 1–166,

Moyer, K. E. *The psychobiology of aggression*. New York: Harper and Row, 1976.

Olweus, D. A critical analysis of the "modern" interactionist position. In D. Magnusson & N. S. Endler (Eds.), *Personality at the crossroads: Current issues in interactional psychology*. Hillsdale, NJ: Erlbaum, 1977.

Olweus, D. *Aggression in the schools: Bullies and whipping boys*. Washington, DC: Hemisphere, 1978.

Olweus, D. Stability of aggressive reaction patterns in males: A review. *Psychological Bulletin*, 1979, *86*, 852–875.

Olweus, D. Familial and temperamental determinants of aggressive behavior in adolescent boys: A causal analysis. *Developmental Psychology*, 1980, *16*, 644–660.

Olweus, D. The role of testosterone in the development of aggressive, antisocial behavior in human adolescents. In K. T. Van Dusen & S. A. Mednick (Eds.), *Prospective studies of crime and delinquency*. Boston: Klüwer-Nijhoff, 1983.

Olweus, D. Development of stable aggressive reaction patterns in males. In R. Blanchard & C. Blanchard (Eds.), *Advances in the study of aggression. Volume I*. New York: Academic Press, 1984.

Olweus, D., Mattsson, A., Schalling, D., & Löw, H. Testosterone, aggression, physical, and personality dimensions in normal adolescent males. *Psychosomatic Medicine*, 1980, *42*, 253–269.

Rose, R. M. Testosterone, aggression, and homosexuality: A review of the literature and implications for future research. In E. J. Sachar (Ed.), *Topics in endocrinology*. New York: Grune & Stratton, 1975.

Routtenberg, A. The two-arousal hypotheses: Reticular formation and limbic system. *Psychological Review*, 1968, *75*, 51–80.

Schalling, D. The trait-situation interaction and the physiological correlates of behavior. In D. Magnusson & N. S. Endler (Eds.), *Personality at the crossroads: Current issues in interactional psychology*. Hillsdale, NJ: Erlbaum, 1977.

Schalling, D., Cronholm, B., & Åsberg, M. Components of state and trait anxiety as related to personality and arousal. In L. Levi (Ed.), *Emotions: Their parameters and measurement*. New York: Raven Press, 1975.

Woodman, D. Urinary catecholamines and test habituation in maximum security hospital patients. *Journal of Psychosomatic Research*, 1979, *23*, 263–266.

Woodman, D. D., & Hinton, J. Catecholamine balance during stress antecipation: An abnormality in maximum security hospital patients. *Journal of Psychosomatic Research*, 1978, *22*, 477–483.

PART II

Early Developmental Patterns

5

The Nurturant Acts of
Very Young Children

HARRIET L. RHEINGOLD and GENA N. EMERY

In this essay we propose to add caregiving to the catalog of prosocial behaviors of very young children, a catalog that now includes comforting others in distress (Zahn-Waxler, Radke-Yarrow, & King, 1979), helping (Rheingold, 1982), sharing (Rheingold, Hay, & West, 1976), and cooperating (Hay, 1979). Caregiving, of course, includes many of these behaviors yet organizes them in another perhaps more inclusive category. Based on the data of formal and informal studies, justification for the proposal is considered, a theoretical account of the behavior's acquisition is sketched with special attention to how component processes are integrated, and the significance of the early acquisition of the behavior for a theory of development is presented.

Caring for the needs of the helpless young of our species constitutes a biological necessity, because upon it depends the preservation of the species. In this requirement *Homo sapiens* is not alone. In many genera of the Class Mammalia the altricial young require extensive care from birth, as well as in some of the class Aves, and even of Pisces, though to a much lesser extent. So demanding and necessary is care of the young in the Family Hominidae that it is legitimized by the laws and customs of human societies. Whether care of the young qualifies as a prosocial behavior may be questioned. In one sense it may be viewed as the most important of the prosocial behaviors, because it demands a sacrifice of time and energy

DEVELOPMENT OF ANTISOCIAL
AND PROSOCIAL BEHAVIOR

and is of paramount significance for the continuation of the species; in another it could be viewed as no more than preservation of one's own genes (the concept of *inclusive fitness*: Hamilton, 1964). This we recognize, but at the level of daily life as we experience it, the prosocial nature of the care of the young seems clear. Here we are more interested in the *proximate* mechanisms that are of consequence for development, that is, in ontogenetic explanations, than in the *ultimate* levels of explanation of how a behavior contributes to individual fitness, that is, the behavior's long-term adaptive significance—its phylogeny rather than its ontogeny.

In the Class Mammalia the young are cared for predominantly but not exclusively by their mothers. In many species other unrelated females contribute to their care (reviewed by Spencer-Booth, 1970), and in a substantial number of mammalian genera— nearly 40% of primate genera—males also offer care such as sleeping in contact with young, retrieving, transporting, cleaning and grooming (including ingesting the excreta of the young), providing food, baby-sitting in the mother's absence, and playing with and defending them (reviewed in Kleiman & Malcolm, 1981). Disregarding gestation and lactation, the summary of male parental behavior indeed closely resembles that of female parental behavior. In Homo sapiens the evidence for parental care includes in addition such behaviors as talking to and smiling (to mention only a few), and occurs from birth on (e.g., Parke & O'Leary, 1976). In many mammalian species, furthermore, siblings also care for each other; they groom one another, share food, guard and baby-sit, and retrieve younger siblings (reviewed in Bekoff, 1981).

REVIEW OF THE CHILD LITERATURE

Within the human species, examples abound of children as young as 2 years of age, and even younger, extending some nurturant acts to their parents and other adults, and to children, including some younger than themselves, as well as to replicas thereof, as in doll play. Children thus offer care at a relatively earlier age and to more varied recipients than has been reported for their mammalian relatives.

For the purposes of this essay, nurturant acts, with the synonym *caregiving,* are defined most simply and reasonably as comprising all the acts that human parents carry out in caring for their relatively helpless infants. These acts include not only those that fulfill the infants' biological needs for food, warmth, cleansing, and protection from harm, but also those more psychologic acts that produce a socialized child such as talking to, playing with, and instructing. All these we call *nurturant acts.*

Early biographers of their own children's development recorded the appearance of nurturant acts directed to their parents, infant siblings, and dolls during the second year of life (summarized in Valentine, 1938). Children reared together in a nursery were also reported to care for each other's needs (Freud & Burlingham, 1944). More recent studies of caregiving in natural settings show that children at this age respond sympathetically to adults and children in distress (Zahn-Waxler et al., 1979), contribute to the care of infant siblings (Dunn, Kendrick, & MacNamee, 1981), and in nursery schools help each other by sharing, aiding, and comforting (Bar-Tal, Raviv, & Goldberg, 1982).

The literature also includes a number of studies on the play of young children with dolls, studies that were set exclusively in the framework of cognitive development. Reports by Sinclair (1970), Inhelder (1971), and Lézine (1973) present data on such behavior by children in a nursery in Paris to demonstrate the transition from sensory-motor behavior to symbolic activity. A study of English children was considered by Lowe (1975) to show trends in the development of representational play. The study of African children by Dasen, Inhelder, Lavallée, and Retschitzki (1978), resembling in many ways Sinclair's study, was also cast as the development of symbolic activity. Similarly, Nicolich (1977) traced the stages of symbolic play with dolls, as did Fein and Apfel (1979) in a study of pretend play, while Fenson and Ramsay (1980) presented their findings in terms of decentration and integration. All these studies showed age trends in more meaningful acts of care accorded dolls and in imbuing the dolls with a life of their own.

In the studies we now present, the first set of data comes from a laboratory study of children at the ages of 18, 24, and 30 months, and the second from observations obtained in the course of collecting samples of children's speech in homes.

THE LABORATORY STUDY

The laboratory rather than the home was chosen to provide a setting conducive to evoking a fair amount of the behavior of interest in a relatively short time, to standardize the number and kinds of stimuli, and to ensure high-fidelity recording. In contrast to other studies of doll play, the setting provided a full complement of objects that was present throughout the session, and the caregiving objects were realistically sized for the age of the children. As in some studies, the setting provided four possible classes of potential recipients: (1) three dolls, (2), an equal number of stuffed animals (not just the teddy bear of some other studies [e.g., Sinclair, 1970]), (3) the parent (explicitly defining the identity of the "others" of previous studies [e.g., Fein & Apfel, 1979; Lowe, 1975]), and, of course, (4) the child's own self. We asked, How would the children distribute their nurturant acts among these classes? Also, to satisfy our definition of caregiving, the children's acts had to resemble what parents actually do for their young offspring. To that end, their nurturant acts were classified by categories measuring maternal care (Rheingold, 1960), such as feeding, grooming, and talking to the child, with the addition of the category of sharing, belatedly recognized as the very common parental behavior of showing and giving objects to the young. The category of talking to, not analyzed in the aforementioned studies of doll play, was divided into classes of speech that could be compared by the recipients of care. Furthermore, in addition to recording the children's talking to the recipients as a category of nurturant acts, the content of all their speech during caretaking was examined for evidence from which their knowledge of the meaning of their acts could be inferred and which would attest to the validity of their acts being interpreted as caregiving rather than as simply random events. Of special interest here were verbalizations that ascribed a measure of animateness to the dolls and animals, referring to, for example, such internal states as needs, wants, and feelings (see Bretherton, McNew, & Beeghly-Smith, 1981), as well as the possible occurrence of those alterations of the voice labeled baby talk (reviewed in Papoušek & Papoušek, 1981). This last measure would apply to the active–passive distinction so prominent in the cognitive studies, that is, whether the children treated the dolls as capable of caring for themselves.

Increases by age were anticipated not only in amounts of nurturant acts, primarily accorded dolls and animals, but especially in accompanying verbal behavior. Then, as in other studies, the diversity of acts, labeled *elaboration* by Lézine (1973), was also expected to increase with age (Fenson, Kagan, Kearsley, & Zelazo, 1976), as was the serial ordering (Lashley, 1951) of related acts in a sequence of caregiving to the same recipient. The emergence of ordered sequences at about 18 months of age had been reported (Dasen et al., 1978; Inhelder, 1971; Lézine, 1973; Lowe, 1975; Nicolich, 1977; Sinclair, 1970) but without frequency counts, except for two-act sequences by Fenson and Ramsay (1980), who labeled them *ordered multischemes*. The criterion in the present study was a temporal ordering of acts resembling that which adults would perform in caring for a child—information here considered revealing of the child's intentions and plans.

Equal numbers of boys and girls were studied at each age, but major differences were not anticipated because none had been reported in studies of other positive social behaviors in children so young (e.g., Bar-Tel et al., 1982; Rheingold, 1982; Rheingold et al., 1976; Zahn-Waxler et al.,

1979). Girls, however, were expected to display more nurturant acts toward dolls than would boys (e.g., Dasen et al., 1978; Lowe, 1975), possessing as they do more lifelike dolls (Rheingold & Cook, 1975)—a finding that echoes parental expectations and approval (Fagot, 1978). Although Valentine (1942) wrote of "the passion of little girls and sometimes of boys for dolls" (p. 306) and wondered if the more common devotion to dolls by girls evinced an innate protective impulse, he too allowed for parental suggestions of the appropriateness of dolls as playthings for girls and not for boys.

METHOD

Subjects

A group of 36 children, comprised of 6 boys and 6 girls at the ages of approximately 18 months (mean, 19.7; range, 18.2 to 21.1), 24 months (mean, 25.5; range, 24.0 to 26.4), and 30 months (mean, 31.6; range, 30.0 to 32.9) were seen individually with a parent present. Six of the 36 children were accompanied by their fathers and the rest by their mothers. The children came from homes above average in educational level: fathers' years of education averaged 17.3 (range, 10–20) and mothers', 15.9 (range, 12–20). Potential subjects' names were obtained from local hospital and county records, and 91% of the parents contacted by telephone agreed to participate.

The Laboratory Setting

The study took place in a suite of three connecting and attractively decorated rooms. The main room contained a low table holding a small baby doll, a child's book, and a chime ball; a doll carriage with mattress; across the room a child's rocker with a doll blanket draped on one arm; a doll cradle with mattress, pillow, and blanket; and a teddy bear and rattle. One smaller room contained a doll's high chair with a Raggedy Ann doll in it; a low table on which were placed a cup, a bowl containing three animal crackers, a spoon, baby food jar, bottle, plastic apple, and bib; and a child's chair on which was seated another teddy bear. The other small room contained a doll's bed with mattress, pillow, and blanket; a stuffed dog; a low table on which sat a baby doll, baby bath tub, towel, wash cloth, soap, baby comb and brush, a facial tissue, and a disposable diaper. All objects were child-sized, placed at the child's eye level, and in the same position for all children. Each room also contained a chair for the parent to sit in.

Procedure

The experimenter met the parent and child in a reception room and explained the purpose of the study in terms the child would not understand. The parent was instructed to respond in a natural fashion without directing the child's activities. The parent was also asked to remain seated, at first in the large room but later moving if the child requested the parent's presence in another room or if the child seemed to have exhausted the possibilities for play in one room. The parent was reassured that whatever the child did was of interest and that we held no fixed expectations. The parent and child were then led into the playrooms where the one-way windows and video cameras were remarked. The trial began as the experimenter left and lasted 30 minutes. The sessions were recorded on audio- and videotape by remotely controlled cameras on pan-and-tilt units that tracked the child in the playrooms. Split-screen imaging and digital timing aided the subsequent analyses.

Measures of Caregiving

The children's acts were coded from videotapes by predefined measures of caregiving, including notation of the recipient of the act. The eight categories and the acts that defined them were (1) *Beds*—the child places doll or animal in bed (or carriage but only if verbally indicated for sleeping); places in cradle; places pillow under recipient's head; covers with, pulls up, straightens, or tucks in blanket or adjusts mattress for recipient; rocks in cradle; kisses goodnight following bedding; or cautions silence for bedded recipient; (2) *Caresses*—kisses, hugs or nuzzles, or pats; (3) *Disciplines*—hits with one or more blows; (4) *Feeds*—places cracker to mouth of recipient; places apple to mouth; places bottle to mouth; places bowl, cup, or jar to mouth; places spoon to mouth; transfers "food" from one utensil to another prior to feeding, or stirs or spoons food from any receptacle prior to feeding; seats recipient in high chair prior to feeding; places bib appropriately; or places utensil or food on high-chair tray of seated recipient; (5) *Grooms*—combs hair, brushes hair, places in bathtub in seated or face-up position, rubs soap on recipient's body, uses washcloth or towel in "bathing," places diaper on recipient, uses facial tissue appropriately, or wraps in blanket; (6) *Positions*—places doll or animal in seated, standing, or propped position so that position is maintained; holds doll or animal against own chest and supports it with an arm across its back, as an adult might hold a baby; pushes or pulls recipient in carriage; or rocks in arms or in rocking chair; (7) *Shares*—points by extending an index finger toward an object, excluding points to structural features of the rooms; holds up or holds out an object while looking at the recipient; or gives an object by releasing it into parent's lap or hand or very close to doll or animal. Some children used feeding items in sharing with the parent (e.g., giving the apple), and such acts could have been coded as feeding had we been less conservative.

Talks To, Category 8, was coded when the child spoke directly to a doll, animal, or parent. For dolls and animals, the act was coded whether or not it accompanied a caregiving act, but for the parent only if it accompanied one, so as to rule out a great deal of speech directed to the parent from a distance. Criteria for coding thus included visual regard, contact with or close proximity to the recipient while talking, as well as the content of the utterance, especially the use of the appropriate proper noun or pronoun. Repetitions, whether exact, partial, or transformed, were not counted, and in general the counts erred on the side of conservatism. The transcribed utterances were assigned to four classes (the first of the examples being typical of speech to dolls and animals, the second, of speech to parents): (1) *commands*—instructs or directs the recipient to do something (e.g., "Sit up, baby," "Mommy, brush hair"); (2) *comments*—imparts information to the recipient (e.g., "Here's cookies," "I wash your face"); (3) *questions*—poses any interrogatives beyond a tag question (e.g., "Want juice?" "What's that?"); and (4) *social phrases*—relatively contentless or conventional phrases (e.g., "Oh, poor baby," "Hi, Daddy").

Special note was made when the children seemed to alter their patterns of speech in addressing a doll or animal resembling those commonly used by adults in speaking to infants (i.e., baby talk). Such patterns included one or more of such characteristics as a higher-than-usual pitch; strongly accentuated stress, tone, or intonation; a lengthening of some syllables; and often a songlike quality.

The children, of course, could not themselves be recipients of the categories of Disciplines, Caresses, Shares, or Talks To, nor the parents of Beds or Positions, but the dolls and animals could be recipients of all eight categories of caregiving.

Diversity of behavior was measured by the number of different caregiving acts a child displayed at least once of the 39 possible within the eight categories, regardless of recipient. Repetitions of the same act, even with different recipients, were not counted; for example, holding the cup to the mouth of a doll, an animal, and oneself here counted as only one act. For the dolls and animals, all 39 acts could be carried out, but only 23 could for the parent and 19 for child's self (e.g., in the category of Grooming, "brushes hair" was possible for the parent and the self, but not "puts in tub").

The serial ordering of acts was defined as a sequence of two or more related acts directed to the same recipient that were carried out consecutively and that included or ended in a defined caregiving act. Sequences could include (1) acts preliminary to the caregiving act, limited to only one such act per sequence, (2) the caregiving act or acts or separate components thereof, omitting repetitions as usual, (3) verbal commands, and (4) such concluding acts as returning an item to its former place. Repeated sequences to the same recipient were not counted unless separated by at least 2 minutes; if, however, a repeated sequence included additional acts, the longer of the two was counted. Furthermore, if two recipients were simultaneously cared for in a sequence, the acts were counted as only one sequence. Thus, sequences were coded conservatively.

Confirming verbal evidence was defined as the children's verbalizations that supported the interpretation of their acts as caregiving. All the children's utterances accompanying or relevant to their nurturant acts were coded into the following classes: (1) *abstract*—those giving their intentions (e.g., "I'm giving my bear a good night"), reasons for their activity (e.g., "Need to comb her hair to go to school"), or descriptions of the consequences of the act (e.g., "He's going sleeping" as puts the bear to bed); (2) *concrete*—those describing in specific terms the child's actions (e.g., "Put the baby on the pamper," "I rockin' the dog"); and (3) *general*—those providing information that was not considered abstract or concrete but was nevertheless relevant, such as referring to one or more of the objects being manipulated (e.g., "This is for little baby" as holds bottle to doll's mouth; "Doggie" as hugs dog). To avoid reading too much into their still-immature speech, this evaluation of children's utterances was extremely conservative.

Ascribing animateness to dolls and animals was estimated by compiling several measures. First, all instances of talking to the dolls and animals were judged to reveal the child's imputing to them the ability to hear. Second, the child's commands to them (e.g., "Sit there, Raggedy Ann"), as well as putting objects such as a rattle in the hand of the doll or animal, or placing food on the high-chair tray with a command to eat, showed that the child assumed the objects could act independently, that is, granted them an active role (see McCune-Nicolich, 1981; Watson & Fischer, 1977). Third, verbalizations during caregiving that contained references to the objects' internal states (e.g., "This one [bear] is sleepy"), feelings (e.g., "Oh, what's wrong, Annie?"), and preferences (e.g., "He didn't like his apple") were considered to attribute some degree of sentience to them. The measure here was the number of children who displayed one or more of these types of acts or verbalizations.

Measures of Observer Agreement

On measures of acts within categories of caregiving, pairs of observers independently coded 18 randomly chosen records, balanced for age and sex. For all other measures 12 records, similarly chosen, were so coded. The median percentages of the number of agreements divided by the number of agreements and disagreements, on only acts that occurred, were 100 for caregiving acts (range, 60–100), 90 for the number of sequences (range, 71–100), 88 for the number of serially ordered acts within sequences (range, 76–100), and 93 for classes of confirming verbal evidence (range, 78–96). For reported data, all disagreements were subsequently resolved.

RESULTS

All the children at each age accorded the dolls and animals, the parents, and themselves a considerable number of nurturant acts, the mean number increasing by only nine from age to age (Table 5.1). The children averaged about 3 acts per minute and displayed behaviors in a mean of 6.4 of the 8 categories of caregiving, with individual scores ranging from 5 to 8 and minimal differences by age.

Dolls and Animals as Recipients

All the children directed nurturant acts toward the dolls and animals. The total number of these acts, summed over categories, increased by age (Kruskal-Wallis, $H(2) = 8.0$, $p < .02$), the increase from 18 to 24 months appearing to be greater than that from 24 to 30 months. The two most common categories of caregiving over the three ages, in order of number of children, were Positions and Grooms, followed closely by Feeds and Talks To (Table 5.1). The order of mean frequencies was similar for the age groups except for the increase in Beds (as well as in number of children), Talks To, and Grooms from 24 to 30 months. Although many children participated in Caresses and Shares with the dolls and animals, the mean frequencies of these categories were low, and Disciplines occurred very rarely indeed.

More than half the children spoke directly to the dolls and animals, and at 30 months almost all did. At 18 months, social phrases accounted for two thirds of all utterances, but at the older ages they accounted for only one third (Table 5.2). In contrast, both commands and comments increased until, at 30 months, they accounted for almost two thirds of all

Table 5.1

Frequency of Nurturant Acts within Categories by Age and Recipient

Category	18 months		24 months		30 months	
	N^a	Mean[b]	N^a	Mean[b]	N^a	Mean[b]
Dolls and animals						
Beds	5	1.7	8	6.3	11	10.3
Caresses	6	1.8	8	1.5	9	2.2
Disciplines	2	0.2	1	0.1	3	0.3
Feeds	8	3.4	9	7.7	10	5.9
Grooms	10	4.6	10	4.8	10	8.9
Positions	12	8.5	11	10.1	12	9.0
Shares	7	1.1	5	0.7	7	1.2
Talks to	8[c]	3.1	7	10.1	10[c]	14.5
	12	24.2	12	41.2	12	52.4
Parent						
Feeds	4	0.4	4	0.5	2	0.6
Grooms	5	1.2	2	0.9	3	1.0
Shares	12	40.8	12	27.1	12	23.2
Talks to	11[c]	14.6	12	21.1	11[c]	21.9
	12	57.3	12	49.6	12	46.7
Self						
Beds	5	1.0	3	0.8	4	1.4
Feeds	12	6.9	11	8.2	11	5.8
Grooms	9	2.9	6	1.2	9	4.1
Positions	5	0.6	9	0.9	2	0.3
	12	11.4	12	11.0	12	11.6
All recipients						
Grand total	12	93.0	12	101.8	12	110.7

[a] Number of children who displayed one or more of the different acts in the category.

[b] Mean frequency for group of 12 children, including those who performed no act in that category.

[c] Records of speech available for only 11 children.

such direct address. At each age the children seldom asked the dolls and animals questions. Thus, with maturity, the children not only spoke to the dolls and animals more often, but the nature of what they said also changed.

At each age the children accorded the dolls more nurturant acts than they did the animals (Wilcoxon matched-pairs signed-ranks test, $z = -3.68, p < .001$). The dolls were fed, groomed, positioned, and shared with

Table 5.2

Frequency of Classes of Direct Address (Talks To) by Age and Recipient

Class	18 months (N = 11)		24 months (N = 12)		30 months (N = 11)	
	N^a	Mean[b]	N^a	Mean[b]	N^a	Mean[b]
Talking to dolls and animals						
Social Phrases	7	2.1	7	3.4	7	5.2
Commands	4	0.7	6	3.8	8	4.4
Comments	2	0.2	4	2.2	8	4.4
Questions	1	0.1	3	0.7	3	0.5
	8	3.1	7	10.1	10	14.5
Talking to parents						
Social Phrases	3	0.6	6	1.1	7	1.2
Commands	6	1.7	8	2.2	8	4.2
Comments	11	10.1	12	13.5	11	12.5
Questions	4	2.2	9	4.2	9	4.0
	11	14.6	12	21.1	11	21.9

[a] Number of children whose utterances fell in the class.

[b] Mean frequency for all children whether or not their utterances fell in the class.

more often but were less often put to bed than the animals. The dolls were also spoken to more often, and the increase by age in the number of commands and comments in relation to social phrases occurred more often in speech to them than to animals. Both classes of recipients, however, were equally often caressed and disciplined. Even though the children performed more nurturant acts for the dolls, only three children at 18 months of age, one at 24 months, and one at 30 months performed none for the animals. Most children, then, at all ages cared for both animals and dolls.

The Parent as Recipient

The children accorded the parents many caregiving acts, at the youngest age more than twice as many as they accorded the dolls and animals (Table 5.1). Although the mean frequency of acts accorded the parents did not differ reliably by age, that accorded the dolls and animals did increase by age, so that by 30 months of age the children were directing relatively more acts to the inanimate objects than to the parents.

The most frequent behavior was sharing objects with the parent by showing and giving, with a mean frequency that surpassed any other category. Of the separate components within Sharing, it was the giving of objects that decreased most precipitously, from a mean of 20 at 18 months of age to a mean of only 7 by both older groups. Showing by pointing to an object or holding it up for the parent's viewing, in contrast, remained a prominent behavior, the means decreasing gradually from 21 to 20 to 16 across the three ages. As for the other categories, only a few children fed or groomed their parents and then infrequently. None caressed a parent, but one 18-month-old boy hit his mother.

All the children also talked to their parents while carrying out nurturant acts. As Table 5.1 shows, they talked more often to their parents than to the dolls and animals (even though the criterion for speech to parents was stricter), and although the mean frequency of utterances increased with age, the increase was smaller than that to dolls and animals. What they said to their parents also differed; the children mostly commented on the objects given or on the caregiving act they were performing for them or for the dolls and animals (Table 5.2). Also, in contrast to their speech to the dolls and animals, they asked their parents more questions but gave fewer commands and scarcely any social phrases.

The Self as Recipient

All the children directed some nurturant acts toward themselves. The mean frequency of the acts for the four possible categories showed negligible differences by age (Table 5.1). Almost all the children fed themselves—not a surprising event given that three animal crackers were provided—a majority groomed themselves, and some lay down in the bed or rocked themsleves in the rocking chair.

Diversity of Acts

Although the number of acts displayed by the children to all recipients differed only slightly by age, the mean number of different acts increased with age from 18.0 to 21.7 to 23.8, respectively (Kruskal-Wallis, $H(2) = 9.01$, $p < .02$). A closer examination, however, showed that the mean number of different acts accorded the parent remained steady across the ages (means varying around 6.7 of the 23 possible), as did those accorded the self (means varying around 5.4 of the 19 possible). In contrast, the number of different acts accorded the dolls and animals increased from 10.4 to 13.8 to 17.2 of the 39 possible (Kruskal-Wallis $H(2) = 8.90$, $p < .02$). Not only did the children accord the dolls and animals more caregiving acts as age increased, but their repertoire of acts became more diversified, a finding that may stem in part from the greater number of categories available for the inanimate objects.

The Serial Ordering of Acts

At 18 months all the children carried out sequences of two or more acts; at 24 months, sequences of three or more; and at 30 months, sequences of five or more acts, a length achieved by only two children of the 18-month-old group and six of the 24-month-old group. The percentages of two-act sequences of all sequences decreased across the ages, from 65 to 50 to 42. The means of the children's mean length of sequences increased from 2.42 to 2.85 to 3.45 across the ages (Kruskal-Wallis, $H(2) = 13.64$, $p < .01$), and the corresponding means for the means of each child's 5 longest sequences were 2.73, 3.47, and 4.63 (Kruskal-Wallis, $H(2) = 16.91$, $p < .001$). In summary, even 18-month-old children coordinated their caregiving acts, but the older children displayed an increasing ability to order their acts in a logical sequence, appearing to act with a plan in mind.

Confirming Verbal Evidence

The children's speech revealed considerable verbal knowledge of their acts, the mean number of such verbalizations increasing across the three ages (Table 5.3). At 18 months of age, general statements constituted 77.8% of these utterances but decreased to 63.5% at 24 months and to 54.8% at 30 months. Concrete utterances, those in which the children put into words what they were doing, coinciding exactly with their visible acts, increased (Kruskal-Wallis, $H(2) = 12.4$, $p < .01$), as did abstract utterances, those from which intentions to perform an act or reasons for it could be inferred (Kruskal-Wallis, $H(2) = 7.6$, $p < .05$). In contrast to the percentages of general statements, those for the combined classes of concrete and abstract utterances rose from 22.2% at 18 months to 36.6% at 24 months to 45.2%, that is, almost half of all utterances, at 30 months. The

Table 5.3

Frequency of Classes of Speech Informative of Caregiving by Age

Class	18 months (N = 11)		24 months (N = 12)		30 months (N = 11)	
	N^a	Mean[b]	N^a	Mean[b]	N^a	Mean[b]
General	11	16.5	12	16.5	11	20.6
Concrete	5	1.7	9	2.7	11	7.4
Abstract	8	3.0	11	6.8	11	9.6
	11	21.2	12	26.0	11	37.6

[a] Number of children whose utterances fell in the class.

[b] Mean frequency for all children whether or not their utterances fell in the class.

increase aside, the simple finding that even at 18 months of age the children spontaneously gave a mean of three verbalizations from which their intention to carry out a caregiving act could be inferred is noteworthy.

Intonational Changes No changes of intonation characteristic of baby talk were recorded for speech to the parent, but some were recorded in the children's speech to the dolls and animals, and increasingly so with age. Across the three ages, the numbers of children who used the register, although few, increased from 4 to 6 and then to 8, with corresponding mean frequencies of 3.2, 5.8, and 11.6. Typical examples were "Nap, bear" at 18 months, "You can have your supper" at 24 months, and "Good baby had a good day" at 30 months.

Ascribing Animateness to Dolls and Animals

Talking to the dolls and animals constituted one major body of evidence that the children ascribed a measure of animateness to them (Table 5.2). The issuing of commands such as "Sit there, Raggedy Ann, and eat," and the asking of questions such as "You ready to go?" before pushing an animal in the carriage were especially telling. In addition, some of the children's speech also revealed an awareness that the dolls and animals were capable of having preferences, feelings, and internal states. Although the speech of only a few children gave such awareness (one at 18 months, four at 24 months, and five at 30 months), the findings provide evidence of the early appearance of affective perspective-taking. Furthermore, when the records of individual children were searched for the combined evidence of direct address (especially the issuing of commands and questions), the ascription of sentience, and such nonverbal acts as trying to put a spoon in the doll's hand, almost all the children (10 at 18 months, 11 at 24 months, and all at 30 months) treated the dolls and animals as though they were animate beings.

Sex Differences

Boys and girls ($N = 18$ each) did not differ reliably in number of caregiving acts, in number of different acts, in number of acts in any category of caregiving, including that of talking to the recipients, or in any of the other measures. A reliable difference occurred, however, in the girls according more nurturant acts to dolls than did the boys (Mann-Whitney U test, $z = -1.95$, $p = .05$). The girls also directed more acts toward the dolls than toward the animals (Wilcoxon matched-pairs signed-ranks test,

$T = 1.5, p < .01$) in contrast to the boys who provided similar amounts of care for both dolls and animals. These differences, not apparent within ages, appeared only when scores were collapsed across all ages.

OBSERVATIONS IN THE HOME

Because doll play was so often reported in baby biographies, accounts of the behavior outside the laboratory seem unnecessary. Still, a contemporary account of such play by several children in their homes, including their caregiving of persons and themselves, supplement the findings from the laboratory. These observations were incidentally recorded during a series of 2-hour visits in homes to collect samples of mothers' speech to their 2-year-old children.

The records, averaging about 13 hours in duration for each child, covered the span of time from 24 to 33 months of age in the lives of five boys and seven girls, four of whom had infant siblings. Of 426 caregiving acts recorded, 421 could be classified by the eight categories of the laboratory study. The most common behavior was Sharing with adults, with the observer being an even more frequent recipient than the parent. Next in order of frequency were Talking to, with dolls almost as frequent recipients as the adults, and Self-grooming, which consisted mostly of dressing. Dolls were fed, put to bed, and positioned much more often than toy animals by both boys and girls. Disciplining was rare—only 3 of the 421 acts. The infant siblings were talked to and given and shown objects, and live animals were fed and caressed. The speech to the dolls and animals contained many examples of ascribing sentience to them. For example, a 30-month-old girl reported of her doll, "She's gonna take the cow to bed with her so she won't cry," and a 28-month-old boy rocking a doll said, "He have a bad dream, hug him, rock him."

In the main, considerable concordance was found between home and laboratory observations. The home offered more classes of recipients; the laboratory, by circumscribing the environment, increased the frequency of the behaviors per unit of time.

DISCUSSION

The boys and girls in this study, even those at 18 months of age, freely extended many nurturant acts to their parents, the dolls, and toy animals—as well as to themselves. In many respects their acts closely resembled those parents extend to their infants and those that had been extended to these very children by their parents. Toward these different recipients, within the constraints of the setting, the children showed a nice appreciation of what was appropriate. Especially in their speech they showed the ability to distinguish among the different recipients, more often sharing information with their parents and less often instructing them in what to do. Furthermore, their speech revealed that their nurturant acts were not aimless or random and that the replicas we provided of living beings were so viewed.

Even though the 18-month-old children exhibited a full complement of behavior, the older children surpassed them in exhibiting a larger repertoire of nurturant acts and in organizing them in longer chains. Although the number of self-directed acts remained steady, the proportion of acts directed to the dolls and animals increased as the proportion directed to their parents decreased. The children's speech became more informative of what they had in mind to do and more appropriate to the recipient, especially in imbuing the dolls and animals with feelings and preferences to be consulted.

These findings agree in the main with findings of others on children of comparable age, specifically on increases with age in amounts of doll play, diversity of acts, lengthening of the serial ordering of acts, assigning of an active role to dolls and animals, and on the absence of an increase in self-directed acts. Differences can be accounted for in part by differences in the setting and in the classes of behavior recorded. In the present study, the children were free to move through a relatively large space and were not seated at a table. Three animals served as potential recipients in contrast to the one of some studies. The caregiving objects were numerous, continuously available, and realistically sized in contrast to the miniature-sized objects of some studies. The nature of the children's acts with dolls, animals, the parent, and the self were organized by categories of care, and their speech was counted as caregiving, analyzed by classes, and searched for evidence of intention. And regarding the children's ascribing animateness to the dolls and animals, evidence was sought in both verbal and nonverbal behavior. Furthermore, the absence of such distractions or other competing stimuli, as might occur in a home or nursery school, contributed to the richness of the children's responses.

The mimicking of nurturant acts that children perform for themselves, such as raising an empty cup to the mouth or lying down in a bed, has been considered as an early stage in the development of symbolic play, preceding doll play and occurring before 18 months of age. When placed in the framework of social behavior, such acts do not, of course, qualify as prosocial behavior. Rather, they may be viewed as developments in caring for oneself that increase rather than decrease with age. The absence of an increase in the laboratory study may be attributed to a setting that did not provide the opportunity for such other classes of self-care as the dressing and undressing observed at home.

Real or Imaginary?

Before we consider the main proposal that the children's acts warrant the appellation prosocial, the findings on care afforded dolls must be reconciled with that afforded real people. Is all the children's behavior, regardless of recipient, just play? Or, more precisely, is care afforded dolls play and care afforded people (and animal pets) real, that is, not play? Or, more precisely still, is care afforded dolls imaginary or, as often characterized, pretend play? Granted that dolls and toy animals are but replicas of the real (an important distinction for Piaget's stage theory of cognitive development), the adjectives *imaginary* or *pretend* depict the adults' view and not necessarily the children's. Children do what they can with what a situation presents. They can offer food, real or not real, to a parent, but they can put only a doll to bed. To the child, play in a doll house (respects to Ibsen) may be serious business. Then, who decides what is play and what is not play? The eye of the beholder? Or, the mind of the child? The children's view, we propose, *is* knowable—by their acts and even more by what they say. To be sure, the situation is imaginary, but it is a situation comprehensible only in the light of a real situation, as "a recollection of something that actually happened . . . more memory in action than a novel imaginary situation" (Vygotsky, 1978, p. 103; from a lecture delivered in 1933). In light of these several considerations, the case is made that, for considering the nurturant acts of very young children as prosocial, the animateness of the recipient is irrelevant.

Defense of Children's Behavior as Prosocial

Now we can turn our attention to the main proposition, that the spontaneous nurturant acts of children in the second year of life deserve to join the category of prosocial behavior. First, we have shown that, given the wherewithal at their disposal, their acts were not random but appropriate to the different recipients. Many of their acts were carried out in orderly and logical sequences, giving evidence of a measure of planning, and were accompanied by speech that revealed a knowledge of the meaning of their acts. Then, the majority of their acts so closely resembled those of adult caretakers that the same benefit would accrue to the recipients as the acts of adult caretakers, acts that in verity they had themselves benefitted from at the hands of their own parents.

To press the matter further, were these nurturant acts performed at some sacrifice? We come now to the nub of the problem. Children so young have few pressing duties. They have lots of time. They have little to sacrifice. Indeed, here it is crucial to point out how inappropriate it is to judge children's behavior by standards of adult behavior. Despite the resemblance of their caregiving acts to those of adults, a child's behavior should not be gauged by how far it must develop to become adult. In a very important sense, for the student of development, adult behavior cannot be viewed as superior to that of children or even infants. Rather, each stage of development should be regarded as functionally complete in its own right (and from the point of view of the evolutionary biologist, as adapted to the environment in which it finds itself). To be faithful to the developmental perspective, our task is to discover when behaviors of interest first appear—however immature their form—and then to ask about their acquisition and conditions of maintenance.

Processes of Acquisition

Although not intentionally taught by parents, caregiving is acquired by learning. To begin at an elementary level, the behavior depends on the acquisition of motor skills, following in broad outline Bruner's (1973) account of the organization of early skilled action during the first year of life. By the second year of life, the serial structuring of acts (Lashley, 1951) contributes to the child's competence in achieving intended results. Goal-directed, skilled action thus may be conceived of as the construction of serially ordered constituent acts whose performance is modified toward less variability, more anticipation, and greater economy by benefit of feed-forward, feedback, and knowledge of results (Bruner, 1973). Piaget's (1952) sensorimotor stages of means and ends and object permanence find a place here. The acquisition of motor skills depends of course on physiological maturation (of brain, hand, and foot), interaction with the physical world and the things in it, and practice. The motor skills necessary to imitate the behavior of others develop accordingly.

As motor skills are acquired, so do cognitive skills develop. With maturation and experience the child's perception of events and their meaning increases, as do memory, learning (that is, the modification of behavior by experience), and linguistic skills. In the second year, children begin to use symbols for real objects in playing and of course in speech, especially as they progress from single word utterances to two- and three-word utterances (Piaget, 1951, 1962). The studies of doll play already referred to (e.g., Fein & Apfel, 1979; Fenson & Ramsay, 1980; Nicolich, 1977; Sinclair, 1970) were proposed to exemplify the concept.

The mechanism proposed by Piaget to account for symbolic play (also labeled *representational play*) was deferred imitation. It is at precisely this point that we can bring in the principles of social learning theory. The important place that imitation plays in social learning theory depends upon the mechanisms of observational learning (Bandura, 1977), including the development of attention, memory, motoric reproduction skills (already referred to), and the role of reinforcement.

Cogent as these theoretical accounts of how the children acquire the ability to accord care to others are, two other matters require special consideration. The first is an emendation; the second a question. The first points out the special nature of what, and whom, the children imitate. They reproduce precisely those behaviors accorded them by their parents, the behaviors of which they themselves were the recipients. This the children accomplished in the laboratory even with dolls, animals, and caregiving objects they had never seen before, so great was their ability to generalize. The second raises the question of the rewards (or reinforcement) children experience in carrying out nurturant acts. When adults are the recipients, a response, however, minimal, may be assumed. When real babies are the recipients, the response is more problematic. But in the case of the dolls and toy animals, the response is actually nonexistent (however real imaginatively). Of course, just the ability to perform adult-type acts may be reinforcing to very young children. Still, children may be vicariously rewarded by carrying out for others acts that as recipients they found rewarding, just as are adults in caring for their real children.

The currently popular concept of social cognition bears some relevance to this account. It could be proposed, for example, that the young child in acting nurturantly is assuming the role of the parent. Certainly the data lend themselves to such a proposal. They supply evidence that the children know what others see (e.g., in attracting their parents' attention to distant objects) and what even the dolls may be thinking and feeling. They speak differently to their parents than to the dolls, and they not only speak to babies and dolls but speak for them. There is evidence too that they are aware of others' emotional states, a fact used to index their empathic feelings. The question remains, however, of how much the concept adds to an understanding of the origins of the behavior of interest, that is, how much it explains. That the very young child can be at the same time both caregiver and the one cared for contributes to knowledge about the development of social behavior. Nevertheless, to claim, as the evidence seems to show, that the child behaves as a caregiver makes a stronger and preferred statement than claiming that the child assumes the parental role. The child behaves *as* a caregiver rather than *as if* a caregiver.

Concluding Statement

How general is the phenomenon? Our own data pertain to children from homes of relatively well-educated and presumably benevolent parents. The same undoubtedly applies to the anecdotes reviewed earlier. Yet the findings of this essay are similar to those of other studies of children from a variety of family backgrounds in the United States, France, Israel, and the Ivory Coast of Africa. The possibility exists, of course, that in other less benign settings children might show fewer nurturant acts than any of the studies reported. It is just at this point that we feel called upon to defend concentrating on the positive rather than the negative side of the coin. The best defense is that, had the topic of this essay been the aggressive behavior of the young, scarcely anyone would have criticized the omission of concurrent prosocial behavior. Such is the orientation of the world, including parents, teachers, observers, and many investigators, that disruptive behaviors command attention while the overwhelmingly more common prosocial behaviors go largely unremarked.

In conclusion, we propose that not only do the behaviors here studied qualify as prosocial behaviors but that, in addition, to offer care to related persons carries enormous significance for the evolution of the *species,* and to offer care to all other persons carries enormous significance for the evolution of *society.* That behaviors of such consequence develop early seems remarkable, but their very consequence may be responsible for their precocity.

ACKNOWLEDGEMENT

This investigation was supported by grant number HDO1107 from the National Institute of Child Health and Human Development to H.L.R. We thank Sarah B. Cornwell for help in coding and Sara D. Peach for invaluable assistance at every stage of the study.

REFERENCES

Bandura, A. *Social learning theory.* Englewood Cliffs, NJ: Prentice-Hall, 1977.
Bar-Tal, D., Raviv, A., & Goldberg, M. Helping behavior among preschool children: An observational study. *Child Development,* 1982, *53,* 396–402.
Bekoff, M. Mammalian sibling interactions: Genes, facilitative environments, and the coefficient of familiarity. In D. J. Gubernick & P. H. Klopfer (Eds.), *Parental care in mammals.* New York: Plenum, 1981.
Bretherton, I., McNew, S., & Beeghly-Smith, M. Early person knowledge as expressed in gestural and verbal communication: When do infants acquire a "theory of mind"? In M. E. Lamb & L. R. Sherrod (Eds.), *Infant social cognition: Empirical and theoretical considerations.* Hillsdale, NJ: Lawrence Erlbaum Associates, 1981.

Bruner, J. S. Organization of early skilled action. *Child Development*, 1973, *44*, 1–11.

Dasen, P. R., Inhelder, B., Lavallée, M., & Retschitzki, J. *Naissance de l'intelligence chez l'enfant baoulé de côte d'ivoire*. Berne: Hans Huber, 1978.

Dunn, J., Kendrick, C., & MacNamee, R. The reaction of first-born children to the birth of a sibling: Mothers' reports. *Journal of Child Psychology and Psychiatry*, 1981, *22*, 1–18.

Fagot, B. I. The influence of sex of child on parental reactions to toddler children. *Child Development*, 1978, *49*, 459–465.

Fein, G. G., & Apfel, N. Some preliminary observations on knowing and pretending. In N. R. Smith & M. B. Franklin (Eds.), *Symbolic functioning in childhood*. Hillsdale, NJ: Lawrence Erlbaum Associates, 1979.

Fenson, L., Kagan, J., Kearsley, R. B., & Zelazo, P. R. The developmental progression of manipulative play in the first two years. *Child Development*, 1976, *47*, 232–236.

Fenson, L., & Ramsay, D. S. Decentration and integration of the child's play in the second year. *Child Development*, 1980, *51*, 171–178.

Freud, A., & Burlingham, D. *Infants without families: The case for and against residential nurseries*. New York: International University Press, 1944.

Hamilton, W. D. The genetical evolution of social behaviour, Parts I and II. *Journal of Theoretical Biology*, 1964, *7*, 1–52.

Hay, D. F. Cooperative interactions and sharing between very young children and their parents. *Developmental Psychology*, 1979, *15*, 647–653.

Inhelder, B. The sensory-motor origins of knowledge. In D. N. Walcher & D. L. Peters (Eds.), *The development of self-regulatory mechanisms*. New York: Academic Press, 1971.

Kleiman, D. G., & Malcolm, J. R. The evolution of male parental investment in mammals. In D. J. Gubernick & P. H. Klopfer (Eds.), *Parental care in mammals*. New York: Plenum, 1981.

Lashley, K. S. The problem of serial order in behavior. In L. A. Jeffress (Ed.), *Cerebral mechanisms in behavior*. New York: Wiley, 1951.

Lézine, I. The transition from sensorimotor to earliest symbolic function in early development. In J. I. Nurnberger (Ed.), *Biological and environmental determinants of early development*. Baltimore: Williams & Wilkins, 1973.

Lowe, M. Trends in the development of representational play in infants from one to three years: An observational study. *Journal of Child Psychology and Psychiatry*, 1975, *16*, 33–47.

McCune-Nicolich, L. Toward symbolic functioning: Structure of early pretend games and potential parallels with language. *Child Development*, 1981, *52*, 785–797.

Nicolich, L. M. Beyond sensorimotor intelligence: Assessment of symbolic maturity through analysis of pretend play. *Merrill-Palmer Quarterly*, 1977, *23*, 89–99.

Papoušek, M., & Papoušek, H. Musical elements in the infant's vocalization: Their significance for communication, cognition, and creativity. In L. P. Lipsitt (Ed.), *Advances in infancy research* (Vol. 1). Norwood, NJ: Ablex, 1981.

Parke, R. D., & O'Leary, S. E. Family interaction in the newborn period: Some findings, some observations, and some unresolved issues. In K. F. Riegel & J. A. Meacham (Eds.), *The developing individual in a changing world* (Vol. 2): *Social and environmental issues*. The Hague: Mouton, 1976.

Piaget, J. *The origins of intelligence in children* (M. Cook, trans.). New York: International Universities Press, 1952.

Piaget, J. *Play, dreams and imitation in childhood* (C. Gattegno & F. M. Hodgson, trans.). New York: Norton, 1962. (Originally published, 1951.)

Rheingold, H. L. The measurement of maternal care. *Child Development*, 1960, *31*, 565–575.

Rheingold, H. L. Little children's participation in the work of adults: a nascent prosocial behavior. *Child Development,* 1982, *53,* 114–125.

Rheingold, H. L., & Cook, K. V. The contents of boys' and girls' rooms as an index of parents' behavior. *Child Development,* 1975, *46,* 459–463.

Rheingold, H. L., Hay, D. F., & West, M. J. Sharing in the second year of life. *Child Development,* 1976, *47,* 1148–1158.

Sinclair, H. The transition from sensory-motor behaviour to symbolic activity. *Interchange: A Journal of Educational Studies,* 1970, *1,* 119–126.

Spencer-Booth, Y. The relationships between mammalian young and conspecifics other than mothers and peers: A review. *Advances in the Study of Behavior,* 1970, *3,* 119–194.

Valentine, C. W. A study of the beginnings and significance of play in infancy. *British Journal of Educational Psychology,* 1938, *8,* 285–306.

Valentine, C. W. *The psychology of early childhood.* London: Methuen, 1942.

Vygotsky, L. S. *Mind in society.* Cambridge, MA: Harvard University Press, 1978.

Watson, M. W., & Fischer, K. W. A developmental sequence of agent use in late infancy. *Child Development,* 1977, *48,* 828–836.

Zahn-Waxler, C., Radke-Yarrow, M., & King, R. A. Child rearing and children's prosocial initiations toward victims of distress. *Child Development,* 1979, *50,* 319–330.

6

Infant–Parent Attachment and the Origins of Prosocial and Antisocial Behavior

EVERETT WATERS, DALE HAY, and JOHN RICHTERS

> *If you can look into the seeds of time and say*
> *which grains will grow and which will not*
> *Speak then to me . . .*
>
> Shakespeare, *Macbeth* I, iii, 58–60

The primary goal of this essay is to outline and examine the implications of attachment theory and research for the development and prediction of socialization outcomes in childhood. As is so often the case in research on social development, speculation and theory about the developmental implications of attachment have tended to outdistance empirical research. Accordingly, we devote a considerable portion of our presentation to issues that lie ahead of us rather than focusing exclusively on the accomplishments we have in hand.

Our presentation is divided into four parts. In the first, we briefly characterize the infant–parent relationship as it has been described within the theoretical traditions of psychoanalysis, learning theory, and ethology. Each of these theoretical perspectives has contributed to contemporary views of infant–parent attachment and to models of socialization. In fact, it is difficult to imagine a persuasive analysis of the links between early attachment relationships and later socialization outcomes that does not build, to some extent, upon Freud's insights into the complexity of social behavior and development, learning analyses of developmental change, and ethological perspectives on species-specific strategies of social adaptation.

In the second part of this essay, we review the studies of individual differences that have related early social interaction to the quality of attachment relationships later in infancy. It is important to identify the interactive processes that underlie the formation and differentiation of attachments, because these processes may continue to contribute to subsequent socialization. As we shall see, attachment relationships differ in the extent to which they are secure and harmonious or anxious and conflict ridden. The infant's role in establishing and maintaining a successful, coordinated relationship with the parent could be viewed as an early prosocial achievement; determinants of that achievement may influence later achievements as well. In the same section we also review the correlational data relating these individual differences in attachment to concurrent and predictive assessments of prosocial and antisocial behavior. These analyses do not necessarily establish causal relationships, but they identify developmental pathways worthy of further investigation.

Insofar as the existing correlational data are neither extensive nor easy to relate decisively to socialization outcomes in childhood or beyond, we devote a third section of this essay to a conceptual analysis of relationships between attachment and socialization. In the final section of the essay, we try to highlight theoretical and methodological issues that must be taken into consideration if the implications of our conceptual analyses are to be translated into new research. We view the job of predicting from very early relationships to prosocial and antisocial outcomes many years later to be a worthy but inherently difficult task.

THEORIES OF INFANT–PARENT ATTACHMENT

Psychoanalytic theory, learning theory, and comparative ethology have inspired the major investigations of human infant attachment. Unfortunately, however, these perspectives are not easily integrated. As world views they make rather different assumptions, set dissimilar tasks for themselves, and invoke different criteria for evidence. They study social phenomena at different levels of analysis and abstraction. As a consequence, several decades of research have not yet led to a unified theory of infants' social attachments. In fact, conceptualizations of infant–parent ties within the three major perspectives remain different enough to warrant distinct labels, almost as if each theory referred to a different phenomenon. Psychoanalysts refer to the infant–mother bond as the primary example of object relations. Learning theorists typically focus on discrete behaviors, not relationships; when they do discuss the parent–child relationship, they conceptualize it in terms of the child's dependency. And, although attachment historically has been used as a generic label for any research concerning the infant–adult relationship, Bowlby has used it with specific reference to the ethological/behavioral systems construct developed in his trilogy, *Attachment and Loss* (Bowlby, 1969, 1972, 1980).

Ainsworth (1969, 1972) has published comprehensive reviews of attachment theory and research, organized along the lines of these three theoretical perspectives. Unfortunately, comparison across perspectives tends to overlook differences within each; they are not as monolithic as they might first appear. Furthermore, Bowlby's ethological theory owes many debts to psychoanalytic thinking. In addition, Ainsworth's tripartite categorization does not adequately characterize the eclectic and largely implicit theory that guides much of contemporary attachment research, nor does she give sufficient recognition of her own major contribution to the theory, the concept of security. To simplify our presentation, however, we maintain the distinction among perspectives and compare them in terms of three defining issues: (1) conceptualization of the nature of the infant's tie to his or her parents, (2) the origins of this tie and the mechanisms through which it develops, and (3) the stability and significance of early social relationships for later development. The reader is referred to Ainsworth (1969, 1972), Maccoby and Masters (1970), Sroufe and Waters (1977), Cairns (1979), Waters (1980), Waters and Deane (1982), and Joffe and Vaughn (1982) for broader reviews, and to Ainsworth (1973), Rajecki, Lamb, and Obsmacher (1978), and Cairns (1979) for a further presentation of the diversity within each of the major perspectives.

Psychoanalytic Theory

Nature of the Infant–Parent Tie Traditional psychoanalytic theory does not view the infant–mother bond as different in kind from subsequent bonds of attachment and love between adults. Infant–mother attachment is viewed as an affective bond and, by virtue of its status as the child's *first* love relationship, it is considered the strongest and longest-lasting bond. As Freud himself characterized it, the infant–mother bond is "the prototype of all later love relationships."

Unfortunately, psychoanalytic theory does not specify—explicitly or implicitly—how either the strength or the quality of such a bond can be mapped into observable patterns of behavior. Obviously, independence does not necessarily imply indifference and clinginess does not necessarily imply either lack of confidence or unqualified positive feelings. Nor does the degree of an infant's or adult's protest over separation or loss necessarily reflect the strength or quality of the bond. And, similarly, a strong, unsatisfied need for parental attention and affection during infancy may very well be associated with either prosocial or antisocial behavior patterns later in life. The inability to translate the notion of a purely affective bond into observable data has been a barrier to the transfer of genuine psychoanalytic insights into the mainstream of developmental research.

Origins of the Infant–Parent Bond   The central developmental mechanism in Freud's theory of attachment, particularly in his earlier writings, is drive reduction. In Freud's view, the emotional bond between infant and mother develops as she satisfies the infant's primary biological needs in the context of feeding.

Freud's drive reduction model has largely been invalidated by empirical evidence that maternal gratification of infant needs per se and subsequent attachment are not that closely related (Caldwell, 1964; Maccoby & Masters, 1970; Sears, Maccoby, & Levin, 1957). For example, Ainsworth (1963, 1967) and Schaffer and Emerson (1964) have shown that infants frequently display attachment behavior to persons who have not been responsible for satisfying the infants' basic needs. These data are consistent with Harlow's demonstration that infant macaques prefer to seek comfort from cloth-covered surrogate mothers rather than from wire-covered surrogates who feed them (Harlow, 1961). At the very least, Harlow's work indicates that importance of feeding per se has been over-estimated in psychoanalytic theory. Whether Harlow's data refute the drive-reduction model or simply establish the existence of a more primary drive for physical contact is perhaps another matter. Ainsworth (1969) has noted that in his later writings Freud himself began to have second thoughts about the primacy of oral gratification in early emotional development.

Stability and Developmental Significance of the Infant–Parent Bond
Psychoanalytic theory places great emphasis on the enduring significance of the infant–parent relationship for later development. If the infant–mother tie is indeed the prototype for all later love relationships, then presumably there should be some connections between this early bond and the subsequent affective bonds that emerge later in life—including friendships, courtship, marriage, and parenthood. But Freud clearly did not intend to limit the significance of the infant–parent relationship to

these. In fact, psychoanalysts have consistently emphasized that conflicts and defenses rooted in early relationships with parents are essential to understanding prosocial and antisocial behavior occuring outside the context of love relationships.

In brief, psychoanalytic theory emphasizes the infant–parent relationship as an affective bond that arises within a social context. It is characterized as the matrix upon which subsequent developmental processes build, and it defines a range of issues that are at the motivational core of a great deal of behavior after infancy. Psychoanalytic theory also paints a vivid portrait of the psychological complexity of overt behavior. As we discuss below, many of these insights can be assimilated into a program for empirical research concerning infant–parent relationships and socialization outcomes.

Learning Theory

Nature of the Infant–Parent Tie   In contrast to the strong emphasis on an unseen affective bond in psychoanalytic theory, behaviorally oriented theorists (e.g., Cairns, 1966; Dollard & Miller, 1950; Gewirtz, 1961; Sears, 1963) have sought evidence for behavioral markers of the infant–parent relationship. Like the psychoanalysts, the learning theorists soon found themselves dealing in abstractions, but these were expressed in terms of functional relationships and generalized response classes, not unseen bonds. Furthermore, the behavioral markers chosen tended to be those that visibly increased or maintained proximity and physical contact between infant and parent. In studies of infants, communicative gestures, locomotor approach, and touching were highlighted. Studies of somewhat older children emphasized more general forms of seeking attention and approval (e.g., Beller, 1955; Heathers, 1955). Affect was involved only insofar as certain behaviors that signal the adult to approach; smiling and crying, incidentally, connote affect. Indeed, rather than viewing affect as an integral part of an organized attachment system, some learning theorists have viewed distress as a form of behavioral *dis*organization (Cairns, 1972; Gewirtz, 1972).

In the learning perspective, attachment has primarily been viewed as a normative developmental process, common to many species, not as a domain in which there are systematic individual differences. When learning theorists turned their thoughts to individual differences, they reasoned that attachment relationships might differ in strength and that the quantity of overt behavior emitted is a useful and valid index of the existence and strength of a bond. (This view probably derives as much from empirical observations of preschoolers judged to vary in dependency as it does from theoretical conviction). So defined, attachments exist when the rate of proximity- and contact-seeking is greater than zero; increases in the frequency, duration, or intensity of such behavior imply a stronger bond. Conversely, the characteristic declines in proximity-seeking and separation distress that occur between ages 2 and 4 years are thought to imply attenuation of the attachment bond, although that process may be delayed more for some children than for others.

Within the learning perspective, the attachment relationship is equated with the parent's and infant's behavioral preferences for each other's company and their mutual control over each other's behavior. These criteria can be used to identify other types of relationships as well; differences among relationships reflect varying degrees of such behavioral preference and control. No special status is accorded the first relationship; except for some differences in the frequency and content of the behaviors shown within it, the attachment relationship has much in common with friendships among peers and love relationships in adulthood, which similarly reflect mutual preference and control. Within this perspective, the attachment bond is viewed more as a predictable developmental outcome than as a special source of subsequent adaptations—that is, more as an effect of certain experiences than as a cause of later development.

Origins of the Behavioral Bond   Within this perspective, attachment formation is viewed as a form of learning. The learning theorists have consistently emphasized external controls over the infant's behavior. By and large, behaviorally oriented theorists have not acknowledged the active roles that infants themselves play in initiating and maintaining their attachment relationships (for an important exception, see Rheingold, 1969). Rather, these theorists have assumed a close, straightforward, essentially rational relationship between parental responsiveness and the infant's contemporaneous behavior. Attachment is thought to arise in the context of interactions and to take the form of systematic relationships among stimuli and responses. In time, the infant's discrete attachment behaviors become consolidated into a more general functional response class. This in turn may merge into a generalized dependency persisting into later childhood. Dependency is still under the control of external events, but they now take the form of persons and classes of persons, not isolated stimulus events.

Several mechanisms have been invoked to explain various dimensions of this learning process—perceptual learning (i.e., coming gradually to distinguish persons from the inanimate world and familiar caregivers from persons in general), contingent reinforcement, generalization, and discrimination. With some exceptions, however (e.g., Cairns, 1972), learning theorists have not tried to account for the less rational, more paradoxical dimensions of the attachment process, such as reactions to reunion after separation (see Ainsworth, 1969).

Stability and Developmental Significance of Attachment Behavior
With the exception of discussing dependency as a generalized trait, learning theorists do not predict any aspect of the parent–infant relationship to be stable across time and context. Rather, primary emphasis is placed on the situational specificity of social behavior. Because learning theorists do not emphasize that the infant can determine its own behavior, they tend not to search for developmental continuities in social competence. Because attachments are viewed as effects rather than as precursors or causes, they are not typically seen as influencing later parent–child relations or as contributors to later prosocial and antisocial development. Nonetheless, behaviorally oriented researchers have suggested a variety of mechanisms that might explain a stable infant–parent bond. These include consistent availability and salience of one or a few adults and/or temporally stable patterns of reinforcement for approach and proximity.

Empirical research on the stability of infants' attachment behavior across time and situation has been an important focus in the theoretical competition between learning perspectives and alternative views that emphasize the infant as an important determiner of his or her own behavior. As we shall see below, there are in fact quite stable individual differences in infants' attachment relationships, and these differences have a wide range of correlates across age and domains of behavior. As strong and consistent data on the stability and correlates of attachment have emerged, interest in the learning perspective on attachment has declined. Unfortunately, there has been a corresponding decline of interest in defining more precisely what actually is learned in the process of forming and maintaining attachments. There has been very little new research, for example, concerning parents as influences on their children's attachment behavior or as mediators of pathways between early attachment and later socialization outcomes.

We view this decline as unfortunate because even if attachment relationships cannot be operationalized successfully as arrays of indifferent responses to prevailing contingencies of reinforcement, they certainly are influenced by learning. What is needed is a better conceptualization of that learning process, since the stability of individual differences in infants' attachment relationships may depend quite heavily upon consistency in the child-rearing environment. Also, perhaps most important for our present purposes, the learning that occurs within the infant–parent relationship may contribute to the development of prosocial and antisocial behavior in later childhood.

Ethological Attachment Theory

Nature of the Infant–Mother Bond   Ethological attachment theory emphasizes the fact that in most environments virtually all infants develop patterns of attachment behavior characterized by a balance between the child's proximity-seeking and exploration across a variety of contexts. Bowlby (1969) has hypothesized that the control system underlying this behavior reflects species-characteristic patterns of learning abilities that evolved under the pressures of predation. A direct test of this evolutionary hypothesis is clearly difficult to imagine (see Hay, 1980), because behavioral adaptations do not leave a fossil record and selective breeding experiments are clearly not in order.

Ethological attachment theory places more emphasis on the goal of maintaining proximity to adults than it does to any particular behavior. Attachment is never equated with either a single behavior or with the quantity of behavioral output per se; it is inferred from the organization of behavior across contexts and across time. Indeed, sufficiently high rates of many behaviors that serve the attachment behavioral system (e.g., crying, signalling, and clinging) can be antithetical to the adaptive function of the parent–infant bond. Like the learning theorists, the ethological attachment theorists recognize the situational specificity of attachment behavior, but draw attention to the appropriateness of such fluctuations and their underlying organization and coherence.

Origins of the Infant–Parent Bond   Although ethological attachment theory is compatible with the notion that attachment is learned, it does not specify in any detail the role that learning plays. In this perspective, however attachment behavior is learned, the process is facilitated by species-specific biases in learning abilities. The acquisition of typical patterns of attachment behavior is assumed to be easier and more likely (given the average expectable environment) than the acquisition of equally complex but randomly constructed sets of behavior. Hypothesizing that attachment has biological substrates does not imply that all attachment behavior is innate, but simply suggests that the innate learning abilities of a species promote the integration of skills that work together as components of the attachment control system.

Stability and Developmental Significance of the Infant–Parent Bond
The notion of species-specific biases in learning abilities implies a degree of similarity among attachment relationships across infants, and probably also a degree of buffering against moderate environmental variation. In addition, the very complexity of the attachment behavioral control sys-

tem lends a certain inertia that might resist temporary changes in the environment. Finally, the interactive nature of the attachment relationship implies that an infant actively operates to maintain the social environment to which its behavior is adapted. Accordingly, in normal and reasonably stable environments, patterns in the use of an adult as a secure base from which to explore should be stable over time. As we indicate below, several sets of empirical data support this expectation.

At the same time, ethological theory identifies attachment with the maintenance of a degree of proximity with the caregiver across time, not with specific behaviors. Consequently, as the infant's behavioral repertoire and cognitive abilities change with development, the content and patterning of attachment behavior will change. Visual and vocal interaction will suffice where proximity and contact were once required. The infant's excursions away from the adult eventually last longer and span wider distances. With the infant's increasing cognitive abilities, the secure base becomes portable. Thus, ethological theory does not predict stability of behavioral detail across time and situations. It does, however, predict that patterns of adaptation fostered by interaction with one or a few supportive adults will be coherent (if not absolutely identical) across time and situations.

Ethological attachment theory per se implies very little about the impact of infant–adult relationships on later social development. At the same time, however, Bowlby and Ainsworth both have continuing interests in psychodynamic analyses of personality development, and have suggested relationships to later development that are consistent with their view of attachment, if not necessarily derived from it. Bowlby's classic study of juvenile thieves illustrates these interests. Waters and Sroufe (1983) have also tried to incorporate ethological attachment theory into an integrative organismic psychology of social development and competence. Although these extrapolations can be useful for the evolution of developmental theory, ethological attachment theory as such remains primarily a theory concerning the nature of the infant's tie to his or her parents. Its implications beyond this, and its boundaries and limitations, are not easily specified.

CORRELATES OF SECURE VERSUS ANXIOUS ATTACHMENT

Bowlby's (1969) emphasis on the adaptive functions of the attachment system implies that essentially every infant raised in an average expectable environment will become attached to one or more caregivers. Thus, research on the origins of attachment has focused on individual differences in the quality of attachment relationships, not on their presence or absence. Ainsworth and Wittig (1969) classified qualitative differences in attachment relationships along a dimension of security. In brief, secure infants are confident in the caregiver's availability and responsiveness. This is most evident in their use of the adult as a secure base from which to explore and as a haven of safety when threatened. In contrast, anxiously attached infants are less confident of the caregiver's availability and responsiveness, and as a result their exploratory behavior and responses to stress are often disorganized.

By incorporating her longstanding interest in security (e.g., Salter, 1939) into Bowlby's ethological theory of attachment, Ainsworth generated a number of testable hypotheses concerning the antecedents and consequences of these qualitative differences in parent–infant relationships. Primary among these hypotheses are (1) that important differences in the quality of attachment arise primarily from patterns of early interaction between parent and infant, and (2) that these differences in the quality of early attachment provide a foundation for the development of subsequent attachment and love relationships throughout the life span. Thus, Ainsworth's interest in the differential security of attachment relationships moved the theory from an evolutionary to a developmental analysis, and permits the study of the effects of these early experiences on later development, including prosocial and antisocial outcomes. We now summarize three sets of studies that pertain to Ainsworth's hypotheses: (1) research on the reliability and validity of the security construct; (2) studies of the antecedents of secure and anxious attachments; and (3) studies of later behaviors and attainments that can be predicted from individual differences in the security of attachment.

Assessment, Stability, and Discriminant Validity

One of the most important developments in research on attachment has been the validation of the Ainsworth Strange Situation procedure (Ainsworth & Wittig, 1969) as a standardized procedure for assessing secure versus anxious attachment. The Strange Situation is composed of a series of eight 3-minute episodes in which the infant is introduced to an unfamiliar room, a set of toys, an unfamiliar adult, and two brief separations from the parent. Infants who are able to use the mother as a secure base and haven of safety at home can be identified in the Strange Situation by their characteristic responses to the parent's return after brief separations. If they are not distressed by separation, secure 1-year-olds greet the mother's return and go back to effective exploration and play, with occasional bouts of interaction with the parent. If they have been distressed by separation, they actively approach the mother when she returns, and actively achieve and maintain physical contact. Physical contact and interaction effectively terminate separation distress in securely attached infants and enables them to return to preseparation levels of exploration and play. In contrast, infants who are unable to use the mother as a secure base and haven of safety in the home can be identified by their displays of anger, inability to reestablish or maintain physical contact after separation, and/or inability to be comforted by physical contact. In some research, it has proved useful to distinguish between infants who actively avoid their mothers on reunion (anxious avoidant) and those who both seek and resist physical contact and are unable to be comforted or return to play (anxious resistant). In any case, in terms of the themes of interest here, secure infants and their parents tend to cooperate harmoniously with a potentially threatening situation, whereas the same set of events tend to provoke conflict, anger, and resistance on the part of anxious infants and their parents.

Several studies (Connell, 1977; Main & Weston, 1981; Waters, 1978) have demonstrated that Strange Situation assessments are quite stable over the second year of life in middle-class families. However, attachment relationships can change from secure to anxious, or anxious to secure, in response to stressful events that intrude into the mother's daily life (Vaughn, Egeland, Sroufe, & Waters, 1980). Furthermore, secure versus anxious attachment to the mother is not highly correlated with the quality of attachment to the father (Lamb, 1978; Main & Weston, 1981) or to extrafamilial caregivers (Sagi, Lamb, Lefkowicz, Shoham, Dvir, & Estes, 1985). These data suggest that the Strange Situation assessment indeed measures the quality of the dynamic relationship between parent and infant, not simply stable traits of individual infants that persist across partners and environmental change. It is important to keep this fact in mind when trying to use the Strange Situation assessment as a predictor of later socialization outcomes—the question is one of links between the quality of an early dyadic relationship and later individual adaptation, not simply a correlation of infant characteristics at two different times. Moreover, when seeking the developmental origins of secure attachment relationships, one must document the contributions of both partners.

Antecedents of Attachment

The Infant's Contributions   Although ethological attachment theory places great emphasis on the role of appropriate (i.e., species characteristic) parental behavior as a determinant of attachment outcomes, it has also emphasized the importance of the infant's contribution to its own caregiving environment. Several recent studies have provided evidence that even the neonate's behavior has important consequences for infant–mother interaction weeks and months later. For example, Vaughn, Crichton, & Egeland (1982) have reported that assessment of development and physiological responses to stress were significantly related to patterns of infant–mother interaction during feeding at ages 3 and 6 months. These neonatal assessments were also related to patterns of interactive play, mother's sensitivity to infant signals, and (of particular interest for our purposes) a dimension of the mother's cooperation versus interference with the infant's ongoing behavior at age 6 months. In addition, Waters, Vaughn, & Egeland (1980) have reported that measures of orienting to the environment, regulatory maturity, and composite measures of neonatal adaptation were all related to patterns of secure versus anxious attachment at 1 year of age.

Maternal Contributions   Ainsworth's research has demonstrated that the most significant antecedents of secure versus anxious attachment are patterns of early interactive experience with a caregiver. In brief, consistency, contingent responsiveness, facilitation and cooperation rather than interference with the infant's ongoing behavior, and an affectively positive context for interaction seem to be the most critical precursors of secure attachment. The most detailed longitudinal data on the mother's contribution to the quality of attachment during the first year is from Ainsworth's intensive, ethological study of 26 middle-class infants and their mothers. In the course of the study, infant–mother dyads were observed in their homes during 4-hour visits, once every 3 weeks, from age 3 weeks through 54 weeks. Detailed recordings were made of infant-directed maternal behaviors such as responses to infant crying, episodes of leaving and entering a room, episodes of picking up and putting down the infant, face-to-face interactions, and episodes involving maternal commands to the infant. In addition, more general characteristics of the mother's behavior patterns were assessed, yielding six general scales: (1) sensitivity/insensitivity to infant signals and communications, (2) acceptance/rejection, (3) accessibility/ignoring, (4) emotional expression, (5) cooperation/interference, (6) and maternal rigidity. At the end of 1 year, the quality of attachment was assessed by the Strange Situation procedure.

Among a wide array of significant results, analyses of early maternal behavior indicated that mothers whose infants were securely attached at the end of the year had (1) responded more rapidly to infant crying, (2) acknowledged their infants more often when entering a room after a period of absence, (3) were more likely to be rated as tender while holding their infants, and (4) were less interfering and abrupt when picking up their infants. In addition, mothers of securely attached infants were less likely to devote themselves to routine activities while holding their infants, and were generally more adept at handling their infants during close physical contact. In terms of more general characteristics, mothers of securely attached infants were rated as more sensitive to infant signals, more cooperative with ongoing behavior, more physically and psychologically accessible, and more accepting of the demands of parenthood than were mothers of anxiously attached infants. These results have been substantially replicated by Grossman and Grossman (1985) in a longitudinal study of infants in northern Germany.

Attachment and Socialization Outcomes

During the last 5 years, a number of longitudinal research projects have produced correlational data relating quality of infant–mother attachment with a wide range of socialization outcomes in infancy and early to middle childhood. These outcomes include early forms of prosocial behavior and cooperation, self-control, and behavior problems.

Positive Social Interaction   Prosocial and antisocial behavior can often best be understood within the context of the relationships in which they occur, and indeed the very first relationships an infant establishes provide the first opportunities for prosocial and antisocial encounters. In fact, the interactions of a parent with a securely attached infant reveal much of a prosocial nature—coordinated interaction, affective sharing, cooperative coping with stress, and the like. Thus, the relationship between security and the infant's own prosocial tendencies is apparent even in the midst of the Strange Situation procedure. In addition, observations of infants in other situations have confirmed this relationship. For example, Stayton, Hogan, & Ainsworth (1971), Londerville & Main (1981), and Matas, Arend, & Sroufe (1978) have demonstrated that secure attachment is related to a child's attentiveness to adults, his or her "disposition to obey," and the development of internalized controls (as inferred from obedience to past commands in the absence of surveillance) at 9 to 12 months, 21 months, and 24 months. Main and Weston (1981) have also shown that secure attachment at 12 months is related to a child's readiness to interact positively with new adults. In particular, they demonstrated that secure infants were more interested, showed more signs of "relatedness," and showed more empathic responses to a playful adult's bids for interaction and expressions of affect than did insecure infants.

In addition to these studies, which highlight infants' positive interactions with adults and responsiveness to their socialization goals, others have related secure attachment to involvement and competence in early peer group interactions. For example, Lieberman (1977) found that security versus anxiety assessed in the home at age 3 years, prior to preschool experience, was related to two components of behavior with peers after 4 months of preschool experience. Security at home was correlated .55 with scores on reciprocal interaction (sharing, successful verbal requests, social initiation, and shared laughter). Moreover, although parents whose children were more secure had arranged for their children to have significantly greater amounts of peer contact prior to preschool, the relations to reciprocal interaction were significant even when peer experience was controlled.

In a similar study, Waters, Wippman, & Sroufe (1979) have demonstrated that secure attachment at 20 months is related to two other important facets of social competence and socialization at age 3 years. As indicated in Table 6.1, secure attachment at 20 months predicts to both positive social motivation (ego strength/effectance) and to social skill and competence.

Whereas most of the recent longitudinal studies have involved stable, middle-class families, similar relationships between patterns of attachment, social competence, and socialization have also been reported in studies of families of lower socioeconomic status. For example, securely attached infants from disadvantaged families have been shown to be more sociable and compliant with their mothers at age 2 years, and with their preschool teachers at age 4½ (Erickson & Crichton, 1981; Erickson, Farber, & Egeland, 1982; Pastor, 1981). Securely attached children from high-risk families have also been found to have better self-control than anxiously attached peers in preschool (Egeland, 1983), and to be less dependent on preschool teachers (Sroufe, Fox, & Pancake, 1983).

Attachment and Behavior Problems   Recent research in both disadvantaged and middle-class families has demonstrated that secure versus anxious attachment in infancy is related to a variety of behavior problems in early and middle childhood. For example, in the study by Lieberman (1977) described above, security of attachment correlated −.48 with scores on negative behavior (violent use of toys, physical aggression, verbal threat, leaving the classroom, and crying) in preschool. The relationship was significant even when the amount of peer experience the children had prior to nursery school was controlled. Erickson, Sroufe, and Egeland (in preparation) have recently reported that children who exhibit patterns of anxious attachment at ages 12 and 18 months are more likely than securely attached children to develop behavior problems in

Table 6.1

Q-Set Item Means by Attachment Classification and Item-Total Score Correlations

	Item-total correlation	Attachment classification group means		p (One-tailed) test
		Secure	Anxious	
Peer competence scale:				
Other children seek his company	.73	6.2	3.8	.001
Socially withdrawn	−.89	3.9	6.2	.002
Suggests activities	.83	6.2	3.5	.005
Hesitates to engage	−.86	3.9	6.2	.007
Peer leader	.71	5.2	3.3	.01
Sympathetic to peers' distress	.43	8.4	4.2	.01
Spectator (versus participant) in social activities	−.90	4.1	6.1	.02
Attracts attention	.87	5.6	3.4	.02
Hesitant with other children	−.88	3.4	5.4	.03
Withdraws from excitement and commotion	−.49	2.7	4.1	.03
Typically in the role of listener (not full participant in group activities)	−.66	4.2	5.9	.05
Characteristically unoccupied	−.55	3.7	4.7	.14
Ego strength effectance scale:				
Self-directed	.81	6.4	4.2	.01
Uncurious about the new	−.55	2.4	3.7	.01
Unaware, turned off, "spaced out"	−.78	2.8	4.2	.03
Forcefully goes after what he wants	.67	6.6	5.1	.04
Likes to learn new cognitive skills	.74	5.9	5.0	.05
Confident of his own ability	.58	6.6	5.7	.15
Sets goals, which stretch his abilities	.76	6.3	5.5	.19
Becomes involved in whatever he does	.88	7.1	6.5	.23
Does not persevere when nonsocial goals are blocked	−.74	2.7	3.1	.25
Samples activities aimlessly, lacks goals	−.81	3.2	4.8	.25
Suggestible	−.72	4.4	4.8	.36
Indirect in asking for help	−.50	3.2	3.5	.38

school. Children who were secure at both 12 and 18 months had the fewest behavior problems, children who were anxious at both ages had the most, and behavior problem outcomes were quite varied in children whose attachment classifications changed between the ages of 12 and 18 months.

In summarizing research on 40 children who were secure or anxious at both 12 and 18 months, Sroufe (1983) has indicated that at 42 months anxiously attached children were less ego-resilient, less independent, less compliant, less empathic, less socially competent, lower in self-esteem, and expressed more negative and less positive affect than did securely attached children. In addition, children who had been classified as anxious–resistant at 12 and 18 months were described by their preschool teachers as either impulsive and tense or helpless and fearful. Children who had been classified as anxious–avoidant in infancy were later described by their preschool teachers as hostile and socially isolated from their peers, Lewis, Feirling, McGuffog, and Jaskir (1984) have also reported significant relationships between attachment in infancy and subsequent behavior problems in a longitudinal study of 113 middle class children seen at age 1 year and again at age 6 years.

In summary, the attachment outcome studies reviewed above yield a number of reliable, predictive links between security of infant–mother attachment and subsequent patterns of social competence, psychopathology, and prosocial as well as antisocial behavior. As indicated earlier, however, these studies are entirely correlational in design. That is, they were neither designed to address specific questions about paths of influence between attachment and socialization outcomes, nor intended to extend beyond a straightforward description of the correlational associations they document. Thus, although the consistency of these findings is impressive and points to the significance of early relationships for later development, they are not in themselves explanations but rather data in search of explanation. Unfortunately, as indicated above, ethological attachment theory does not specify the mechanisms through which security of early attachment could exert an influence on the subsequent emergence of prosocial or antisocial behavior patterns. The other theoretical perspectives—psychoanalysis and learning theory—must be consulted, and new theoretical postulates must be set forth.

PROCESS-LEVEL MODELS OF THE RELATIONSHIP
BETWEEN ATTACHMENT AND SOCIALIZATION

In the discussion that follows we introduce and examine two conceptual models that could account for the reported correlations between early parent–child interaction, security of infant–parent attachment, and socialization outcomes. Our point of departure for this analysis lies in the following four propositions derived from the correlational studies just reviewed: (1) the quality of early infant–parent interaction contributes to the security of attachment; (2) the security of attachment relates to contemporary and later socialization outcomes; (3) parental child-rearing practices remain consistent across significant periods of time; and (4) parental child-rearing practices affect prosocial and antisocial behavior throughout childhood.

Both of the models discussed below reflect our contention that security per se cannot explain either the acquisition or the maintenance of prosocial or antisocial behavior later in development. Moreover, both models emphasize that paths of influence between parent and child are bidirectional, throughout the history of their relationship. In this sense, the models outlined here resemble the theoretical models set forth by Sears (e.g., Sears, 1951). The two models differ from each other principally in the extent to which they implicate the child's prior achievements as determinants of his or her later learning experiences, and in the extent to which they focus on the child's perceptions and internalization of the rearing experience as well as the actual interactions that occur.

Figure 6.1: Consistent Parent–Child Relations over Time

The essence of the model outlined in Figure 6.1 is that correlations among a child's characteristics across age could always be interpreted as a series of independent effects, arising from stable components of parent–child interaction. Figure 6.1 describes a progression of bidirectional relations between parental child-rearing practices and characteristics of the

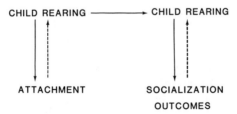

Figure 6.1. This figure portrays a model relating the security of early attachment relations to both positive and negative socialization outcomes. In this model, both of these variables are under the control of parental child-rearing strategies and behavior. It is assumed that parental behavior is reasonably consistent over time, although there will exist bidirectional patterns of influence at any one point in the child's development. This model, which does not posit any direct causal link between attachment and later social achievements and deficits, can completely account for the observed correlational data.

child who is being reared, in early infancy, in the second year of life when the attachment has been formed, and later in development. As outlined above, the child-rearing practices that are most relevant to the development of secure versus anxious attachment are sensitivity to signals, cooperation with ongoing behavior, acceptance of responsibility, responsiveness to the infant's demands over time, and physical and psychological availability. In other words, parents whose infants are secure provide consistent, contingent, appropriate responses to the infants' behavior. Furthermore, by behaving in this way, the parents are also providing clear prosocial models of empathic, cooperative, nurturant behavior. It is likely that such tendencies to provide consistent reinforcement and model prosocial behavior remain stable within parents over time. They are likely to be continuous with the patterns of parental control that are reflected in infants' obedience, good performance by parent and child in teaching tasks, and other positive socialization outcomes that can be predicted from the security of attachment. At the same time, characteristics of the infant that promote secure versus anxious attachment, such as responsiveness to the environment and emotional regulation, may also be stable over childhood and may elicit particular types of parental behavior that facilitate successful socialization at various points in time.

Although Figure 6.1 has the virtue of proposing a parsimonious explanation for the correlation between attachment and socialization outcomes, and this could completely account for the available correlational data, it could nonetheless be expanded upon in several ways. In particular, cognitive mediational factors could be invoked. Figure 6.1 does not clearly explain how parental child-rearing practices continue to exert an influence on the older child's and adolescent's social behavior, outside of the family situation (e.g., Block, this volume; Farrington, this volume; McCord, this volume). Furthermore, it does not specify fully how the dyad's early achievements may influence the child's subsequent rearing experiences. Thus Figure 6.2 was constructed to speak to these additional issues.

Figure 6.2: Parental Expectations and Child Identification as Mediators

Figure 6.2 emphasizes that the products of early socialization (i.e., the child's acquired characteristics and the quality of the relationship that has been established between parent and child) are themselves significant influences on later development. In this second model, patterns of sensitive early care and certain infant characteristics promote secure attachment. In turn, secure attachment combined with age-appropriate child-

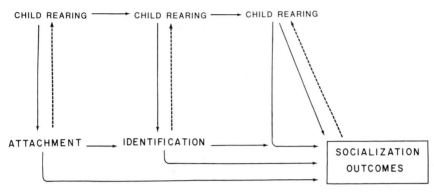

Figure 6.2. The figure expands upon Figure 6.1 by incorporating the child's identification with the parent as a mediating variable. Again, parental behavior is assumed to be reasonably consistent over time, and again there are assumed to be bidirectional pathways of influence between parent and child at any one point in time. In addition, we speculate that the security or insecurity of early attachment relationships may either facilitate or inhibit identification with the parent, which in turn may mediate socialization outcomes. A critical test of this second figure versus the simpler one must await further data.

rearing practices serve to initiate processes of identification in early childhood. Although the psychoanalytic concept of identification is a useful link in building a model, we do not need to conceptualize completely in terms of unseen forces; it can be operationalized in terms of variables such as (1) differential attention to the parent, (2) preference for the parent, (3) familiarity with parental behavior, (4) reproduction of characteristic parental actions, (5) responsiveness to parental control, and (6) avoidance of parental censure.

Figure 6.2 proposes that both the child's identification with the parent and the parent's expectations for the child, based on the child's early achievements, are key processes that mediate the influence of secure attachment on socialization outcomes in later childhood. That is, when early parent-child interactions have been harmonious, (1) the child will develop a secure attachment and its correlates, including confidence, self-esteem, and a positive orientation toward parents as socializing agents; (2) the parent will develop positive expectations and confidence about the task of socializing this particular child; (3) the child will *consequently* acquire the behaviors and attitudes summarized by the term identification; and (4) the child will *consequently* be receptive to the parent's later socialization practices, which will in turn be affected by the parent's positive regard. Hence, in middle childhood, the child will tend to adopt parental standards and values as his or her own. In contrast, if early interactions are not harmonious, and parent and child do not develop a mutually agreeable, supportive relationship, then the child might prove resistant to parental control and tutelage later in childhood, even if the parents' socialization skills improve. Furthermore, in this model, subsequent socialization builds upon early achievements, and, if they are stymied, both identification and the learning of social skills may suffer. Parents who do not expect good things of their children, based on past interactions, may not be so inclined to provide facilitating, age-appropriate rearing experiences, not to mention ones that compensate for earlier deficits and failures.

Thus, both models emphasize the role children play in their own socialization, and highlight the relevance of individual differences data and observations of dyadic relationships over time for the construction of normative models of development. Figure 6.1 is a parsimonious account of the available correlational data. However, by introducing the constructs of identification and parental expectations, Figure 6.2 helps explain both the persistence of parental influence over time and the differential degrees of susceptibility of particular children to peer versus parental influences.

SOCIALIZATION OUTCOMES ARE INHERENTLY DIFFICULT TO PREDICT

The figures outlined in the preceding section are conceptually straightforward. Figure 6.1 points to the consistent effects of parental childrearing practices over time; Figure 6.2 draws attention to the mediating roles of the parent–child relationship and the child's identification with the parent in the course of socialization. Both point to attachment as socialization outcome and mediator rather than the sole cause of the child's later prosocial and antisocial behavior. If data were gathered to provide multiple independent measures of each construct in the models, a causal modeling analysis could be used to compare their effectiveness in explaining a common set of data.

This venture, however, is more complicated than it might first seem. Consider the simplest case for such an analysis, involving the child and just one parent. Such a causal analysis would require assessments of the child's and parent's characteristics and behavior and of qualities of their dyadic relationship at at least two points in time. We would have to construct measurement models that informed us how reciprocal influences between parent and child could be specified at any one time. Only then could we test a prediction model that relates antecedent influences to consequent outcomes and identifies mediated paths of influence.

Furthermore, the enterprise soon becomes even more complex, in that whatever analytic strategies are adopted, they rest on prior empirical decisions. Are the actual data being collected reliable, valid, and theoretically relevant? The correlational studies we review above examine a host of discrete variables, which makes comparison across studies difficult. Research on attachment has benefitted from attention to the stability and construct validity of Strange Situation behavior; the prosocial and antisocial outcomes to be predicted deserve equally careful scrutiny.

Specifying What Is To Be Predicted

Throughout this essay we have tended to beg the question of what exactly constitutes prosocial and antisocial behavior, which is fine when proposing very general models, but less adequate when trying to test those models. Future research must deal with the following questions.

1. Are prosocial and antisocial behavior unitary phenomena? A variety of phenomena have fallen under the rubric of prosocial and antisocial behavior, as the other chapters in this volume attest. Are they equally good markers of a general prosocial or antisocial tendency? If so, how could we tell? Simple correlations may be misleading because they would not take into account the frequency of antecedent events calling for different types of action. For example, sharing possessions, protecting younger children, cooperating to solve problems, and rescuing animals who have been hurt may all qualify as prosocial acts. But how frequently do younger children require protection, problems arise to be solved, wounded birds appear in one's back yard? At the same time, even if these diverse behaviors do intercorrelate at any one point in development, is there any a priori reason to believe that they have common antecedents? Perhaps those early experiences that predict, for example, generosity, do not predict cooperative problem solving.

2. Can the models predict both activity and reactivity? The foregoing consideration suggests that the social phenomena one is trying to predict may not simply be individual classes of action but also certain types of reactions to specified environmental events, such as the needs of other persons or perceived threats. Both activity and reactivity define the nature of a social interaction (Cairns, 1979), and both may reveal stable individual differences over time. Is there any reason to believe, however, that they share the same developmental antecedents?

3. Do the models predict ordinary as well as extraordinary behavior? Prosocial and antisocial behavior include events that occur in the course of ordinary social interaction and those that occur much more rarely. Are

the antecedents of cooperative peer relations identical to those of dramatic rescue attempts? Are the antecedents of quarreling in a peer group
identical to those of street violence? Do extraordinary social acts (such as
murder) stem from prior ordinary tendencies, and, if so, must that fact be
taken into account in constructing and testing developmental models?

4. Does the success of prediction depend on the choice of measures?
Assume that we wish to understand the socialization processes that yield
a "prosocial" child. Would we be most interested in whether the child in
question *ever* shows certain behaviors, or in the rate of occurrence of
those behaviors? Or is latency to react to opportunities a better measure?
Should we perhaps examine the pattern of different variables working
together? Should we focus on interactive phenomena, not the discrete
acts of individuals? Perhaps it would make sense to examine prosocial
and antisocial *relationships* rather than acts or interactions. The use of
frequency counts of discrete acts is a common practice in studying social
phenomena, but is not always the most suitable approach to the problem
at hand (Hay, 1980; Waters, 1978).

Discerning Learning Processes within the
Attachment Relationship

Consideration of the foregoing questions will help develop sensitive
causal models of the relationships among child rearing practices, attachment, identification, and socialization outcomes. However, at some
point, even these more sophisticated correlational designs will probably
have to be supplemented with experimental analyses of socialization processes. However, this statement is not a call for unidimensional analyses
of complex phenomena, studied in impoverished laboratory simulations.
At various points in our argument we have invoked learning principles.
Nonetheless, it would be a mistake to reduce the complexity of events
taking place in socialization to a simplistic mechanistic account. Rather,
both of the models we have constructed imply that we must analyze how
learning principles actually operate in natural settings and how children
contribute to their own socialization (see also Maccoby, Chapter 12; Patterson, Chapter 11; Radke-Yarrow & Zahn-Waxler, Chapter 10;
Rheingold & Emery, Chapter 5). In particular, in designing future research, it is important to keep in mind that the human child's first experience of being a member of a social community traditionally occurs within
the family setting. Experimental analyses of learning and identificatory
processes must be done in tandem with controlled observational studies
of how such processes actually operate in the child's ordinary experience.
That is, any analysis of the relationship between early parent–child inter-

action, attachment, and later development must take into account the fact that the attachment relationship itself is a domain in which important social learning—in the fullest sense of that term—is highly likely to occur. The following questions about modeling and reinforcement processes within parent–infant relationships illustrate the kind of research that needs to be done.

What Prosocial and Antisocial Models are Habitually Provided and Attended to within the Family setting?   Family members often act in ways that further each other's well being, but at other times find themselves working at cross-purposes. The reunion behavior of anxiously attached infants and their parents exemplifies the latter, but conflicts may occur even within secure relationships on occasion. Hence, very young children are constantly surrounded by both prosocial and antisocial models, and analyses of early child-rearing practices should include documentation of such modeling. Good parenting is almost by definition prosocial, and young children show in their actions that they have learned much by watching their parents parent (Rheingold & Emery, this volume). However, parents cannot possibly be uniformly giving, sympathetic, and cooperative. They have complex socializing agenda that require them to interfere with or resist their children's activities—to protect the children from harm, to teach them self-control, and to discourage dependence. By seeking to meet these long-range socialization goals, parents are frequently forced in the short run to model "unsympathetic" or "uncooperative" behavior. This paradoxical feature of child rearing must be taken into account in predicting socialization outcomes.

It is not enough, however, to document the models that parents provide. In addition, an analysis of social learning must specify why young children seem affected by some experiences more than others. For example, modeling a prosocial action is sometimes less effective than other procedures in encouraging a child to perform that action (e.g., Hay & Murray, 1982). Children are not slavish imitators of everything they see, but rather they appear to select events from which to learn.

Evidence regarding modeling and imitation in the context of the attachment relationship is important for an analysis of the development of identification, which we have viewed as a potential mediator of socialization outcomes. Even without invoking the construct of identification, however, characteristics of early attachment relationships may constrain the social learning that occurs within them. The degree of security the infant experiences may influence the nature and frequency of social acts enacted within that relationship, which in turn determines the models available to the child. This bidirectional process alluded to in both models deserves more careful scrutiny and experimental analysis.

What Consequences Accure to Children's Own social Actions? From the first year of life on, children themselves demonstrate socially desirable and undesirable actions, and thus their own behavior takes on "prosocial" and "antisocial" meaning within the family context. In the course of their everyday activities with attachment figures and other persons, 1-year-olds show behaviors that resemble the prosocial acts of adults: They offer tangible objects to other persons, enter into cooperative games, attempt to comfort companions who are distressed, and help their parents with common household tasks (for a review of the evidence, see Hay & Rheingold, 1983). At the same time, of course, children at this early age sometimes engage in conflict with family members and others (Hay & Ross, 1982; Kendrick & Dunn, 1983).

These phenomena are readily documented, but not so easily interpreted. Do these particular early prosocial behaviors that are so clearly seen within attachment relationships qualify as precursors to the prosocial and aggressive behaviors of later life? If so, are the early forms somewhat analogous or exactly homologous to the later appearing behaviors? Are individual differences in the frequency, latency, or duration with which these behaviors are shown in early life systematically related to later differences, and thus should their occurrence be incorporated into our developmental models? Although that is a testable question, there is no a priori reason to believe it may be so; other attributes that on the surface do not resemble the later behaviors may in fact be better predictors of them. Furthermore, it is not always easy to trace the fate of discrete classes of behaviors over time (see Hay, 1980; Waters, 1978).

Nonetheless, the absence of predictability would not imply that these early social actions are devoid of social meaning. Rather, their reliable occurrence provides the occasions for studies of parental responses to their children's early social efforts, which in turn may index processes that continue to contribute to socialization. Research to date indicates that parents appear to treat these early analogs to prosocial and antisocial behavior fairly seriously, in that they acknowledge certain actions as socially appropriate and discourage others (e.g., West & Rheingold, 1978; Zahn-Waxler, Radke-Yarrow, & King, 1979). It seems likely, however, that parents respond to their young children's social actions in inconsistent ways, just as humans have a habit of doing in adult life as well. For example, parents may react with disdain or repugnance to some "gifts" from their infants (youth do not always share the aesthetic tastes of their elders) or with impatience when their "helpful" toddlers delay the accomplishment of important tasks. These reactions teach children about the value to be placed on certain behaviors. In addition, at approximately the same time that parents are designating certain behaviors as socially desirable, children may be learning from peers that quite different actions are socially effective; for example, a combination of distal communication and actual hands-on contact is more effective than distal communication alone in inducing a peer to give up a disputed toy (Hay & Ross, 1982). More detailed observations and experimental manipulations of such social learning processes in early life will clearly aid in constructing developmental models.

In sum, process analyses such as the ones we have sketched out are not easy to put into practice. Causal modeling procedures require careful attention to issues of selecting and measuring indicator variables, as well as including latent variables to be tested. Furthermore, they must be supplemented by controlled observational and experimental analyses of the ways in which the processes they invoke actually operate in ordinary social environments.

SUMMARY AND CONCLUSIONS

Our charge in writing this essay was to discuss the relationship between infant–parent attachment and the development of prosocial and antisocial behavior. This of course is one variant of the classic question about the role of early experience in socialization, and so we have tried both to summarize the evidence at hand and to speculate about the most profitable conceptual and methodological approaches to that classic question. We began by considering the three major theoretical perspectives on attachment, highlighting their similarities and differences. Although most contemporary research on attachment has been conducted within Bowlby's ethological tradition, the goals of the researchers have outdistanced the theory; ethological theory is primarily an account of the nature and adaptive functions of the parent–infant tie. When considering the role attachment plays in concurrent and subsequent socialization, it is necessary to supplement Bowlby's theory with an appreciation of Freud's insights into the paradoxes and complexities of social development and the learning theorists' emphasis on change and underlying processes. With respect to socialization, attachment in a sense is both a form of biologically constrained learning and an arena within which much additional learning about the social world proceeds apace.

Next we reviewed recent research on attachment and its correlates. This research indicates that, by the second year of life, there exist stable individual differences in infant–parent relationships that can be classified along a dimension of security. Security characterizes relationships and does not reduce to characteristics of individual infants or parents. Nonetheless, the security of a 1-year-old's attachment to a parent can be predicted reliably from earlier infant characteristics and parental child-rearing practices, and it is associated with concurrent and subsequent manifestations of prosocial and antisocial behavior.

These correlational studies highlight interesting associations but do not necessarily imply causal relationships. We therefore outlined two conceptual models that illustrate possible paths of influence between early interactive experiences, attachment, and subsequent behavior. The basic model emphasizes consistent patterns of parent–child interaction, which are associated with various outcomes at various points in development. The expanded model emphasizes the impact of early attainments on later socializing experiences, as well as the mediating role of identificatory processes. Both models stressed the contributions children make to their own socialization. We then posed several questions that would need to be considered before either model can be tested, and called for supplementary experimental work on contributing processes. This experimental work in turn would have to be informed by careful observations of the social nature and functions of the social learning that habitually occurs within the family setting.

In sum, we have not answered the question posed with a simple yes or no. However, in neither of the models we offer do we posit early attachment as the sole cause of subsequent social adjustment. The picture is simply more complex than that. Rather, we believe that the question can only be answered completely through an integration of theoretical perspectives and methodologies. Ethological attachment theory can and should be supplemented with insights from other perspectives, and correlational studies of individual differences must be linked with a search for underlying processes. This undertaking is clearly a worthy one—indeed, it is central for a unified theory of social development—but it is by no means an easy task.

REFERENCES

Ainsworth, M. D. S. The development of infant-mother interaction among the Ganda. In B. M. Foss (Ed.), *Determinants of infant behaviour.* Vol. 4. London: Methuen, 1963 (New York: Wiley).
Ainsworth, M. D. S. *Infancy in Uganda: Infant care and the growth of love.* Baltimore: Johns Hopkins University Press, 1967.
Ainsworth, M. D. S. Object relations, dependency, and attachment: A theoretical review of the infant-mother relationship. *Child Development,* 1969, *40,* 969–1025.
Ainsworth, M. D. S. Attachment and dependency: A comparison. In J. Gewirtz (Ed.), *Attachment and dependency.* Washington, DC: V. H. Winston, 1972.

Ainsworth, M. D. S. The development of infant-mother attachment. In B. Caldwell & H. Ricciuti (Eds.), *Review of child development research* (Vol. 3). Chicago: University of Chicago Press, 1973.

Ainsworth, M. D. S., & Wittig, B. A. Attachment and exploratory behavior of 1-year-olds in a strange situation. In B. M. Foss (Ed.), *Determinants of infant behaviour.* Vol. 4. London: Methuen, 1969.

Ainsworth, M. D. S., Blehar, M., Waters, E., & Wall, S. *Patterns of attachment.* Hillsdale, NJ: Lawrence Erlbaum Associates, 1978.

Beller, E. K. Dependency and independence in young children. *Journal of Genetic Psychology,* 1955, *87,* 23–35.

Bowlby, J. *Attachment and loss* (Vol. 1, *Attachment*). New York: Basic Books, 1969.

Bowlby, J. *Attachment and loss* (Vol. 2, *Separation*). New York: Basic Books, 1972.

Bowlby, J. *Attachment and loss* (Vol. 3, *Loss*). New York: Basic Books, 1980.

Cairns, R. Attachment behavior of mammals. *Psychological Review,* 1966, *73,* 409–426.

Cairns, R. Attachment and dependency: A psychological and social-learning synthesis. In J. L. Gewirtz (Ed.), *Attachment and dependency.* Washington, DC: V. H. Winston, 1972.

Caldwell, B. M. The effects of infant care. In M. L. Hoffman and L. W. Hoffman (Eds.), *Review of child development research,* Vol. 1. New York: Russell Sage Foundation, 1964.

Connell, D. Individual differences in attachment: An investigation into stability, implications, and relationships to structure of early language development. Unpublished doctoral dissertation, Syracuse University, 1976.

Dollard, J., & Miller, N. E. *Personality and psychotherapy.* New York: McGraw Hill, 1950.

Egeland, B. Discussion of Kipp et al.'s paper, Patterns of self-control in young handicapped children. In M. Perlmutter (Ed.), *Minnesota Symposium in Child Psychology,* Vol. 16, 1983.

Erickson, M. F., & Crichton, B. Antecedents of compliance in two-year-olds from a high risk sample. Paper presented at the meeting of the Society for Research in Child Development, Boston, April 1983.

Erickson, M. F., Farber, E. A., & Egeland, B. Antecedents and concomitants of compliance in high risk preschool children. Paper presented at the annual meeting of the American Psychological Association, Washington, DC, August 1982.

Erickson, M. F., Sroufe, L. & Egeland, B. The relationship between quality of attachment and behavior problems in preschool in a high risk sample. In I. Bretherton & E. Waters (Eds.), *Growing points in attachment theory and research.* Monographs of the Society for Research in Child Development, 1985.

Gewirtz, J. L. A learning analysis of the effects of normal stimulation, privation, and deprivation on the acquisition of social motivation and attachment. In B. M. Foss (Ed.), *Determinants of infant behavior.* New York: Wiley, 1961.

Gewirtz, J. L. On the selection and use of attachment and dependence indicators. In J. Gewirtz (Ed.), *Attachment and dependency.* Washington, DC: Winston, 1972.

Grossman, K., & Grossman, K. E. Maternal sensitivity and newborn's orientation responses as related to quality of attachment in northern Germany. In I. Bretherton & E. Waters (Eds.), *Growing points in attachment theory and research.* Monographs of the Society for Research in Child Development, 1985.

Harlow, H. F. The development of affectional patterns in infant monkeys. In B. M. Foss (Ed.), *Determinants of infant behavior.* New York: Wiley, 1961.

Hay, D. F. Multiple functions of proximity-seeking in infancy. *Child Development,* 1980, *51,* 636–645.

Hay, D. F., & Murray, P. Giving and requesting: Social facilitation of infants' offers to adults. *Infant Behavior and Development*, 1982, *5*, 301–310.

Hay, D. F., & Rheingold, H. The early appearance of some valued social behaviors. In D. Bridgeman (Ed.), *The development of prosocial behavior: Interdisciplinary theories and strategies*. New York: Academic Press, 1983.

Hay, D. F., & Ross, H. The social nature of early conflict. *Child Development*, 1982, *53*, 105–113.

Heathers, G. Emotional dependence and independence in nursery school play. *Journal of Genetic Psychology*, 1955, *87*, 37–57.

Joffe, L., & Vaughn, B. Infant mother attachment: Theory, assessment, and implications for development. In B. Wolman (Ed.), *Handbook of developmental psychology*. Englewood Cliffs, NJ: Prentice Hall, 1982.

Kendrick, K., & Dunn, J. Sibling quarrels and maternal responses. *Developmental Psychology*, 1983, *19*, 62–70.

Lamb, M. E. Qualitative aspects of mother- and father-infant attachments. *Infant Behavior and Development*, 1978, *1*, 266–275.

Lieberman, A. F. Preschoolers' competence with a peer: Influence of attachment and social experience. *Child Development*, 1977, *48*, 1277–1287.

Lewis, M., Feiring, C., McGuffog, C., & Jaskir, J. Predicting psychopathology in 6-year-olds from early social relations. *Child Development*, 1984, *55*, 123–136.

Londerville, S., & Main, M. Security of attachment, compliance, and maternal training methods in the second year of life. *Developmental Psychology*, 1981, *17*, 289–299.

Maccoby, E., & Masters, J. Attachment and dependency. In P. Mussen (Ed.), *Carmichael's manual of child psychology*, Vol. 2. New York: Wiley, 1970.

Main, M., & Weston, D. R. Security of attachment to mother and father: Related to conflict behavior and the readiness to form new relationships. *Child Development*, 1981, *52*, 932–940.

Matas, L., Arend, R. E., & Sroufe, L. A. Continuity of adaption in the second year: The relationship between quality of attachment and later competence. *Child Development*, 1978, *49*, 547–556.

Pastor, D. The quality of infant-mother attachment and its relationship to toddlers' initial sociability with peers. *Developmental Psychology*, 1981, *17*, 326–335.

Radke-Yarrow & Zahn-Waxler (This volume)

Rajecki, D., Lamb, M., & Obmascher, P. Toward and general theory of infantile attachment: A comparative review of aspects of the social bond. *The Behavioral and Brain Sciences*, 1978, *3*, 417–446.

Rheingold, H. The social and socializing infant. In D. Goslin (Ed.), *Handbook of socialization theory and research*. Chicago: Rand McNally, 1969.

Sagi, A., Lamb, M. E., Lewkowicz, K. S., Shoham, R., Dvir, R., & Estes, D. Security of infant-mother, -father, and -metapelet attachments among kibbutz-reared Isreali children. In I. Bretherton & E. Waters (Eds.), *Growing points in attachment theory and research*. Monographs of the Society for Research in Child Development, 1985.

Salter, M. D. The concept of security as a basis for the evaluation of adjustment. Unpublished doctoral dissertation. University of Toronto, 1939.

Schaffer, H. R., & Emerson, P. E. Patterns of response to physical contact in early development. *Journal of Child Psychology and Psychiatry*, 1964, *5*, 1–13.

Sears, R. R. Dependency and motivation. In M. R. Jones (Ed.), *Nebraska Symposium on Motivation*. Lincoln: University of Nebraska Press, 1963.

Sears, R. R., Maccoby, E. E., & Lewin, H. *Patterns of child-rearing*. Evanston IL: Row Peterson, 1957.

Sroufe, L. Infant caregiver attachment and patterns of adaption in preschool: The roots of maladaption and competence. In M. Perlmutter (Ed.), *Minnesota Symposium on Child Psychology,* Vol. 16. Hillsdale, NJ: Erlbaum, 1982.

Sroufe, L. A., Fox, N., Pancake, V. Attachment and dependency in developmental perspective. *Child Development,* 1983, *54,* 1615–1627.

Sroufe, L. A., & Waters, E. Attachment as an organizational construct. *Child Development,* 1977, *48,* 1184–1199.

Stayton, D. J., Hogan, R., & Ainsworth, M. D. S. Infant obedience and maternal behavior: The origins of socialization reconsidered. *Child Development,* 1971, *42,* 1057–1069.

Vaughn, B., Crichton, L., & Egeland, B. Individual differences in qualities of caregiving during the first six months of life: Antecedents in maternal and infant behavior during the newborn period. *Infant Behavior and Development,* 1982, *5,* 77–95.

Vaughn, B., Egeland, B., Sroufe, L. A., & Waters, E. Individual differences in infant-mother attachment at 12 and 18 months: Stability and change in families under stress. *Child Development,* 1979, *50,* 971–975.

Waters, E. The reliability and stability of individual differences in infant-mother attachment. *Child Development,* 1978, *48,* 489–494.

Waters, E. Traits, behavioral systems, and relationships: Three models of infant-mother attachment. In K. Immelmann, G. Barlow, L. Petrinovitch, & M. Main (Eds.), *Behavioral development.* Cambridge: Cambridge University Press, 1980.

Waters, E., & Deane, K. E. Attachment: Theories, models, recent data, and some tasks for comparative developmental analysis. In L. W. Hoffman, R. Gandelman, & H. F. Schiffman (Eds.), *Parenting: Its causes and consequences.* Hillsdale, NJ: Erlbaum Associates, 1982.

Waters, E., & Sroufe, L. A. Social competence as a developmental construct. *Developmental Review,* 1983, *3,* 79–97.

Waters, E., Vaughn, B., & Egeland, B. Individual differences in infant-mother attachment: Antecedents in neonatal behavior in an urban economically disadvantaged sample. *Child Development,* 1980, *51,* 208–216.

Waters, E., Wippman, J., & Sroufe, L. A. Attachment, positive affect and competence in the peer group: Two studies in construct validation. *Child Development,* 1979, *50,* 821–829.

West, M., & Rheingold, H. Infant stimulation of maternal instruction. *Infant Behavior and Development,* 1978, *1,* 205–215.

7

Behavior at Home and Friendly or Hostile Behavior in Preschool

J. STEVENSON-HINDE, R. A. HINDE, and A. E. SIMPSON

INTRODUCTION

Preschool often provides the first opportunity for children to interact with others away from home and without their mothers. Given the probable importance of peer relationships for social development (e.g., Youniss, 1980), children's abilities to meet the demands placed on them in these circumstances may set the tone for much that is important later. However, once they are in preschool, children show individual differences in their behavior to peers and teachers (Hinde, Easton, Meller, & Tamplin, 1983), and at least some of this variation has roots in the home (Hinde & Tamplin, 1983).

One may view relationships at home as influencing, and being influenced by the child's personality, in an "ongoing dialectic" (Hinde, 1982, p. 66). Aspects of the child as an individual, such as his or her competence, ego resilience, or mood become intervening variables, tying together interactions in different contexts. For example, children with authoritative parents (who direct the child's activities in a rational manner, encourage verbal give and take, recognize the child's individual interests, etc.) were competent at nursery school, as revealed by their social responsibility and independence (Baumrind, 1971). Another predictor of competence in preschool is the quality of a child's attachment to the mother, assessed in the Ainsworth Strange Situation. That is, children who were classified at 15 months as securely, rather than insecurely, attached to their mothers scored higher on Q-sort items concerning peer competence and ego strength/effectance in a preschool playgroup 2 years later (Waters, Wippmann, & Sroufe, 1979). Similarly, children who were securely attached to their mothers at 18 months had higher ego-control and ego-resiliency in a school setting $3\frac{1}{2}$ years later (Arend, Gove, & Sroufe, 1979). Finally, within the framework of Thomas and Chess (1977), links have been found between family interactions and temperamental characteristics on the one hand (e.g., Dunn & Kendrick, 1982a; Hinde, Easton, Meller, & Tamplin, 1982) and characteristics and interactions at school on the other (e.g., Billman & McDevitt, 1980; Hinde, Stevenson-Hinde, & Tamplin, 1985). This chapter further explores such links within the home and from home to preschool. It is based on a study involving home interviews (Simpson & Stevenson-Hinde, 1985) and observations (Hinde & Tamplin, 1983) as well as school observations (Hinde et al., 1983). For the purposes of this volume, we omit interactions that may be considered neutral and focus on those that have positive or negative connotations.

THE STUDY

Sample

Thirty-seven children, 16 girls and 21 boys, all 50 months of age (plus or minus 3 weeks) were studied. They came from intact, two-child families, with a sibling aged between 2 years and 7 years, 8 months. No mothers worked fulltime, and all fathers were employed, in occupations ranging from unskilled to professional. All children attended the same preschool playgroup, in a Cambridgeshire village, for several mornings a week.

Data Collection

Two interviews were administered to the mother at home: (1) a Relationships Interview (based on Richman, Stevenson, & Graham, 1982) given on one visit and (2) a Temperamental Characteristics Interview (based on Garside, Birch, Scott, Chambers, Kolvin, Tweddle, & Barber, 1975) given on a second visit.

Interviews were followed by two unstructured observation sessions (60 minutes each) of mother–child interactions in the home (by a person different from the interviewer). Their verbal behavior and spoken commentary by the observer were tape recorded. Immediately after each set of visits, the interviewer and the observer independently completed a questionnaire about the home setting.

Preschool observations took place during the same weeks as the home visits, using an observation system similar to that used at home. Classroom behavior was observed for four mornings (40+ minutes each), and playground behavior was observed for a minimum of three mornings (30+ minutes each).

Coding, Choice of Measures, and Analysis

Table 7.1 lists the measures chosen to fit into a framework of positive or negative behavior. Interview measures were either reported frequencies of behavior or ratings of behavior. The ratings were made by the interviewer and were based on the mother's tape-recorded descriptions of recent behavior. All but three interview measures listed in Table 7.1 were significantly ($p < .05$, two-tailed) consistent across the previous 8 months. That is, correlation coefficients between these measures, taken at 42 months and at 50 months, ranged from .32 to .73, except for the Squabble rate with sibling (.19), Aggression with peers (.13), and frequency of Tantrums (.12).

Two measures from the home questionnaire completed by the interviewer and the observer were chosen, because they related to mother–child interactions and had high interrater agreement. These were (1) mother Sensitive to child, a sum of ratings over five behaviorally based items and (2) mother Enjoys child, a global rating.

Observations at home and at school were coded by a further modification of Lytton's (1973) modification of Caldwell's (1969) coding scheme. In addition to being positive or negative, each observation measure had to meet the following criteria: more than half the children showed the behavior, and the split-half reliability was significant ($p < .05$, one-tailed). For school observations, each behavior occurred in four settings: directed to peers inside the classroom; to adults inside the classroom; to peers outside in the playground; and to adults outside in the playground. Application of the above criteria left us with 12 school measures of positive and negative behavior (see Table 7.1). Observation measures were expressed either as absolute frequencies per unit time observed or as the proportion of total interactions with others. Here, we focus on absolute frequencies, because we feel that the absolute frequency of positive or negative interactions in school is what primarily matters to others, and because these particular interactions form only a small part of the total interactions. At school, positive and negative interactions formed only 11% and 12%,

Table 7.1

List of Measures: At Home and at School

HOME

Positive mother to child (60%)[a]

	Interview
Joint Activities	frequency in past week
Mother Accepts child	accepts child's offers of help: (1–5)[b]
	Observer ratings
Mother Sensitive to child	sensitive, warm, gentle, meshing, rapport:
	5 items, (1–7) each
Mother Enjoys child	enjoyment of child's company: (1–7)
	Direct observations
Mother Expresses Pleasure	expresses pleasure, smiles, laughs, etc.
Mother Verbally Friendly	expresses affection, approval, etc.

Negative mother to child (100%)

	Direct observations
Mother Noncomplies (%)	noncomplies per total control statements
Mother Inhibits	cautions, inhibits, threatens, etc.
Mother Reactively Hostile	resists, refuses, expresses displeasure, etc.
Mother Actively Hostile	criticizes, interferes, threatens, hits, etc.

Negative child to mother (33%)

	Direct observations
Child Disconfirms	ignores, turns away
Child Noncomplies (%)	noncomplies per total control statements
Child Inhibits	cautions, inhibits, threatens, etc.
Child Reactively Hostile	resists, refuses, expresses displeasure, etc.

Negative child to sibling/peer (67%)

	Interview
Squabble rate with sibling	frequency of squabbles per time together
Relationship with sibling	mostly enjoy to mostly aggressive: (1–5)
Aggression with peers	mostly enjoy to mostly aggressive: (1–4)
Assertive[c]	fights; bullies peers: 2 items, (1–5) each

Problem behavior (23%)

	Interview
Night Waking	frequency in past month
Night Wetting	frequency in past month
Worries	number of different ones, each weighted 1 or 2
Fears	number of different ones, each weighted 1 or 2
Dependent[c]	asks help; cries if left: 2 items, (1–5) each
Demanding	never demanding to very (1–5)
Refuses/difficult	frequency in past week
Tantrums	frequency in past week

(Continued)

Table 7.1 (*Continued*)

Unmalleable[c]	strength of refusal, from obeys to kicks and screams: in 2 settings, (1–5) each
Intense[c]	over-intense expression of feelings: in 4 settings, (1–5) each
Moody[c]	sulky; inequable, irritable in 5 settings: 6 items, (1–5) each
Poor Attention Span[c]	time at one thing on own: (1–5)
Active[c]	on the move: in 5 settings, (1–5) each

SCHOOL[d]

Positive behavior

Child Friendly to peers (inside, outside)	expresses pleasure, affection, approval
Child Friendly to adults (inside, outside)	

Negative behavior

Child Disconfirms peers (inside, outside)	ignores, turns away
Child Disconfirms adults (inside)	
Child Reactively Hostile to peers (inside, outside)	resists, refuses, expresses displeasure, etc.
Child Reactively Hostile to adults (inside)	
Child Actively Hostile to peers (inside, outside)	criticizes, interferes, threatens, hits, etc.

All interactions

Total Interactions with peers (inside, outside)	the sum of all interactions given and received
Total Interactions with adults (inside, outside)	

[a] Intercorrelations within groups of home measures: The percentage of possible pairs that were significantly correlated ($r_s \geq .32$).

[b] Numbers in parentheses denote ratings made by the interviewer or observer.

[c] From the Temperamental Characteristics Interview.

[d] All direct observations.

respectively, of total interactions to peers inside and even less to peers outside and to adults. Therefore, we did not want to weight these interactions by relatively large and varying denominators. In any case, correlations between frequencies and corresponding proportions were high, ranging from .78 to .94 for home observation measures and from .68 to .97 for school observation measures. Where a correlation coefficient reached significance for measures expressed as proportions as well as absolute frequencies, this was noted.

ASSOCIATIONS AMONG THE HOME MEASURES

Although the six mother-to-child measures labelled positive were collected from three data sources—interview, ratings of observed behavior, and direct observations (see Table 7.1)—they showed a considerable degree of intercorrelation. Nine out of 15 intercorrelations (i.e., 60%) reached significance and ranged from .33 to .81. This suggests that mothers were quite consistent in the extent to which they showed positive behavior. This was also true for measures of negative behavior from mother to child. Here, all six possible intercorrelations were significant and ranged from .33 to .68. The negative child-to-mother behavior was not so tightly organized, with only two out of six possible correlations (i.e., 33%) reaching significance. Finally, the degree of intercorrelation among the negative child–sibling/peers measures was 67% and 23% for measures of problem behavior. The latter set may be thought of as being comprised of two subsets, with the first five measures concerned with anxious (or in extreme cases, neurotic) behavior and the last eight measures with difficult behavior (Richman et al., 1982). The degree of intercorrelation was 20% for the first subset and 39% for the second.

Rather than showing correlations between all possible sets, we ask how the first two sets, with the mother as subject, relate to the other sets, with the child as subject (Table 7.2). First, the negative child-to-mother interactions were positively correlated with observations of both positive (i.e., mother Expresses Pleasure and mother Verbally Friendly) and negative (i.e., mother Inhibits and mother Reactively Hostile) mother-to-child interactions. (As this suggests, mother Expresses Pleasure was somewhat associated with mother Inhibits [.21] and mother Reactively Hostile [.35]. However, this was not the case for mother Verbally Friendly, where correlations with mother Inhibits [.02] and mother Reactively Hostile (−.03 were low.)

The remaining sets of child's behavior, which involve negative behavior with sibling and peers and problem behavior, were not significantly correlated with any of the four negative mother-to-child interactions. (Even when boys and girls were considered separately, there were only $\frac{4}{68}$ [6%] significant correlations for girls and none for boys.) However, the child's behavior with sibling and peers and problem behavior were negatively correlated with the six positive mother-to-child interactions. In particular, the more the mother did with the child and the more sensitive

Table 7.2

Significant Correlations between Mother-to-Child Measures with Child as Subject[a]

Mother to child	Child to mother			Child with sib	Child with peers		Problem behavior									
	Dis-con-firms	In-hib-its	Reac-tively Hos-tile	Squab-bles	Poor Rela-tion-ship	Ag-gres-sion	Wor-ries	Fears	De-mand-ing	Tan-trums	Re-fuses	Un-mal-lea-ble	In-tense	Moody	Ac-tive
Positive															
Joint Activities															
Mother Accepts child				−		−	−	−	−		−	−	−	−	
Mother Sensitive to child					−								−	−	
Mother Enjoys child					−										
Mother Expresses Pleasure	+	+								−b					
Mother Verbally Friendly	+	+b													−b
Negative															
Mother Noncomplies (%)															
Mother Inhibits	+	+	+												
Mother Reactively Hostile			+b												
Mother Actively Hostile															

[a] Significant Spearman correlation coefficients are entered as positive or negative symbols. Coefficients range from .32, $p < .05$, to .52, $p < .001$, two-tailed, $N = 37$.

[b] The correlation is also significant when the frequency of an observed interaction is expressed as a ratio of the total interactions.

she was to the child, the less Moody it was. The more Accepting the mother, the less Squabbling with sibling and peers, the less Worries, Fears, Demanding, and Refusals, and the less Unmalleable, Intense, and Moody the child. The more mothers appeared to Enjoy the child, the less Aggressive the sibling relationship and the less Active the child. Activity was also negatively correlated with the frequency and proportion of the observation measure, mother Expresses Pleasure. The higher the frequency of mother Verbally Friendly, the fewer Tantrums and the less Moody the child. With temperamental characteristics, such as mood and activity, which tend to be seen as relatively enduring aspects of the child, it is tempting to say that children who are not moody or more active than normal have mothers who enjoy them more. However, it is also likely that aspects of the mother–child relationship influence characteristics of the developing child.

Within the category of problem behavior, the Anxious subset produced only 2 significant correlations out of 30 (7%), whereas the Difficult subset produced 23%. Overall, difficult children tended to have fewer positive interactions with mothers, whether the interactions were assessed by interview or by direct observation. Similar correlations have been reported for younger children (e.g., Campbell, 1979; Dunn & Kendrick, 1980; Milliones, 1978). However, some studies have reported no association between the temperamental characteristic Difficult and mother–infant interaction (e.g., Bates, Olson, Pettit, & Bayles, 1982; Vaughn, Taraldson, Crichton, & Egeland, 1981), and Bates (1980) concludes that "the data are so far mixed in support of the hypothesis that maternal perceptions of difficultness are concurrently associated with negative aspects of the mother infant relationship" (p. 312). Lack of agreement may be partly due to measurement problems (see Hubert, Wachs, Peters-Martin, & Gandour, 1982).

LOOKING FROM HOME TO PRESCHOOL

Within preschool, interactions occurred in two settings: (1) the classroom, where adults exerted moderate control and (2) the playground, where there was much less adult supervision. Frequencies of positive (Friendly) and negative behavior (Disconfirm, Reactively Hostile, and Actively Hostile) to peers were somewhat correlated, with the three correlation coefficients in each setting (inside and outside) ranging from +.15 to +.41. This is compatible with other findings with children of this age (e.g., Jacklin & Maccoby, 1978; Feshbach & Feshbach, 1969). However, when total activity was controlled for by making each measure a ratio of total interactions, each of the six correlations between positive and negative behavior to peers decreased (ranging from $-.24$ to $+.08$).

Table 7.3 indicates which measures from home were significantly correlated with positive and negative behavior at school. Of the 372 possible correlations between the 31 home and 12 school measures, 62 (17%) were significant. However, because of the intercorrelations among the home measures and among the school measures, it is not possible to compare this with an expected number of significant correlations.

In considering the association between home and school measures, we made use of a simple prediction that positive behavior at home would be positively associated, and negative and problem behavior would be negatively associated, with positive behavior at school; whereas the opposite would hold for negative behavior at school. Each significant coefficient that supported the prediction is described here as being in the "expected" direction, and those that did not, as in the "wrong" direction.

Looking first at the correlations between home measures and Friendly behavior to peers at school (Table 7.3, Columns 1 and 2), there were only $\frac{4}{62}$ (6%) significant correlations, of which none was in the expected direction. With Friendly behavior to adults, $\frac{9}{62}$ (15%) correlations were significant, with 7 in the expected direction. For negative behavior to adults (Table 7.3, Columns 11 and 12), there were $\frac{6}{62}$ (10%) significant correlations, with 5 in the expected direction. (Most forms of negative behavior to adults hardly occurred. Twenty-seven or more children showed none of the following behavior categories: Actively Hostile to adults inside, Disconfirm, Reactively Hostile, or Actively Hostile to adults outside.) In summary, we cannot say that the tabled measures of positive or negative behavior used at home helped to predict the absolute frequencies of Friendly behavior to peers at school. The home measures went some way toward predicting behavior to adults at school.

However, between home measures and negative behavior to peers at school, there were $\frac{43}{186}$ (23%) significant correlations, with 40 in an expected direction. We now look more closely at these correlations and attempt to narrow down which home behaviors predicted negative behavior to peers at school. For positive mother–child interactions at home, $\frac{16}{36}$ (44%) correlations with negative behavior to peers were significant and negative. The positive mother–child set included three different types of data—the maternal interview (Joint Activities, mother Accepts child), the home questionnaire completed by the observer and interviewer (mother Sensitive to child, mother Enjoys child), and direct observations (mother Expresses Pleasure, mother Verbally Friendly). Each of these six measures produced at least one significant correlation. The best single predictor was mother Verbally Friendly, which was significantly negatively

Table 7.3

Significant Correlations between Home Measures and School Measures[a,b]

Home	Positive				Negative								Total interactions			
	To Peers		To Adults		To Peers						To Adults		With Peers		With Adults	
	Friendly		Friendly		In (67%)			Out (33%)			In (0%)					
	In	Out	In	Out	DIS	RH	AH	DIS	RH	AH	DIS	RH	In	Out	In	Out
Positive M–C (60%)[d]																
Joint Activities	−												−			
Mother Accepts child	−												−	−		
Mother Sensitive to child					−c				−c							
Mother Enjoys child						−			−c							
Mother Expresses Pleasure									−c							
Mother Verbally Friendly			−		−		−				−		−c		−	
Negative M–C (100%)																
Mother Noncomplies (%)																
Mother Inhibits			−c							+c						
Mother Reactively Hostile			−c							+c						
Mother Actively Hostile										+c		+c				+
Negative C-M (33%)																
Child Disconfirms			−				−									
Child Noncomplies (%)			+				+c				+c					+
Child Inhibits							−						−c			
Child Reactively Hostile											+					

Significant Spearman coefficients for child behavior measures (rotated table)

Negative C–S, P (67%)									
Squabble rate with sib									
Relationship with sib	+								
Aggression with peers	+	+	+						
Assertive	+	+^{c}	+^{c}			+^{c}	+	+	+
Problem behavior (23%)									
Night Waking							–^{c}		
Night Wetting									
Worries								+	
Fears	–								
Dependent	+	+							
Demanding	+^{c}	+					+		
Refuses/difficult	+^{c}	+	+^{c}				+		
Tantrums	+			+					+
Unmalleable	–^{c}	–							–
Intense		+		+	+	+^{c}	+		
Moody	+	+	+^{c}	+^{c}				+	+
Poor Attention Span	–^{c}	+							
Active		+	+^{c}	+^{c}	+^{c}				+

^{a} Significant Spearman coefficients are entered as positive or negative symbols. Coefficients range from .32, $p < .05$, to .53, $p < .001$, two-tailed, $N = 37$.

^{b} In = in classroom; Out = outside on playground. DIS = Disconfirms; RH = Reactively Hostile; AH = Actively Hostile; M–C = Mother–Child; and C–S, P = Child–Sibling, Peer.

^{c} The correlation is also significant when the frequency of an observed interaction is expressed as a ratio of the total interactions.

^{d} Intercorrelations within groups of measures: the percentage of possible pairs that were significantly correlated ($r_s \geq .32$).

correlated with $\frac{5}{6}$ negative measures. Thus, positive mother–child interactions did predict a relatively low frequency of negative behavior to peers at school.

The second home set, negative mother–child, was correlated with only the most extreme negative behavior in the school playground, namely Actively Hostile to peers. In particular, the more Inhibiting, Reactively Hostile, and Actively Hostile the mother at home, the more Actively Hostile the child to peers at school. This held for both the absolute frequencies and the proportions of total interactions. Such correlations could imply modelling (see Radke-Yarrow & Zahn-Waxler; Waters & Hay, this volume). For the negative child–mother measures, child Noncomplies predicted Active Hostility to peers inside, but there were only three other significant correlations, all negative.

The negative child–sibling, peer home set showed an interesting split: the sibling measures were unrelated to negative behavior to peers in school, whereas the two measures of behavior with peers at home correlated especially well with negative behavior to peers inside school (with $\frac{3}{4}$ significant correlations).

Finally, within the set of problem behavior, 15 out of 78 (19%) correlations were significant, even though there were six measures that were not significantly correlated with any of the measures of negative behavior to peers at school. Five of these six measures (Night Waking, Night Wetting, Worries, Fears, and Dependent) formed the anxious subset, which did not "map on" to the negative behavior at school. The sixth measure that did not correlate significantly with negative behavior to peers at school was the frequency of Tantrums reported by mothers. Three of these six measures (i.e., Fears, Dependent, Tantrums) did not show significant overall correlations with negative behavior to peers, because the coefficients went in one direction for girls and another for boys. In particular, Fearful and Dependent boys were more Reactively Hostile to peers inside (.11; .44), while girls were less (−.59; −.45), and Dependent boys were more Actively Hostile inside (.36), while girls were less (−.46). Outside, more Active Hostility was shown the more Fearful (.16) and Dependent (.46) the boys, while girls showed less (−.54; −.38). For Tantrums, the direction was different, with boys showing a negative correlation with Reactive Hostility, both inside (−.41) and outside (−.33), while for girls it was positive (.59; .41).

The remaining seven measures in the problem-behavior set produced no large sex differences in correlations with negative behavior to peers at school, and all the significant correlations were positive. In particular, Demanding, Refuses, Unmalleable, Moody, Poor Attention Span, and

Active were all positively correlated with negative behavior to peers inside the classroom. Outside, positive correlations occurred for Intense, Moody, and Active. That the correlations involving Active were not simply due to more total interactions of every kind at school is shown by significant correlations for the proportion of negative behavior to total interactions (indicated by c in Table 7.3), as well as by the absolute frequency of the behavior.

In summary, positive mother–child interactions predicted less negative behavior to peers both inside and outside the classroom, as well as less squabbling and difficult behavior at home (Table 7.2). Although negative mother–child observations were not associated with negative behavior to peers inside school, they were the best predictor of the most antisocial behavior in the playground, Actively Hostile. Agonistic interactions with peers at home and problem behavior of a similar nature to the school behavior predicted a relatively high frequency of negative behavior to peers at school, especially in the classroom.

FRIENDLY INTERACTIONS AT SCHOOL

Whilst links were found between behavior at home and negative behavior at school, we must consider why the frequency of friendly behavior to peers at school was not well predicted. Some associations did emerge for proportions, over a wider range of home observation measures. The proportion of each child's interactions with peers that were friendly was correlated not only with frequent positive and neutral interactions with the mother but also with infrequent negative interactions (Hinde & Tamplin, 1983). Furthermore, friendly behavior in school is likely to be better predicted by patterns of home variables than by any single one. For example, Baumrind (1971) found that parents who were both nurturant and controlling were likely to have children who were self-reliant, explorative, and contented. Although our methods of data collection did not permit exact parallels with her categories, we found some support for her view. By selecting mothers who were above or below the median on various observed interactions, it was possible to fit some of them into Baumrind's three categories of Permissive, Authoritative, or Authoritarian mothers. It was found that friendly behavior at school was associated with mother's gentle and positive control combined with warmth. The associations between maternal control and hostility in school were more complex, perhaps because the pattern of maternal control may be either a cause or a consequence of child aggressiveness (Hinde & Tamplin, 1983).

NEGATIVE INTERACTIONS AT SCHOOL

A low frequency of negative interactions at school was associated with positive mother–child interactions at home (Table 7.3). Similarly, Manning found that children with a low level of hostility in nursery school had mothers who were "friendly but not fussy" (Manning, Heron & Marshall, 1978, p. 55). She called such children *specific specialists,* because their hostility tended to be restricted to situations in which they were frustrated or annoyed. Other children fell into other groups, according to their predominant type of hostility: *games specialists,* who showed rough intimidating behavior during games; *harassment specialists,* who showed hostility which seemed unprovoked, at least in the immediate situation, and which tended to be directed at a particular person, often repeatedly; and *harassment-specific specialists,* who were bossy as well as teasing but were relatively unsuccessful in disputes. Unlike the specific specialists, the other three groups showed behavior problems in nursery school and 3 years later in primary school and/or at home. Manning's careful work shows how predictions may be refined by incorporating context into direct observations.

Problem behavior at home, including the style of behavior reflected in the temperamental characteristics Unmalleable, Intense, Moody, and Active, was associated with a high frequency of negative behavior to peers at school (Table 7.3).

Billman & McDevitt (1980) found relations between temperamental characteristics of the child as rated by mothers and observations of social behavior in nursery school. Taking only those characteristics similar to the ones used here, it was found that Intense children were "physical'—hitting, taking, and touching more than less-intense children. Active children were involved in more hitting and taking and watched others less. A compatible picture of negative social behavior of Active children has been found by others (e.g., Buss, Block, & Block, 1980). Unlike the present study, or Billman et al.'s study, the Buss et al. study relied not on maternal reports of activity but on actometers. Children with high actometer levels were those who

> try to stretch limits, try to take advantage of others, try to be the centre of attention, like to compete, are self-assertive, and somewhat aggressive, and are not obedient, compliant, shy or reserved. Thus active children are seen as relatively outgoing, but also they tend to resist adult demands and strive to dominate their peers. (p. 406)

Looking over time, similar associations have been found from preschool to middle-school age. Richman et al. (1982) have shown that "early restlessness" predicts later antisocial disorder, whereas fearfulness predicts neurotic disorder. Olweus (this volume) found that an active, intense boy is more likely to develop aggressive modes of action later on than a calm and quiet boy.

CONCLUSIONS

In attempting to relate home influences to school behavior, our initial assumption has been that the former are multiple and interrelated, and that we must not expect any one facet of home experience to be prepotent. We must hope to find the links through child characteristics that both influence, and are influenced by, home interactions and relationships and which also influence (and perhaps are in due course influenced by) interactions in school. Given our present inability to identify the precise pattern of child characteristics relevant to given aspects of behavior in school, it is also profitable to make direct comparisons between interactions at home and school. However, we must not think in terms of direct effects of home experiences on school behavior, but rather of home experiences affecting and producing both temporary responses and longer-term predispositions in the child that affect behavior in school. In fact, when a broad spectrum of behavior at home and school is considered, we are able to find relatively little evidence of children behaving at school either as they behave at home or as their mothers behave to them, but considerable evidence that patterns of home variables are related in meaningful ways to behaviors in school (Hinde & Tamplin, 1983).

The variables we have tapped inevitably represent only a small proportion of those that are relevant. Nevertheless, we have shown that certain characteristics of the child are related to aspects of the mother–child relationship, and that the child characteristics and the mother–child relationship are related to some interactions in preschool.

The direction of effects cannot be assessed from such correlational data. Nevertheless, in many cases working assumptions can be made. It would be reasonable to proceed on the assumption that reshaping home relationships might affect the dialectic between home relationships and child characteristics and thus affect friendly and hostile behavior in school (e.g., Carey, 1982; Patterson, 1980). However, it must not necessarily be assumed that the mother–child relationship is the only, or even the central, issue. For instance, at an earlier age, children's behavior may be markedly affected by the birth of a younger sibling (Dunn & Kendrick, 1982b).

Although we have emphasized the complex nexus of variables to which the child is responding at home, the issues considered in this chapter represent only a small fraction of those that are important. We have noted that girls who were Fearful and Dependent initiated fewer negative interactions at school, whereas boys initiated more. This also held for the characteristic Shy, which involved slow initial approach and slow adjustment to new people and/or situations (Hinde, Stevenson-Hinde, & Tamplin, 1985). Similarly at home, boys with high Shy scores had tensionful mother–child interactions, whereas girls with high scores had positive interactions (Simpson & Stevenson-Hinde, 1985). For certain other characteristics (Active, Irregular Attention Span, Unmalleable, Intense, Moody, and Assertive), there was a stronger tendency for girls with high scores to have tensionful mother–child interactions than there was for boys with high scores (Hinde & Stevenson-Hinde, 1985). Such sex differences can be accounted for in part by the differing expectations that mothers have concerning behavior appropriate for boys and girls. This is in keeping with a concept of "goodness of fit" between temperament and environment (Lerner, Lerner, & Zabski, 1985; Plomin, 1982). In his review of childhood temperament. Plomin suggests an approach that incorporates assessments of the expectations of relevant others and emphasizes the interaction component of a temperament × environment analysis.

Finally, it should again be stressed that our children did not show clinical behavior problems. Bates (1980) points out that the development of severe behavior problems may require a conjunction of variables, such as a difficult temperament, adverse parental attitudes, and practices (e.g., Cameron, 1978), and/or stressful events such as parental divorce or birth of a sibling (Dunn & Kendrick, 1982b). Thus, one might develop a model comparable with that of Brown (e.g., 1982) for predicting the onset of depression in women, involving a combination of variables from both the past and the present.

Such a model to predict the occurrence of a clinical disorder is compatible with Thomas and Chess's (1977) view of temperament. In the New York Longitudinal Study, Thomas and Chess found that parental practices could determine whether a child became more or less difficult. Similarly, in the present study, when children were assessed at 3.5 years and 8 months later, there was an indication that characteristics and negative family interactions become more tightly linked as the child gets older (Stevenson-Hinde & Simpson, 1982). Such links, and changes in them over time, emphasize the transactional nature of development (Stevenson-Hinde & Hinde, 1985).

SUMMARY

We have focused on positive and negative behavior of 50-month-old children at home and at preschool. At home, positive mother-to-child interactions were associated with less squabbling with siblings and peers as well as with less problem behavior. When home measures were related to positive and negative behavior to peers or to adults at preschool, a meaningful pattern emerged for some aspects of school behavior, especially negative behavior to peers. The sets of home measures that best predicted negative behavior to peers at school were (1) positive mother–child interactions (from three different sources of data), (2) agonistic behavior with peers at home, and (3) mild behavior problems of a similar nature to the school behaviors. Although negative mother–child interactions were not associated with negative behavior to peers inside the classroom, they were the best predictor of the most antisocial behavior in the playground—active hostility.

ACKNOWLEDGMENTS

We would like to thank A. M. Tamplin for help with the analysis, and D. F. Easton and G. Titmus for statistical advice.

REFERENCES

Arend, R., Gove, F. L., & Sroufe, L. A. Continuity of individual adaptation from infancy to kindergarten: A predictive study of ego-resiliency and curiosity in preschoolers. *Child Development*, 1979, *50*, 950–959.
Bates, J. E. The concept of difficult temperament. *Merrill-Palmer Quarterly*, 1980, *26*, 299–319.
Bates, J. E., Olson, S. L., Pettit, G. S., & Bayles. K. Dimensions of individuality in the mother/infant relationship at 6 months of age. *Child Development*, 1982, *52*, 446–461.
Baumrind, D. Current patterns of parental authority. *Developmental Psychology Monographs*, 1971, *4*, (1, Pt. 2).
Billman, J., & McDevitt, S. C. Convergence of parent and observer ratings of temperament with observations of peer interaction in nursery school. *Child Development*, 1980, *51*, 395–400.
Brown, G. W. Early loss and depression. In C. M. Parkes, and J. Stevenson-Hinde (Eds.). *The place of attachment in human behavior*. New York: Basic Books, 1982.

Buss, D. M., Block, J. H., & Block, J. Preschool activity levels: Personality correlates and developmental implications. *Child Development,* 1980, *51,* 401–408.

Caldwell, B. M. A new "APPROACH" to behavioral ecology. In I. P. Hill, (Ed.), *Minnesota Symposia of Child Psychology,* Vol 2, Minneapolis: University of Minnesota Press, 1969.

Cameron, J. R. Parental treatment, children's temperament, and the risk of childhood behavioral problems: 2. Initial temperament, parental attitudes, and the incidence and form of behavioral problems. *American Journal of Orthopsychiatry,* 1978, *48,* 140–147.

Campbell, S. B. G. Mother–infant interaction as a function of maternal ratings of temperament. *Child Psychiatry and Human Development,* 1979, *10,* 67–76.

Carey, W. B. Clinical use of temperament data in paediatrics. In Ciba Foundation Symposium, 89, *Temperamental differences in infants and young children,* London: Pitman, 1982.

Dunn, J., & Kendrick, C. Studying temperament and parent–child interaction: Comparison of interview and direct observation. *Developmental Medicine and Child Neurology,* 1980, *22,* 484–496.

Dunn, J., & Kendrick, C. Temperamental differences, family relationships, and young children's response to change within the family. In Ciba Foundation Symposium 89 *Temperamental differences in infants and young children,* London: Pitman, 1982(a).

Dunn, J., & Kendrick, C. *Siblings: Love, envy, and understanding.* Cambridge, MA: Harvard University Press, 1982(b).

Feshbach, N. D., & Feshbach, S. The relationship between empathy and aggression in two age groups. *Developmental Psychology,* 1969, *1,* 102–107.

Garside, R. F., Birch, H., Scott, D., Chambers, S., Kolvin, I., Tweddle, E. G., & Barber, L. M. Dimensions of temperament in infant school children. *Journal of Child Psychology and Psychiatry,* 1975, *16,* 219–231.

Hinde, R. A. Attachment: Some conceptual and biological issues. In C. M. Parkes, and J. Stevenson-Hinde (Eds.), *The place of attachment in human behavior,* New York: Basic Books, 1982.

Hinde, R. A., Easton, D. F., Meller, R. E., & Tamplin, A. M. Temperamental characteristics of 3–4-year-olds and mother–child interaction. In Ciba Foundation Symposium, 89, *Temperamental differences in infants and young children,* London: Pitman, 1982.

Hinde, R. A., Easton, D. F., Meller, R. E., & Tamplin A. M. Nature and determinants of preschoolers' differential behaviour to adults and peers. *British Journal of Developmental Psychology,* 1983, *1,* 3–19.

Hinde, R. A., and Stevenson-Hinde, J. Relationships, personality, and the social situation. In R. Gilmour and S. Duck (Eds.), *Key issues in personal relationships.* Hillsdale, NJ: Erlbaum, 1985.

Hinde, R. A., Stevenson-Hinde, J., & Tamplin, A. M. Characteristics of 3 to 4-year-olds assessed at home and their interactions in preschool. *Developmental Psychology,* 1985, *21,* 130–140.

Hinde, R. A., & Tamplin A. M. Relations between mother–child interactions and behaviour in preschool. *British Journal of Developmental Psychology,* 1983, *1,* 231–257.

Hubert, N. C., Wachs, T. D., Peters-Martin, P. & Gandour, M. J. The study of early temperment: Measurement and conceptual issues. *Child Development,* 1982, *53,* 571–600.

Jacklin, C. N., & Maccoby, E. E. Social behavior at 33 months in same-sex and mixed-sex dyads. *Child Development,* 1978, *49,* 557–569.

Lerner, J. V., Lerner, R. M., & Zabski, S. Temperament and elementary school children's actual and rated academic performance: A test of a 'goodness-of-fit' model. *Journal of Child Psychology and Psychiatry*, 1985, *26*, 125–136.

Lytton, H. Three approaches to the study of parent–child interaction: Ethological, interview and experimental. *Journal of Child Psychology and Psychiatry*, 1973, *14*, 1–17.

Manning, M., Heron, J., & Marshall, T. Styles of hostility and social interactions at nursery, at school, and at home. An extended study of children. In L. A. Hersov, M. Berger, and D. Shaffer (Eds.), *Aggression and anti-social behavior in childhood and adolescence*, London: Pergamon, 1973.

Milliones, J. Relationship between perceived child temperament and maternal behavior. *Child Development*, 1978, *49*, 1255–1257.

Patterson, G. R. Mothers: The unacknowledged victims. *Monographs of the Society for Research in Child Development*, Serial No. 186, 1980.

Plomin, R. Childhood temperament. In B. B. Lakey and A. E. Kazdin (Eds.), *Advances in clinical child psychology* (Vol. 6), New York: Plenum, 1982.

Richman, N., Stevenson, J., & Graham, P. J. *Preschool to school: A behavioural study*, London: Academic Press, 1982.

Simpson, A. E., & Stevenson-Hinde, J. Temperamental characteristics of 3- to 4-year-old boys and girls and child–family interactions. *Journal of Child Psychology and Psychiatry*, 1985, *26*, 43–53.

Stevenson-Hinde, J., & Hinde, R. A. Changes in associations between characteristics and interactions. In R. Plomin and J. Dunn (Eds.), *The study of temperament: Changes, continuities, and challenges*, Hillsdale, New Jersey: Erlbaum, 1985.

Stevenson-Hinde, J., & Simpson, A. E. Temperament and relationships. In Ciba Foundation Symposium 89, *Temperamental differences in infants and young children*, London: Pitman Books, 1982.

Thomas, A., & Chess, S. *Temperament and development*, New York: Brunner/Mazel, 1977.

Vaughn, B., Taraldson, B., Crichton, L., & Egeland, B. The assessment of infant temperament: A critique of the Carey Infant Temperament Questionnaire. *Infant Behavior and Development*, 1981, *4*, 1–18.

Waters, E., Wippmann, J., & Sroufe, L. A. Attachment, positive affect, and competence in the peer group: Two studies in construct validation. *Child Development*, 1979, *50*, 821–829.

Youniss, J, *Parents and peers in social development*, Chicago: University of Chicago Press, 1980.

PART III

Impulse Control

8

The Role of Impulse Control in the Development of Antisocial and Prosocial Behavior

LEA PULKKINEN

Although many behavioral problems are thought to be related to impulse control, research on this topic has not been extensive. The concept of impulse control has been of heuristic value in clinical contexts. As an operationalized, empirical concept, however, its psychological meaning remains unclear. The concept itself derives from psychoanalytic theory. The purpose of psychoanalysis is to illuminate the determinants of impulses that consist of external stimuli, internal stimuli, or certain cognitive goals in order to study ego resistance and the derivatives of warded-off impulses (see Fenichel, 1945, p. 23).

The empirical study of impulsivity, on the other hand, has proceeded within a number of unrelated research traditions. Although impulse control is generally conceptualized as an opposite to impulsivity, research on impulsivity has generally not examined the acquisition of impulse control. This essay reviews different empirical approaches to the study of impulsivity and self-control and examines their relationship to social development (the study of psychomotor impulsivity is excluded).

APPROACHES TO CONCEPTUALIZING IMPULSIVITY

Psychoanalytical Approaches to Impulse Expression

In psychoanalytic theory, an *impulse* is conceptualized as a discharge of psychic energy. The source of this energy—the id—is closely related to bodily processes from which it derives its energy. The id, it is argued, cannot tolerate increases in energy, which are experienced as uncomfortable states of tension. If external stimuli or internally produced excitations raise the level of tension, the id tries to return the organism to a constant energy level through energy discharge. The id functions according to the pleasure principle. The ego is that part of the id that has been modified by influences deriving from the external world (Freud, 1961). The ego seeks to reduce the levels of tension and to substitute the reality principle for the pleasure principle. The ego decides the extent of immediate instinctual satisfaction, postpones satisfaction until more favorable circumstances can be achieved, or suppresses the excitations completely (Freud, 1949).

There have been various attempts to operationalize psychoanalytical constructs. Dombrose & Slobin (1958) constructed the IES test in order to measure the relative strength of the id, the ego, and the superego. The battery consists of four subtests. An example is the Arrow-Dot test. This task consists of diagrams containing arrows and dots and, interposed between them, various bars and straight and dashed lines. The subject is instructed to draw the shortest line possible from the arrow to the dot. A line through a barrier counts as an I(id)-score. In accordance with hypotheses, delinquent, disturbed, and learning-disabled adolescents have higher I-scores and lower E(ego)-scores than normal controls. High E-scores correlate positively with intellectual effectiveness. In addition, female nursing students have higher E-scores and lower I-scores than other female groups, suggesting a relationship between realistic control of behavior and prosocial development (see Mangold, 1966; McCormick, Klappauf, Schnobrich, & Harvey, 1971; Rankin & Wioff, 1964; Signori, Smordin, Rempel, & Sampson, 1964; Stawar & Lamp, 1974).

Developmental trends in performance on the Arrow-Dot test have been demonstrated. Pulkkinen (1980) showed that E-scores increased and I-scores declined from age 4 to age 6 years. High E-scores correlated with moral judgment, affective and cognitive role-taking, constructive behavior, and vocabulary. I-scores correlated negatively with these variables and, in addition, positively with aggressiveness and disobedience. In my view, the IES test, particularly the Arrow-Dot subtest, holds some promise for the operationalization of the psychoanalytic id and ego functions. Further validity studies are needed, however.

Another approach to the operationalization of the psychoanalytical concept of impulse control has been presented by Getsinger (1980). Getsinger maintains that ego delay—a metapsychological and dynamic construct—can usefully be employed to describe individual differences along a continuum from low to high ego delay. *Ego delay* is defined as "the temporal duration during which the executive dimension of psyche (the ego) mobilizes its resources and functions in order to act on reality in such a way that drive and tension can be safely reduced" (Getsinger, 1980, pp. 350–351).

Two ideal types of individuals differing in their degree of ego delay are specified:

> The prototype of low ego delay (LED) is characterized by little tendency toward inhibition between stimulation and response . . . Behaviorally, the LED type is impulsive, hyperactive, reckless, and aggressive. Because of erratic psychophysiological rhythms, the biological clock is frequently accelerated. Internal time goes much faster than objective time, and there is a tendency toward boredom . . . Although primarily directed toward the environment (extraversive), the LED type frequently conditions poorly and may appear unable to learn from experience.
>
> At the other end of the continuum is the high ego delay type (HED). This type is characterized by a highly introversive tendency relevant to the handling of impulses. Oriented toward the cognitive (as contrasted with the affective) realm, the HED type is highly controlled and prefers to avoid intense levels of stimulation . . . The HED type shows more infrequent oscillations in autonomic nervous system activity. (Getsinger, 1980, pp. 352–354)

Getsinger recommends the use of a multitechnical approach to assess ego delay, including observation, clinical interviews, and psychological tests (e.g., the TAT, the Rorschach (F+, M/C scores), the MMPI (Psychopathic Deviate and Hypomania subscales), and the Eysenck Personality Inventory). As a special addition, he also includes two methods of time estimation—production and verbal estimation. In the former, subjects are asked to produce a specified interval of time (e.g., 30 seconds) by starting and stopping an unseen clock. The LED type, Getsinger argues, will produce shorter time intervals than the HED type because of a faster internal clock. In verbal time estimation, subjects are required to estimate the length of an elapsed time interval.

Assessing psychiatric patients, Getsinger found that ego delay is positively correlated with long-term adjustment following psychiatric hospitalization (Getsinger & Leon, 1979) and with vocational readjustment following disability (Getsinger, 1977). Using the production method, he also observed that sociopaths were less accurate in estimating time intervals and, further, they were less able to delay temporal judgments than self-actualizers selected according to Block's Ego-Resiliency scale (Getsinger, 1977).

Experimental work on the Getsinger measure, however, has provided inconsistent results. For example, Barabasz (1970) was not able to replicate the differences in time estimation between delinquents and nondelinquents previously reported by Siegman (1961). Nor were Senior, Towne, and Huessy (1979) successful in replicating the differences in time estimation between normal and hyperactive children previously reported by Cappella, Gentile, and Juliano (1977). Trying to relate time estimation to the Cattell 16 PF test (Cattell, Saunders, & Stice, 1957), Bell (1972) emphasized the many inconsistencies in the time-estimation literature. He called for further, more sophisticated research prior to formulating a theory relating personality characteristics to time estimation. Hence, far-reaching generalizations based on the ego-delay construct appear premature at the present time.

Impulsivity as a Personality Trait

In the psychoanalytic conception, an *impulse* is associated with an instinct that has a source, an aim, and an impetus. Therefore, an impulse is considered to have a certain degree of content. In contrast, studies of *impulsivity* as a personality trait have emphasized the individual's style of behavior at the expense of behavioral content.

In Murray's (1938) theory of personality, impulsion is classified as a general personality trait and scored as the ratio of impulsion to deliberation. *Impulsion* is defined as the "tendency to act quickly without reflection. Short reaction time, intuitive or emotional decisions. The inability to inhibit an impulse" (p. 148). *Deliberation* is defined as the "inhibition and reflection before action. Slow reaction time, spastic contraction, compulsive thinking" (p. 148). Questionnaire items were used to examine both impulsion (e.g., "I often act on the spur of the moment without stopping to think") and deliberation (e.g., "When suddenly confronted by a crisis I often become inhibited and do nothing").

A focus on the stylistic characteristics of behavior makes it more difficult to operationalize impulsivity. Perhaps due to this problem, studies of impulsivity have generally employed questionnaires to measure its construct. Due to the diverse nature of the items included in these tests, however, factor analytic studies of impulsivity have been difficult to interpret.

Sanford, Webster, and Freedman (1957) regard impulse expression as a broad personality variable. They constructed an impulse-expression scale (J) consisting of 123 items drawn from prior impulsivity inventories. Their aim was to construct an instrument that would "measure a general readiness to express, to seek gratification of, impulses, in overt action or in conscious feeling and attitude. This readiness . . . might . . . discriminate those subjects . . . who seem to be in need of self-discipline and integration . . . (p. 2)." The J scale correlates negatively with the Socialization and the Social Responsibility scales of the California Psychological Inventory (Gough, 1957). Sanford et al. (1957) interpreted their findings in terms of Freud's libidinal types. However, their interpretation was complicated by the recognition that the J scale measures both spontaneous or "free" as well as defensive or "driven" impulse expression. On the whole, narcissistic individuals have received high scores on this test, whereas compulsive individuals have received low scores.

Other questionnaire studies have operationalized impulsivity in a more narrow manner. Buss and Plomin (1975) concluded that the concept has been indexed primarily by decision time, sensation seeking, persistence, and inhibitory control. According to Buss and Plomin (1975) and Plomin (1976), the Rhathymia scale of the Guilford–Martin personality questionnaire (Guilford, 1940) has influenced the content of subsequent impulsivity scales. When the Thurstone Temperament Schedule was developed on the basis of factor analyses of Guilford's items in the early 1950s, one of the Thurstone scales (the "impulsive" scale) replicated Guilford's Rhathymia scale. Eysenck has also incorporated Rhathymia items in the Maudsley Personality Inventory (H. J. Eysenck, 1959), the Eysenck Personality Inventory (EPI) (H. J. Eysenck & S. B. G. Eysenck, 1963), and the Eysenck Personality Questionnaire (EPQ) (H. J. Eysenck & S. B. G. Eysenck, 1975).

Questioning the unidimensionality of Eysenck's Extraversion factor, Carrigan (1960) suggested that at least two factors underlly extraversion. A few years later, S. B. G. Eysenck and H. J. Eysenck (1963) described two separate but correlated subclusters of extraversion items: sociability and impulsivity. Items with high loadings on the Impulsivity scale refer primarily to decision time (e.g., "Are you inclined to stop and think things over before acting?"). As noted by Guilford (1975), the confounding of sociability and impulsivity complicates the interpretation of extraversion.

S. B. G. Eysenck and H. J. Eysenck (1977) related impulsivity to their three-dimensional system of extraversion, neuroticism, and psychoticism. They reported that impulsivity can be partitioned into four factors: impulsivity defined narrowly (e.g., "Do you generally do and say things without stopping to think?), risk-taking, non-planning, and liveliness. Impulsivity, broadly defined, correlated positively with extraversion and psychoticism, whereas impulsivity, narrowly defined, correlated with neuroticism and psychoticism.

Recently, Block (1978) criticized the three-dimensional system of personality advanced by the Eysencks. The EPQ Extraversion scale, Block argued, is not equivalent to earlier E scales because the presence of impulsivity has been reduced. Items measuring impulsivity have instead been included in the psychoticism scale. Psychoticism items seem to depict an aggressive and impulsive individual without appreciable conscience. The problems inherent in the P scale were demonstrated when diagnosed psychotics received lower scores on this measure than prisoners in the standardization sample (H. J. Eysenck & S. B. G. Eysenck, 1976). The Eysencks admit that the label "psychoticism", as they use it, does not correspond to the general content of the concept. But, then, why use it?

Results of other questionnaire studies indicate that convicted criminals are invariably more impulsive, hostile, self-centered, and immature than non-delinquent controls (see Laufer, Johnson, & Hogan, 1981). Impulsive individuals are less able to recognize or consciously monitor anger than non-impulsive individuals (Drury, 1981). Nevertheless, it is unlikely that antisocial behavior can be predicted solely on the basis of impulsivity (Toch, 1979).

Sensation Seeking

A recent approach to the study of impulsivity—the construct of *sensation seeking*—refers to individuals' need for optimal levels of stimulation (Zuckerman, 1978; Zuckerman, Buchsbaum, & Murphy, 1980). The sensation seeker, it is argued, searches for novel experiences in order to reach an optimal level of arousal. The Sensation Seeking Scale (SSS) was developed to measure this construct. The SSS consists of four components: (1) thrill and adventure seeking (a desire to engage in outdoor activities with elements of risk), (2) experience seeking (exemplified by the following item, "I like to have new and exciting experiences and sensations even if they are a little frightening, unconventional or illegal"), (3) disinhibition (the use of alcohol for social disinhibition and interest in sex), and (4) boredom susceptibility (a dislike of routine work and repetitions).

In Zuckerman's (1978) view, sensation seeking is related to the impulsive component of extraversion and, moreover, to nonconformity, unconventionality, and lack of concern with social mores, responsibility, and self-control. Conversely, absence of sensation seeking is illustrated by overly conforming, conventional, and controlled behavior. Empirical studies have examined the relationship between sensation seeking and other domains of behavior (Zuckerman, 1978). High sensation seekers report a greater variety of heterosexual activities than low sensation seekers. Heavy drug use and smoking are also associated with sensation seeking. However, heavy drinking has only been related to the Disinhibition scale. High sensation seeking also correlates with betting behavior, volunteering for dangerous activities, and with originality.

Psychophysiological and biochemical correlates of sensation seeking suggest that "involved in the genotype of sensation seeking is an excitable CNS [central nervous system] as expressed in strong orienting reflexes to novel stimuli and an augmenting reaction to increasing intensities of stimulation. The excitability of the CNS seems to be related to biochemical characteristics of the sensation seeker including low MAO [monoamine oxidase] levels and high levels of gonadal hormones" (Zuckerman, 1978, p. 541). Zuckerman et al. (1980) concluded that varied sexual experience, interest in new situations, experimentation with drugs, manic–depressive tendencies, and psychopathy are associated with both sensation seeking and its biological correlates.

S. B. G. Eysenck and Zuckerman (1978) examined the relationship between impulsivity and sensation seeking. A factor analytic study of Zuckerman's sensation seeking scale and Eysenck's Impulsivity scale yielded two factors: impulsivity and venturesomeness. The latter factor included most of the thrill and adventure seeking items plus some risk-taking items. The Impulsivity factor, on the other hand, included items defining impulsivity in a more narrow manner (i.e., lack of deliberation). Both venturesomeness and impulsivity correlated positively with psychoticism and extraversion (S. B. G. Eysenck & H. J. Eysenck, 1978). In addition, neuroticism correlated negatively with venturesomeness and positively with impulsivity. Additional research is needed to determine the relationship between these aspects of personality and their relationship to prosocial and antisocial development.

Impulsivity as a Temperament

According to temperament theories of personality, certain behavioral tendencies originate in inherited dispositions. These dispositions are not specific traits but broad personality types. Buss and Plomin (1975) have outlined four temperaments: activity, emotionality, sociability, and impulsivity. Following Murray (1938), Buss and Plomin consider impulsivity as a dimension defined by the polar opposites of impulsivity and deliberateness. However, both the unitary nature of impulsivity as a temperament and the extent of it's heritability remain uncertain. As Buss and Plomin noted, "Impulsivity is the most troublesome of the four temperaments" (p. 122).

According to Buss and Plomin (1975), inhibitory control is the essential component of impulsivity. Other, less important aspects include fast versus slow decision time, attention fluctuation versus attention persistence, and sensation seeking versus boredom. Reviewing the relationships among the components of impulsivity, Buss and Plomin conclude that persistence, decision time, and sensation seeking are modestly related. In addition, they note that inhibitory control (e.g., resistance to temptation, delay of gratification) has not been adequately measured in existing impulsivity scales.

Buss and Plomin (1975) based their study of heritability on maternal ratings of twins' temperaments. Their rating instrument included only 20 items classified a priori into different temperamental categories. The impulsivity items referred to aspects of impulsivity and self-control that may not have been interpreted uniformly by all mothers (e.g., "Child tends to be impulsive", "Learning self-control is difficult for the child", "Child gets bored easily", "Child learns to resist temptation easily" (reversed), "Child goes from toy to toy quickly" (Buss & Plomin, 1975, p. 17). Each item was rated on a scale from 1 (a little) to 5 (a lot). Because the age of the subjects varied considerably in this study (from 1 to 9 years), the relevance of individual items for children of different ages may have varied. Also, the authors did not include reliability estimates. Later, Lyon and Plomin (1981) reported that the average agreement between ratings completed by mothers and fathers was only .51, even when corrected for attenuation due to the unreliability of the ratings. Using reliable and objective assessment methods, Plomin and Foch (1980) reported that contrary to previous results of questionnaire studies, they found little evidence for genetic influences on activity level, fidgeting, vigilance, selective attention, and aggression in a sample of 7-year-old twin pairs. Between-family environmental sources of variance were far more important than within-family factors.

In the New York Longitudinal Study (NYLS) (Thomas, Chess, & Birch, 1968; Thomas & Chess, 1977), nine dimensions of temperament were studied in young children: activity level, rhythmicity, approach or withdrawal, adaptability, threshold of responsiveness, intensity, quality of mood, distractability, and persistence. None of these dimensions fits clearly the concept of impulsivity, with the possible exception of distractability. Activity level and distractability showed the least temporal stability. In addition, the child's behavior during the first year did not predict behavior at age 5 years. Perhaps the child's CNS develops and stabilizes so gradually that constitutional temperaments can only be discerned after the age of 2 or 3 years (see Schmidt-Kolmer, 1972).

The Colorado Temperament Inventory (Plomin & Rowe, 1978) attempts to combine the NYLS dimensions with Buss and Plomin's (1975) temperament dimensions. However, impulsivity was not included in the

Colorado study. Although Gray (1972) believes that impulsiveness and not extraversion is a personality "primary," the results regarding impulsivity as an inherited temperament are inconclusive.

Buss and Plomin (1975) limited the concept of temperament to behaviorally active characteristics. Although they note (Buss & Plomin, 1975, p. 8) that the bipolar opposites of activity, emotionality, sociability, and impulsivity, were active–lethargic, emotional–impassive, gregarious–detached, and impulsive–deliberate, Buss and Plomin did not examine the passive end of the continuum. Restricting the concept of temperament to its active manifestations excludes passive but perhaps equally relevant manifestations of temperaments.

In the Buss and Plomin study, the correlations among the a priori based temperament scales were sometimes moderately high. For example, activity and impulsivity correlated .49–.59, emotionality and impulsivity correlated .32–.36, and emotionality and sociability correlated −.19––.40. On the other hand, emotionality and sociability, and sociability and impulsivity were mutually independent. These correlations are comparable with expectations made on the basis of the circular ordering of personality traits presented by Eysenck (1965) (see also Wilson, 1978).

Despite these various research efforts, the conceptual meaning of the construct of temperament remains unclear. O'Connor, Foch, Sherry, and Plomin (1980), for example, concluded that significant genetic influences exist with regard to some behavior problems (e.g., bullying, emotionality, tenseness, shyness, restlessness, school problems, and sleep disturbance). If heritability is one of the central criteria defining a temperament, we need to understand how these behavior problems are related to temperaments.

Impulsivity as a Cognitive Style

In the early 1960s, Kagan and his colleagues advanced the cognitive style of "reflection–impulsivity" (Kagan, 1965; Kagan, Moss, & Sigel, 1963). Operationalized by decision time under conditions of uncertainty, the Matching Familiar Figures test (MFFT) (Kagan, Rosman, Day, Albert, & Phillips, 1964) was devised to measure this construct. The MFFT is a matching-to-sample task in which the child is shown a drawing of a familiar object (the standard figure) and instructed to select an identical figure from several comparison figures. Kagan assumed that impulsive children respond more quickly and make more errors than reflective children because of their failure to examine thoroughly the various alternatives. Based on a median split on the two MFFT variables—latency of response and accuracy of response—four groups of subjects are frequently generated. Usually, two thirds of the subjects, labeled *reflectives* (the slow–accurate children) and *impulsives* (the fast–inaccurate children), fall into the two diagonal cells. The remaining third of the children fall in the counter-diagonal cells and are labeled fast–accurate and slow–inaccurate children, respectively. However, this operationalization, which confounds two sources of variance—response accuracy and response latency—obscures the meaning of subsequently observed difference among children. (see Block, Block, & Harrington, 1974).

Based on a thorough review of the empirical literature, as well as on their own empirical findings, Block et al. (1974) concluded that empirical evidence for the construct validity of the MFFT was sparse and inconsistent. Contrary to Kagan's view, the personality implications of MFFT accuracy scores were shown to be more appreciable than those of MFFT latency scores. Fast–inaccurate children were not impulsive, minimally concerned, and unanxious, as Kagan had claimed; rather, they were anxious, hypersensitive, and vulnerable. In the conceptual framework outlined by J. H. Block and J. Block (1980), accurate children are ego resilient, whereas inaccurate children are brittle, rigid, susceptible to anxiety, and less resourceful.

According to Messer's review (1976) of the MFFT literature, performance on the MFFT task correlates with performance on other response uncertainty tasks suggesting that reflective children evaluate alternative hypotheses more carefully than impulsive children before responding. Also, impulsivity is related to reading difficulties, learning disabilities, and to school failure. According to Messer, however, latency does not become a reliable index of the cognitive style of reflection–impulsivity until school age.

Kagan's view of reflection–impulsivity has been critically appraised in recent studies. Generally, the results of these studies are consistent with the position taken by Block et al. (1974). For example, MFFT accuracy, but not MFFT latency, is related to intelligence (Genser, Hafele, & Hafele, 1978) and learning disability (Nagle & Thwaite, 1979; Quay & Brown, 1980; Quay & Weld, 1980). Nagle and Thwaite concluded that children with learning disabilities are not more impulsive than other children. Instead, they use inadequate strategies in processing information. Correspondingly, O'Donnell, Paulsen, and McGann (1978) believe that MFFT response accuracy measures a maturational dimension of task-oriented attention at preschool age. None of these studies, however, have related performance on the MFFT to behavioral impulsivity.

According to Losel (1980), response latency is partially a task-dependent and partially an individual characteristic. In particular, latency seems to reflect a cognitive style variable on moderately difficult to difficult tasks. Losel based his conclusion on the finding that, relative to impulsive children, reflective children were more likely to modify their response latencies according to the difficulty level of the task. Consistent with Losel's (1980) results, Kendall, Hooke, Rymer, and Finch (1980) found that when the number of task alternatives increased from 6 to 10, only adults who had previously been categorized as reflective increased their decision times. In contrast, impulsive subjects emphasized speed at the expense of successful task completion. The authors concluded that "these data suggest a latency-related response inhibition deficit associated with cognitive problem-solving" (Kendall et al., 1980, p. 179).

In a longitudinal study conducted by Hopkins, Perlman, Hechtman, and Weiss (1979), three cognitive style tests—the MFFT, the Embedded Figures Test, and the Stroop Colour Test—were administered to 70 adults who had been diagnosed as hyperactive 10–13 years earlier and to 42 control subjects. Contrary to expectations, the hyperactive subjects did not have significantly shorter MFFT latencies than the control subjects. However, the hyperactive subjects made significantly more errors ($p <$ .05) than the controls. They were also more field dependent and more constricted (*constriction* refers here to an inability to ignore distractions).

Other studies have yielded similar results. For example, in a study of 10-year-old children, reflection–impulsivity was unrelated to hyperactivity (Sergeant, van Velthoven, & Virginia, 1979). In addition to administering the MFFT, teacher ratings and other observational data were obtained in this study. According to the results, the MFFT accuracy score predicted teacher ratings of talkativeness. Note, however, that response accuracy was unrelated to hyperactivity, impulsivity, and distractability. Equally significant, MFFT performance did not predict any observation variable. Consistent with the Sergeant et al. study, Quay and Brown (1980) reported that none of the MFFT scoring procedures (accuracy of response, latency of response, or the separate analysis of the four MFFT groups: fast–accurate, fast–inaccurate, slow–accurate, and slow–inaccurate children) differentiated between severely disordered boys and normal controls at ages 7 and 12 years. Consistent with these findings, Moore, Haskins, and McKinney (1980) concluded that the implications of reflection–impulsivity, as operationalized by the MFFT, should be limited to tasks involving response uncertainty. MFFT performance, these authors noted, does not imply differences in classroom behavior. Susman, Huston-Stein, and Friedrich-Cofer (1980) also showed that performance on the Kansas Reflection–Impulsivity Scale for Preschoolers cannot be equated with behavioral impulsivity.

APPROACHES TO CONCEPTUALIZING
SELF-CONTROL

Social Development

Maccoby (1980) has outlined the characteristics of impulsive behavior. According to Maccoby, impulsive children act without thinking, respond to immediate stimuli without remembering the lessons of the past or without considering future consequences, fail to integrate their pursuit of larger goals with smaller subgoals, move quickly among unrelated activities, and do not impose organization on their actions. The last characteristic—the absence of an hierarchical organization of plans (see Miller, Galanter, & Pribram, 1960)—distinguishes the behavior of children from the behavior of adults.

The developmental ability to organize and regulate actions presupposes that the child learns (1) to delay certain actions, (2) to weigh future consequences in light of the present, (3) to overcome barriers, (4) to avoid behavioral disorganization due to arousal, (5) to integrate elements of behavior, and (6) to concentrate (Maccoby, 1980). Parents may assist their young child in achieving impulse control by situational management, by carrying out for their children the ego functions they still do not possess themselves, teaching coping skills, helping children to anticipate consequences, and exposing children to adequate models of self-control.

Kopp (1982) has differentiated between different phases in the development of self-control. The first phase (birth to 2–3 months)—*neurophysiological modulation*—"subsumes processes that safeguard the immature organism from intrusive or strong stimulation" (Kopp, p. 202). Some infants have low thresholds. Therefore, they become easily aroused and are difficult to quiet. At this age, control is aided by parents' social interactions and caregiving routines. The second phase (3 to 9–12 months)—*sensorimotor modulation*—"signifies the child's ability to engage in a voluntary motor act (e.g., reach and grasp) and change the act in response to events that arise" (Kopp, p. 203). The term modulation is used because this process does not involve awareness of situational meaning. The role of the caregivers is important in promoting infants' awareness of situational demands and of their own actions.

The third phase (9–12 to 18 months)—*control*—"characterizes the emerging ability of children to show awareness of social or task demands that have been defined by caregivers, and to initiate, maintain, modulate, or cease physical acts, communication, and emotional signals accordingly" (Kopp, p. 204). Control is viewed as a derivative of qualitative and quantitative changes in cognitive-processing abilities. It includes compliance as well as self-initiated inhibition of previously prohibited behavior. The cognitive capacity for reflection does not yet exist but the child depends on the presence of key signals. Limitations in control arise as a function of memory constraints. During this age period, parents may foster control by repeatedly communicating expectations about acceptable forms of child behavior.

The fourth phase (24+ months) signifies the emergence of self-control and the progression toward self-regulation. Self-control differs from control "by virtue of the appearance of representational thinking and evocative (recall) memory" (Kopp, p. 206). Self-control, on the other hand, differs from self-regulation "in degree, not in kind . . . self-control means that the child has limited flexibility in adapting acts to meet new situational demands and a limited capacity for delay and waiting. In contrast, self-regulation is . . . more mature form of control and presumably implicates the use of reflection and strategies involving introspection, consciousness, or metacognition" (p. 207). Self-regulation differs from self-control in that the former is more adaptive to changes. The latter signifies self-initiated modification of behavior as a result of remembered information—a shift toward an internally generated monitoring system. Caregivers and other sources of social influence have a continuing and major role in promoting childrens' progression toward self-regulation. According to Kopp (1982), the nature of their influence is facilitating rather than causative.

Delay of Gratification

Using behavioral measures, Mischel (1974) and his colleagues have examined delay of gratification. In their research, subjects are required to choose between rewards that vary both in delay time and in value. The subject must usually choose between an immediate but small reward and a delayed but larger reward. Mischel (1974) assumes that inadequate delay patterns often are partial causes of antisocial and criminal behavior. His theoretical orientation consists of a synthesis of social learning theory and cognitive principles influenced by expectancy-value theory. This approach draws attention to both the cognitive and the developmental processes through which self-control is acquired, as well as to the motivational factors that guide the individual's choices. According to Mischel (1974), impulsivity and delay can be conceptualized as two contrasting behavior patterns both of which may be maladjustive in their extreme forms. The impulsive pattern is more typical of members of lower socioeconomic classes than of members of middle or upper classes. This pattern correlates with low achievement orientation and weak social and cognitive competence. Delinquents and psychopaths are often characterized by an extreme pattern of impulsive responding. At the other end of the continuum are individuals who are more likely to be oriented toward future goals. This latter pattern of behavior correlates with high scores on ego-control measures, high achievement motivation, high level of aspiration, strong social responsibility, and general maturity.

Using the interview method, Mischel and his colleagues (Mischel, 1979; Yates & Mischel, 1979) have studied how individuals develop their understanding of effective self-regulation strategies. According to these studies, most preschoolers do not yet possess strategies for effective delay. On the contrary, they increase the difficulty of delay by focusing on what they want but cannot have. Children, it appears, do not develop delay strategies until the age of 9 or 10 years. At that relatively late age, they may avoid looking at the rewards, they may concentrate on another task, or they may generate negative ideations of the object. In a study of delay tolerance, Gallagher (1981) demonstrated that behaviorally disordered kindergarten children understood situational contingencies less well and were less aware of useful strategies than adjusted children. This metacognitive approach, pioneered by Flavell in the 1970s, holds promise for future research in the area of self-control.

Theoretical Perspectives on Self-Control in Cognitive–Behavioral Interventions

In the 1960s, several researchers began to examine the role of cognitive processes in children's control over motoric behavior (see Hobbs, Moguin, Tyroler, & Lahey, 1980). Based on Vygotsky's theory (1962) of the controlling function of speech, Luria (1961) presented a developmental sequence of self-regulation. According to this model, the child achieves self-control in two stages. In the first stage, other persons' regulating speech becomes part of the child's self-verbalizing. In the second stage, the child's covert speech gradually comes to guide and control his or her behavior. The practical implications of this theory, however, remain uncertain. For example, a training program of self-control based on Luria's principles has given mixed results with delinquents (Little & Kendall, 1979). In spite of recent criticism of the stage model (Wozniak, 1972), Luria's model has served to change the focus of behavior therapy toward more cognitively oriented interventions.

Rational emotive therapy (Ellis, 1962) has also influenced the development of the cognitive–behavioral approach. Ellis assumes that nonpsychotic psychological disturbances, such as intense anger, result from irrational patterns of thought. Rational emotive therapy attempts to alter these faulty belief systems.

Finally, the cognitive–behavioral approach was influenced by learning theorists, especially by Kanfer and Karoly's (1972) notion of self-regulation and by Bandura's (1977) theory of self-efficacy. Kanfer and Karoly (1972) approached self-control from the point of view of a closed-loop learning paradigm. Kanfer's (1975) method for self-management and self-control includes self-monitoring, establishment of specific rules of conduct, environmental support, self-evaluation, and strong schedules of reinforcement. Kanfer differentiates between self-management and self-control. The former is used to rearrange behavioral schedules, acquire new skills, and engage in activities without pronounced behavioral consequences. Self-control, on the other hand, refers to a person's attempt to acquire a controlling response in a specific situation and to the conflicting consequences of the current behavior.

Recently, Kanfer (1979) extended his analysis of self-regulation to altruism. He advanced a system-oriented paradigm that integrates intrapsychic dynamic processes with the kind of environmental control emphasized by behaviorists. He maintains that altruistic acts can be conceptualized as behaviors that inherently involve conflict situations similar to those encountered in the domain of self-control. According to Kanfer, neither self-control nor altruism should be regarded as an individual trait. Depending on the person and the situation, *alpha* variables (e.g., social norms or expected social reinforcements contingencies), *beta* variables (e.g., self-generated standards or self-evaluative feedback), and *gamma* variables (e.g., empathy and emotional arousal) vary in their importance for achieving conflict resolution.

Willpower is often associated with self-control. Behavioristically oriented researchers, however, note that "the key to self-mastery is not to be found in appeals to willpower and other presumed inner resources, but rather in awareness, the knowledge of how to use various stimuli to increase and decrease certain responses" (Thoresen & Mahoney, 1974, p. 142). Self-control is displayed when a person engages in behaviors whose previous probability has been less than alternative behaviors involving delayed rewards. Correspondingly, the behavioral theory presented by Ainslie (1975) views impulsivity as the choice of a less rewarding alternative when more rewarding alternatives are available but delayed. Impulsivity is accounted for by a decline in the effectiveness of the reward as a result of temporal delay. Self-control, it is argued, can be established through a rearrangement of reward contingencies and by training individuals to evaluate alternatives, reach decisions, and get small immediate rewards.

IMPULSE CONTROL WITHIN A TWO-DIMENSIONAL
FRAME OF REFERENCE

Ego-Control and Ego-Resiliency

Conceptualization of impulsivity as a personality characteristic considers impulsive behavior as a unidimensional construct with different
labels attached to the two opposite ends of the continuum. Although it has
generally not been acknowledged, both ends of this dimension—absence
of control and presence of control—may in their extreme involve pathology. Neither end of the continuum describes well-adapted, flexible behaviors. The constructs of ego-control and ego-resiliency (J. H. Block & J.
Block, 1980) illustrate this position. These constructs derive from an integration of psychoanalytic ego theory (Fenichel, 1945) and Lewin's field
theory. From a psychoanalytic perspective, *ego-control* refers to the control of impulse through specific ego structures, including delay of gratification, inhibition of aggression, and so on. *Ego-resiliency,* on the other
hand, refers to ego functions more strongly related to adaptation.

According to Lewin, psychological boundaries have two characteristics—permeability and elasticity. J. H. Block and J. Block (1980) incorporated these Lewinian notions into their constructs of ego-control and ego-
resiliency. Undercontrol derives from excessive boundary
permeability—the failure of a boundary to contain psychological tension.
The manifestations of undercontrol include immediate expression of motivations and affects, inability to delay gratification, and insufficient modulation of impulse. The other end of the continuum—overcontrol—is
caused by excessive boundary impermeability. Its manifestations include
inhibition of action and affect, delay of gratification, and excessive containment of impulse. In their conceptual analysis, J. H. Block and J.
Block differentiate between the construct of ego-control and related constructs, such as extraversion versus introversion, externalizing versus
internalizing, reflection versus impulsivity, and activity level.

The construct of ego-resiliency refers to the elasticity of psychological
boundaries, the capacity of a boundary to change its characteristic level
of permeability (i.e., degree of control) depending on environmental demands. At the one end of the continuum, ego-resiliency implies the ability
to adapt to changing circumstances; the opposite end of the continuum—
ego-brittleness—implies the inability to respond dynamically to situational requirements. Although ego-resiliency involves problem-solving
ability, it cannot be equated with intelligence. Ego-resiliency, however, is
related to the effective use of intelligence. Nor can ego-resiliency be
equated with the broad construct of ego strength, or with the more con-
text-bound construct of competence (White, 1963).

According to J. H. Block and J. Block (1980), the antecedents of ego-control and ego-resiliency include both constitutional and experiential factors. Children have to learn impulse control and to regulate self-expression. Child-rearing practices are likely to influence both the acquisition of control and the adaptability of behavior.

A Model of Impulse Control

A different two-dimensional model of impulse control was advanced by the present author (Pitkänen, 1969; Pulkkinen, 1982c). This model emphasizes the availability of alternative responses for the expression of frustration. When external events instigate aggression, two kinds of aggression-inhibitory tendencies are considered: (1) suppression of the *extrinsic* aspect of aggression (or the overt response) and (2) neutralization of the *intrinsic* aspect of aggression (or the emotional reaction). Suppression of aggression, it is argued, depends on external control and is manifested in avoidance behavior. Stimulus activation is more closely tied to emotional reactions, fear of the threatening stimulus, and anxiety about one's inability to defend oneself. In contrast, neutralization of aggression is assumed to be the result of an individual's cognitive appraisal efforts. According to this theory, an individual considers alternative ways of coping with threatening situations and chooses a course of action that takes into account the different elements involved.

Figure 8.1 describes the two-dimensional model. When excitation is present, an individual may either express his or her intents without inhibition or choose (often unconsciously) one of the inhibitory tendencies. Behavioral indicators of these constructs depict behavioral alternatives to aggression. The model describes how behavior varies from situation to situation depending on excitation, situational cues and constraints, and the individual's actual state. It is also hypothesized that individuals react differently to excitation due to variations in socialization experiences and in constitutional factors.

In a Finnish longitudinal study of social development, significant behavioral continuity was obtained between the ages of 8 and 20 years. The continuity demonstrated in this study is *heterotypic,* which, according to Kagan (1969), means that a particular attribute is predictive of a phenotypically different but theoretically expectable attribute. Uncontrolled expression of impulse was related to aggressive behavior at age 8 years, to close peer relations at age 14 years, and to revelling behavior at age 20 years. Moreover, aggressive behavior predicted delinquency, smoking, and heavy drinking (Pulkkinen, 1982, 1983a, 1983b). Correspondingly, submissive behavior at age 8 years, pronounced dependence on the home

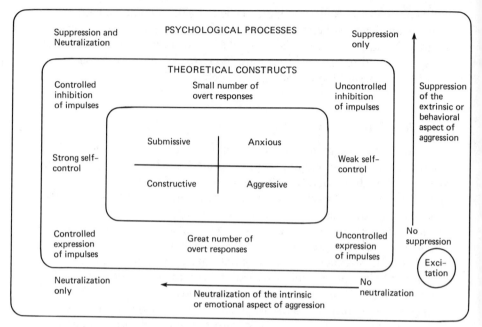

Figure 8.1. A model of impulse control (Pulkkinen, 1982).

environment at age 14 years, and "the way of life of a Loner" at age 20 years were interpreted as manifestations of impulse inhibition. Constructive behavior at age 8 years, different orientation toward responsibility at age 14 years, and "the way of life of a Striver" at age 20 years were related to controlled expression of impulse. Finally, social helplessness and anxiety at age 8 years, negativism at age 14 years, and "the way of life of a Loser" at age 20 years were associated with uncontrolled inhibition of impulse (Pulkkinen, 1982). A change from constructive tendencies toward a behavior pattern characteristic of the "Striver" personality took both place when parental child-rearing practices were characterized by sustained interest in, and control of, the child's activities, trust, warmth, advice, and consideration of the child's opinion; and, further, when parents granted the child a gradual increase in independence and responsibility. This pattern of child-rearing was called *child-centered guidance.* Its opposite—relating to the child in a short-sighted way—was related to weak self-control.

Adler's Four Life Styles

Some 50 years ago, Adler presented a two-dimensional model of social behavior (Adler, 1929, 1935; Kannarkat & Bayton, 1979). Although this model is not explicitly related to impulse control, the personality types described by Adler resemble those obtained by the present author. Adler differentiated "for teaching purposes" between four life styles based on "(1) the degree of an individual's approach to social integration, and (2) the form of movement that he develops (with greater or lesser activity) to maintain that degree of approach in a manner that he regards as most likely to achieve success (in their own interpretation)" (Adler, 1935, p. 70).

The first type—the active–destructive personalities—manifest throughout their lifespan a dominant or "ruling" attitude. This attitude appears in all interpersonal relationships. Active–destructive persons are, as the label implies, active, but lack social interest. Therefore, when confronted directly by an examination-like situation, a test of their social value, or by a judgment of their social usefulness, they act in an antisocial manner. They may attack others directly, become a delinquent, a tyrant, a sadist, a drug addict, or an alcoholic. The second type—the passive–constructive personalities—expect a great deal from others and depend on others for achieving personal goals. Adler calls such people the "getting" types. This personality type is inactive and lacks social interest. The third type—the passive–destructive personality—typically avoids problem solution. Instead of struggling with a problem, they merely try to "side-step" challenges in order to avoid direct defeat. This personality type is passive and lacks social interest. The three types described above lack the ability to cooperate. The conflict between a life style characterized by lack of social interest and external problems—often demanding social interest—has severe repercussions in the long run. In the case of the second and the third type, these consequences are often neurosis and psychosis.

The fourth type—the active–constructive personality—is prepared for cooperation and social contribution. Hence, a certain amount of their activities is used for the benefit of others and is compatible with their needs; it is useful, normal, and correctly imbedded in the stream of evolution.

Alder's concept of social interest (*Gemeinschaftsgefühl* in German) refers to a feeling of communion. The person experiences social belonging, a prerequisite for effective participation in social interchange. Although social interest is an innate potentiality, individuals need to develop it (Dreikurs, 1963). Rather than being static, it changes in relationship to how successful an individual is in satisfying societal demands. It is likely that parental socialization practices influence whether children become active or passive, constructive or destructive. An atmosphere of mutual trust and respect (closely related to the notion of child-centered guidance presented above) encourages constructiveness; lack of trust and respect, on the other hand, encourages destructiveness. In addition, familial emphasis upon personal initiative encourages active attitudes (Maddi, 1968).

Using personality inventories, Kannarkat and Bayton (1979) have validated Alder's four life styles. However, they emphasize Adler's cautious attitude toward his theory of types and warn against viewing the four types as something "ordained and independent" (p. 359). Adler stated explicitly that although one cannot avoid using the concept of types for purposes of generalization, its informational value may be limited in concrete instances.

CONCLUSION

In considering the study of impulsivity and control from the point of view of prosocial and antisocial development, this review outlines several conceptual problems characteristic of this research area. Several generalizations can be made. First, the concept of impulsivity as a personality trait is vaguely defined. In psychoanalytic theory, an impulse is understood as a discharge of psychic energy from the id. This discharge is controlled by the ego. Accordingly, impulsivity might signify frequent impulse expression since a main cause of impulsivity is the weakness of the ego in controlling the expression of impulses.

Although psychodynamically oriented research has attempted to operationalize impulse expression (e.g., via projective tests), empirical measures of impulsivity have more often been based on different theoretical orientations. However, some exceptions to this trend exist. The IES test (Dombrose & Slobin, 1958), for example, operationalizes the construct of impulse control by using simple motion tasks. As noted above, impulse control scores on the Arrow-Dot subtest increase with age and are related to intellectual effectiveness and prosocial orientation. Weak control, on the other hand, correlates with less socialized behavior. In many cases, attempts to operationalize impulsivity and self-control have relied on temporal concepts. Getsinger (1980), for example, introduced the constructs of high and low ego delay. He defined delay as the period during which the ego mobilizes its resources in order to reduce drive strength and tension. According to this approach, a person characterized by low ego delay is behaviorally impulsive, hyperactive, reckless, and aggressive. Getsinger's broad, heuristic constructs, however, do not appear to have been validly operationalized by his time estimation method, an approach that is hypothetically related to psychophysiological rhythms and to individuals' subjective time experience.

Cognitive style measures of impulsivity have also relied extensively on differences in response time (e.g., Kagan, 1965). As previously noted, reflection–impulsivity was operationalized by decision time under conditions of uncertainty. However, response latency is associated with far less important personality correlates than response accuracy (Block et al., 1974). Even response accuracy can not be unanimously accepted as an indicator of impulsivity. Rather, this variable appears to describe resourcefulness and the quality of the individual's information-processing strategies. Neither response latency nor response accuracy on cognitive task have been related to behavioral impulsivity.

Personality questionnaires have also relied on decision time as a major indicator of impulsivity. For example, Murray (1938) defined impulsion as the tendency to act quickly without reflection. Its opposite—deliberation—was defined as the tendency to reflect before deciding upon a course of action. It is associated with slow reaction time, Since then, decision time, sensation seeking, persistence, and inhibitory control have constituted the main ingredients of impulsivity scales (Buss & Plomin, 1975). According to S. B. G. Eysenck and H. J. Eysenck (1977), short decision time constitutes a narrowly defined version of impulsivity. Impulsivity in a broader sense includes other aspects of behavior as well (e.g., risk-taking).

Researchers have sometimes used the term impulsivity without providing an adequate conceptual definition. For example, in their study of impulsivity as a temperament, Buss and Plomin (1975) did not define this construct, although the words ''impulsive'' and ''self-control'' were used in their parental rating scales. A central problem in defining impulsivity in terms of response time resides in the assumption that everything done quickly is weakly controlled. However, one should not exclude the possibility that certain individuals may have well-developed moral principles that they are able to apply quickly to problems of decision making. Alternatively, response time may reflect differences in personal tempo. However, because impulsivity refers to lack of behavioral control, this construct cannot be reduced to differences in personal tempo.

From the perspective of attribution theory, poor performance on cognitive tasks is impulsive if the following conditions are satisfied (see Table 8.1): (1) The individual responds to irrelevant cues; (2) Poor performance is not a consequence of inadequate skills or knowledge; (3) Positive attention to the task is inferred from the individual's behavior.

Impulsivity cannot be accepted as the main reason for inadequate performance when the individual is indifferent toward the task or lacks the necessary skills. Impulsivity implies lack of internal control of behavior and, according to my views, is manifested in responses to irrelevant task cues in spite of the positive attention to a task and necessary skills for an

Table 8.1

Attribution of Impulsivity in Cognitive Tasks

Capacity for a good performance	Attention to a task	Cues for responses	Impulsivity as a mediating factor
Yes	Positive	Irrelevant	Yes
No	Negative	Irrelevant	No

adequate performance. That is, the individual responds to exciting aspects of stimulation without giving sufficient consideration to situational demands or without following a well-defined plan of action. Correspondingly, social behavior should only be labeled impulsive if the following conditions are satisfied (see Table 8.2): (1) The individual does not take situational demands into consideration but responds immediately and directly to stimulation; (2) The individual understands relevant situational demands; (3) Attitudes toward situational demands are basically positive.

When the individual's attitude toward situational demands are negative, impulsivity should not be inferred. Hence, antisocial behavior and legal offenses are not necessarily impulsive.

A one-dimensional conceptualization of impulsivity fails to consider behavioral variation in impulse control. In the two-dimensional model of impulse control presented above (Pulkkinen, 1982), behavioral alternatives are described in terms of social expectations and variations in impulse control. In the case of uncontrolled impulse expression (see Figure 8.1), impulsivity can reasonably be inferred. In the case of controlled impulse expression, on the other hand, behavior is modulated according to situational demands. Control of impulse may also involve suppression of behavior, that is, the psychic energy associated with the impulse is not relieved in action. In this case, arousal is experienced as internal tension.

The two-dimensional model confounds, however, the construct of temperament and the process of socialization. Problems of social behavior in

Table 8.3

Attribution of Impulsivity in Social Behavior

Understanding situational demands	Attitudes toward situational demands	Taking situational demands into consideration	Impulsivity as a mediating factor
Yes	Positive	No	Yes
No	Negative	No	No

children correlate with parental socialization practices. However, the educability of a child may depend on his or her temperamental characteristics. For example, it is difficult to teach self-control to an easily excitable child. Although such children may understand and accept situational demands, they have nevertheless a tendency to act without sufficient consideration of such demands. When this temperamental characteristic co-occurs with inadequate parenting, children are at an especially strong risk for adopting unorganized, impulsive behavior.

Antisocial behavior is frequently related to negative experiences of socialization. Consequently, antisocial behavior may reflect lack of social interest. Prosocial behavior, on the other hand, is characterized by strong social interest. Both antisocial and prosocial behavior may occur impulsively or deliberately. Hence, prosocial or antisocial motivations should be kept distinct from the construct of impulsivity. The results of adequate socialization cannot be identified either with impulsivity or with its opposite, impulse control. Children characterized by inadequate controls are, however, at greatest risk for behaving without consideration of social norms. Correspondingly, strong behavioral control may frequently be associated with prosocial development.

REFERENCES

Adler, A. *Problems of neurosis.* New York: Harper Torchbooks, 1964.
Adler, A. A typology of meeting life problems. In H. L. Ansbacher & R. R. Ansbacher (Eds.), *Superiority and social interest. A collection of later writings.* London: Routledge & Kegan, 1965.
Ainslie, G. Specious reward: A behavioral theory of impulsiveness and impulse control. *Psychological Bulletin,* 1975, *82,* 463–496.
Bandura, A. *Social learning theory.* Englewood Cliffs, NJ: Prentice Hall, 1977.
Barabasz, A. F. Time estimation and temporal orientation in delinquents and nondelinquents. *Journal of General Psychology,* 1970, *82,* 265–267.
Bell, C. R. Accurate performance of a time-estimation task in relation to sex, age, and personality variables. *Perceptual and Motor Skills,* 1972, *35,* 175–178.
Block, J. Review of the Eysenck Personality Questionnaire. In O. Buros (Ed.), *The eight mental measurement handbook.* Highland Park, NJ: The Gryphon Press, 1978.
Block, J., Block J. H., & Harrington D. M. Some misgivings about the Matching Familiar Figures Test as a measure of reflection-impulsivity. *Developmental Psychology,* 1974, *10,* 611–632.
Block, J. H., & Block, J. The role of ego-control and ego-resiliency in the organization of behavior. In W. A. Collins (Ed.), *Minnesota Symposia on Child Psychology,* (Vol. 13). New York: Lawrence Erlbaum, 1980.
Buss, A. H., & Plomin, R. *A temperament theory of personality development.* New York: Wiley, 1975.
Cappella, B., Gentile, J. R. & Juliano, D. B. Time estimation by hyperactive and normal children. *Perceptual and Motor Skills,* 1977, *44,* 789–790.

Carrigan, P. M. Extraversion-introversion as a dimension of personality. *Psychological Bulletin*, 1960, *57*, 329–360.

Cattell, R. B., Saunders, D. R., & Stice, G. *Handbook for the Sixteen Personality Factor Questionnaire*, Champaign, IL: Institute for Personality and Ability Testing, 1957.

Dombrose, L. A., & Slobin, M. S. The IES Test. *Perceptual and Motor Skills*, 1958, *8*, 347–389. (Monogr. Suppl. 3).

Dreikurs, R. Individual psychology: The Adlerian point of view. In J. M. Wepman & R. W. Heine (Eds.), *Concepts of personality*. Chicago: Aldine, 1963.

Drury, C. B. An investigation of the relationships between impulsivity and anger potential. *Dissertation Abstracts*, 1981, *42*, 76 (4-B).

Ellis, A. *Reason and emotion in psychotherapy*. New York: Lyle Stuart, 1962.

Eysenck, H. J. *The Maudsley Personality Inventory*. London: University of London Press, 1959.

Eysenck, H. J. *Fact and fiction in psychology*. New York: Penguin Books, 1965.

Eysenck, H. J. *Smoking, health and personality*. London: Weidenfeld and Nicolson, 1965.

Eysenck, H. J., & Eysenck, S. B. G. *Manual for the Eysenck Personality Inventory*. San Diego: Educational and Industrial Testing Service, 1963.

Eysenck, H. J., & Eysenck, S. B. G. *Manual of the Eysenck Personality Questionnaire* (Junior and adult). London: Hodder & Stoughton, 1975.

Eysenck, H. J., & Eysenck, S. B. G. *Psychoticism as a dimension of personality*. London: Hodder & Stoughton, 1976.

Eysenck, S. B. G., & Eysenck, H. J. On the dual nature of extraversion. *British Journal of Social and Clinical Psychology*, 1963, *2*, 46–55.

Eysenck, S. B. G., & Eysenck, H. J. The place of impulsiveness in a dimensional system of personality description. *British Journal of Social and Clinical Psychology*, 1977, *16*, 57–68.

Eysenck, S. B. G., & Eysenck, H. J. Impulsiveness and venturesomeness: Their position in a dimensional system of personality description. *Psychological Reports*, 1978, *43*, 1247–1255.

Eysenck, S. B. G., & Zuckerman, M. The relationship between sensation seeking and Eysenck's Dimensions of Personality. *British Journal of Psychology*, 1978, *69*, 483–487.

Fenichel, O. *The psychoanalytic theory of neurosis*. New York: Norton, 1945.

Freud, S. *The ego and the id* (Standard Edition). London: Hogarth, 1961.

Freud, S. *An outline of psychoanalysis*. New York: Norton, 1949.

Gallagher, R. An evaluation of self-control strategies in behaviorally-disordered and adjusted kindergarten children. *Dissertation Abstracts*, 1981, *42*, 76 (6-B).

Genser, B., Hafele, A., & Hafele, M. Reflexivität–Impulsivität: Fähigkeit oder kognitiver Stil? *Zeitschrift für Entwicklungspsychologie und Pädagogische Psychologie*, 1978, *10*, 114–123.

Getsinger, S. H. Ego-delay and vocational behavior. *Journal of Personality Assessment*, 1977, *41*, 91–95.

Getsinger, S. H., & Leon, R. Impulsivity, temporal perspective, and post-hospital adjustment of neuropsychiatric patients. *Journal of Psychology*, 1979, *103*, 221–225.

Getsinger, S. H. Ego delay. In R. H. Woody (Ed.), *Encyclopedia of clinical assessment* (Vol. 1). San Francisco: Jossey Bass, 1980.

Gough, H. G. *Manual for the California Psychological Inventory*. Palo Alto, CA: Consulting Psychologists Press, 1957.

Gray, J. A. The psychophysiological nature of introversion–extraversion: A modification of Eysenck's theory. In V. D. Nebylitsyn & J. A. Gray (Eds.), *Biological basis of individual behavior*. New York: Academic Press, 1972.

Guilford, J. P. *An inventory of factors STDCR*. Beverly Hills, CA: Sheridan Supply Co, 1940.

Guilford, J. P. Factors and factors of personality. *Psychological Bulletin*, 1975, *82*, 802–814.

Hobbs, S. A., Moguin, L. E., Tyroler, M., & Lahey, B. B. Cognitive behavior therapy with children: Has clinical utility been demonstrated? *Psychological Bulletin*, 1980, *87*, 147–165.

Hopkins, J., Perlman, T., Hechtman, L., & Weiss, G. Cognitive style in adults originally diagnosed as hyperactives. *Journal of Child Psychology and Psychiatry and Allied Disciplines*, 1979, *20*, 209–216.

Kagan, J. Impulsive and reflective children. Significance of conceptual tempo. In J. Krumboltz (Ed.), *Learning and the educational process*. Chicago: Rand McNally, 1965.

Kagan, J. C. The three faces of continuity in human development. In D. A. Goslin (Ed.), *Handbook of socialization theory and research*. Chicago: Rand McNally, 1969.

Kagan, J., Moss, H. A., & Sigel, I. E. Psychological significance of style of conceptualization. In J. C. Wright & J. Kagan (Eds.) *Basic cognitive processes in children. Monographs of the Society of Research in Child Development*, 28. (2, Serial No. 86), 1963.

Kagan, J., Rosman, B. L., Day, D., Albert, J., & Phillips, W. Information processing in the child: Significance of analytic and reflective attitudes. *Psychological Monographs, 78*, (1, Whole No. 578), 1964.

Kanfer, F. H. Self-management methods. In F. H. Kanfer & A. P. Goldstein (Eds.), *Helping people change*. New York: Pergamon Press, 1975.

Kanfer, F. H. Personal control, social control, and altruism. Can society survive the age of individualism? *American Psychologist*, 1979, *34*, 231–239.

Kanfer, F. H., & Karoly, R. Self-control: A behavioristic excursion into the lion's den. *Behavior Therapy*, 1972, *3*, 398–416.

Kannarkat, J. P. & Bayton, J. A. Validity of Adler's active–constructive, active–destructive, passive–constructive, and passive–destructive typology. *Journal of Research in Personality*, 1979, *13*, 351–360.

Kendall, P. C., Hooke, J. F., Rymer, R., & Finch, A. J. Cognitive styles in adults: Task alternatives, task strategy, and time-estimation. *Journal of Personality Assessment*, 1980, *44*, 175–181.

Kopp, C. B. Antecedents of self-regulation: A developmental perspective. *Developmental Psychology*, 1982, *18*, 199–214.

Laufer, W. S., Johnson, J. A., & Hogan, R. Ego control and criminal behavior. *Journal of Personality and Social Psychology*, 1981, *41*, 179–184.

Little, V. L., & Kendall, P. C. Cognitive-behavioral interventions with delinquents: Problem solving, role-taking, and self-control. In P. C. Kendall & S. D. Hollon (Eds.), *Cognitive-behavioral interventions: Theory, research, and procedures*. New York: Academic Press, 1979.

Luria, A. R. *The role of speech in the regulation of normal and abnormal behavior*. New York: Leveright, 1961.

Lyon, M. E., & Plomin, R. The measurement of temperament using parental ratings. *Journal of Child Psychology and Psychiatry and Allied Disciplines*, 1981, *22*, 47–53.

Losel, F. On the differentiation of cognitive reflection-impulsivity. *Perceptual and Motor Skills*, 1980, *50*, 1311–1324.

Maccoby, E. E. *Social development. Psychological growth and the parent-child relationship*. New York: Harcourt Brace Jovanovich, 1980.

Maddi, S. R. *Personality theories. A comparative analysis*. Homewood, IL: Dorsey, 1968.

Mangold, K. M. Comparison of delinquents and non-delinquents on the IES Test. *Perceptual and Motor Skills*, 1966, *22*, 817–818.

McCormick, C. C., Klappauf, J., Schnobrich, J., & Harvey, J. Relationships among Arrow-

Dot IES scores and Wechsler IQS and MMPI scales for hospitalized, disturbed adolescents. *Perceptual and Motor Skills*, 1971, *33*, 1227–1234.

Messer, S. B. Reflection-impulsivity: A review. *Psychological Bulletin*, 1976, *83*, 1026–1052.

Miller, G. A., Galanter, E., & Pribram, K. *Plans and the structure of behavior.* New York: Holt, Rinehart & Winston, 1960.

Mischel, W. Processes in delay of gratification. In L. Berkowitz (Ed.), *Advances in experimental social psychology*, (Vol. 7). New York: Academic Press, 1974.

Mischel, W. On the interface of cognition and personality. Beyond the person-situation debate. *American Psychologist*, 1979, *34*, 740–754.

Moore, M., Haskins, R., & McKinney, J. D. Classroom behavior of reflective and impulsive children. *Journal of Applied Developmental Psychology*, 1980, *1*, 59–75.

Murray, H. *Explorations in Personality.* New York: Oxford University Press, 1938.

Nagle, R. J., & Thwaite, B. C. Are learning-disabled children more impulsive? A comparison of learning-disabled and normal-achieving children on Kagan's Matching Familiar Figures Test. *Psychology in the Schools*, 1979, *16*, 351–355.

O'Connor, M., Foch, T., Sherry, T., & Plomin, R. A twin study of specific behavioral problems of socialization as viewed by parents. *Journal of Abnormal Child Psychology*, 1980, *8*, 189–199.

O'Donnell, J. P., Paulsen, K. A., & McGann, J. D. (1978). Matching Familiar Figures Test: A unidimensional measure of reflection inpulsivity? *Perceptual and Motor Skills*, 1978, *47*, 1247–1253.

Pitkänen, L. A descriptive model of aggression and nonaggression with applications to children's behaviour. *Jyväskylä Studies in Education, Psychology and Social Research*, (Whole No. 19). Jyväskylä, Finland: University of Jyväskylä, 1969.

Plomin, R. Extraversion: Sociability and impulsivity? *Journal of Personality Assessment*, 1976, *40*, 24–30.

Plomin, R., & Foch, T. T. A twin study of objectively assessed personality in childhood. *Journal of Personality and Social Psychology*, 1980, *39*, 680–688.

Plomin, R., & Rowe, D. A twin study of temperament in young children. *Annual progress in child psychiatry and child development.* New York: Brunner/Mazel, 1978.

Pulkkinen, L. Myönteisen sosiaalisen käyttäytymisen varhaiskehitys. [Early development in prosocial behavior.] *Reports from the Department of Psychology, University of Jyväskylä, Finland*, (Whole No. 230), 1980.

Pulkkinen, L. Self-control and continuity from childhood to late adolescence. In P. B. Baltes & O. G. Brim, Jr. (Eds.), *Life-span development and behavior*, Vol. 4. New York: Academic Press, 1982.

Pulkkinen, L. Finland: The search for alternatives to aggression. In A. P. Goldstein & M. Segall (Eds.), *Aggression in global perspective.* New York: Pergamon Press, 1983a.

Pulkkinen, L. Youthful smoking and drinking in a longitudinal perspective. *Journal of Youth and Adolescence*, 1983, *12*, 253–283.(b)

Quay, L. C., & Brown, R. T. Hyperactive and normal children and the error, latency, and double median split scoring procedures of the Matching Familiar Figures Test. *Journal of School Psychology*, 1980, *18*, 12–16.

Quay, L. C., & Weld, G. L. Visual and auditory selective attention and reflection-impulsivity in normal and learning-disabled boys at two age levels. *Journal of Abnormal Child Psychology*, 1980, *8*, 117–125.

Rankin, R. J., & Wikoff, R. L. The IES Arrow-Dot performance of delinquents and nondelinquents. *Perceptual and Motor Skills*, 1964, *18*, 207–210.

Sanford, N., Webster, H., & Freedman, M. Impulse expression as a variable of personality. *Psychological Monographs*, *71*, 11 (Whole No. 440), 1957.

Schmidt-Kolmer, E. (Ed.). *Pädagogische Aufgaben und Arbeitsweise der Krippen.* Berlin: VEB Verlag Volk und Gesundheit, 1972.

Senior, N., Towne, D., & Huessy, H. Time estimation and hyperactivity, replication. *Perceptual and Motor Skills,* 1979, *49,* 289–290.

Sergeant, J. A., van Veltoven, R., & Virginia, A. Hyperactivity, impulsivity and reflectivity. An examination of their relationship and implications for clinical child psychology. *Journal of Child Psychology and Psychiatry and Allied Disciplines,* 1979, *20,* 47–60.

Siegman, A. W. The relationship between future time perspective, time estimation, and impulse control in a group of young offenders and in a control group. *Journal of Consulting Psychology,* 1961, *25,* 470–474.

Signori, E. J., Smordin, M. M., Rempel, H., & Sampson, D. L. G. Comparison of impulse, ego, and superego functions in better adjusted and more poorly adjusted delinquent adolescent girls. *Perceptual and Motor Skills,* 1964, *18,* 485–488.

Stawar, T. L., & Lamp, R. E. IES Test performance by learning disabled boys. *Perceptual and Motor Skills,* 1974, *38,* 695–699.

Susman, E., Huston-Stein, A., & Friedrich-Cofer, L. Relation of conceptual tempo to social behaviors of Head Start children. *Journal of Genetic Psychology,* 1980, *137,* 17–20.

Thomas, A., Chess, S., & Birch, H. G. *Temperament and behavior disorders in children.* New York: New York University Press, 1968.

Thomas, A., & Chess, S. *Temperament and development.* New York: Bruner/Mazel, 1977.

Thoresen, C. E., & Mahoney, M. J. *Behavioral self-control.* New York: Holt, Rinehart & Winston, 1974.

Toch, H. *Psychology of crime and criminal justice.* New York: Holt, Rinehart & Winston, 1979.

Vygotsky, L. S. *Thought and language.* New York: Wiley, 1962.

White, R. W. Ego and reality in psycho-analytic theory. *Psychological Issues,* 1963, *3,* (entire issue).

Wilson, G. Introversion/Extroversion. In H. London & J. E. Exner (Eds.), *Dimensions of personality.* New York: Wiley & Sons, 1978.

Wozniak, R. Verbal regulation of motor behavior: Soviet research and non-Soviet replications. *Human Development* 1972, *15,* 13–57.

Yates, B. T., & Mischel, W. Young children's preferred attentional strategies for delaying gratification. *Journal of Personality and Social Psychology,* 1979, *37,* 286–300.

Zuckerman, M. *Sensation seeking.* In H. London & J. E. Exner (Eds.), Dimensions of personality. New York: Wiley, 1978.

Zuckerman, M., Buchsbaum, M. S., & Murphy, D. L. Sensation seeking and its biological correlates. *Psychological Bulletin,* 1980, *88,* 187–214.

9

Distinguishing between Antisocial Behavior and Undercontrol*

JACK BLOCK and PER F. GJERDE

This essay is a first attempt to respond to a longstanding concern we have had with the way the study of antisocial and prosocial behavior has proceeded over the years. We believe there has been a general failure to consider closely enough the relationship between what is called poor impulse control and what is called antisocial behavior. In our view theory and research on the antisocial personality (or for that matter, on the prosocial personality) has too casually equated or assimilated antisocial behavior to the notion of undercontrol of impulse. We believe there is an important linkage between the societally defined category called antisocial behavior and the construct of undercontrol, but this relationship is far from an equivalence. The main purpose of this essay, therefore, is to articulate the differences between these two constructs and to evaluate the utility, empirically, of maintaining their distinctiveness. We first es-

* This study was supported by National Institute of Mental Health Grant MH 16080 to Jack Block and Jeanne H. Block. Per F. Gjerde was partly supported by Grant B68-80-006 from the Norwegian Research Council for Science and the Humanities. We would like to thank Ruth Butler, Phillip Cowan, Peter Feld, Pat Kerig, Kevin Lanning, Avril Thorne, and Denise Watson for providing prototypical descriptions of the antisocial and the prosocial child. We also gratefully acknowledge the contribution of Susan Keyes in creating the illegal substance use index. Requests for reprints should be sent to Jack Block, Department of Psychology, Tolman Hall, University of California, Berkeley, CA 94720.

DEVELOPMENT OF ANTISOCIAL
AND PROSOCIAL BEHAVIOR

Copyright © 1986 by Academic Press, Inc.
All rights of reproduction in any form reserved.

tablish the personality characteristics that psychologists consider to distinguish between undercontrol of impulse and antisocial behavior. We then present some empirical relationships differentially associated with the two constructs.

Theorists of many persuasions have found it necessary to invoke as an explanatory construct something akin to the construct of impulse control. Because many of these invocations have been ad hoc and casual rather than systematic theoretically and descriptively, the construct has required a conceptual and behavioral basis, which we have sought to offer (see J. Block, 1950; J. H. Block, 1951; J. H. Block & J. Block, 1980).

Our own formulation, termed *ego-control,* derives from an attempt to integrate aspects of psychoanalytic theory (Fenichel, 1945) with the theorizing of Lewin regarding the dynamics of motivational states (Lewin, 1935, 1936, 1938, 1951). Based on the Lewinian formulation of boundary permeability (the degree of mutual influence between subsystems), ego control refers to the modal degree of impulse control characterizing an individual's ego organization. When dimensionalized, the underlying continuum at the one end—overcontrol—implies excessive boundary impermeability resulting in containment of impulse, delay of gratification, inhibition of behavior, and insulation from environmental distractors. The opposite end of the continuum—undercontrol—implies excessive boundary permeability resulting in insufficient modulation of impulse, immediate and direct translation of needs into behavior, and vulnerability to distractors. Whereas each of these two modes of behavior can serve adaptive functions under a restricted set of circumstances, extreme placement at either end of the continuum can be expected to be dysfunctional in the long run.

The location of individuals on this dimension of ego control provides implicative and predictive informations about how individuals will behave in a wide variety of situations, about cognitive functioning and the articulation of experience, and about psychosocial adaptation. Behaviorally, the *overcontroller* appears to be constrained and inhibited, to show minimal expression of personal emotions, to be highly organized, to tend toward categorical thinking, to be able to continue working on uninteresting tasks for relatively long periods of time, to be intolerant of ambiguity, to be over-conforming and indecisive, and to have relatively narrow and unchanging interests. Behaviorally, the *undercontroller* appears to be unduly spontaneous, to readily manifest emotional reactions, to tend to disregard social customs, to tend toward the immediate gratification of personal desires, even when such gratifications are at odds with ultimate goals, and to have widely ranging associative processes that often produce unusual thoughts (that may or may not be of high "quality").

Considerable clinical and research effort has been devoted to understanding the nature of individuals societally labeled as antisocial. Descriptions of the antisocial or the psychopathic individual generally converge in finding insufficient impulse control to be a central personality characteristic. For example, the most recent version of the highly influential psychiatric Diagnostic and Statistical Manual (DSM-III) includes impulsivity as one of the major diagnostic criteria defining the DSM-III category Antisocial Personality Disorder (American Psychiatric Association, 1980). DSM-III discourages the use of the term *antisocial personality disorder* with individuals less than 18 years of age. With regard to children, the term tension-discharge disorder has been recommended (Group for the Advancement of Psychiatry, 1966). McCord and McCord have suggested that antisocial behavior can be traced to an individual's search for immediate pleasure: "The psychopath is highly impulsive. He is a man for whom the moment is a segment of time detached from all others. His actions are unplanned and guided by whims" (McCord & McCord, 1964, p. 16). Rabin also has placed major emphasis on the inability of antisocial individuals to develop an adequate capacity for self-control. The psychopath "continues to be egocentric and impulsive, being solely concerned with the immediate fulfillment of his needs. Since he can suffer no delay or postponement and cannot tolerate frustration when thwarted by the environment, he remains rather childish in this respect" (Rabin, 1979, p. 327).

It is easy conceptually to recognize why these various societally oriented descriptions of the antisocial personality find inadequate impulse control to be a central component. Societal definitions of antisocial behavior generally have referred to obvious, flagrant, immediately disruptive behaviors such as face-to-face violence, criminal behaviors, and violations of social codes designed to facilitate the everyday functioning of the society. Given this (generally held) definition of antisocial behavior, it follows that undercontrol may set the stage for a variety of antisocial behaviors. Yet, looked at conceptually rather than in the narrow terms set by operationalizing antisocial behavior in terms of reported violations or encounters with police or number of traffic violations or recorded drunkenness, it may well be that the current emphasis on the relationship between undercontrol and antisocial behavior is excessive and prevents deeper recognitions. By viewing an antisocial predisposition largely in terms of insufficient impulse control, important psychological insights regarding different kinds of antisocial behavior may be lost. Conceiving of antisocial behavior in broader terms, involving rejection or unawareness of the social contract, inability to empathize with unfortunate others, and an absence of inhibitions regarding the manipulation and exploitation of others, one can readily see how an individual—antisocial in this latter way—could well have sufficient ability to modulate impulse. A configuration of personality qualities of this kind, conjoining control of impulse with an absence of empathy and internalization of social codes, is likely to set the stage for premeditated, consequential, (and sinister) antisocial behaviors ultimately, in contrast to the spontaneous, local, and generally self-defeating behaviors characteristic of antisocial undercontrollers.

J. H. Block and J. Block (1980) and earlier Cleckley (1964) have noted that psychopaths can be planful and premeditated as well as short-sighted and impulsive. But, due to an absence of introspection during affective moments, psychopaths are unable to place themselves in the affective situation of others and are, therefore, less constrained in their behavior than more empathic individuals. When it is further recognized that ego-control is functionally unrelated to introspectiveness—there can be introspective or non-introspective undercontrollers, introspective or non-introspective overcontrollers—it follows that the two constructs of impulse control and antisociality should be kept separate and the separate implications of the two constructs established. Such efforts are likely to provide understanding of the differential developmental factors that foretell individuals later characterized as undercontrolled and as antisocial, respectively.

In addition to ample anecdotal evidence suggesting that the extremely assaultive person often appeared mild mannered and well controlled prior to the aggressive act, some empiricism has been brought to bear on this topic. Megargee (Megargee, 1966; Megargee, Cook, & Mendelsohn, 1967; Megargee & Mendelsohn, 1962) reported that extremely violent criminals were more controlled than either nonassaultive criminals or normal individuals. The overcontrolled type may be "more of a menace than the verbally aggressive, 'chip-on-the-shoulder' type who releases his aggression in small doses" (Megargee & Mendelsohn, 1962, p. 437). Correspondingly, Laufer, Johnson, and Hogan (1981) found that compared to drug offenders, murderers scored higher on a measure of ego control.

We recognize that the utility of distinguishing between impulse control and antisocial behavior is likely to depend on the age of the subject. The two constructs may be difficult to keep separate when very young subjects (i.e., preschool and elementary school children) are studied, because at these early ages, there is relatively little internalization of experience and affect. With the advent of late childhood and early adolescence, however, undercontrol and antisociality can be expected to be more clearly distinguishable and thus more closely identified with different behavioral patterns, different views on self and the world, and different types of family environments. The increased separation of the two constructs in late childhood may at least partly be due to the emerging conception of other persons' ability to experience both pleasure and pain, an understanding related to the increased capacity for empathy (Hoffman, 1975).

The longitudinal study of ego and cognitive development initiated by Jeanne and Jack Block in 1968 provides a unique opportunity to test some of these hypotheses. In this project, children were assessed on a wide range of experimental measures in the domains of personality and cognitive development at the ages of 3, 4, 7, 5, 11, and 14 years. The children, now adolescents, are currently being assessed at the age of 18 years. In addition, independent observer-based personality evaluations in the Q-sort format were obtained at each of these age levels excepting age 5 years. In addition, data on parental child-rearing practices and interactive patterns were collected both in preschool and in early adolescence.

The current study employs the Q-sort methodology to distinguish between the behavioral implications of the concepts of undercontrol and the antisocial character. Almost three decades ago, one of us (J. Block, 1957, 1961/1978) advanced a method whereby the defining behavioral attributes of psychological constructs could be compared in a quantitative and objective manner by the use of the Q-sort methodology. Qualified judges, it was suggested, could use the Q-sort to formulate a construct or the personality implications associated with a construct. These Q-sort–based definitions, if consensual, demonstrated that the construct was equivalently meaningful to the several judges. The several Q-sort definitions then warranted averaging across judges and could serve as a criterion or prototypical definition of the construct. Subsequently, by correlating the Q-sort descriptions of actual subjects with this consensus-based criterion definition, scores ordering subjects on this construct (or a new variable) could be developed. A high correlation between a subject's Q-sort profile and the criterion definition would mean that the subject is close to, or congruent with the construct; a low correlation would mean the opposite. In the Block and Block longitudinal study (see, e.g., J. H. Block & J. Block, 1980), this method has been employed to provide criterion-based definitions of ego control and ego resiliency, among other constructs. This methodological approach also has been used to establish the conceptual and empirical similarities between the related constructs of social competence and self-esteem in normals (Vaughn & Gallagher, 1983; Waters, Noyes, Vaughn & Ricks, 1985).

THE Q-SORT METHODOLOGY

Because some readers may be unfamiliar with the Q-sort method, a brief description may be helpful. The Q-sort is an "ipsative procedure" (J. Block, 1957, 1961/1978; Cattell, 1944; Stephenson, 1953). The term *ipsative measurement* can best be understood by contrasting it to the more common *normative measurement*. In normative measurement, "there is a scale for every *trait* and a population of individuals is distributed about the mean of that population. In ipsative measurement, there is a scale for every *individual* and a population of an individual's trait scores is distributed about that individual's mean" (Guilford, 1952, p. 30). In other words, in ipsative measurement a score, or a Q-sort item, reflects the salience of that score, or Q-item, relative to other scores, or Q-items, with reference to the particular subject under study. The Q-sort as an ipsative method has therefore been said to provide "person-centered" rather than "variable-centered" data (J. Block, 1961/1978). It is important to note that despite the ipsative nature of the Q-sort, individual Q-items can be employed in a normative manner (J. Block, 1957).

A set of Q-items can be viewed as constituting a general language for describing individual differences within a particular domain. Most often, the focus of Q-sets has been on personality characteristics (see, e.g., the California Q-sort, J. Block, 1961/1978; California Child Q-sort, J. Block & J. H. Block, 1969/1980). But Q-sorts have also been developed to describe the domains of child-rearing orientations, selfconcepts, home environments, and teaching strategies, among others.

The Procedure of Q-Sorting In Q-sort methodology, the assessor is provided with a set of statements, printed on separate cards, which contains the entire vocabulary that the assessor is permitted to employ (J. Block, 1961/1978). The assessor is required to arrange the Q-sort items according to a predetermined distribution that specifies the number of cards allowed to be included in each pile. The items are arranged by the sorter according to their judged salience and representativeness with reference to the individual, or construct, being evaluated. Those items deemed by the Q-judge to be most characteristic of the subject are assigned high scores, those items deemed least characteristic of the subject are assigned low scores. The "forced" distribution of items need not be "normal", or Gaussian, as is sometimes assumed. Indeed, a distribution that approaches rectangularity is preferable because it permits the assessor to make finer and more frequent discriminations at the ends of the distribution.

The requirement that different assessors use identical Q-sort distributions confers several advantages: A large number of discriminations can be gained from each Q-sorter, and because all participants employ the same scaling metric, comparisons among raters (and averaging of raters) can proceed straightforwardly. In addition, the forced distribution reduces response sets and problems associated with the social desirability of ratings. The reader is referred to J. Block (1956, 1961/1978) for a detailed description of the Q-sort rationale.

METHOD

Subjects

Subjects were participants in the longitudinal study of ego and cognitive development conducted by Jeanne and Jack Block at the University of California, Berkeley.

Subjects were initially recruited into the study at age 3 years, while attending either a university-run nursery school or a parent cooperative school, and were assessed on wide-ranging batteries of personality and cognitive measures at ages 3, 4, 5, 7, 11, and 14 years. Subjects were equally distributed as to sex, lived primarily in urban settings, and were heterogeneous with respect to social class and parent education. The exact number of subjects in any analysis varies somewhat. About two-thirds of the subjects are white, one-quarter are black, and one-twelfth are Asian. For a more detailed description of this study, see J. H. Block and J. Block (1980).

Procedures

Measuring Personality: The California Child Q-Set   Personality characteristics of the children were described by their nursery school teachers at ages 3 and 4 years, by their public school teachers and project examiners at ages 7 and 11 years, and by project examiners at age 14 years, using the standard vocabulary of the California Child Q-Set (CCQ) (J. Block & J. H. Block, 1969, 1980). The CCQ is an age-appropriate modification of the California Q-Set (J. Block, 1961/1978) and consists of 100 (or 63) widely ranging statements about the personality, cognitive, and social characteristics of children.

At age 3 years the children were each described by three nursery school teachers who had worked with them a minimum of 5 months before completing the descriptions. Teachers also received training and met with the project director who explained the rationale, provided written instructions to the CCQ, and answered questions about item meanings. Each teacher then independently did a Q-sort for a child who was not in the study (usually from a previous year) but who was known to all the teachers. The item descriptions were discussed, and usually a second child was described to check understandings. At age 4 years, each child was again described via the CCQ procedure but by an entirely different set of three nursery school teachers equivalently trained.

When the children were age 7 years and in public school, one teacher and two examiners provided the Q-sort characterizations of a child. When the children were 11 years old, each child was described by four or five examiners who had observed him or her while administering a variety of experimental procedures tapping different aspects of cognitive and personality functioning. Similarly, when the children were 14 years old, each child was described by four examiners who had observed him or her during experimental sessions.

When the children were brought in for assessment at ages 7, 11, and 14 years, the examiners Q-sorted them using only 63 of the original 100 CCQ items. The 37 CCQ items excluded were those for which the examiners believed reliable judgments could not be formulated given the necessary constraints set by the laboratory environment. To insure commensurativeness of the Q-data, as in earlier assessments, a nine-step rectangular distribution was employed by the examiners in sorting the 63 CCQ items. In addition, during the age-14-year assessment, examiners also described each subject using the 100 items of the original adult form of the California Q-set (J. Block, 1961/1978).

Judges described each child by arranging the Q-set items into a forced nine-step, rectangular distribution according to the evaluated salience of each item with respect to a particular child. They worked independently of each other. At each age, the independent Q-sort formulations were averaged to form composite Q-sort descriptions. The CCQ descriptions were completed by a total of 11 different nursery school teachers when the children were aged 3 years; an entirely different set of 9 nursery school teachers completed the Q sorts when the children were aged 4 years; 67 different public school teachers and 2 examiners offered their personality evaluations when the children were aged 7 years; 5 different examiners offered Q-sort formulations when the children were aged 11 years; and still another set of 4 examiners provided Q-sort descriptions when the children were aged 14 years. (Note that no information from the clinical interview influenced the 14-year composite.) Thus, the assessments at each time period are strictly independent of each other and of all other measures. The estimated internal consistency reliabilities of the Q-items, based on the correlations among observers, averaged .65 at ages 3 and 4 years. At age 7 years, the average item reliability was .47; at 11 years, it was .70; and at 14 years, it was .72.

This reliability information not only provides important information about the relative quality of the personality data employed, but also places perspective on the possible magnitude of correlations that can be expected when these measures are related to criterion variables. It is insufficiently recognized that obtained correlations may be considerably attenuated as a function of the inevitable unreliability of the measures employed (J. Block, 1963, 1964; Epstein, 1979, 1980).

Operationalizing the Construct of Undercontrol   Indexing the construct of undercontrol was accomplished in two steps. First, the personality characteristics considered to be associated with the construct of undercontrol were specified, beforehand, by three clinical psychologists who used the CCQ to describe, independently, a prototypical undercontrolling child. These criterion-definers showed high levels of agreement in their conceptualization of undercontrol; the alpha reliability of the consensus prototype was .89. The second step toward creating an undercontrol score for each subject involved correlating the composited CCQ description of each subject in the study with the undercontrol prototype across all 100 CCQ items. For each subject, the correlation or congruence between his or her Q-descriptions by teachers or examiners and the undercontrol prototype was taken as a score indexing the similarity between the personality of the subject and the construct of undercontrol. A high correlation means that the subject is similar or close to the prototypical definition (i.e., is undercontrolled); a low or negative correlation indicates that the subject is dissimilar or far from the prototypical definition (i.e., is overcontrolled).

Operationalizing the Construct of Antisocial Behavior   Indexing the construct of antisocial behavior was accomplished in a manner identical to the one described above for undercontrol. First, criterion definitions of the construct of antisocial behavior were obtained from seven psychology graduate students and doctoral-level professionals, each of whom described independently a prototypical antisocial child. There was high agreement among these seven criterion definers in their conceptualization of this construct; the alpha reliability of the prototype was .90. For each subject, the correlation or congruence between his or her Q-description was taken as a score indexing the similarity of his or her personality to the prototypical definition of an antisocial subject. A high correlation indicates that the subject is similar to the prototype (i.e., antisocial); a low or negative correlation indicates that the subject is dissimilar to the prototype (i.e., prosocial).

The same criterion definers also described the personality characteristics associated with a prosocial child. The prototypes of antisocial and prosocial behavior were highly negatively correlated ($r = -.92$). We decided, therefore, that the prototypical definition of the antisocial personality was sufficient alone to adequately represent the antisocial–prosocial continuum.

Creating "Pure" Indices of Undercontrol and Antisocial Behavior   The CCQ-based prototypical definitions of undercontrol and antisocial behavior were only moderately related; the correlation between the two prototypes was .33. With this level of correlation, the mean values associated with many CCQ items in the two prototypes were often close and did not clearly discriminate between undercontrol and antisocial behavior. To obtain indices differentiating sharply between these two constructs, we identified two subsets of CCQ items. The first subset contained only those CCQ items either highly characteristic (item placement = Category 7, 8, and 9) or highly uncharacteristic (item placement = Category 1, 2, and 3) of undercontrol and placed in the middle categories (neither highly characteristic nor highly uncharacteristic, item placement = Category 4, 5, and 6) in the prototypical definition of antisocial behavior. Thirteen CCQ items met these criteria and served to represent the "pure" construct of undercontrol in this study. The second subset contained 14 other CCQ items either highly characteristic or highly uncharacteristic of antisocial behavior and placed in one of the three middle categories in the prototypical definition of undercontrol. These 14 CCQ items served to represent the pure construct of antisocial behavior in this study. However, of the 27 CCQ items included in the two item subsets, only 16 could be employed at all age levels given the constraints of the laboratory setting in which the children were evaluated at ages 7, 11, and 14 years. In order to make our indices of undercontrol and antisocial behavior fully commensurate over time, the 11 CCQ items not employed at ages 7, 11, and 14 years were excluded from further analyses. Ten of the 16 retained CCQ items characterized undercontrol; the remaining 6 were indicative of antisocial behavior.

Using this method to differentiate between undercontrol and antisocial behavior, the undercontrolled child is described by the following 10 CCQ items (used at all age levels): rapid personal tempo; emotionally expressive; talkative; vital, energetic and lively; curious and exploring; anxious in unpredictable environments (reflected); shy and reserved (reflected); keeps thoughts, feelings to self (reflected); inhibited and constricted (reflected); and reflective (reflected). Three additional CCQ items also defining of undercontrol were not employable at ages 7, 11, and 14 years; cries easily; tends to brood, ruminate, worry (reflected); and likes to be alone (reflected).

The qualities of antisocial behavior that differentiate between this construct and undercontrol are mostly descriptive of disturbances in interpersonal relationships. The following six items used at all age levels described the antisocial child: suspicious and distrustful; stubborn, sulky and whiny; warm and responsive (reflected); arouses liking in adults (reflected); and helpful and cooperative (reflected). Eight additional CCQ items that had been judged intially to discriminate between undercontrol and antisocial behavior were not employable at ages 7, 11, and 14 years: attempts to transfer blame to others; tries to take advantage of others; is afraid of being deprived; is jealous and envious; emotional reactions are inappropriate; behaves in a dominating manner; shows recognition of others' feelings (reflected); and tends to give, lend, and share (reflected).

Two composite measures—one indexing undercontrol and one indexing antisocial behavior—were created by summing the items included in each subset (reflecting those items where it was conceptually appropriate to do so), then taking their average.

As mentioned above, of the 14 items initially selected as discriminating antisocial behavior from undercontrol, only 6 were available at all five age levels. Most of the items defining antisocial behavior not included in the final composite refer to qualities of interpersonal relationships, qualities judges felt could not be evaluated reliably in a laboratory setting. However, because the ratings of these behaviors when available were highly correlated with the composite based on the six CCQ items available at all age levels, and because we considered it to be of essential importance that the same composite of antisocial behavior be used in all analyses, we excluded these eight CCQ items, restricting ourselves to the six CCQ items always available.

Measuring Drug Usage: Coding and Scoring a Clinical Interview   Included in the assessment battery at age 14 years was an extensive individual interview conducted by a skilled clinician and typically lasting 55–75 minutes (range: 40 minutes to over 2 hours). All interviews were videotaped. The interview included such topics as school work, family dynamics, peer relations, current activities, and future aspirations. Within the interview subjects also were asked about their use of the following substances: wine and/or beer, liquor, tobacco, marijuana, and other "harder" drugs. In addition to their verbal responses, subjects also were asked to indicate which substances they had used by checking off the appropriate items on a substance use checklist, the items of which are noted in Table 9.1.

Although self-report data on substance use are always subject to underreporting, a number of investigators indicate that these data have a high concordance with more objective measures (e.g., Jessor & Jessor, 1977;

Table 9.1

Substances Included on the Substance Use Checklist

Tobacco
Beer
Wine
Hard liquor (e.g., whiskey, gin)
Marijuana
Hashish
Hallucinogens (e.g., LSD, peyote, mescaline)
Inhalants (e.g., glue, gasoline, nitrous oxide, amyl nitrate)
Barbiturates (e.g., Seconal, Quaaludes)
Tranquilizers (e.g., Valium, Librium)
Amphetamines (e.g., Dexedrin, Methedrine)
Cocaine
Codeine-type medicines
Heroin
Other

Perry, Killen, & Slinkard, 1980; Single, Kandel, & Johnson, 1975). Subjects in this study appeared to answer our questions about substance use with candor. The interviewer was skilled in gaining rapport, eliciting information without inducing discomfort, and recognizing when a subject wished to close off a topic. Thus, although information varies in specificity from subject to subject, the data that were recorded are likely to reflect honest answers to our queries, or to reflect somewhat the under-reporting phenomenon. To the extent the latter effect is operative, it seems likely the relationships subsequently to be reported are attenuated in strength but not biased.

Data from the substance use portion of the interview were independently coded or scored by two raters. Agreement on coding was high, and in the few cases of discrepancy, items were discussed to reach consensus. For each of the substances listed in Table 9.1 information was coded on (1) frequency of use, (2) context of use, and (3) school grade in which use was initiated. Of particular interest in this report is the information on use of marijuana and the harder drugs (i.e., hashish through heroin). A more complete report focusing on the pattern of usage of all substances by our adolescent subjects can be found in Keyes and J. Block (1984).

For marijuana, information on use and frequency of use was scored on a scale of 0–5 as follows: (0) never used marijuana; (1) used once or twice; (2) used sometimes, occasionally; (3) used once a month; (4) used once a week; and (5) used more than once a week. Only one subject noted usage without providing an indication of frequency of use. This individual was classified in group 2: used sometimes, occasionally. (Examination of other items from this subject's protocol indicated that this procedure was somewhat likely to under-represent, not over-represent, her usage of marijuana.) Scores on the marijuana use variable thus ranged from 0 to 5, with a mean of 1.33 and standard deviation of 1.68. As the relationship between the mean and standard deviation indicates, the score distribution was highly skewed.

For the harder drugs, information on frequency of use was less complete. As a result, a score was derived that was simply the sum of the number of these harder substances that had been tried at least once on a recreational, nonprescription basis. Scores thus ranged from 0 to 9, with a mean of .71 and a standard of 1.49. As the relationship between the mean and the standard deviation indicates, the score distribution was highly skewed.

An illegal substance use summary score was then calculated as the sum of the marijuana and drug use variables. This score ranged from 0 to 14, with a mean of 2.07 and a standard deviation of 2.87. The skewness of this score fairly reflects the skewness in usage of these substances within the sample studied.

Measuring the Self-Concept: The Self-Descriptive Q-Sort   When the children were approximately 14 years old, they described their self-concepts using the Self-Descriptive Q-Set (SQ) (J. H. Block & J. Block, 1977). The SQ consists of 43 widely ranging adjectives relevant to a person's self-concept. Subjects described themselves by arranging the SQ items in a forced-choice, seven-step, rectangular distribution according to the evaluated salience of each item with reference to their self-concept. The subjects completed the SQ twice. They described first their actual self-concept. Later, in a separate session, they used the SQ to describe their ideal self-concept (ego ideal). The correlation between subjects' actual self-concept and their ideal self-concept provides us with an estimate of self-esteem.

Measuring Child-Rearing Practices: The Child-Rearing Practices Q-Sort   When the children were approximately 12 years old, mothers and fathers independently described their child-rearing values, using the Child-Rearing Practices Report (CRPR) (J. H. Block, 1965). The CRPR was developed to provide a self-descriptive instrument that would tap both common and uncommon child-rearing dimensions. The CRPR consists of 91 items that are arranged by parents in a forced-choice, seven-step, rectangular distribution according to the perceived salience of each item with reference to particular child-rearing orientations.

RESULTS

Two types of analyses are reported. First, we examined the longitudinal consistency of the observer-based undercontrol and antisocial behavior scores from age 3 to 14 years. Second, the pure undercontrol and antisocial scores, specified at age 14 years, were correlated with independently obtained information on the children and their parents. These independent data sources include (1) the illegal substance use index, (2) the adolescents' descriptions of their self-concept and ideal self, and (3) the parent's descriptions of their child-rearing practices. Since the major purpose of this study is to identify parental and adolescent characteristics that discriminate between pure undercontrol and pure antisocial behavior, results are only reported if the correlation of undercontrol with a second variable is significantly different from the correlation of antisocial behavior with that same variable.

Reliabilities of the Pure Indices of Undercontrol and Antisocial Behavior

The 10 CCQ items defining undercontrol were intercorrelated separately at each of the five age levels. The average correlation among the items at each age was .54 at age 3 years, .42 at 4 years, .53 at 7 years, .75 at 11 years, and .66 at 14 years. The Spearman–Brown adjusted reliabilities at these five ages were .92, .88, .92, .96, and .95, respectively.

The six CCQ items defining antisocial behavior were also intercorrelated at each of the five age levels. The average correlation among the six items at each age was .50 at age 3 years, .42 at 4 years, .55 at 7 years, .72 at 11 years, and .68 at 14 years. The Spearman–Brown adjusted reliabilities at these five ages were .86, .81, .86, .94, and .92, respectively.

The consistently somewhat higher reliabilities obtained for the undercontrol index are due to the greater number of items included in this measure compared to the measure of antisocial behavior; they are not caused by differences in the magnitude of the average correlations. If we equalize the two measures with respect to number of items, the size of the reliabilities becomes comparable.

The Relationship between the Pure Undercontrol and Antisocial Behavior Indices from Age 3 to 14 Years

Next, we calculated the intercorrelations between the relatively pure undercontrol and antisocial behavior scores at each of the five age levels. Among girls, the correlations were −.16 (ns) at age 3 years, .14 (ns) at 4 years, $-.37$ ($p < .01$) at 7 years, $-.57$ ($p < .001$) at 11 years, and $-.40$ ($p < .01$) at 14 years. Among boys, these correlations were .42 ($p < .01$), .23 (ns), $-.35$ ($p < .01$), $-.50$ ($p < .001$), and $-.41$ ($p < .01$), respectively. These correlations indicate, as hypothesized, that the personality descriptions generated by these two indices become more clearly distinguishable as the child approaches late childhood and adolescence.

Longitudinal Consistency of the Constructs of Undercontrol and Antisocial Behavior from Age 3 to 14 Years

The measures of undercontrol and antisocial behavior, generated separately for each of the five age levels, were intercorrelated in order to examine the longitudinal consistency of the two constructs. Table 9.2 shows the correlations for the two measures over the 11-year time span, separately for girls and boys.

With regard to undercontrol, the correlations for girls range from .74 to .31, with an average correlation of .52. For boys, these correlations range from .86 to .26, with an average of .54. With regard to antisocial behavior, the correlations are appreciably less consistent for both sexes. For girls,

Table 9.2

Longitudinal Consistency of Undercontrol and Antisocial Behavior Indexes from Age 3 to 14 Years[a]

	Age				
	3	4	7	11	14
Undercontrol Index					
Age 3	—	.67****	.50***	.41**	.38*
Age 4	.86****	—	.50***	.31*	.31*
Age 7	.57***	.44**	—	.53****	.74****
Age 11	.40**	.43**	.60****	—	.65****
Age 14	.47**	.26	.55****	.61****	—
Antisocial Behavior Index					
Age 3	—	.67****	.37*	.06	.02
Age 4	.58****	—	.37**	−.12	.02
Age 7	.25	.26	—	.27	.35*
Age 11	.16	.08	.38**	—	.48***
Age 14	.11	.24	.44**	.66**	—

[a] The correlations for girls are above the diagonal; the correlations for boys are below the diagonal. Ns range from 39 to 52 for both sexes.
* $p < .05$, ** $p < .01$, *** $p < .001$, **** $p < .0001$.

they range from .67 to −.12, with an average of .27; for boys, they range from .66 to .08, with an average of .33.

Sex Differences in Undercontrol and Antisocial Behavior

Table 9.3 shows the means and standard deviations for undercontrol and antisocial behavior from age 3 to 14 years, separately for girls and boys.

No sex differences were observed in the undercontrol scores. With regard to antisocial behavior, boys received higher scores at all age levels, the difference between the two sexes reaching statistical significance at ages 3 and 11 years. Thus, there is a tendency for boys to manifest more pure antisocial characteristics than girls.

Indices of Undercontrol and Antisocial Behavior Related to Illegal Substance Use

The pure undercontrol and antisocial indices at age 14 years were correlated with the illegal substance use score. The results show that undercontrol is unrelated to illegal substance use in both sexes. For girls, the

Table 9.3

Descriptive Statistics for Undercontrol and Antisocial Behavior Indexes[a]

Girls			Boys				
M	SD	n	M	SD	n	t	
							Undercontrol Index (age in years)
57.35	15.00	61	58.70	15.93	55	ns	3
55.98	12.96	64	57.95	15.26	64	ns	4
51.87	5.25	50	52.89	5.85	52	ns	7
50.51	18.97	52	54.54	16.80	54	ns	11
49.91	18.44	54	50.06	17.41	52	ns	14
							Antisocial Behavior Index (age in years)
32.28	14.88	61	37.45	10.48	55	2.14**	3
40.06	14.53	64	40.77	12.42	64	ns	4
43.86	4.78	50	44.66	4.87	52	ns	7
34.51	12.58	52	39.75	16.23	54	1.85*	11
36.71	14.26	54	40.52	14.79	52	ns	14

[a] M = Mean; SD = Standard Deviation; n = number of subjects; and t = t-test value.
* p < .10, ** p < .05.

correlation was $-.05$; for boys, it was $-.01$. Use of illegal drugs at age 14 years, however, was significantly related to antisocial behavior. The correlation between the drug use score and the index of antisocial behavior was .30 ($p < .05$; $N = 53$) for girls, and .39 ($p < .01$; $N = 50$) for boys. When the separate correlations of drug use with undercontrol and antisocial behavior were compared, using McNemar's formula (McNemar, 1969) for comparing independent correlations, the difference in the magnitude between the two correlations was significant in both sexes (for girls, the t value was 1.80, $p < .10$; for boys, the t value was 2.04, $p < .05$).

Indices of Undercontrol and Antisocial Behavior Related to Self-Descriptions

At age 14 years, the subjects were asked to provide descriptions of self-concepts, both *actual* self and *ideal* self, using the 43-item Self-Description Q-Sort (SQ). These self-report data were related to the observation-based pure indices of undercontrol and antisocial behavior, identified concurrently at age 14 years. Table 9.4 and 9.5 display the results of these analyses separately for girls and boys. For each Q-sort item, the correlations associated with undercontrol and antisocial behavior were compared using McNemar's formula.

As seen in Table 9.4, the indices of undercontrol and antisocial behavior are associated with significantly different descriptions of self in both sexes. Among girls, 12 (28%) of the 43 SQ items discriminated significantly between the two constructs. Female adolescents scoring high on the pure antisocial composite were, relative to same-aged undercontrolled girls, likely to describe themselves as *more* critical, rebellious, and reserved; more likely to be distractable; and more mischievous and masculine. They were also likely to describe themselves as *less* adventurous, assertive, and responsible; less likely to be a show off; and less feminine and competent. Among boys, a different pattern of 14 (33%) SQ items discriminated between undercontrol and antisocial behavior. Antisocial male adolescents were, relative to undercontrolled male adolescents, likely to describe themselves as *more* competitive and self-controlled, more likely to plan, orderly, reserved, and self-confident. These boys were also likely to describe themselves as *less* energetic, sociable, and restless; less likely to be a show off; and less talkative, fearful, distractible, and impulsive. It is of particular interest to note that the self-report item that discriminated most strongly between the two groups is self-controlled, the antisocial scores being higher on this characteristic.

We turn now to the descriptions of ideal self displayed in Table 9.5. Among girls, 8 (19%) SQ items discriminated significantly between undercontrol and antisocial behavior; among boys, the number was 11 (26%). Antisocial adolescent girls were, relative to same-aged undercontrolled girls, likely to describe their ideal self as *more* logical, mischievous, and obedient. They also described their ideal self as *less* energetic and self-centered, generous, sympathetic, and distractible. Antisocial male adolescents were, relative to same-aged undercontrolled boys, likely to describe themselves as *more* competitive, critical, and fearful; and more

Table 9.4

Undercontrol and Antisocial Behavior Indices Related to Descriptions of Actual Self at Age 14 Years

SQ-Item[a]	Under-control	Anti-social behavior	z
Girls			
Adventurous	.21	−.21	2.15**
Assertive	.43***	.01	2.27**
Responsible	.17	−.21	1.94**
Show off	.32	−.13	2.34**
Feminine	.14	−.39***	2.79***
Competent	.30**	−.11	2.12**
Critical	−.27*	.22	2.42**
Rebellious	−.07	.25*	1.64*
Reserved, shy	−.57***	.15	2.51***
Distractable	−.09	.25*	1.74*
Mischievous	−.16	.37***	2.78***
Masculine	−.09	.23*	1.64*
Boys			
Energetic	.31**	−.15	2.31**
Restless	.13	−.29**	2.10**
Sociable	.27*	−.11	1.90*
Show off	.34**	−.16	2.53***
Talkative	.38***	−.24*	3.16***
Fearful, worrying	.08	−.33**	2.07**
Distractable	.22	−.15	1.83*
Impulsive	.30**	−.23*	2.66***
Self confident	−.12	.34**	2.33**
Competitive	−.22	.19	2.03**
Self-controlled	−.33**	.51***	4.44***
Likely to plan	−.29**	.14	2.15**
Orderly, neat	−.32**	.28**	3.03***
Reserved, shy	−.35***	.13	2.43**

[a] SQ = Self-Descriptive Q-Sort. For the sample of girls, Ns are 54. For the sample of boys, Ns are 51.
* $p < .10$, ** $p < .05$, *** $p < .01$.

Table 9.5

Uncercontrol and Antisocial Behavior Indices Related to Descriptions of Ideal Self at Age 14 Years[a]

SQ-Item	Under-control	Anti-social behavior	z
Girls			
Energetic	.24*	−.22	2.37**
Self-centered	.14	−.20	1.74*
Generous	.15	−.22	1.89*
Sympathetic	.04	−.38***	2.22**
Distractable	.15	−.29**	2.27**
Logical	−.08	.26*	1.75*
Mischievous	−.22	.38***	3.15***
Obedient	−.24*	.18	2.16**
Boys			
Affectionate	.23	−.37***	3.02***
Planful	.27*	−.39***	3.34***
Considerate	.06	−.50***	2.95***
Generous	.06	−.35**	2.06**
Helpful	.03	−.37***	2.02**
Sympathetic	.13	−.32**	2.24**
Trusting	.06	−.28**	1.69*
Fearful	−.21	.15	1.77*
Gets upset easily	−.03	.40***	2.20**
Critical	−.33**	.43***	3.83***
Competitive	−.27*	.33**	3.00***

[a] SQ = Self-Descriptive Q-Sort; z = z-score value. For the sample of girls, Ns are 54. For the sample of boys, Ns are 50.
* $p < .10$, ** $p < .05$, *** $p < .01$.

likely to get upset easily. These male adolescents were also likely to describe themselves as *less* affectionate, planful, considerate, generous, helpful, sympathetic, and trusting.

Indices of Undercontrol and Antisocial Behavior Related to Parental Child-Rearing Practices

When the children were 12 years old, mothers and fathers described their child-rearing practice using the 91-Item Child-rearing Practice Q-Sort (CRPR). These parental self-reported child-rearing orientations were related to the pure undercontrol and antisocial behavior scores identified 2 years later. The results of these analyses, completed separately for girls and boys, are reported in Table 9.6 for fathers and in Table 9.7 for moth-

Table 9.6

Undercontrol and Antisocial Behavior Indices Related to Fathers' Child-Rearing Practices at Age 12 Years

CRPR item[a]	Under-control	Anti-social behavior	z
Daughters			
Child should be comforted when scared	.60***	.02	1.96**
Respects child's opinions	.47**	−.07	1.69*
Insulates child from different ideas	.02	−.64***	2.27**
Shows affection by hugging, kissing child	.45**	−.10	1.71*
Lets child decide many things for self	.49**	−.16	2.03**
Enjoys home full of children	.29	−.50**	2.47**
Expects a great deal of child	.39*	−.25	1.95**
Is easy going, relaxed with child	.43*	−.49**	2.90***
Child reasoned with when misbehaves	.66***	−.08	2.55***
Trusts child to be well-behaved	.33	−.46**	2.48**
Jokes and plays with child	.52**	−.32	2.65***
Parent and child share warm ties	.38*	−.37*	2.33**
Supernaturality used to explain to child	.17	−.52**	2.18**
Encourages child to talk about troubles	.50**	−.31	2.54***
Child not allowed to question parental decisions	.07	.60***	−1.81*
Stays home if child left alone with stranger	.23	−.50**	2.28**
Child should be aware of sacrifices	−.20	.51**	2.23**
Much conflict between parent and child	−.49**	.53**	3.28****
Thinks child must learn early not to cry	−.44**	.36	2.48**
Child expected to appreciate advantages	−.36	.23	1.78*
Teaches child to control feelings always	−.32	.42*	2.27**
Keeps child from fights	−.15	.45**	1.85*
Controls child by warning bad can occur	−.57***	.04	2.01**
Child not allowed to get angry with me	−.04	.61***	2.18**
Prevents rough games	−.46**	.37	2.58***
Sometimes forgets promises to child	−.35	.42*	2.37**
Often feels angry with child	−.47**	.49**	2.94***
Punishes child by violating her	−.07	.55***	2.01**
Watches closely what and when child eats	−.21	.43*	1.96**
Children of different sex shouldn't see each other naked	−.59***	.01	2.01**
Sons			
Respects child's opinions	.60***	−.17	3.00***
Sometimes forgets promises to child	.16	−.34*	1.78*
Encourages child to muse about adult life	.26	−.29	1.96**
Child given time to think, day dream	.33*	−.25	2.07**
Too much "TLC" can harm, weaken child	.27	−.28	1.96**
Child should not play alone without adult supervision	.29	−.18	1.67*

(Continued)

Table 9.6 (*Continued*)

CRPR item[a]	Under-control	Anti-social behavior	z
Wish child not have to grow up fast	−.53**	.25	2.93***
Prefers child not to risk failure	−.21	.30	1.81*
Worries regarding sad, bad things in his life	−.33*	.42**	2.73***
Child not allowed to get angry with me	−.53**	.04	2.22**
Extra privileges given for good behavior	−.36*	.57***	3.55****
Keeps child from fights	−.24	.40**	2.32**
Lets child know when angry with him	−.37*	.21	2.08**

[a] CRPR = Child-Rearing Practices Report. For the sample of girls, Ns are 20. For the sample of boys, Ns are 27.
* $p < .10$, ** $p < .05$, *** $p < .01$, **** $p < .001$.

ers. Again, we have only included Q-items that discriminated significantly ($p < .10$, or beyond) between undercontrol and antisocial behavior.

Inspection of Table 9.6 shows that more paternal child-rearing practices discriminated between undercontrol and antisocial behavior in the sample of girls than in the sample of boys. Among girls, 30 (33%) paternal CRPR items discriminated between undercontrol and antisocial behavior; among boys, the number was considerably lower, only 13 (14%). Girls described as antisocial have, relative to same-aged undercontrolled girls, fathers who were *more* likely to describe the father–daughter relationship as conflictual, to teach the daughter to control her feelings at all times, to feel angry with the daughter, to make her aware of parental sacrifices, and to expect her to appreciate such sacrifices. These fathers were also more likely to prevent rough games and to control the daughter by warning that bad consequences can occur. Relative to fathers of undercontrolled female adolescents, fathers of antisocial female adolescents were also *less* likely to be affectionate; they were less relaxed; they joked less, and were less playful and protective of their daughter. At the same time, these fathers were also less likely to expect a great deal from their daughter, to let her decide many things by herself, and to allow questioning of paternal decisions. In general, these results portray fathers of antisocial daughters as less affectionate and less caring, and yet less encouraging of independence than fathers of undercontrolled girls. We note that the especially significant item, "Teaches child to keep control of feelings at all times," was significantly less associated with undercontrol than with antisocial behavior.

Among males, fewer paternal CRPR items discriminated between pure

Table 9.7

Undercontrol and Antisocial Behavior Indices Related to Mothers' Child-Rearing Practices at Age 14 Years

CRPR item[a]	Under-control	Anti-social behavior	z
Daughters			
Prefers child not to risk failure	.11	−.37**	1.93*
Future plans include child's preferences	.24	−.29*	2.10**
Wishes child not to grow up fast	.19	−.34**	2.12**
Is easy going, relaxed with child	.21	−.28	1.94**
Some of own interests abandoned for child	.39**	−.06	1.83*
Trusts child to be well behaved with parents	.11	−.53***	2.71***
Many duties given to child	.30	−.18	1.86*
Lets child know when angry with child	.43***	−.05	1.98**
Encourages child to be curious	−.34**	.28	2.49**
Worries regarding sad, bad things in child's life	−.21	.26	1.86*
Scolding, criticism improves child	−.16	.34**	1.99**
Much conflict between child and parent	−.21	.27	1.90*
Sons			
Helps child when being teased by friends	.39**	−.09	2.10**
Sibling jealously, quarreling punished	.14	−.33**	2.02**
Child not blamed for others' trouble making	.08	−.56***	2.98***
Child reasoned with when misbehaves	−.52***	.39**	4.13****
Encourages child to do his best	−.33**	.29*	2.68***
Sometimes teases, makes fun of child	−.25	.21	1.83*
Supernaturality used to explain to child	−.35**	.11	2.03**
Makes child aware of shame/disapproval of misbehavior	−.36**	.05	1.79*

[a] CRPR = Child-Rearing Practices Report. For the sample of girls, Ns are 34. For the sample of boys, Ns are 38.

* $p < .10$, ** $p < .05$, *** $p < .01$, **** $p < .001$.

undercontrol and pure antisocial characteristics. Relative to fathers of undercontrollers, fathers of antisocial male adolescents were *more* likely to wish the son had not grown up so fast, to see him risk failure, to worry about sad things in his life, and to keep him from fights. They were also more likely to give the son extra privileges, to let him get angry with father, and to let him know when the father is angry. On the other hand, these fathers were *less* likely to respect their antisocial son's opinions and less likely to forget promises, but also less likely to encourage the son to muse, daydream, and think. We sense, in these data, a growing worry among fathers of antisocial boys about the future of their sons and increased efforts to encourage prosocial behaviors.

Table 9.7 displays the maternal child-rearing practices, identified at age 12 years, that discriminated between undercontrol and antisocial behavior. Compared to paternal child-rearing practices, maternal child-rearing orientations differentiated less frequently between the two behavior patterns, especially in the sample of boys.

Among girls 12 (13%) CRPR items were differentially related to undercontrol and antisocial behavior; among boys the number was only 8 (9%), or less than could be expected by chance. These eight items are included in Table 9.7 but they are not interpreted. Relative to mothers of undercontrolled girls, mothers of antisocial girls described themselves as *more* likely to encourage the daughter to be curious, to worry about sad things in her life, to think that scolding would improve the daughter, and to report the mother–daughter relationship as conflictual. These mothers were also likely to describe themselves as *less* relaxed with their daughter, less likely to trust her to behave, to give her duties and to include her preferences, to let her know when the mother is angry, to prefer the daughter to not risk failure, to abandon own interests for her, and to wish she had not grown up so fast. This group of items describes mothers' relationship with their antisocial daughters as relatively conflictual and lacking in trust. However, these maternal descriptions do not convey the same lack of warmth, affection, and stress on independence evident in the descriptions of fathers' relationship with their antisocial daughters.

DISCUSSION

This essay has several purposes: (1) The development of age-appropriate, consensus-based criterion descriptions of pure undercontrol and pure antisocial characteristics; (2) the description of a method for evaluating the similarities and differences between these two constructs; and (3) the presentation of some empirical relationships differentially associated with undercontrol and antisocial tendencies in early adolescence. The high levels of agreement achieved by the two groups of criterion definers reiterate the usefulness of the Q-methodology in generating reliable, precise, and meaningful definitions of complex psychological constructs. Consistent with other recent studies (e.g., Cantor, Smith, French, & Mezzich, 1980; Clarkin, Widiger, Frances, Hunt, & Gilmore, 1983; Horowitz, Wright, Lowenstein, & Parad, 1981; Vaughn & Gallager, 1983; Waters et al., 1985), this essay provides strong evidence for the utility of criterion definitions, or conceptual prototypes, in defining individual difference constructs. This approach, we believe, provides a useful alternative to other methods by which individuals are ranked according to their relative standing on individual difference constructs (e.g., self-reports, personality inventories, experimental procedures, etc.).

In the first part of this study, we specified the personality characteristics distinguishing between undercontrol and antisocial tendencies. Consistent with our hypothesis, numerous Q-items discriminated between the two constructs. There is no indication in these Q-descriptions provided by clinical and developmental psychologists that difficulty in maintaining an adequate level of impulse control is a centrally important characteristic of the antisocial individual. Antisocial individuals are defined above all by lack of empathy and by poor interpersonal relations. This description of the antisocial person is consistent with Gough's (1948) emphasis on the incapacity to form interpersonal relationships, deficient role-playing ability, and absence of social emotions (e.g., group identification) as the most important signs of an antisocial disposition.

The undercontrolled individual is, not unexpectedly, described in more positive terms than the antisocial individual. The absence of anxiety and lack of emotional constriction (e.g., expressiveness, vitality, curiosity, rapid social tempo, etc.) are the most salient characteristics that separate undercontrollers from antisocial individuals. The quality of interpersonal relationships is comparatively less important in defining undercontrol than in defining the antisocial type. The undercontroller is by definition neither more nor less likely to have good interpersonal relations than the overcontroller. In sum, the modest overlap between the two constructs being compared indicates that further analyses—based on different combinations of undercontrol and antisocial behavior (e.g., undercontrolled–antisocial, undercontrolled–prosocial, overcontrolled–antisocial, and overcontrolled–prosocial)—should be undertaken to evaluate further the possibility that different patterns of antisocial behavior characterize overcontrolled and undercontrolled individuals.

The criterion-definition approach has several advantages over pervious methods used to identify antisocial individuals. In their review of research on children's prosocial dispositions, Radke-Yarrow, Zahn-Waxler, and Chapman (1983) noted that one of the most serious limitations on research in this area is how prosocial (and by implication, antisocial) behavior has been indexed. Rarely, these authors concluded, has prosocial behavior been evaluated in terms other than frequency of observed social transgressions. Hence, other, perhaps equally relevant factors, such as motivation and behavioral intensity, have been excluded from consideration. Although frequency counts of simple behaviors often yield higher interrater agreement than observer-based ratings of complex constructs, accumulating evidence indicates that observer-based evaluations of personality, when provided by knowledgeable, context-sensitive informants whose multiple observations are composited, provide reliable and valid estimates of complex behaviors (J. Block, 1977; J. H. Block & J. Block, 1980a; Epstein, 1979, 1980; Moskowitz & Schwarz, 1982). In particular, broadband assessment procedures are often superior to microanalytic, context-blind strategies when generalizations across situations (Moskowitz & Schwarz, 1982; Waters & Sroufe, 1983) or predictability over time (Bakeman & Brown, 1980) are evaluated. The outcome of this study indicates that antisocial behavior should be evaluated in terms others than simple, fallible, equivocal counts of recorded antisocial episodes. Since the Q-sort methodology takes into account a wide variety of affects, cognitions, and behaviors in defining antisocial behavior, the resulting criterion definition is likely to provide a more valid and psychologically meaningful definition of antisocial proclivities.

The pattern of relationships differentially associated with the indices of undercontrol and antisocial behavior clearly attests to the empirical utility of keeping the two constructs conceptually distinct. Of the two indices—undercontrol and antisocial behavior—only the antisocial index predicted illegal substance use, a finding providing strong evidence for the discriminant validity of the two constructs. The undercontrol index was unrelated to drug use, indicating that behavioral dispositions not specifically related to undercontrol (e.g., lack of empathy and interpersonal distrust) appear to have greater implications for whether adolescents engage in antisocial activities, such as drug use.

These results extend previous findings regarding the relationship between drug usage and personality characteristics (for recent reviews on this topic, see Braucht, Brakarsh, Follingstad, & Perry, 1973; Gorsuch & Butler, 1976). Enhanced understanding of these relationships has been achieved by recent longitudinal studies employing nonclinical samples. In a 4-year longitudinal study of junior and senior high school students, Jessor and Jessor (1977) reported that marijuana use was associated with an inadequate personal control structure. In a longitudinal examination of the preschool and middle childhood precursors of adolescent drug usage, J. Block, Keyes, and J. H. Block (1985) reported that drug users, identified at age 14 years, were seen by their nursery and elementary school teachers over the preceding decade as more rebellious and less socially competent, resourceful, and adult-oriented than nonusers. Whereas these studies have provided substantial evidence that personality factors precede and influence substance use, and not vice versa, they did not evaluate the relative importance of the constructs of undercontrol and antisocial behavior. In the study conducted by Block et al., however, the antisocial quality of the personality characteristics associated with illegal substance use emerged clearly. The results presented in this chapter show even more clearly the greater importance of antisocial dispositions compared to inadequate impulse control as a predisposing factor to drug usage.

The characteristics of the self-concept differentially associated with the two indices are important for several reasons. First, they connect the observer-based indices of undercontrol and antisociality with entirely independent and fundamentally different kinds of data, the subjects' perceptions of their real and ideal selves. The content of the correlates associated with undercontrol and antisocial tendencies, respectively, provides important validation for the observer-based measures of these two constructs.

Second, sex-differentiated relationships are evident in these analyses. The hypothesis that antisocial individuals do not necessarily have difficulties in maintaining an adequate level of self-control receives strong support from the self-descriptions provided by antisocial adolescent boys. These boys view themselves as significantly more self-controlled, more likely to plan, orderly, and also as significantly less impulsive than undercontrolled adolescent boys—a finding that is likely to cast serious doubt on the widespread and oversimplified notion that antisocial behavior derives strongly from insufficient ability to modulate impulse. In the sample of girls, on the other hand, the dimension of self-control appears less relevant than sex-role identification in distinguishing between the self-concept of undercontrolled and antisocial adolescents. Antisocial girls, these results indicate, perceive themselves as less conventionally sex-typed (i.e., more masculine and less feminine) than undercontrolled girls. This emphasis on a more unconventional sex-role orientation in antisocial girls is consistent with other studies suggesting that less sex-typed adolescent females are more likely to engage in illegal behavior, such as drug usage (e.g., Block et al., 1985).

Third, the descriptions of ideal self provide important information about how undercontrolled and antisocial adolescents perceive their ego ideal. The interpersonal wariness and alienation so strongly characteristic of the antisocial criterion definition were reflected in these descriptions, especially in the sample of boys. Relative to undercontrolled boys, antisocial boys were less likely to describe their ideal selves as affectionate, considerate, generous, and sympathetic. The set of values reflected in this ego ideal indicates a strong identification with an antisocial role orientation, even at this relatively early age. In the ego ideals of girls, on the other hand, contradictory aspirations were evident. Although antisocial female adolescents described their ideal self as less generous and sympathetic than undercontrolled girls, they also aspired to become more obedient and planful. This finding suggests that antisocial girls experience some problems of impulse control not seen in same-aged antisocial boys. Moreover, since the identification of these girls with an antisocial role orientation appears less complete than for boys, a high score on the antisocial index may be less predictive of future antisocial activities for adolescent girls than for adolescent boys.

In her study of the young sociopath, Robins (1966) reported results that underscored the importance of father's behavior in predicting antisocial behavior in the offspring, both male and female. Antisocial behavior in the father predicted both juvenile antisocial behavior and antisocial behavior in adults who had been minimally antisocial as children. Moreover, antisocial behavior in the father was the only childhood variable that predicted that the degree of antisocial behavior would not decrease with age. The current study differs from that of Robins' insofar as our subjects represent an unselected sample of young adolescents and, hence, are characterized by a much lower level of antisocial behavior. In addition, we did not evaluate the degree of antisocial behavior characterizing the father. Instead, we examined the relationship between paternal child-rearing orientations and antisocial behavior in the offspring. Despite this difference in subject selection and predictor variables, our results are consistent with Robins' conclusion in its emphasis on the father–child relationship. Another parallel in outcome also suggests itself. In summarizing her results, Robins concluded that girls' orientations appeared to be somewhat more dependent on problem behaviors in the parent, especially in the father, than did boys. In the current study, the relationship between paternal child-rearing orientations and adolescent development was stronger for girls than boys. This congruence in results across studies using different subject samples and different assessment procedures suggests that future studies of antisocial behavior might do well to examine closely the father–daughter relationship, especially in studies of adolescent populations because the need for a father figure may become more important as the adolescent prepares for a more mature adult role (J. Block, 1971).

J. Block (1971) reported that psychologically maladjusted individuals often experienced neurotic and brittle parents of the opposite sex. Although not directly concerned with parental personality antecedents of maladjustment in the offspring, our findings pertain to the relative importance of the same-sexed versus the opposite-sexed parent for the subsequent adjustment of the child. For girls, our results are consistent with Block's observation that the adjustment of the offspring is strongly related to the qualities of the opposite-sexed parent. For boys, indications for the greater importance of either parent did not emerge.

The numerous relationships that emerged between fathers' child-rearing orientations and adolescent undercontrol and antisocial proclivities in the female sample are consistent with a trend in developmental psychology stressing the role of paternal influences on child development and with the finding that positively involved fathers are important for the social and personal adjustment of girls (J. Block, 1971; J. Block, von der Lippe, & J. H. Block, 1973; Gjerde, 1984; Lamb, Owen, & Chase-Lansdale, 1979). The evidence agrees quite well with Becker's (1964) conclusion that when both mothers and father have been included, paternal influences at least equal maternal influences. Psychologists have often assumed that because father–child contacts are less frequent and of shorter duration than mother–child contacts, paternal influences have less impact on the child. But as one of us (J. Block, 1971) has remarked, paternal influences may gain in their effect by virtue of their timing, nature, and context, and by the emphasis they are accorded in anticipation by the mother and the child.

REFERENCES

American Psychiatric Association. *Diagnostic and statistical manual of mental disorders, Third Edition*. Washington, DC: American Psychiatric Association, 1980.

Bakeman, R., & Brown, J. V. Early interaction: Consequences for social and mental development. *Child Development, 1980, 51,* 437–447.

Becker, W. C. Consequences of different kinds of parental discipline. In M. L. Hoffman and L. W. Hoffman (Eds.), *Review of child development,* (Vol. 1). New York: Russel Sage Foundation, 1964.

Block, J. *An experimental investigation of the construct of ego-control*. Unpublished doctoral dissertation, Stanford University, 1950.

Block, J. A comparison of forced and unforced Q-sorting procedures. *Educational and Psychological Measurement, 1956, 16,* 481–493.

Block, J. A comparison between ipsative and normative ratings of personality. *The Journal of Abnormal and Social Psychology, 1957, 54,* 50–54.

Block, J. *The Q-sort method in personality assessment and psychiatric research*. Springfield, IL: C. C. Thomas, 1961.

Block, J. The equivalence of measures and the correction for attenuation. *Psychological Bulletin, 1963, 60,* 152–156.

Block, J. Recognizing attentuation effects in the strategy of research. *Psychological Bulletin, 1964, 61,* 214–216.

Block, J. *Lives through time*. Berkeley, CA: Bancroft Books, 1971.

Block, J. Advancing the psychology of personality: Paradigmatic shift or improving the quality of research? In D. Magnusson and N. S. Endler (Eds.), *Personality at the crossroads: Current issues in interactional psychology*. Hillsdale, NJ: L. Erlbaum, 1977.

Block, J. *The Q-sort method in personality assessment and psychiatric research*. Palo Alto, CA: Consulting Psychologists Press, 1978.

Block, J., & Block, J. H. *The California Child Q-Set*. Institute of Human Development, University of California, Berkeley, 1969. (in mimeo)

Block, J., & Block, J. H. *The California Child Q-set*. Palo Alto, CA: Consulting Psychologist Press, 1980.

Block, J., Keyes, S., & Block, J. H. *Childhood personality and environmental antecedents of drug use: A prospective longitudinal study*. Unpublished manuscript, University of California, Berkeley, 1985.

Block, J., von der Lippe, A., & Block, J. H. Sex-role and socialization patterns: Some personality concomitants and environmental antecedents. *Journal of Consulting and Clinical Psychology*, 1973, *41*, 321–341.

Block, J. H. *An experimental study of a topological representation of ego structure*. Unpublished doctoral dissertation, Stanford University, 1951.

Block, J. H. *The Child-Rearing Practices Report (CRPR)*. Institute of Human Development, University of California, Berkeley, 1965. (in mimeo)

Block, J. H., & Block, J. *The Self-Descriptive Q-sort*. Department of Psychology, University of California, Berkeley, 1977. (in mimeo)

Block, J. H., & Block, J. The role of ego-control and ego-resiliency in the organization of behavior. In W. A. Collins (Ed.), *Development of cognition, affect, and social relations: The Minnesota Symposia on Child Psychology*, Vol. 13. Hillsdale, NJ: L. Erlbaum, 1980.

Braucht, G. N., Brakarsh, D., Follingstad, D., & Perry, K. L. Deviant drug use in adolescence: A review of psychosocial correlates. *Psychological Bulletin*, 1973, *79*, 92–106.

Cantor, N., Smith, E., French, R., & Mezzich, J. Psychiatric diagnosis as prototype categorization. *Journal of Abnormal Psychology*, 1980, *89*, 181–193.

Cattell, R. B. Psychological measurement: Ipsative, normative, and interactive. *Psychological Review*, 1944, *51*, 292–303.

Clarkin, J. F., Widiger, T. A., Frances, A., Hunt, St. W., & Gilmore, M. Prototypic typology and the borderline personality disorder. *Journal of Abnormal Psychology*, 1983, *92*, 263–275.

Cleckley, H. M. *The mask of sanity*, (4th Ed.). St. Louis: C. V. Mosby Co, 1964.

Epstein, S. The stability of behavior: I. On predicting most of the people much of the time. *Journal of Personality and Social Psychology*, 1979, *37*, 1097–1126.

Epstein, S. The stability of behavior: II. Implications for psychological research. *American Psychologist*, 1980, *35*, 790–806.

Fenichel, O. *The psychoanalytic theory of neurosis*. New York: Norton, 1945.

Gjerde, P. F. *The effect of second parent presence on parent-adolescent interaction: Developmental implications*. Unpublished doctoral dissertation, University of California, Berkeley, 1984.

Gorsuch, R. L., & Butler, M. C. Initial drug abuse: A review of predisposing psychological factors. *Psychological Bulletin*, 1976, *83*, 120–137.

Gough, H. G. A sociological theory of psychopathy. *American Journal of Sociology*, 1948, *53*, 359–366.

Group for the Advancement of Psychiatry. *Psychological disorders in children: Theoretical considerations and a proposed classification*. New York: Aronson, 1966.

Guilford, J. P. When to factor analyze. *Psychological Bulletin*, 1952, *49*, 26–37.

Hoffman, M. L. Moral internalization, parental power, and the nature of parent-child interaction. *Developmental Psychology*, 1975, *11*, 228–239.

Horowitz, L., Wright, J., Lowenstein, E., & Parad, H. The prototype as a construct in abnormal psychology: 1. A method for deriving prototypes. *Journal of Abnormal Psychology*, 1981, *90*, 568–574.

Jessor, R., & Jessor, S. L. *Problem behavior and psychological development*. New York: Academic Press, 1977.

Keyes, S., & Block, J. Prevalence and patterns of substance use among early adolescents. *Journal of Youth and Adolescence*, 1984, *13*, 1–14.

Lamb, M., Owen, M. T., & Chase-Lansdale, L. Fathers and daughters. In C. B. Kipp (Ed.), *Becoming female: Perspectives on development*. New York: Plenum, 1979.

Laufer, W. S., Johnson, J. A. & Hogan, R. Ego control and criminal behavior. *Journal of Personality and Social Psychology*, 1981, *41*, 179–184.

Lewin, K. *A dynamic theory of personality*. New York: McGraw-Hill, 1935.

Lewin, K. *Principles of topological psychology*. New York: McGraw-Hill, 1936.

Lewin, K. *The conceptual representation and the measurement of psychological forces*. Durham, NC: Duke University Press, 1938.

Lewin, K. *Field theory in social science*. New York: Harper, 1951.

McCord, W., & McCord, J. *The psychopath: An essay on the criminal mind*. Princeton, NJ: Van Norstrand, 1964.

Megargee, E. I. Undercontrolled and overcontrolled personality types in extreme antisocial aggression. *Psychological Monographs, 80*, (3, Whole No. 66), 1966.

Megargee, E. I., Cook, P. E., & Mendelsohn, G. A. Development and validation of an MMPI scale of assaultiveness in overcontrolled individuals. *Journal of Abnormal Psychology*, 1967, *72*, 519–528.

Megargee, E. I. & Mendelsohn, G. A. A cross validation of twelve MMPI indices of hostility and control. *Journal of Abnormal and Social Psychology*, 1962, *65*, 431–438.

Moskowitz, D. S., & Schwarz, J. C. Validity comparison of behavior counts and ratings by knowledgeable informants. *Journal of Personality and Social Psychology*, 1982, *42*, 518–528.

Perry, C. L., Killen, J., & Slinkard, L. A. Peer teaching and smoking among junior high students. *Adolescence*, 1980, *15*, 277–281.

Rabin, A. I. Psychopathic (Sociopathic) personalities. In H. Toch (Ed.), *Psychology of crime and criminal justice*, New York: Holt, Rinehart & Winston, 1979.

Radke-Yarrow, M., Zahn-Waxler, C., & Chapman, M. Children's prosocial dispositions and behavior. In P. Mussen (Ed.), *Handbook of Child Psychology*, Vol. 4, 4th ed. New York: Wiley, 1983.

Robins, L. N. *Deviant children grow up*. Baltimore: Williams & Wilkins, 1966.

Single, E., Kandel, D., & Johnson, B. D. The reliability and validity of drug responses in a large scale longitudinal survey. *Journal of Drug Issues*, 1975, *5*, 426–443.

Stephenson, W. *The study of behavior*. Chicago: University of Chicago Press, 1953.

Vaughn, B. E., & Gallagher, R. J. *Measuring social competence and self-esteem in young mentally retarded children: Discriminating between constructs and populations*. Paper presented at the biennial meeting of the Society for Research in Child Development, Detroit, MI, 1983.

Waters, E., Noyes, D. M., Vaughn, B. E., & Ricks, M. Social competence and self-esteem: A Q-sort analysis of conceptual and empirical similarities between related constructs. *Developmental Psychology*, 1985, *21*, 508–522.

Waters, E., & Sroufe, A. Social competence as a developmental construct. *Developmental Review*, 1983, *3*, 79–97.

The Role of Familial Factors in the Development of Prosocial Behavior: Research Findings and Questions

MARIAN RADKE-YARROW and **CAROLYN ZAHN-WAXLER**

The belief that childhood experiences in the family have profound and lasting influences unifies many theories of human development and creates a pact of agreement between science and common wisdom. There is less certainty, however, about how these effects are accomplished.

In the past half-century, research has taken various paths to attempt to understand the links between childhood experiences and later behavioral outcomes. One approach has been through retrospective methods, hoping through adult recall to identify lines of continuity. Another method has been longitudinal research in which behavior of normal and disturbed parents and children has been followed over time, attempting in this way to establish linkages. Parent and child behaviors are also studied for brief intervals of time; the sampled behavior is assumed to provide a valid indicator of more general and enduring behavioral characteristics. Still another research strategy is represented in laboratory analogue rearing studies in which parental (experimenter) impact on child behavior has been telescoped into techniques of influence varied experimentally in brief laboratory encounters. Through each of these strategies has come information about familial influences on the child's social and emotional behavior and development.

Views of family influences on children have changed over the years. Traditionally, the problem has been framed in terms of rearing variables, suggesting that what parents do to and with the child are the determinants of the child's outcome. Such an interpretation has come under criticism: Mutual influences of parents and children are increasingly recognized. Likewise, "built-in" characteristics of the participants are considered as aspects of the systems of influences that contribute to individual development.

The kinds of behavior that have been investigated as "consequences" of familial experiences have often been problem behaviors, such as psychopathologies, aggression, and delinquency. Less attention has been given to positive characteristics of individuals. For example, social responsibility and altruism, the dimensions that concern us here, have not been much represented in these kinds of research.

In the present essay, we are interested in these latter behaviors and factors in the family that contribute to their development. We define this domain as behaviors that are positively responsive to others' needs and welfare. They can be viewed as somewhat parallel, but opposite to, antisocial, aggressive actions. They are behaviors of helping as opposed to hurting or neglecting, of respecting as opposed to denigrating, and of being psychologically supportive and protective as opposed to dominating or exploitative. At a descriptive level, they are behaviors that are helpful and affiliative responses to others: responses to signs of suffering, need, or danger in another person or animal, such as, assisting, sharing, being kind and considerate, comforting, cooperating, protecting someone from harm, rescuing someone from danger, and feeling empathy and sympathy. These descriptions alert one to the vast variety of behaviors that share the common dimension of a positive, responsible orientation to others. The behaviors are of many forms, involve diverse psychological processes, have a variety of origins, and serve various functions.

The recent re-entry of these topics into psychological research is interesting. When this class of behaviors came into American social psychology in the 1960s, it acquired the new label of *prosocial*. The social psychologists who initiated experimental studies behavioristically defined the class by the outcomes: behaviors that aid or benefit another person. Philosophical arguments of innate selfish or altruistic properties of human nature were avoided. Sometimes a conditional factor was added to the definition in which motives were considered; namely, the individual anticipates no extrinsic reward for the action, and the action itself involves some cost to the doer. It is possible to find fault with these definitions by asking "what if" questions: What if a man plans to harm someone and, because of his miscalculations, his actions result ultimately in benefiting his grateful "victim"? What if, in helping you, I know that I will save myself? What if good intentions to aid are harmful to the recipient? What if, in order to protect someone from harm, I have to attack the aggressor? Thus, there are shifting definitional grounds, depending on whether prosocial behavior is regarded from the perspective of consequences, individual motivations and determinants, or moral philosophy. In developmental psychology of the period of the 1960s and 1970s, social learning formulations directed studies to specific adult influence techniques (e.g., adult modeling, social reinforcement). Studies in social psychology stressed situational determinants or the influences of an equity principle or the effects of presumed social norms. Little attention was given to the prosocial behaviors themselves, to the various functions they might serve for the individual, or to characteristics of the individual.

The field of prosocial research has changed. Conceptions of prosocial behavior and the conditions that foster it have broadened to include both the external environmental influences and the internal characteristics or mechanisms in individual behavior. This has made the issue of the role of familial experiences in children's prosocial development a far more challenging and complicated one. Also, changing subject matter in psychology, such as interest in emotions and in cognitive and affective interrelations has brought new questions, concepts, and paradigms into the research. These changes are important to the subject concerning us here. They tell us that we are not dealing with a single kind of interpersonal behavior, and that we should not search for a single or uniform set of family influences.

As already noted, the influences of early experience on the development of the individual's prosocial "attachments", in the sense of empathy and responsibility for others and for society, have neither been emphasized in psychological and psychiatric theories nor figured prominently among the outcome variables in longitudinal research. Indeed, most of the research on prosocial behavior has not been developmental in design. This is a particularly unfortunate state of affairs for an analysis of family influences, which is inherently a developmental question. It tells us that, at this point in research history, there are only the beginnings of a body of systematic knowledge. These beginnings constitute a base, however, from which to begin to view a very important kind of positive interpersonal attribute.

This paper has two major purposes. One is to review and integrate the research knowledge that we now have about family influences. The second is to give equal consideration to a critique of existing research and to an identification of needed research. Since a number of lengthy reviews of research on prosocial behavior exist in the literature (Mussen & Eisenberg-Berg, 1977; Radke-Yarrow, Zahn-Waxler, & Chapman, 1983; Rushton, 1980; Rushton & Sorrentino, 1981; Staub, 1979; Wispe, 1978), comprehensive review is not our primary emphasis.

A FRAMEWORK FOR VIEWING FAMILY INFLUENCES

"Family influences" conjure up various images. Theoreticians and investigators interested in familial contributions to individual human development have used formulations and variables that differ remarkably, depending on the discipline—genetics, sociology, psychology, psychiatry. We have drawn most heavily on research in psychology. This places a selectivity on our review. Within the framework of psychological studies we have tried to sort out the several perspectives that have guided prosocial research.

A first perspective has been to view the family as a self-contained unit that involves a time line that is a biological or developmental line as well as a history of learning. Although often seen only as a constellation of environmental factors, family influences are at the same time a set of influences of family genetics and developmental–biological conditions that constrain and interact with the behaviors of parents and children with each other. With a developmental view uppermost in mind, a central question for psychological research on prosocial behavior is: How well does the family provide for (take into account) the child's inherent capabilities of responding positively to others; that is, how well are the modes of influence used by parents adapted to the child's constitutionally unique capabilities and sensitivites as well as those reflecting normative developmental changes in the child?

Another question of family impact, one less conscious of development, is simply: What modes of influence used by parents promote prosocial behavior? With either of these questions, family can be dealt with as a group, or it can be one parent's interaction with one child. For the most part, studies have focused on interaction of parent and child, without regard to the larger family entity, and without reference to developmental level of the child.

A second perspective in the research literature is to view the family as a mediator of culture and society. Prosocial behavior involves children's views of their social worlds and children's systems of relating to persons beyond the family as well as within. Parents carry society within them and bring it to their parental roles via their backgrounds and traditions, and their present statuses and experiences in society. Family and society are also a combination in history. The family is functioning at a given moment in time. This fact, in large or small degree, may override the influence that the individual parent can exert upon the child; it modifies parents' methods of influence, and it changes parents' objectives in child behavior. The historical moment is relevant not only to descriptive data on family functioning, but also to relations obtaining between familial conditions and outcomes in child personality. This broader context provides many clues to understanding the weight and quality of parent influence on the child's altruism.

In the third perspective family influences can be seen in another light. The first two views emphasize the continuities in family functioning (even continuity in chaos) that derive from the personality dynamics of family members and from the dynamics of society. We make use of this continuity for prediction. However, families also suffer disequilibria by virtue of events, internal and external to the family, that alter family life (e.g., illness, economic depression, divorce, death, etc.). Such disruptions are very common in family experience, and they are very likely to affect children's abilities to relate to other persons and specifically their abilities to relate in positive ways.

Thus, family is a many-sided source of influence. At present, there is no unifying approach that satisfactorily links these several kinds and levels of influences. The many pieces of information from research begin to form lines of evidence that are important in developmental psychological theory, for child-rearing practices, and for social policies of child care. In the following discussions we use these three perspectives in viewing family influences on children's prosocial behavior.

FAMILY AS A UNIT OF INTERACTION

Development and Parental Influence

We begin with a pair of questions to which we have only very partial answers from research: (1) Are parents effectively in touch with their children's inherent and developmentally changing capacities for prosocial behavior? and (2) How are parents' behaviors and their effects on children's prosocial behaviors modified in relation to children's developmental levels and individual child characteristics?

It is now well documented that children have an inherent or innate interest (or at least an interest manifested in the first year) in other social beings. Moreover, there are data to indicate that beginning with newborns, responses akin to empathy make their appearance. Thus, Simner (1971) and Sagi and Hoffman (1976) report distress cries from newborns in response to cries of other infants. Data reported by Radke-Yarrow and Zahn-Waxler (1983) similarly document emotional distress and positive interventions by children in the second and third years of life when in the presence of suffering and distress emotions in others. The evidence poses a very interesting question; namely, how influential are caregiver conditions in these early months and years in determining how these inherent tendencies are enhanced, retarded, warped, or extinguished? In an insightful discussion of maturing infant functions and caregiver influences, Sroufe (1979) describes how a complex of caregiving may be of critical importance for the beginnings of prosocial behavior. He describes the infant as developing "systems" of behavior (e.g., attachment, affiliation, exploration) that interact and become organized into patterns. He has proposed that this development is organized around the quality of the caregiver relationship with the child. In a good relationship, "what seems to be learned is the trustworthiness and dependability of the surround" (p. 502). Further, caregivers' effectiveness in promoting healthy emotional development is seen as deriving from the ways in which caregivers "create" the appropriate affective climate and tune their behaviors to the infant's tension level, catching it at the peak of organized engagement" (p. 507).

We would speculate about parental effects on very early underpinnings of the child's positive orientations to other persons: The parental variables found to be generally influential in infants' social and emotional growth, are equally relevant as facilitating conditions for prosocial development. Drawing upon Sroufe's work, we have a bit of evidence. He and his colleagues (Waters, Wippman, & Sroufe, 1979) have traced from positive caregiver–child relationships (secure attachment) in the first year, an increased likelihood of outgoing positive interactions with peers in the third and fourth years. This kind of information needs to be elaborated and detailed, specifically with regard to empathic and altruistic interactions.

There is an important set of unknowns about early family environment in relation to the child's prosocial development that concerns parents' expectations and their recognition of empathic and prosocial attempts by their infants and toddlers. Parents have been alerted to many kinds of infant capabilities and needs, but not with respect to prosocial behavior. Little information exists concerning parents' beliefs about very young children (or children of any age) as empathic and altruistic organisms. Yet these beliefs most certainly affect not only parents' awareness of the child's positive other-oriented behavior but also parent's responses to such behavior.

Having begun our discussion with infancy, it is logical to continue in a developmental framework. Throughout childhood, family factors affecting children's prosocial behavior operate cumulatively within the developmental structure of the child. As other behavior systems are developing, and as developmentally changing socialization demands are made on the child, how do prosocial motivations and actions fit into the scheme of development? Children are exposed to interpersonal and social–moral problems of increasing variety and complexity. How do parents contribute to children's abilities and motives to deal with them, specifically in relation to empathy and prosocial interactions? We assume that the influence of any given parental factor will depend on the child's developmental level. How do parents modify their practices to accommodate to developmental changes in the child? How do children's changing capacities limit or enhance the effects of specific parental behaviors? Unfortunately we cannot move forward along developmental lines to answer these questions directly. There is virtually no research in which socialization practices and influences have been investigated developmentally in relation to empathy and altruism. At present we must be satisfied with the data from nondevelopmental studies of associations between family variables and prosocial child behavior. From them we can only infer about developmental dimensions of family influence.

Parental Modes of Influence

Specific parental methods of influence are the focus of the vast majority of socialization studies. It is assumed that parents influence child behavior most certainly by *intending* to influence: by instructing the child, providing opportunities for experience, and disciplining. Parents influence also by *nonintention,* by the "side effects" of what they are as persons and how they behave. Cutting across parental intentionality are two modes of influence that we distinguish as (1) actions taken by the parent that are *not in reaction* to the child's behavior but that expose the child to cognitive structures and behavioral and affective contexts, and (2) actions by the parent that are *reactive* to child behaviors that the parent tries to encourage or inhibit or redirect. We look at the research on parental influences in terms of these classes of parental behavior. It should be pointed out that, in most of the research, parental influence has been measured primarily in terms of the child's actions in a relatively short time frame. Children's emotions, cognitive structures, beliefs, and values have not often been considered.

Nonreactive Modes of Influence: Parent as Model   In lay terms, the child learns from the kind of example set by the parent. In psychoanalytic theory, imitation by the child involves the dynamics of identification with the loved or feared parent. In observational learning, the parent provides the representation or model of behavior that can be adopted by the child. In each, it is a process of the child's incorporating into his or her own repertoire of behavior and orientations, the content observed in the parent.

Research on the effects of a model is mainly to be found in the publications of developmental psychologists. There are two bodies of information: one from experimental studies and the other from naturalistic and clinical sources. The experimental studies, for better or worse, are overwhelmingly uniform in their approach and specific manipulations. The prosocial act is usually sharing toys, pennies, candy, and the like that have been "won" in a game. The sharing is with someone (not present) who is said to be in need. An adult has just played the game and has modeled the sharing, before leaving the child to play. In studies of honesty, the procedures have involved games with rules in which an adult models either cheating or adherence to the rules. In all of the studies, the model's action is extraordinarily salient by virtue of the confined experimental setting. There are not other competing modeled acts, no other persons, no real context with which the experimental situation is continuous. The paradigm is interpreted as a child-rearing analogue. (For review of these studies, see Mussen & Eisenberg-Berg, 1977; Radke-Yarrow, et al., 1983; Rushton, 1980).

The results show that children who are exposed to a model, compared with children in control groups, are more likely to show the behavior manifested by the models—whether the modeled behavior is honesty, generosity, cheating, selfishness, helping, or rescuing behavior. There is evidence that the effect of the model sometimes remains over a few weeks or months of time and that it sometimes generalizes to other kinds of prosocial behaviors. To these positive findings we must add further evidence; namely, that children's imitation is not automatic or universal. As many as 40–50% of the children do not follow the model's lead (Bryan & Walbek, 1970; Rosenhan & White, 1967). Some children only imitate in a token way (Poulos & Liebert, 1972), and still others behave oppositely from the adult example (Bryan & Walbek, 1970). In summary, the findings from the laboratory (the positive effects of the model on prosocial behavior and the individual differences in being influenced by the model) are not unexpected; they seem to represent common experience. Exactly what mechanisms are involved in imitation and what changes in the child are brought about by imitation of the adult are not much elucidated by these studies.

Studies of imitation of prosocial behavior in which parents are the models are few. In a naturalistic study of toddlers' prosocial actions, Zahn-Waxler, Radke-Yarrow, and King (1979) found no association between frequency measures of mothers' modeling of prosocial behavior and children's prosocial responses. However, in the same data, there was striking evidence of delayed imitation by the children in which nearly exact reproductions of mothers' ways of comforting and helping appeared spontaneously in children's efforts to cope with others' distress and to comfort them. Here the techniques of how to comfort seem to have been observed and adopted. A further bit of evidence on parents as models comes from Hartshorne and May (1928). Children whose honesty or dishonesty tended to be relatively more consistent than that of other children, suggesting perhaps the acquisition of some guiding principle in their behavior, had parents who presented themselves in ways that could be interpreted as models of honesty or dishonesty. Two often-cited studies of remarkable self-sacrifice and compassion are London's (1970) study of Christians who rescued Jews in the period of Nazi terror, and Rosenhan's (1969) study of youth who were deeply involved in the Civil Rights Movement in the United States. Retrospective accounts of childhood by these altruists elaborate a theme that might be interpreted as parental modeling influences. They described their parents as being involved in activities addressing human needs and as being "highly principled."

As is apparent, we are left with many questions concerning the process of prosocial learning through observation in the family. How important is the parental model relative to other parental influences in the child's acquisition of prosocial behaviors? Given the child's pervasive exposure to parent behavior, one might assume a high potential for observational learning. Does the relative importance and nature of the child's imitation change with age? Are young children more or less likely to learn through imitation? We do not know. Yando, Seitz, and Zigler (1978) speculate that there is possibly less "spontaneous" imitation as the child matures. These authors also propose that, as part of polarizations that occur between parent and adolescent, there may be motivations not to imitate.

Another largely unstudied question concerns what is imitated. As is well known, imitation is not a passive process; a child does not imitate every parental behavior that is observed. Yet little research information exists about the selectivity that occurs. In laboratory studies of modeling in which the adult's relationship with the child has been varied experimentally, the model's effectiveness has been shown to be enhanced by the adult's power and competence (Eisenberg-Berg & Geisheker, 1979; Grusec, 1971), sometimes diminished by friendliness just preceding experimental modeling (Crusec & Skubiski, 1979; Weissbrod, 1976), enhanced by long-term nurturance (Yarrow, Scott, & Waxler, 1973, and diminished by affectless, lackluster behavior (Waxler & Yarrow, 1975). The point made by these studies is that what the adult is like is an important factor determining how much a child learns through imitation. The studies address children's selectivity among models but not selectivity in the behavior that is imitated, or when or to whom the imitated behavior is directed.

With regard to the susceptibility of different children to modeling influences, Akamatsu and Thelen (1974) have reviewed research for child characteristics that contribute to increased or decreased receptivity to imitative learning. With the exception of child dependency, which related positively to amount of imitation (in the laboratory), no consistent relations appear in the literature. These findings must not be considered final, however, for the variables studied have not been extensively probing of children's cognitive and social–emotional characteristics.

In summary, despite an extensive research literature on children's imitation of the adult's prosocial behavior, the conclusions we are able to draw are not precise. To understand children's imitation as a significant process in socialization, there is need to observe imitation in the family context in relation to variables within the child and the parents, and in relation to the kinds of prosocial behaviors being modeled and imitated. Analyses are needed of what is learned in observing parents' prosocial behavior. Does the child learn the skills (i.e., how to help) by this process? Is sensitivity to interpersonal cues enhanced? Does the child acquire motives to help by observing parental example? Since prosocial behavior is differently manifested and motivated in different families, what is learned imitatively may vary considerably. Prosocial behavior in some families is adherence to a prescribed set of codes. In this instance, imitation by the child would be learning rules, conventions, and skills. In other families, prosocial behaving is a general mode of relating positively, empathically, and easily to others. In other families, it may be a consuming emotional commitment to a humanitarian cause. In these various family settings, imitation would seem to involve quite different kinds of learning by the child and might, therefore, be differently influenced by characteristics of both child and parent.

Nonreactive Modes of Influence: The Behavior Setting   A second mode of family influence on prosocial development is the parent's structural and anticipatory management of the behavior settings and the experiences that comprise the child's life. Parents are in almost complete control of the environment of young children and they continue to have a managerial role into late childhood. In the group life of the family, there are settings and activities in which prosocial behaviors (sharing, aiding, cooperating) occur by virtue of the nature of the task (e.g., taking care of a young child, aiding a grandparent, helping a neighbor or parent, contributing to charity) or in which there are opportunities or provocations for behaving prosocially (e.g., a pleasant companion is present, someone is unhappy or is being treated unjustly).

From piecemeal and scattered reports, there is evidence to the effect that children's participation in prosocial activities that are integral aspects of the family's functioning increases the likelihood of their prosocial behavior. One often-cited piece of evidence comes from the research of the Whitings (1973, 1975). Children were observed in six cultures. Among other behaviors, children's altruistic and egoistic acts were recorded, and family practices were also observed. Those cultures in which children were responsible for tasks helpful to family maintenance, and particularly tasks of taking care of younger siblings, were the cultures in which children were significantly more altruistic. This difference maintained also for comparisons of individual children within a culture. Staub (1970) replicated this relationship in a laboratory study. Children who were given the responsibility for "taking care of things" while the experimenter was out of the room showed a greater tendency to respond to cries of a child in an adjoining room than children without such responsibility. Supportive of the same idea—that responsibility within the family generalizes to social responsibility to others—is found in Baumrind's studies of rearing (1978). Responsibility with a different flavor is found in an early study by Bathurst (1933). Children who had and those who did not have a pet were compared. Children who cared for a pet showed higher levels of sympathetic behaviors with their peers than children without a pet. This finding has been interpreted as deriving from responsibility for the pet, but it may also be either the result of experiencing reciprocal affectionate contact and interaction with the pet, or a reflection of the different characteristics of persons who choose to have a pet.

The preceding examples have in common the child's being in a setting in which the requirements and expectations incorporate positive other-oriented behavior. There are similar findings regarding the effects on the child of participating *with* parents in responding to needs of others. Such participation in prosocial activities was described by Rosenhan, in the study cited earlier (1969), in which participation with parents was a childhood experience characteristic in the recollections of youth deeply involved in the Civil Rights Movement. Staub (1979) took this idea to the laboratory and had children participate in making puzzles for hospitalized children and in teaching younger children. The results were variable, but more often positive than not. Data from Johnson and Johnson (1974), Crockenberg, Bryant, and Wilce (1976), and others point to the favorable consequences of children's participation in cooperative learning experiences in school. Such experiences increased children's cooperation in circumstances other than those in which the learning had taken place.

Tangential perhaps but possibly similar to the influence of participation in family prosocial activities is the influence of a "group code" in fostering and maintaining prosocial standards. In citing data from Hartshorne and May, Burton (1976) noted that the honesty scores of members within a social unit (e.g., siblings) were highly correlated. Although this may be the result of many factors, one might assume that members of the family unit develop common expectations and standards regarding each others' behavior. Such shared codes and expectations would support similar behavior from members of the group.

On a similar theme of participation, Hoffman (1976) advises that children not be shielded from the experiences of distress that the family encounters in the natural course of events. His assumption is that sensitivity to others' feelings will be fostered by such experiences. Some qualifications may be necessary, however, regarding the intensity of such encounters and the kinds of buffer or support provided the child in circumstances of distress. The experimental work on giving young children role training in responding to others' emotional needs (presumed to increase their sensitivities to others' psychological states) lends some support to Hoffman's suggestion. Role training (Iannotti, 1978; Staub, 1971) had some positive influence on children's subsequent helping and generosity.

The effects of participation and responsibility require analysis in order to identify the component processes involved. Such analysis would undoubtedly bring in many variables: The child is practicing skills, developing acuities, observing models, acquiring norms or codes of behaving, and experiencing feedback.

The way of life and the behavior settings that we have been describing assume family practices and standards in which prosocial behaviors are endorsed. Family functioning that interferes with prosocial behaviors could just as well adversely influence the child. Participation in a family in which the child has no responsibilities in the life of the family, or has no opportunities for sharing in affective experiences, or in which selfish and callous behaviors are practiced would be expected to result in less empathy and altruism.

Nonreactive Modes of Influence: Affective Relationships   In considering possible influences of parents' affective behaviors on children's prosocial development, we are looking now at affective behaviors in a nonreactive sense, not as techniques of control in disciplining or rewarding the child for specific responses. Parents' affective states are expressed in the behavior settings they create for the child, in the kinds of models they present to the child, and the kinds of feeling states they produce in the child. How do these affective dimensions influence children's prosocial behavior?

The research literature provides mainly studies in which parental warmth (or lack of it) and prosocial behavior have been examined. Studies in which maternal warmth or nurturance is inferred from mothers' responses to interview questions have tended to show low positive associations with children's moral behaviors (honesty, conscience, altruism). From laboratory studies in which mild and brief manipulations of nurturance have been added to reinforcement and modeling procedures, the effects on children's generosity and helping have been slight and variable. (More extensive coverage of the experimental literature is found in reviews by Burton [1976] and Radke-Yarrow et al. [1983].) Studies of child rearing in which parental nurturance is dealt with as a part of patterns of parental rearing variables yield somewhat different findings. A parental pattern of responsiveness, demandingness, firmness, *and* warm affect relates to children's social responsibility in Baumrind's (1978) work and to altruism in the research of Yarrow et al. (1973) and Zahn-Waxler et al. (1979). It appears that nurturance is frequently in patterns of parental behaviors that are related to children's prosocial qualities, but when considered alone, warmth is not predictive.

The sum of evidence, experimental and naturalistic, would seem to call for a reformulation of the question of whether the child's prosocial behavior is fostered by parental warmth and affection. The question must be asked with consideration of the total rearing context. Although a loving parent is an invaluable asset to the developing child, there is ample evidence that "love is not enough" to facilitate prosocial development, and probably, lack of love is not enough to prevent its development. Parental love can be packaged many ways in rearing: It can be part of a sensitive, firm, and prosocially oriented rearing pattern, and just as easily part of a disorganized indulgent parent with an egoistic orientation. Likewise, lack of parental love can be combined with variable rearing conditions which, on their own, promote or hinder the learning of empathy and altruism.

The relevance of parents' positive affect may depend also on the kind of prosocial behavior that is being learned. For prosocial behaviors of self-sacrifice, sympathy, and compassion that are themselves strongly affective in nature, affective aspects of parents are probably critical. For learning prosocial behaviors that are rules, social expectations, and reciprocity considerations, affective parental variables may be of relatively less importance.

One might regard nurturance and non-nurturance as "chronic" or relatively continuous affective factors in the rearing of the child. Similarly chronic are other affective characteristics of parents, such as parents' feelings of happiness and self-worth, of anxiety, anger, and depression. Because such affects enter into many aspects of parental functioning, they could be of considerable significance for the child's prosocial behaviors.

Our comments on parents' affects in relation to children's prosocial development must be mainly conjectural. We would ask: How does happiness or chronic anxiety or anger affect the parent's abilities to be a model of prosocial behavior or to engage the child in prosocial family activities? Affective states that make social relationships difficult for the parent may interfere with the parent's engagement in prosocial behaviors, thus providing no model of these behaviors. The converse may to some extent be true for parental states of well-being. Also, chronic affective states of anger, depression, happiness enter into parent's functioning as disciplinarians, as they control prosocial and antisocial child behaviors. How does affect modify the effectiveness of control techniques?

Something more specific can be said about the impact of parental depressive states on the child's prosocial behavior. Clinical observations and systematic observations of depressed mother–child interactions indicate high frequencies of disturbances in the young child's social relations and emotional responses to others (Zahn-Waxler, McKnew, Cummings, Davenport, Radke-Yarrow, 1984). Another influence has also been observed: Manic-depressive mothers sometimes manifest intense need for nurturance and they turn to their children for nurturance. At times, in these families, child and parent roles are reversed and the young child assumes the caregiving role. Children from these families tend to show intense preoccupation with adult suffering. For these children, such prosocial responsibilities may be a heavy emotional burden. Intense involvement with emotional needs within the family may make the development of adequate social relationships outside the family difficult. Children's prosocial behavior may be at a high cost. On the other hand, the needed and required caregiving by them may provide some children with a satisfying and fulfilling task (Rachman, 1979).

Reactive Modes of Parental Influence   Much of the research on family influences on children's social development has proceeded on the implicit assumption that parents' greatest impact on the child's social behavior comes through their reactive methods of controlling or disciplining child, that is, techniques used by parents when children are engaged in inappropriate behavior, or when compliance to a parental direction is desired.

In relation to children's prosocial development, there is literature on parental techniques. In many ways it dates from Hoffman's (1963) early work in which he examined the ways by which parents dealt with their preschool-age children's transgressions against persons. He obtained mothers' descriptions of their disciplinary methods, which he typed as either power-assertive or reasoning techniques. Reasoning involved alerting the children to the consequences of their "bad" actions for other persons. Power assertion consisted of threats, physical punishment, and isolation. He found that use of reasoning, when considered without regard to use of power assertion, was not associated with children's considerate behavior toward their peers, but when both techniques were considered, the findings were different. When parents were rated low in power assertion, there was a significant positive association between reported use of reasoning and children's altruism with peers. For children whose parents rated high in power assertion, parental reasoning and children's altruism were negatively related. These findings clearly point to the necessity of considering disciplinary techniques as a pattern of relationships and interventions, not single techniques in isolation.

Hoffman and Saltzstein (1967) and Hoffman (1975) followed this study with studies of older children. Children's reputations among peers on altruistic qualities, children's moral reasoning, and their (projective) guilt over wrong-doing were measured and related to reported parental discipline. With this work as stimulus, other investigators carried out similar studies. The theoretical orientations in almost all of these studies are the same: (1) that power techniques would be negatively related to prosocial behavior, because with external authority as the motivating condition for the child's prosocial behavior, this behavior would not be internalized; and (2) the other-oriented reasoning would be positively related to prosocial behavior, because reasoning was believed to develop sensitivity and empathy on the part of the child. Motivations for prosocial behavior would develop and reside within the child. The findings do not unfailingly fall in line with these predictions.

Let us consider first the evidence on power assertion. In Hoffman and Saltzstein's (1967) study, there are negative associations with children's moral reasoning and (projective) guilt over wrong-doing, in line with predictions. However, it is only with middle-class girls that mother's power assertion relates negatively to peer assessments of the child's altruism. Dlugokinski and Firestone (1973) found that parental power assertion was negatively associated both with children's other-oriented values and understanding of kindness, and with their behavior on an experimental measure of sharing. In a retrospective study, Block (1969), too, found negative associations between college students' involvement in humanitarian causes and their recollections of their parents' use of punishment and power. Power assertion was unrelated to children's altruism in the Dlugo-kinski and Firestone study when altruism was indexed by peer nomina-tions. Generally nonsignificant associations were found in studies by Mussen, Harris, Rutherford, and Keasey (1970); Feshbach (1975); and Zahn-Waxler et al. (1979). Middle-class mothers' and fathers' power as-sertion was positively related to peer measures of altruism in boys in Hoffman and Saltzstein's study. When power was defined as stern de-mands combined with explanation, it was positively related to children's altruism in the Zahn-Waxler et al. study.

Based on data from many of these same studies, reasoning techniques and children's altruism are either positively related or unrelated. In the Hoffman and Saltzstein study, parental reasoning and children's level of moral reasoning and guilt tended to be positively associated, but this was only in a middle-class sample. In the same study, peer judgments of altruism and parental reasoning were positively related only for girls. In Hoffman's 1975 study, positive associations were found between girls' altruism and fathers' reported reasoning and between boys' altruism and mothers' reasoning. Dlugokinski and Firestone, Block, and Zahn-Waxler et al. (the studies previously cited) found positive associations. Reasoning by parents and boys' altruism were unrelated in the study of Hoffman and Saltzstein. These variables were unrelated also in studies of Mussen et al. (1970), Feshbach (1975), and Staub (1971).

Such less-than-decisive findings on power and reasoning require stock-taking of hypotheses and concepts, and most certainly of research strate-gies. Some of the continuing ambiguities arise from the fact that research has proceeded without clarifying the concepts or obtaining more direct measures of parent's behavior. Moreover, the research has not taken the important clue furnished in the first Hoffman study; namely, that power assertion and reasoning are both likely to be used to some degree by parents and that these methods need to be studied in their interactive effects. Further, the kinds of prosocial behavior and the kinds of motiva-tions for behaving prosocially need also to be considered in relation to parental power-assertive and reasoning methods.

Reasoning approaches in the rearing of children seem "civilized" and appeal to the rational human. Moreover, in the value system of many investigators, there is an equation of external power or authority with harmful control of children. It has been advocated, for example, that through attributional techniques the adult can accomplish compliance from the child with a minimal perception of external power and that this is the optimal approach (Perry & Perry, 1983). However, the scientific task is to proceed to an analysis of the various forms of assertive authority and of reasoning, and in so doing, to give close consideration to the consequences of these interventions in terms of the cognitive, affective, and motivational processes affected by them. Henry's (1980) theoretical critique of the concepts of power assertion and reasoning is one such effort. She challenges the presumed opposition or mutually exclusive nature of power and reasoning: Reasoning, she says, is always authority.

One troubling aspect of the present evidence and theorizing about power and reasoning in relation to prosocial behavior is that there is little information about when and how the control techniques are actually used by parents. In the total of the child's rearing conditions, how often and for what provocations are the techniques used? With what parental emotion are the techniques administered? What affects are engendered in the child by these methods? For example, some parental reasoning is administered with anxiety and guilt, and probably engenders such feelings in the child. In some of these instances, the child may be led to feel realistically guilty about an act committed, which may create the motive to make prosocial reparation either in the immediate or more general sense. In this case, one might speculate that realistic guilt has an important role in moral development (Hoffman, 1976). In other instances, parents' use of guilt induction may be such as to generate in children irrational and unresolvable guilt feelings. How these affective qualities of parents' power-assertion and reasoning influence children's prosocial behavior we do not know.

An observation made by Tomkins (1963) is most relevant in bringing another perspective to the issue of parental affective variables and child's prosocial development. He focuses on parents' affective communications with their children specifically in circumstances in which the child is feeling helpless or distressed. Tomkins suggests that when the parent responds to the distressed child nurturantly and sympathetically, the child can express distress without feelings of shame and guilt, and can, therefore, respond, like the parent, with open sympathy and help to another person's distress. Parents who respond to their children's feelings of distress coldly or with contempt may be teaching children to suppress their own feelings and to avoid getting involved in another person's distress. There is some research evidence supporting this formulation (Zahn-Waxler et al., 1979) but mainly it is an important question awaiting research.

Until research is done that allows one to make the kinds of distinctions that have been enumerated with regard to parents' reactive disciplinary techniques, and until parental discipline is observed rather than reported, it is necessary to refrain from generalizing broadly about the socialization of prosocial behavior through specific power or reasoning techniques.

Let us return for a moment to "reasoning," disregarding flaws in definitions and procedures. As we have seen in the research just reviewed, the reported use of reasoning in discipline was often unrelated to prosocial behavior, but when there were significant associations the direction of association was always positive. Let us consider parents' reasoning in a broader sense; namely, as teaching and discussing, and not tied to discipline. A different kind of investigation of reasoning in relation to prosocial values and behavior is thereby suggested. One might expect family discourse about interpersonal relations and social events to influence children's sensitivities and empathic feelings, perhaps as much as or more so than reasoning in disciplinary encounters. Burton (1976) and Staub (1979) have suggested that parents, by the ways in which they interpret social information and reason about social and moral dilemmas, influence the kinds of categories of moral acts and the kinds of generalizations about prosocial behavior that children develop. In fact, parental reasoning in discourse should influence the consistencies and inconsistencies in a child's prosocial behavior. A kind of research is needed that concerns itself with how parents teach children so as to translate principles and moral reasoning into behavior.

The findings discussed earlier regarding children's participation with their parents in altruistic activities and children's being given social responsibilities become relevant here. Both provide circumstances in which social information is likely to be given and discussed by the parent, *and* both are circumstances that combine discourse with translation into behavior. It would be interesting to analyze the reasoning in which parents engage with their children in such nondisciplinary situations. These situations may be as significant for the learning and practice of mature moral judgments as settings of emotional stress that accompany discipline. A few studies may be tapping family discourse when they investigated moral values in the family. Olejnik and McKinney (1973) described parents in terms of their general orientation to controlling their children—as valuing either a prescriptive orientation (presumably conveying information to their children) or a proscriptive orientation. The more generous children were found in the families of prescriptive orientation. Hoffman (1975) also reported on parent values. When parents' espousal of altruistic values, their affection toward their children, and their disciplinary techniques were examined in relation to children's altruism toward their peers, it was parents' values that were most closely related to peer assessments of altruism. These studies suggest that the discipline setting has perhaps been unduly emphasized as the locus of learning.

A final comment on the family as a self-contained unit of influence on the child's development of prosocial behavior: The data we have reviewed and the hypotheses we have suggested have dealt with parental factors in promoting prosocial behavior as if all other aspects of the child's person were "held constant." This is obviously not reality. What parents provide that is contributing positively or negatively to their children's prosocial development is also contributing to other facets of their children's behavior. As children differ in aggression, ego strength, intelligence, sex role, level of anxiety, etc. (whether we assume constitutional or rearing origins), they will be socialized differently and will be different in outcome. The combination of variables of child personality and parental behavior in relation to the child's prosocial behavior has not been dealt with. Research looking only at child personality and prosocial behavior shows modest relations. Among the personality characteristics found to be positively related to altruism are ego strength and ego resiliency (Block & Block, 1973; Mussen et al., 1970), and affiliativeness (Bond & Phillips, 1971). Positive and negative associations have been found between aggression and altruism (Feshbach & Feshbach, 1969; Muste & Sharpe, 1947; Yarrow & Zahn-Waxler, 1976). Children's immediate momentary affective state (Barnett, King, & Howard, 1979; Rosenhan, Underwood, & Moore, 1974) is linked in complicated and inconsistent ways with their prosocial responding.

FAMILY AS MEDIATOR OF SOCIETY AND CULTURE

This formulation of family influences as mediators of society and culture is more likely from sociologists and anthropologists than psychologists. However, regardless of discipline, it is generally accepted that children learn norms, skills, and motivations that are to some degree uniquely patterned by the culture, society, or class into which they are born. Precisely what this entails regarding prosocial values and behaviors is hard to say. The prescriptions and proscriptions of different social groups concerning charity, helping, honesty, compassion, and so on are not well documented. Although there are nationwide economic indicators, and national and cross-national statistics on crime and delinquency to provide bases for group comparisons of current status and change over time, there are no similar descriptive societal statistics for prosocial behavior. Without such indicators it is difficult to describe families as adhering or not to the standards and practices of their class and culture. If descriptive data on prosocial norms and conduct were available, one might ask very interesting questions concerning the types of family practices that are associated with social–cultural differences in the behavior of children and youth. If different social groups develop (or fail to develop) prosocial behaviors of various kinds in their children and youth, what parental values and practices are associated with such differences? If different social groups achieve similar outcomes in their children's prosocial behaviors, do they achieve these outcomes by the same routes?

Among the studies of parental values and practices in which culture and social class have been used as classificatory variables, a small number are relevant to prosocial socialization. The six-culture study by the Whitings (1975) (mentioned earlier) compared children on frequency of helping behaviors. Differences in the extent to which children were assigned family responsibilities were viewed as the rearing link that explained cultural differences in children's prosocial responding. In a long series of studies initiated by Madsen (1967), children of Mexican, Mexican–American, and Anglo–American cultures were compared on a test of cooperation. Group differences in children's cooperation favoring the Mexican cultures were explained in terms of differences in the living conditions in the cultures (e.g., the bare subsistence level of the Mexican rural poor demand cooperation from everyone in order to stay alive; hence, it was reasoned, the higher level of cooperation among children of this background). Studies of social class in relation to children's selfish or unselfish behavior have been carried out in British, American, and Israeli cultures (see review in Radke-Yarrow et al., 1983) with very inconsistent findings. Sometimes prosocial behavior is more frequent in the advantaged classes, sometimes it is less frequent, and sometimes there are no class differences. Further research pursuits along these descriptive, comparative lines seem to be unpromising. If we are to understand the family as a mediator of culture and class, it will be necessary to formulate research strategies that deal directly with the linkages between society, family interactions, and child behavior.

This brings us back to the kinds of family influences (parental model, disciplinary techniques, content of family experience) discussed earlier. Now, however, we are concerned with how the social institutions and conditions that govern the lives of parents are influential in shaping these parental behaviors. We would assume that parents bring to their family roles elements and patterns of experience from their occupational daily lives, their negotiations in daily interactions in the neighborhood or city in which they live, their participation in organized groups (e.g., religion, union, club), their daily meeting of economic needs, and so on. Some of the experiences affect parents' own positive, negative, or callous orientations toward other persons. All of these experiences are relatively routinized in parents' lives and are shared by other adults of similar class or culture. The research problems and strategies are then matters of investigating the nature of these routinized and shared experiences and how they translate into specific behaviors and values in the parent role.

One interesting beginning toward linking societal experiences with parents' child-rearing philosophies and practices if found in the work of Kohn (1969/1977) and Kohn and Schooler (1973). The merit of this work is that societal and interpersonal variables begin to appear in research as comparable units or levels of behavior. In this research, fathers' occupational lives were operationalized in terms of the kinds of supervision the men were given and the kinds of authority relations under which they lived on the job. These interpersonal experiences were the backdrop in analyzing the men's interpersonal behavior in their family roles: when they became the authority figures. The men were interviewed about their methods of controlling their children and their valued child behaviors. Fathers who in their work life were highly self-directed and who had little supervision valued self-control in their children. They were also less likely to report using physical punishment than were fathers in highly supervised and authoritarian job settings. These findings have been replicated in a number of countries (reviewed in Kohn, 1977). Kohn's study did not proceed to the next possible link in a chain of influences; namely, did the children behave differently? One might assume that for fathers with these different job experiences, different child-rearing practices would be in effect, and their children, possibly, would perceive these practices in different lights and would behave differently.

This model seems especially appropriate in the investigation of origins of empathic or callous orientations toward other persons. Such analyses would give us some understanding of the inconsistent correlational findings (cited above) relating culture and prosocial behavior. They would provide insight into some of the conditions maintaining and motivating parental conduct. They would also enable us to deal with a society–individual issue that appears not infrequently in child-rearing research, and that is seldom explored. It is the finding that relations between given parental techniques and child behavior in one social class or culture are not obtained in another group; also that relations that are obtained for a group at one time in history are not done so at another. Two examples are (1) in the research of Hoffman and Saltzstein (1967) (cited earlier) parental techniques of power and reasoning had different effects on boys and girls from families of middle and working classes, and (2) the 1955 Havinghurst and Davis study of social class and parental practices failed to replicate 10 years later. For interpretations of these differences one might turn to analyses of the social contexts in which rearing takes place. For instance, when one observes a parent's disciplinary approach to a child, it is important to know how that approach is regarded by the parents' and the child's reference groups. A given parental disciplinary act may produce guilt in one social group, but be fully accepted in another. Likewise, for some families, certain environmental realities are such that socialization of trusting behavior and helpfulness could endanger the child. Viewing parental behavior from two vantage points simultaneously—the interpersonal dynamics of parent and child and the impinging personal—societal experiences of parent and child—has promise of leading to better comprehension of how children's social behaviors are learned.

FAMILY CHANGE

Family factors in the development of prosocial children and youth have been treated almost like "traits," as if the family were a stable set of conditions and influences. There are the expected developmental changes in family life and functioning but, in addition, families experience severe changes of a nonnormative or nondevelopmental sort. Some changes suddenly and unexpectedly punctuate the status quo; other changes are progressive. Some changes are individual in origin, such as illness or death of a parent, or sudden occupational success or failure. Other changes come as the result of events of history or social change (e.g., war, natural calamity, economic collapse).

Children in the throes and aftermath of family disruption have interested investigators over the years. Examples are Stolz, et al. (1954) studies of children of war-absent and war-returned fathers, Elder's (1974) follow-up of children who lived through the economic depression of the 1930s, and Hetherington, Cox, and Cox's (1979) children of divorce and of newly constructed families. It is not our purpose to review this research; moreover, in these studies, children's positive other-oriented behaviors have not been emphasized in the context of family change. Instead, we pose as an important unmapped area of problems the kinds of impact that major experiences of family disruption are likely to have on children's capacities for empathy and altruism.

There are reasons to assume that other-oriented behaviors are particularly vulnerable in such circumstances, since in many of the disruptions the child loses a parent, or an intimate relationship with a parent, or the parent's own competencies and well-being have suffered. This can mean loss of parental support in the child's learning prosocial behavior. The family disequilibrium may so threaten the child's self-concept and coping skills that positive other-oriented behavior may be sacrificed.

At least three general questions deserve study in relation to disrupted family experience: First, what are preconditions in the family that sustain children through family disturbance, and allow them to emerge with a basically positive self-concept and with empathy and positive other-oriented responding remaining intact? Second, what are critical factors during and after the disruption that affect the fate of childrens' prosocial orientations? The third question is probably a slice of the first two: It is the old issue of hardship and deprivation as contributors to moral growth. When does adversity contribute to positive outcome, when not?

We are very limited in our knowledge with respect to these questions. The questions themselves need to become more integrated into the mainstream of child-rearing theory and research, because most families suffer and succeed at various points in the family life cycle, and children's social development is influenced by both the regular and the unusual in family life.

CONCLUSIONS

Research on prosocial behavior represents a scientific investment in understanding the humaneness of humans. The research reviewed begins with the assumption that relationships and experiences in the family contribute significantly to the prosocial qualities of its members. It is not an extreme position; it is not assumed that family influences stand alone in responsibility or even that they are most important in all circumstances. Family influence on prosocial development is a typical "socialization" problem in psychological research. What is unique to prosocial behavior? Might we have found research problems and research results very similar for almost any positive dimension of social behavior? How advanced and precise is our knowledge in this area?

A major advance is the fact of the topic itself. The child's ability and motivation to extend the self, to be concerned with the well-being of others is now an acknowledged aspect of social and personality development, along with ego strength, achievement motivation, competence, extroversion, and so on. Empathy and the inability to be empathic have come under scrutiny in child development as serious components of interpersonal functioning. Although there have been no startling breakthroughs regarding parental influences, there has been a slow accumulation of understanding concerning conditions that foster and those that interfere with prosocial development. There is overwhelming evidence of multiple routes to prosocial motivations and behavior as aspects of the individual. Many of the socialization processes contributing to children's prosocial development are also important in the development of other positive facets of social development. This is not surprising since one assumes interrelations of different aspects of personality. It is perhaps to be hoped that considerations of empathic prosocial behavior would be further integrated into personality studies.

As a field of investigation compared with research on aggression, research on prosocial behavior is quite primitive. A major short-coming in the existing research is its criteria of "prosocial." There have been only a few studies in which family influences have been measured against prosocial outcomes of great consequence or robustness. Criteria need to be overhauled in two respects: The first is to give up reliance on the very innocuous and almost conventionalized prosocial behaviors that reappear in studies, and to attempt to index more spontaneous and more serious caregiving. The second is to differentiate among prosocial behaviors on psychological bases in terms of motivational and cognitive content. Until both changes are made, this field of research will be relatively limited in predicting or controlling prosocial behavior in ways that make a difference in the lives of individuals and groups.

Issues of research strategy and design are closely linked with problems of criterion measures. Experimental social learning paradigms of the past decades have been played out. New experimental and field approaches and new problem formulations will determine the future directions of research. In a number of respects, prosocial research is especially challenging. One such challenge pertains to the further investigation of cognitive and affective processes in prosocial actions. Another lies in investigation of the child's capacities and incapacities for empathy and prosocial behavior in both normal and psychopathological development. There is promise, too, in research endeavors in which interpersonal dynamics of parent–child interaction are investigated in their broader contexts—biological and societal–cultural. Evolutionary and genetic contributions should not be overlooked as possibly inherent sources of altruism, interacting with environment. Societal factors have received far too little attention. A further challenge for research lies in interventions that foster and support children's prosocial behavior in ways that balance the interests of self and others.

REFERENCES

Akamatsu, T. J., & Thelen, M. A review of the literature on observer characteristics and imitation. *Developmental Psychology,* 1974, *10*(1), 38–47.
Barnett, M. A., King, L. M., & Howard, J. A. Inducing affect about self or other: Effects on generosity in children. *Developmental Psychology,* 1979, *15,* 164–167.
Bathurst, J. E. A study of sympathy and resistance (negativism) among children. *Psychological Bulletin,* 1933, *30,* 625–626.
Baumrind, D. Parental disciplinary patterns and social competence in children. *Youth and Society,* 1978, *9,* 239–276.
Block, J., & Block, J. H. Ego development and the provenance of thought: A longitudinal study of ego and cognitive development in young children. Progress report for National Institute of Mental Health, Grant No. MH 16080, January, 1973.

Block, J. H., Haan, N., & Smith, M. B. Socialization correlates of student activism. *Journal of Social Issues*, 1969, *25*, 143–177.

Bond, N. D., & Phillips, B. N. Personality traits associated with altruistic behavior of children. *Journal of School Psychology*, 1971, *9*, 24–34.

Bryan, J. H., & Walbek, N. H. Preaching and practicing generosity: Children's actions and reactions. *Child Development*, 1970, *41*, 329–353.

Burton, R. V. Honesty and dishonesty. In T. Lickona (Ed.), *Moral development and behavior*. New York: Holt, Rinehart & Winston, 1976.

Crockenberg, S. B., Bryant, B. K., & Wilce, L. S. The effects of cooperatively and competively structured learning environments on inter- and intrapersonal behavior. *Child Development*, 1976, *47*, 386–396.

Dlugokinski, E. L., & Firestone, I. J. Congruence among four methods of measuring other-centeredness. *Child Development*, 1973, *44*, 304–308.

Eisenberg-Berg, N., & Geisheker, E. Content of preachings and power of the model/preacher: The effect on children's generosity. *Developmental Psychology*, 1979, *15*, 168–175.

Elder, G. H., Jr. *Children of the great depression*. Chicago: University of Chicago Press, 1974.

Feshbach, N. D. The relationship of child-rearing factors in children's aggression, empathy, and related positive and negative behaviors. In J. de Wit & W. W. Hartup (Eds.), *Determinants and origins of aggressive behavior*. The Hague, Netherlands: Mouton, 1975.

Feshbach, N. D., & Feshbach, S. The relationship between empathy and aggression in two age groups. *Developmental Psychology*, 1969, *1*, 102–107.

Grusec, J. E. Power and the internalization of self-denial. *Child Development*, 1971, *42*, 93–105.

Grusec, J. E., & Skubiski, S. L. Model nurturance, demand characteristics of the modeling experiment, and altruism. *Journal of Personality and Social Psychology*, 1970, *14*, 352–359.

Hartshorne, H., & May, M. A. *Studies on the nature of character: Studies in deceit*, (Vol. 1). New York: Macmillan, 1928.

Havighurst, R., & Davis, A. A comparison of the Chicago and Harvard studies of social class differences in child rearing. *American Sociological Review*, 1955, *20*, 438–442.

Henry, R. M. A theoretical and empirical analysis of 'reasoning' in the socialization of young children. *Human Development*, 1980, *23*, 105–125.

Hetherington, E. M., Cox, M., & Cox, R. Stress and coping in divorce: A focus on women. In J. E. Gullihorn (Ed.), *Psychology and women: In transition*. Washington, DC: Winston & Sons, 1979.

Hoffman, M. L. Parent discipline and the child's consideration for others. *Child Development*, 1963, *34*, 573–588.

Hoffman, M. L. Altruistic behavior and the parent-child relationship. *Journal of Personality and Social Psychology*, 1975, *31*, 937–943.

Hoffman, M. L. Empathy, role taking, guilt, and development of altruistic motives. In T. Lickona (Ed.), *Moral development and behavior*. New York: Holt, Rinehart, & Winston, 1976.

Hoffman, M. L., & Saltzstein, H. D. Parent discipline and the child's moral development. *Journal of Personality and Social Psychology*, 1967, *5*, 45–57.

Iannotti, R. J. Effect of role-taking experiences on role taking, empathy, altruism, and aggression. *Developmental Psychology*, 1978, *14*, 119–124.

Johnson, D. W., & Johnson, R. T. Instructional goal structure: Cooperative, competitive, or individualistic. *Review of Education Research*, 1974, *44*, 213–240.

Kohn, M. L. Class and Conformity: A study in values. Chicago: University of Chicago Press, 1977. (Originally published in 1969).

Kohn, M. L., & Schooler, C. Occupational experience and psychological functioning: An assessment of reciprocal effects. *American Sociological Review*, 1973, *38*, 97–118.

London, P. The rescuers: Motivational hypotheses about Christians who saved Jews from the Nazis. In J. Macaulay & L. Berkowitz (Eds.), *Altruism and helping behavior*. New York: Academic Press, 1970.

Madsen, M. C. Cooperative and competitive motivation of children in three Mexican subcultures. *Psychological Reports*, 1967, *20*, 1307–1320.

Muste, M. J., & Sharpe, D. F. Some influential factors in the determination of aggressive behavior in preschool children. *Child Development*, 1947, *18*, 11–28.

Mussen, P., & Eisenberg-Berg, N. *Caring, sharing, and helping*. San Francisco: W. H. Freeman, 1977.

Mussen, P., Harris, S., Rutherford, E., & Keasey, C. B. Honesty and altruism among preadolescents. *Developmental Psychology*, 1970, *3*, 169–194.

Olejnik, A. B., & McKinney, J. P. Parental value orientation and generosity in children. *Developmental Psychology*, 1973, *8*, 311.

Perry, D. G., & Perry, L. C. Social learning, causal attribution and moral internalization. In G. L. Bisanz, J. Bisanz, & R. V. Kail (Eds.), *Learning in children: Progress in cognitive development research*. New York: Springer-Verlag, 1983.

Poulos, R. W., & Liebert, R. M. Influence of modeling, exhortative verbalization, and surveillance on children's sharing. *Developmental Psychology*, 1972, *6*, 402–408.

Rachman, S. The concept of required helpfulness. *Behavior Research and Therapy*, 1979, *17*, 1–6.

Radke-Yarrow, M., & Zahn-Waxler, C. Roots, motives and patterns in children's prosocial behavior. In E. Staub, D. Bar-Tal, J. Karylowski, & J. Reykowski (Eds.), *The development and maintenance of prosocial behavior: International perspectives*. New York: Plenum Press, 1984.

Radke-Yarrow, M., Zahn-Waxler, C., Chapman, M. Children's prosocial dispositions and behavior. In P. H. Mussen (Ed.), *Manual of Child Psychology*. New York: Wiley, 1983.

Rosenhan, D. Some origins of concern for others. In P. H. Mussen, J. Laanger, and M. Covington (Eds.), *Trends and issues in developmental psychology*. New York: Holt, Rinehart and Winston, 1969.

Rosenhan, D., & White, G. M. Observation and rehearsal as determinants of prosocial behavior. *Journal of Personality and Social Psychology*, 1967, *5*, 424–431.

Rosenhan, D. L., Underwood, B., & Moore, B. Affect moderates self-gratification and altruism. *Journal of Personality and Social Psychology*, 1974, *30*, 546–552.

Rushton, J. P. *Altruism, socialization, and society*. Englewood Cliffs, NJ: Prentice-Hall, 1980.

Rushton, J. P., & Sorrentino, R. M. (Eds.). *Altruism and helping behavior: Social, personality, and developmental perspectives*. Hillsdale, NJ: Lawrence Erlbaum Associates, 1981.

Sagi, A., & Hoffman, M. L. Empathic distress in the newborn. *Developmental Psychology*, 1976, *12*, 175–176.

Simner, M. Newborn's response to the cry of another infant. *Developmental Psychology*, 1971, *5*, 136–150.

Staub, E. A child in distress: The effects of focusing responsibility on children on their attempts to help. *Developmental Psychology*, 1970, *2*, 152–154.

Staub, E. The use of role playing and induction in children's learning of helping and sharing behavior. *Child Development*, 1971, *42*, 805–816.

Staub, E. *Positive social behavior and morality: Socialization and development*, (Vol. 2). New York: Academic Press, 1979.

Stolz, L. *Father relations of war-born children*. Stanford: Stanford University Press, 1954.

Sroufe, L. A. Socioemotional development. In J. Osofsky (Ed.), *Handbook of infant development*. New York: John Wiley & Sons, 1979.

Tomkins, S. S. *Affect imagery, consciousness, Vol. II. The negative affects*. New York: Springer, 1963.

Waters, E., Wippman, J., & Sroufe, L. A. Attachment, positive affect, and competence in the peer group: Two studies in construct validation. *Child Development*, 1979, *50*, 821–829.

Waxler, C. Z., & Yarrow, M. R. An observational study of maternal models. *Developmental Psychology*, 1975, *11*, 485–494.

Weissbrod, C. S. Noncontingent warmth induction, cognitive style, and children's imitative donation and rescue effort behaviors. *Journal of Personality and Social Psychology*, 1976, *34*, 274–281.

Whiting, B., & Whiting, J. W. M. *Children of six cultures*. Cambridge, MA: Harvard University Press, 1975.

Whiting, J. W. M., & Whiting, B. B. Altruistic and egoistic behavior in six cultures. In L. Nader & T. W. Maretzki (Eds.), *Cultural illness and health: Essays in human adaptation*. Washington, DC: American Anthropological Association, 1973.

Wolf, T., & Cheyne, J. Persistence of effects of live behavioral, televised behavioral, and live verbal models on resistance in deviation. *Child Development*, 1972, *43*, 1429–1436.

Wispe, L. (Ed.). *Altruism, sympathy, and helping: Psychological and sociological principles*. New York: Academic Press, 1978.

Yando, R., Seitz, B., & Zigler, E. *Imitation: A developmental perspective*. New York: Wiley & Sons, 1978.

Yarrow, M. R., Scott, P. M., & Waxler, C. Z. Learning concern for others. *Developmental Psychology*, 1973, *8*, 240–260.

Zahn-Waxler, C. *The social–emotional development of young children with a manic-depressive parent*. Paper presented at Review of the Board of Scientific Counselors, NIMH, May 1981, Maryland, Bethesda.

Zahn-Waxler, C., McKnew, D. H., Cummings, E. M., & Radke-Yarrow, M. Problem behaviors and peer interactions of young children with a manic-depressive parent. *American Journal of Psychiatry*, 1984, *141*, 235–240.

Zahn-Waxler, C., Radke-Yarrow, M., & King, R. Child rearing and children's prosocial initiations toward victims of distress. *Child Development*, 1979, *50*, 319–330.

11

The Contribution of Siblings to Training for Fighting: A Microsocial Analysis

G. R. PATTERSON

There is a growing consensus to the effect that much of a child's antisocial behavior is learned and that much of the early training takes place in the home (McCord, 1978; Pulkkinen, 1982; Robins & Ratcliff, 1978; West & Farrington, 1973). However, it is not clear which conditions within the home actually facilitate the child's learning of fighting behavior. There are two hypotheses explored in the present essay that relate to this issue. The first, briefly explored, is that disruptions in specific child-rearing practices produce increases in antisocial behavior. The hypothesis is that parental failure to monitor and to discipline antisocial behaviors contributes directly to these increases. The second hypothesis, and the major focus for this essay, is that the microsocial processes define the means by which disruptions in family management lead to increases in fighting both within and outside the home (e.g., they explain why inept discipline leads to fighting). Molecular analyses of the exchanges between the problem children and their siblings describe how this comes about.

A microsocial analysis is based upon interactional sequences; the data are collected over repeated sessions in the home. Typically, a code system categorizes the behavior of the target person and the reaction of a family member. A computer analysis typically reveals that there are certain patterns of action and reaction that repeat themselves frequently enough to be identifiable. The assumption is that the behavior of each participant serves in a dual role of stimulus for the reaction that follows and possibly as a reinforcer or punisher of the event that preceded it (Patterson, 1982). Given even a moderately consistent set of contingencies, it is reasonable to believe that, over repeated trails, one or both persons may show alterations in the probability of occurrence of certain reactions to the other person. This, in fact, has been demonstrated by Snyder and Patterson (1984). In the present context the behaviors of concern would be increases in the likelihood of certain coercive behaviors that commonly occur in the children of distressed and nondistressed families. Observation studies routinely demonstrate that these coercive behaviors are found more frequently in the interactions of all members from families of antisocial (Burgess & Conger, 1976; Patterson, 1982; Snyder, 1977) and abused children (Reid, Patterson, & Loeber, 1982;) as compared to normal families. What is of particular interest in the present report is the means by which these high rates of such relatively trivial events as yelling, threatening, teasing, and temper tantrums become transformed into such high-amplitude behaviors as hitting, pushing, and attack with an object.

The intent of the report is to present a general formulation about how the training might occur and then to identify empirical referrents from existing data sets to determine whether the findings are consistent with the hypotheses. An appropriate test for the causal contribution of siblings to fight training would require a longitudinal design. Such a study is currently under way for a sample of 10-year-old boys in a follow-up design with repeated probes at 2-year intervals.

One implication of the sibling-trainer hypothesis is that there should be significant covariation in the antisocial symptoms for the problem child and siblings. In effect, although siblings train the problem child to be increasingly antisocial, it is also the case that they, in turn, are subjected to the effects of the same program.

Similarity of Siblings and Problem Child

The sibling-trainer hypothesis requires significant covariation between the target child and his or her siblings in the incidence of antisocial behavior. It should be noted, however, that significant findings would equally support hypotheses concerning shared biological determinants (Mednick & Christiansen, 1977) and almost any other formulation that includes family variables as determinants for antisocial behavior.

A number of studies have noted similarities in various trait behaviors such as nervous habits (Olson, 1929), interests (Grotevant, Sears, & Weinberg, 1977), and acceptance by peers (Sells & Roff, 1967). Typically these correlations range in magnitude from .20 to .35. Lurie (1970) found that 70% of the siblings of problem children were perceived by parents as emotionally impaired. In addition, the severity of impairment for the labeled problem child covaried with the severity of impairment for the siblings.

Neilsen and Gerber (1979) found that brothers and sisters of chronic truants also tended to be truant. Three studies found correlations between the incidence of delinquent behavior in the target child and siblings (Reid, Patterson, & Weinrott, 1984; Wadsworth, 1979; West & Farrington, 1973). The Wadsworth (1979) study also showed that problem children with older siblings were at greater risk for delinquency than were those with younger siblings.

Observation data collected in the homes of 22 families of antisocial children referred for treatment also provide support for the similarity hypothesis (Patterson, 1982). The Total Aversive Behavior score (the sum of 14 coercive categories) for the problem child correlated .61 ($p < .01$) with the comparable score for male siblings and .63 ($p < .01$) with the score for female siblings. The survey studies by Dengerink and Covey (1981) showed that subjects who had an early history of violence with their siblings also tended to report more violence toward people outside the family. A similar finding was obtained in the retrospective comparison study of adolescent assaulters or thieves (Loeber, Weissman, & Reid, 1983). When initially referred to a clinic for treatment, 64% of the mothers of boys who later became assaulters indicated that they considered their son's fighting with siblings a serious problem. The comparable figure for the mothers of boys who later became thieves was 20%. These two likelihoods differed significantly, as shown by the probability value of .06 for the Fisher exact test.

The findings are consistent with the hypothesis that siblings and the target child are similar across a considerable range of traits including antisocial behavior. Given that one child is labeled delinquent and/or antisocial, there is a significant likelihood that one or more of the siblings will be similarily labeled.

Family Size and Ordinal Ranking and Sex of Sibling

The sibling-trainer hypothesis implies that target children without siblings would be less likely to learn to hit than would children from families where siblings are present. In the same vein, larger family size would mean not only that more trainers are available but that, in addition, perhaps the adults would have more difficulty in carrying out effective family management practices.

Several studies have shown that family size is significantly correlated with parental reports and official records of antisocial behavior (Rutter, Tizard, & Whitmore, 1970; West & Farrington, 1973). Observations in the homes of normal and clinical samples also showed a significant correlation between family size and observed rates of coercive child behavior (Burgess, Kimball, & Burgess, 1978).

The next hypothesis examined is that only children are at less risk for antisocial behavior than are children at other ordinal rankings (e.g., middle, youngest, etc.). Anderson (1969) cited her own findings as well as those from several other studies in support of the fact that children referred for treatment as aggressive tended to be the middle children. "Neurotics" tended to be first born. Consistent with these findings, a sample of children with conduct problems referred to the Oregon Social Learning Center tended to be the second born (Patterson, 1976). However, none of these studies corrected for the base rates or expected occurrences of an only child, a middle child, or a youngest child, etc. The large-scale survey of the Isle of Wight by Rutter, et al. (1970) showed that even when corrected for expected values, highly aggressive boys tended to occupy the middle position significantly more often than expected by chance and less often than the youngest or only child positions. It may be that the middle position is so facilitative because such a child would have both older and younger siblings to serve as both models and victims.

Are the rates of antisocial behavior higher for cross-sex sibling interactions? The observation study by Pepler, Abramovitch, and Corter (1981) showed that interactions among mixed-sex sibling pairs were significantly more aggressive than those between like-sex siblings. Furthermore, this aggressivity increased over an 18-month follow-up period. The study by Dunn and Kendrick (1981) also showed significantly greater aggressivity for mixed-sex sibling pairs. However, observation data collected in the homes of normal and clinical samples showed no difference in rates for the target child coercing male or female siblings (Patterson, in 1984). A comparable analysis involving different samples by Reid (1983b) also failed to demonstrate significant differences in the selection of male or female siblings as targets. However, Reid noted that females (siblings plus mother) are the target for roughly two-thirds of the problem child's aggression.

SETTING THE STAGE: FAMILY MANAGEMENT
PROCEDURES ARE DISRUPTED

For decades, one of the major tenets of developmental psychology has been that measures of child-rearing practices will account for significant variance in measures of child deviant behavior. However, the first decade's effort to establish this linkage was disappointing. The review by Frank (1965) showed inconsistent findings and a failure to replicate. Those correlations that did appear generally accounted for less than 5% of the variance. I believe that part of the difficulty arose from each investigator relying on the use of single assessment modes (e.g., an interview or questionnaire completed by *one* family member). The recent emphasis by Sullivan (1974) and others upon the use of multiple indicators to assess complex constructs, such as parenting practices, is an attempt to redress these earlier oversights (e.g., Patterson & Dishion, 1984; Patterson & Stouthamer-Loeber, 1984). The second problem lay in the fact that most of the child-rearing variables defined global variables such as warmth. These global concepts were selected on an a priori basis as being relevant to the understanding of antisocial behavior. The selected variables were not based on intensive study of families of aggressive children.

A decade of observations in the homes of antisocial and normal boys, plus treating several hundred families of antisocial and abused children, led us to the identification of four key family-management practices (Patterson, 1982). These families as compared to the normal families we studied seemed deficient in each of the four practices: providing consistent and effective discipline contingent upon antisocial behavior, monitoring or tracking the whereabouts of the child, providing positive reinforcement for prosocial skills, and effective problem solving (as a family).

The general model emphasizes the need for the parents, or at least the caretaker, to be contingent in some of their interactions with the child. The field studies emphasized the fact that normal parents tended to be contingent in two crucial areas, and in both respects differed from parents of antisocial boys. The normal parents reacted in a supportive or reinforcing manner to prosocial behaviors observed in the home; parents in the clinical samples were not only less reinforcing (e.g., approving) but they were also less likely to be contingent in their use of these social reinforcers (Patterson, 1982; Taplin & Reid, 1977). According to the model, these parental failures directly produce a child who is antisocial and very likely lacking in social survival skills in such areas as work, relationships, and academics.

In the present context, the key idea is that, even in normal families, parent failure to discipline coercive exchanges occurring at the rate of one every 3 minutes quickly sets the stage for extensive fight training. The coercive exchanges between parents and the problem child build in rate, duration, and amplitude as do the exchanges among siblings. Presumably, it is in the exchanges with the siblings that the participants learn to hit (when, how, whom, where) and to be hit. Given a failure on the part of

adults in the school and/or the home to use effective discipline generates a
setting in which the participants quickly learn the ways that accrue to the
effective use of pain control techniques, including physical assault.

First, there are two hypotheses that need to be examined. One is the
idea that the failure in the use of family management techniques can be
thought of as a low-order parental "trait." If this is the case, then one
would expect positive and significant correlations to hold among the four
measures of family management. The second hypothesis is that parental
failure to track and to discipline will covary with high rates of antisocial
behavior. To test these hypotheses multilevel assessments were made in
the families of several hundred preadolescent and adolescent boys (Patterson & Dishion, 1984). Each of the four family-management constructs
was defined by at least three variables (see Table 11.1); two of them
(monitor, positive parenting) were defined by multiple modes of assessment from several different agents.

The findings pertinent to the first hypothesis are summarized in Table
11.1. The median intercorrelation among the family management practices was .41. The range was .14–.73. The findings provide strong support
for the idea that disruptions in one kind of parent practice tend to be
accompanied by disruptions in other practices as well. In passing, it is
interesting to note that the parental traits with the highest correlation,
discipline and positive parenting, both drew heavily from the same assessment mode, observation in the home. Our current efforts include the

Table 11.1

Intercorrelations among Family Management Variables

	1	2	3	4
1. Monitoring[a]	1.0			
2. Discipline	.42** (50)	1.0		
3. Positive parenting	.36*** (71)	.73*** (52)	1.0	
4. Problem solve	.14* (148)	.40 (52)	.42*** (79)	1.0

[a] Variables are scored such that high scores represent poor skills.
The indicators that define each construct are labeled as follows: *monitor:* interview child, interview mother, interviewer rating, telephone
daily; *discipline:* interview child, observe in home; and *problem solve:*
three global ratings by coders of videotaped family and problem solving.

* $p \} .05.$
** $p \} .01.$
*** $p \} .001.$

ble 11.2

rrelation between Family Management and Child Antisocial Variables

Grades	Antisocial (general)[a] across settings				Multirespondent measure of stealing			
	4th	7th	10th	Total	4th	7th	10th	Total
onitoring	.28**	.44***	.51***	.37****	.08	.52****	.43***	.34****
	(53)	(53)	(41)	(137)	(57)	(55)	(37)	(149)
iscipline	.45***	.35***	.28*	.35****	.24	.62****	.30*	.38****
	(25)	(27)	(21)	(73)	(24)	(28)	(26)	(78)
sitive parenting	.39**	.45***	.32*	.40****	.19	.51***	.12	.29****
	(21)	(26)	(21)	(68)	(21)	(27)	(26)	(74)
oblem solving	.38***	.27**	.06	.27****	.15	.09	−.04	.06
	(54)	(65)	(36)	(155)	(58)	(67)	(44)	(169)

[a] The numbers in parentheses describe the size of the sample. The multiple indicators for the iterion scores were *antisocial:* mother, teacher, peer ratings; and *stealing:* mother and child.
* p } .10.

design of some additional assessment modes to expand the empirical definition for both of these constructs, but as it stands, the correlation suggests that failure to discipline may be highly related to parent failure to reinforce.

Table 11.2 summarizes the correlational data that tests the hypothesis that parenting practices covary with antisocial behavior. Here the findings are presented separately for three age groups: families of 4th-grade, 7th-grade, and 10th-grade boys. To test the hypothesis the family-management scores were correlated with two criterion measures of antisocial behavior. Both criterion measures also reflect the emphasis upon multiple indicators in defining constructs. Antisocial is a composite score assessing general aggressivity based upon the sum of the standardized ratings by parents, teachers, and peers. The stealing score is a summary of the ratings by teachers and by peers. Prior analyses had shown that for these samples there were significant decreases by age for fighting and significant increases in stealing.

The findings provide firm support for the hypothesis that disruptions in parental monitoring and discipline were associated with higher rates of general antisocial behavior. However, the findings for stealing provided only limited support for the hypothesis in that the correlations of both family management variables were nonsignificant for the youngest age group. Additional analyses have also shown that the positive parenting and problem-solving scores correlated significantly with criterion scores measuring academic and social skills (Patterson & Dishion, 1984).

The data provide reasonable support for both hypotheses; with one exception, each of the two key family-management variables correlated, as expected, with each of the criterion measures of antisocial behavior, separately for each of the three age groups. The major question addressed in the present essay concerns the means by which disruption in family management might produce increases in antisocial behavior. It is not intuitively obvious just how faulty discipline and monitoring of coercive exchanges with family members could produce boys who fight. One might grant that failure to discipline coercive exchanges might conceivably produce a rather immature and/or hyperactive child who is unpleasant to be around. But why should these disruptions relate to hitting or fighting? These are the issues considered in the sections that follow.

SOME ASSUMPTIONS UNDERLYING MICROSOCIAL ANALYSIS OF AGGRESSION

There are a number of assumptions implicit in the formulation of the sibling trainer. The assumptions are discussed in detail in the outline of coercion theory presented in Patterson (1982). One of the key assumptions is that some forms of "pathology," such as antisocial behavior, are thought to be the outcome of exchanges among family members. Microsocial analyses are designed to explicate this process. Processes of this kind have only been explored for depressed (Hautzinger, Linden, & Hoffman, 1984), antisocial (Patterson, 1982; Snyder, 1977), and abused child samples (Reid, Taplin, & Lorber, 1981; Reid et al., 1982). From this viewpoint, antisocial, depressive, and withdrawal symptoms are thought to be maintained by interactions with family members. A stronger statement of the position, the one ascribed to antisocial symptoms, is that the behavior of family members is the primary determinant in the initiation of the process that produced the symptoms. At a molecular level, the reactions of other family members serve to elicit and model the deviant behaviors; their reactions also reinforce and punish these behaviors. In effect, the family member who suffers because of the depressed and aggressive exchanges with the identified patient may in a sense be responsible for eliciting and maintaining the very symptoms that lead him or her to refer the family member to the clinic for help.

In the coercion formulation, the prior behavior of the other person is thought of as a stimulus (S) for the reaction (R) that follows it in time. At the third juncture in this sequence, the consequence provided by the other person can function in any one of three ways; each will alter the relation between the S and the R. The consequence can function as a positive reinforcer and will strengthen the connection such that given a future presentation of a similar S, the R is more likely to occur (i.e., the p (R/S) is increased). The recent studies of clinical and normal families by Reid (1983—a) showed that parents and siblings in the clinical samples were more likely than normals to provide positive consequences for coercive child behaviors (e.g., talk, attend, approve). If the consequence is neutral and/or positive whereas the antecedent was aversive, the arrangement defines negative reinforcement, which has been shown in experiments with both animals (Knutson & Viken, 1984) and family members (Patterson, 1982) to have a powerful effect in increasing the p (R/S) in a surprisingly small number of trials. Observations in the home also showed the schedule for negative reinforcement of coercive behavior was significantly greater in clinical than in normal samples (Patterson, 1982). If the consequence provided consists of a punishment such as time out or withdrawal of privileges, this weakens the connection between the S and the R. This is in keeping with the reformulation of the role of punishment by Church (1969) and Rachlin and Herrnstein (1969). Experimental studies of parents and children also demonstrate that such punishments reduce the likelihood of R given a future presentation of the S (Patterson, 1982). It is also the case that scoldings and threats do not seem to function as punishment, per se, but rather serve to extend the duration of coercive sequences.

On the average day there are hundreds of "trials" in which such connections are strengthened. Patterns of action and reactions begin to assume the status of "predictability" among family members and can also be detected by microanalytic techniques. The requirement is that extensive observations be carried out in the field setting and that the data be available for computer analyses. There are certain reliable patterns or structures that have been identified for mother's reactions to child behaviors (Patterson, 1984) and for children's reactions to siblings and to mothers (Patterson, 1977; 1982). One of these structures is discussed in a later section of this report.

These actions and reactions repeated hundreds of times produce patterns that have several interesting characteristics. After a period of time coercive actions tend increasingly to elicit coercive reactions, which in turn elicit further coercive reactions (i.e., the aversive exchanges are extended). The analyses demonstrate that coercive exchanges are significantly longer for the clinical than for the normal families (Patterson, 1982). It is assumed that during these extended exchanges it becomes increasingly likely that one member of the dyad will escalate the amplitude of their behavior and "win" the conflict (i.e., the other person terminates the aversive behavior and temporarily withdraws from the combat). The laboratory test of this hypothesis by Knutson, Fordyce, and Anderson (1982) provided a convincing demonstration of the fact that negative reinforcement can significantly strengthen the amplitude of attack behavior. Extended durations of coercive exchange and negative reinforcement strengthening the amplitude of the behavior for first one and then the other member are thought to be the key mechanisms involved in both spouse abuse and child abuse. They are also considered to be key components in the problem child and sibling interchanges. Presumably, it is during some extended interchange that either the sibling or the problem child increases the amplitude of coercive behavior. If the other member then backs off, the likelihood is increased that in future trials that member will employ high-amplitude behaviors of a similar kind. In keeping with the hypothesis, Reid et al. (1982) recently showed the likelihood of high-amplitude aggression increasing directly as a function of length of coercive sequences. We hypothesize that, if the two members are relatively equal in power, then each increase in amplitude is followed by the other member becoming increasingly likely to react at a higher amplitude. What we have then is an increasing spiral of high-amplitude aggression in which both members begin to use hit and attack with an object at increasing frequencies.

The general formulation about escalation in amplitude implies, in turn, a progression in the development of aggression. It probably begins with high rates of noncompliance, then moves to high rates of (nonphysical) behaviors such as yelling, teasing, and so forth to physical aggression such as pushing, shoving, hitting, attacking with an object, and physical injury to the victim. The progression is assumed to be transitive, such that all children who hit also yell and tease at high rates and are noncompliant, but not all high-rate teasers hit. For fight training the progression moves from low- to high-intensity aggression. As noted earlier, irritable exchanges, first with the caretaker and then with the siblings, are thought to play a key role in moving the target child along this progression.

The next assumption is a corollary of the others. Presumably, both members in an interaction are altered by coercive exchanges. It would follow then that both the target child and the siblings become increasingly aggressive. The findings presented earlier support this idea. However, it goes without saying that correlations such as these do not prove that they trained each other to be that way. However, it is also the case that the hypothesis would require that such correlations exist and that they be positive and significant.

The fifth assumption is that the more extreme the progression reached at home, the more likely the child is to be successful in efforts to generalize the antisocial behaviors to settings outside the home. The extremely aggressive child performs these behaviors at higher rates and amplitude in settings such as the neighborhood and school. They are therefore more likely to be effective in producing consequences similar to those provided by family members. In keeping with this assumption, the findings from several observation studies, reviewed in Patterson (1982), showed that 30–50% of the children referred for antisocial behaviors in the school also displayed these behaviors at home. Given a base rate of .10 for extreme aggression in either setting, the likelihood of obtaining it in both would be .01. It is interesting in this regard to note that boys identified as problems in both the home and the school have been shown to be at greater risk for delinquency than those boys identified only in one setting or the other.

MICROSOCIAL ANALYSES

Data are presented in this section that relate directly or indirectly to the assumptions presented above. Are there reliable patterns of sibling–problem child actions and reactions that can be identified across families? One of the key assumptions in the sibling as trainer formulation is that such structures exist and that they are significantly different from the contributions made by other family members. If such structures were not identified, it would mean that sibling fight training is carried on in a manner idiosyncratic to each family; a state of affairs hardly designed to delight the investigator.

The sibling as trainer formulation would require several additional distinctive features characterizing the interchanges. First, it should be the case that both members contribute significantly to extending the duration of coercive exchanges. Second, it would also be that the problem child exchanges higher rates of hitting with siblings than do normal children with their siblings. It would also require that the problem child hits siblings more othen than parents.

Finally, it should be the case that the likelihood of coercive sibling–problem child exchanges would covary significantly with measures of parent discipline. The formulation presented earlier would have it that it is disruptions in parental discipline that create the situation in which the sibling–problem child training exchanges can occur. In addition, it is also the case that as siblings and problem children become more coercive in rate and amplitude, they become increasingly difficult to discipline. On both counts, then, a significant correlation would be required. In the sections that follow, empirical tests are provided for each of these hypotheses.

Sibling-Problem Child Structure

The findings reviewed here suggest that in some sense there may be a cultural consensus about teasing and hitting exchanges being appropriate behavior for siblings. Most families seem to allow a certain amount; where clinical and normal families seem to differ is in the level or rate at which they allow these behaviors to occur. Although no effort has been made to directly test this hypothesis about cultural programming, it is implicit in much of the discussion that follows.

The special contribution of siblings to aggression emerged in functional analyses carried out a decade ago, but at that time its significance was not recognized by us. Observation studies of families of antisocial and normal children showed that there was a network of antecedent behaviors of family members that reliably elicited (in a probabilistic sense) the problem child's initiation of both hitting and teasing. Both responses were controlled by the same network of stimuli (i.e., these shared functional relations defined a response class) (Patterson & Cobb, 1973). Later studies showed that the family members primarily involved in this particular enterprise were siblings (Patterson, 1977). The target child's hitting or teasing reaction, in turn, also produced a set of reliable reactions (consequences) from siblings. These sibling reactions, in turn, were associated with the increased likelihood of a recurrence of problem child hitting or teasing (accelerators).

The four-stage functional relations are summarized in Figure 11.1. They describe the structure that has presumably emerged as the result of hundreds of training trials. On the left side of Figure 11.1 are listed five sibling behaviors that reliably elicit both Physical Negative and Tease reactions from the problem child. For example, the base rate of occurrence for problem child Physical Negative is .011 and for Tease .003. However, given that the immediate prior behavior of the sibling is Tease, then the conditionals for problem child reactions are .060 and .149, respectively. The prior behavior of the sibling produces a six-fold increase in the likelihood of problem child Physical Negative. Note that inclusion in the network of controlling stimuli requires that the event control both members of the target response class (Pn and Te). One might think of this procedure as an alternative to factor or cluster analyses in constructing response classes. Those responses controlled by similar antecedent and/or consequence events can be said to form a functionally defined class of responses. An analogous, functionally defined class of maternal behavior was identified in Patterson (1985).

Given that the problem child reacts with either Tease or Physical Negative, is there a reliable increase in the likelihood that siblings will react to these events in a homogeneous fashion? One might think of such a network of shared consequences as having some special functional value in perhaps "turning off" the behavior of the problem child. However, it must be said that establishing the correlation between events in no way identifies the reason for the connection. In any case, as shown in Figure 11.1, there are three sibling reactions that are reliably elicited at t_{+1}. These are sibling Physical Negative, Tease, and Yell. Notice again that the base-rate values for these sibling behaviors are listed in parentheses and that generally they are quite low. However, given either of the prior target behaviors of the problem child, there is at least a six-fold increase in likelihood for each of the sibling reactions.

Finally, there is the question of what determines a recurrence, or persistence, of the target responses into the adjacent time interval (i.e., what relates to the extended duration of these responses?). As shown in Figure 11.1, sibling Laugh and Physical Negative both significantly increase the likelihood that the problem child will repeat the performance of Physical Negative or Tease. These detailed findings describe the conditions under which teasing–hitting exchanges among siblings and problem children may be extended. As noted earlier, it is assumed that during these extended episodes the amplitude of the behavior may be increased. In passing, it is interesting to note that a functional analysis of social aggressive

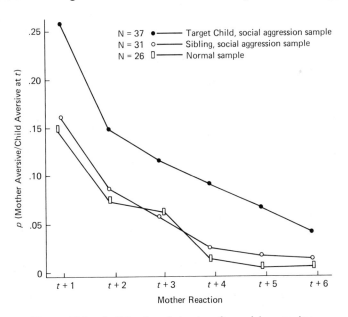

Figure 11.1. A sibling-based structure for social aggression.

behavior identified younger siblings, particularly females, as being the primary contributors to the intitiation and maintenance of the structure (Patterson, 1977). However, as we shall see in a later section (Table 11.4), half the hits given and received by the problem child in clinical samples involve the male sibling.

The sibling contribution to "structure" defined a sequence of not one but three functional relations. At each juncture, the reaction of one member of the dyad produced a reliable increase in the probability that the other would react in a certain way.

In the present context, aggressive children would be characterized by siblings who present higher densities of "controlling stimuli." Presumably the days the target child is observed to be most aggressive would be characterized as days on which the mother and/or sibling present the highest density of these controlling stimuli. In Figure 11.1 the controlling stimuli are Tease, Noncomply, Physical Negative, Laugh, and Comply. All of these sibling behaviors reliably elicit Tease or Hit reactions from the problem child (i.e., are controlling). The controlling aspects of these statistical relationships have been tested in a series of experimental manipulations and suggest, in conclusion, that the use of the term *control* is indeed warranted (Patterson, 1982).

Fight Cycles

It is certainly useful to have information about determinants for extended episodes involving Physical Negative and Tease. Although much of the increasing amplitude in Hitting may be learned in these specific exchanges, it is probably also the case that much of the learning for high-amplitude hitting arises in coercive exchanges with siblings that involve none of the sibling events depicted in Figure 11.1. This section explores a general set of coercive variables that relate directly to extended duration in such episodes.

The general idea is that there are certain dispositions for both members of a dyad that determine their likelihood of starting a fight and then keeping the fight going once it has started. The combined set of dispositions define a *fight cycle*. The formulation is partially based upon the research by Gottman (1979). In his analyses of differences between distressed and nondistressed married couples, he found that it was the disposition to initiate and to continue fights that most clearly differentiated the samples.

Members of antisocial families are significantly more likely to initiate and/or react aversively than are members of normal families. Once started, they are significantly more likely to continue (Patterson, 1976, 1982). Actually, there are three measures of irritable reactions thought to be most pertinent as determinants for extended chains. The first variable, *Start Up,* describes the likelihood that conflict will begin. If one person, such as the problem child, is being neutral or prosocial, how likely is another family member—say, the sibling—to initiate an aversive "attack?" The second variable is *counterattack.* If the other member initiated an attack, how likely is the subject to react aversively? The third variable is *continuance.* If the subject initiates an aversive exchange, how likely is he or she to continue being aversive?

These dispositions define what is meant by a fight cycle. The data show that families of antisocial children are characterized by coercion episodes of longer duration than are normal families (Patterson, 1976, 1982). Furthermore, fight-cycle data analyzed for problem children and mothers showed that, given that they are interacting with each other in a neutral or prosocial fashion, the likelihood was .09 that one or the other would initiate an attack (Patterson, 1982). Once a conflict began, both the child and the mother tended to persist in their irritable reactions. In fact, once started there was about one chance in four of an *extended* interchange. It would seem that the mother and problem child finding a peaceful interlude is a precarious business indeed.

The mean probability values were calculated for each of the fight-cycle variables for the target child and siblings. The data included observations from one normal and two clinical samples (Patterson, 1982). The mean values for start up, counterattack, continuance, and the outcome for the ANOVA are summarized for these problem child–sibling dyads in Table 11.3.

The problem children were consistently more irritable in their reactions to siblings than were normal children to their siblings. These differences

Table 11.3
Three Fight-Cycle Variables for Sibling–Problem Child Exchanges[a]

Irritability variable	Reaction of A to B	Normals (N = 33)	Aggressors (N = 36)	Stealers (N = 35)	F value
Start up	Sib to PC	.01	.03	.03	5.97*
	PC to Sib	.01	.02	.02	1.67
Counterattack	Sib to PC	.19	.21	.28	2.84
	PC to Sib	.10	.19	.19	5.89*
Continuance	Sib to PC	.21	.28	.26	1.50
	PC to Sib	.14	.30	.27	8.29*

[a] Patterson, 1982.
* $p \} .01$.

were significant for two of the three comparisons. For the siblings, it was their dispositions to start up conflicts with the problem child that significantly differentiated them from siblings in more normal families.

Note the interesting fact that in both clinical samples there were very few differences between problem children and siblings in how they reacted to each other. Siblings and problem children from the clinical samples were approximately equally likely to start conflicts and to react in such a way as to extend them. As noted in earlier studies, what differentiates problem children from siblings is the quantity of coercive interchanges with the mother; here the problem children are significantly more heavily engaged than are their siblings (Patterson, 1984).

In 100 minutes of interaction, the problem children are likely to start about three conflicts and their siblings about two. Given three or four children in a family, the likelihood that someone would start up a conflict with someone else would be on the order of every few minutes. Given that one member does initiate a conflict, there is a sizeable increment in the likelihood that the next reaction by the other will be a coercive one.

As shown in Figure 11.2, given the start up and the counterattack, the likelihood is about one in four that the initiator will press forward and an extended coercive encounter will begin. As noted earlier, extended interchanges are thought to be the vehicle by which children learn high-amplitude aggressive behaviors.

Animal studies involving trained fighters as well as clinical studies of assaultive adult prisoners (Toch, 1969) suggest that one of the characteristics of the experienced aggressor is a very rapid escalation in the amplitude of the coercive sequence. This hypothesis was examined as it relates to problem child and sibling exchanges in a study by Patterson (1980). From a sample of families of antisocial boys a set of all coercive chains involving four or more coercive behaviors in sequence by the problem child were rated for the intensity of the reactions at each point in the

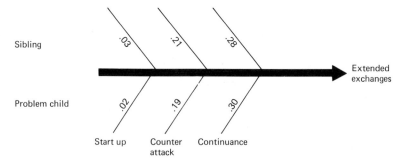

Figure 11.2.   Fight cycle for problem child and sibling from the social aggressor sample.

chain. The ratings ranged from 1 to 9, with the high end of the scale defined as "very annoying" (note that this is analogous to, but not the same as, intensity or amplitude). The findings showed that the antecedent for the extended chain provided by the sibling was rated on the average as only moderately annoying. However, this was followed by an escalation to almost maximum value by the problem child. The siblings' second and third reactions approximate this level. It could be said that both the identified problem children and their siblings function like well-trained fighters in that they quickly escalate the amplitude of their attacks.

Hitting

The sibling-trainer hypothesis would have it that the bulk of the problem childrens' experience in hitting and being hit is based upon their exchanges with siblings. To test this hypothesis, observation data were collected in the homes of 37 families referred for treatment of social aggressors. The comparison sample was 37 families of normals. The two samples were matched for age of target child, family size, father absence, and occupation of the parent. The term *Social Aggressor* as used throughout the discussion refers to a sample of problem boys identified by a two-step sequence. All of them were referred to the center for treatment because of problems of antisocial behavior and a series of three or more observation sessions in the home that showed their rates of coercion exceeded .45 per minute. This places the child one-half standard deviation above the mean for normal children.

The data in Table 11.4 summarize the findings from a comparison of families of social aggressive and normal boys. The two columns describe the likelihood of Hits for normal boys. In keeping with conventional wisdom, the data showed that the fathers of normal boys were much more likely to hit than to be hit by their sons. It is also the case that the likelihood of hitting or being hit was highest when the child was interacting with siblings. An examination of the 164 instances of the target child hitting showed that 48% were directed to male siblings, 20% to female siblings, 23% to mothers, and 9% to fathers.

The picture that emerges for the identified problem children was very different. First, the sheer amount of hitting was dramatically higher. Furthermore, they were even more likely to hit their fathers than to be hit by them. Equally surprising, to us, was the fact that their mothers were more likely to strike them than they were to strike her. However, in keeping with the training hypothesis, the children were much more likely to hit a sibling, particulary male siblings, than they were to hit their parents. These descriptive data are consistent with the training hypothesis. The

Table 11.4

Hitting[a] Exchanges of Target Child and Other Family Members for Normal and Social Aggressor Samples

| | Hitting rate per minute | | | |
| | Normal (N = 37) | | Social aggressor (N = 37) | |
Family member	They hit	He hits	They hit	He hits
Father	.008	.0000	.0026	.0032
Mother	.0002	.0002	.0050	.0022
Female sibling	.0008	.0015	.0030	.0048
Male sibling	.0015	.0013	.0109	.0103

[a] The home observation code category is physical negative, which includes bite, kick, slap, hit, spank, and take object roughly from another (Reid, 1978).

findings are also consistent with the results of the large-scale survey study by Steinmetz (1978) who found that a family's total violence among siblings usually exceeds the amount of violence involving parents.

Covariation of Irritable Exchanges with Fighting

The data have shown that the level of irritable exchange for problem children and siblings is significantly higher in the clinical than in the normal samples. The findings also showed that hitting between problem children and siblings was higher than that in normal families. However, the sibling-trainer hypothesis would require that the two sets of variables covary. Those families in which the mean level of irritable exchanges occur should also be characterized by problem children who do the most fighting at home and in the school.

An earlier study gave a preliminary test of the hypothesis (Patterson, 1982). In that analysis samples of clinical and normal cases were combined as a data base for assessing the target child's irritable reactions to siblings. The Start Up, Counterattack, and Continuance scores for target child–sibling exchanges were then correlated with the observation based Total Aversive Behavior score (a sum of 14 coercive behaviors). The six correlations were in the .2–.5 range. These findings are hardly convincing, because it was the data from the same observations that were used to generate the Irritability probability values. Furthermore, none of the six

Irritability scores accounted for significant amounts of variance in a parent telephone report measure of child deviancy occurring in the home within the past 24 hours.

As a further test for the hypothesis, correlations were calculated between the six measures of irritable exchange and the composite score for physical fighting (peers, teachers, mothers). The analysis was carried out separately for each of three age groups of 4th-, 7th-, and 10th-grade boys. The findings are summarized in Table 11.5. Only those exchanges in which the denominator equaled or exceeded 4 were included in the analyses. An examination of the test–retest stability scores collected at 4- and 8-week intervals for these p values indicated that the reliabilities fell off appreciably when the denominator was less than this value (Patterson, 1984). In fact, the use of this decision rule resulted in dropping the irritability variable Continuance from the analyses. There were simply not

Table 11.5

Correlations of Irritability Variables with Physical Fighting

	Correlations by grades		
Irritability variables[a]	4th	7th	10th
Target child to the siblings			
Start up	.36**	.41**	.64
	(22)	(20)	(17)
Counteraggression	.41**	.05	.23
	(22)	(21)	(17)
Composite[b]	.51***	.31*	.51**
	(22)	(20)	(17)
Siblings to the target child			
Start up	.20	.09	.31
	(21)	(21)	(17)
Counteraggression	.35**	.37**	.15
	(22)	(21)	(17)
Composite	.32**	.40**	.27
	(21)	(21)	(17)

[a] Only those subjects included for whom the denominator used to calculate the p value was equal to or greater than four (see Patterson, 1984).

[b] The sum of the p values for start up and counteraggression.

   * p } .10.

  ** p } .05.

 *** p } .01.

enough subjects for whom the data base was adequate to provide a proper estimate for the *p* value.

Setting up the data to examine developmental trends in the correlations results in very small size samples at each of the three age levels. However, it can be seen that the outcome provides some useful insights into the nature of the covariation. The correlations of target children to sibling variables to Fighting was significant and appreciable in magnitude for all grade levels. Generally, the composite score measuring irritable reactions seemed to give a good estimate of the relation to fighting. Note, too, that the magnitude of the correlation for measures of sibling to problem child exchanges were usually lower than the magnitude for target child reactions to the siblings.

A self-report measure of Delinquency Life Style, based upon the work of Ageton and Elliott (1982), was correlated with all six variables for each of the three age samples. The disposition of the sibling to counter attack was correlated .64 ($p = .001$) with the delinquent life style score for the 7th-grade sample and .42 ($p = .05$) with the scores for the 10th-grade sample. The likelihood of sibling counter attacks correlated with a greater likelihood of the problem child reporting a career delinquency pattern.

THE LABEL "DEVIANT"

Given that problem children tend to have siblings with similar problems raises the interesting question of why one child is identified as the problem child and the others are not. Coercion theory provides two hypotheses that relate to the differential perception of deviancy. First, it is assumed that the prime determinant for labeling one child as deviant is if the observed rate of deviant behavior is higher for one child than for the others. In a sense, the mother correctly perceives that the target child is more deviant than are his siblings as shown by Arnold, Levine, and Patterson (1975) and by Patterson (1982). The latter used a large sample of Oregon Social Learning Center (OSLC) referrals showing a mean Total Aversive Behavior (TAB) score of .99 for the problem child and .66 for siblings. In keeping with the relative standing hypothesis, problem children were half again more deviant than were siblings. One might assume that the bulk of the coercive behaviors that make up this score are relatively innocuous and therefore of little importance in determining parental perception of deviancy. However, the data for hitting from Reid (1978) for a sample of referred families showed rates of .029 for male siblings, .019 for female siblings, and .042 for the identified problem boy. The findings are consistent with those from the study by Speer (1971) in which ratings showed that parents of children referred for diagnosis and treatment perceived their problem child to be significantly more deviant than did parents of normal children. They also perceived the problem child to be significantly more deviant than the siblings.

The second hypothesis is that the target child directs a disproportionate amount of coercive behavior to the *mother* whereas the siblings' interest with her is at the level appropriate for normal children. This is the "special niche" hypothesis (i.e., the problem child has a special niche in the family, particulary for the mother). One study showed that on the average, boys from normal families are coercive in about 5% of their interactions with mothers, fathers, and male and female siblings (Patterson, 1984). In that study, boys referred for antisocial problems were coercive in 12% of the interactions with their mothers whereas male siblings were coercive in 8% and female siblings in 7% of their interactions with her. These findings are in keeping with the hypothesis. This is also in keeping with the recent analyses by Larson (1983). He compared samples of normal and socially aggressive boys from the OSLC data files and found an average likelihood of being coercive to mothers of .2 for siblings in both samples. However, the likelihood of the target child being coercive with the mother was .11 for the normal sample and .26 for problem children from the clinical sample ($F = 10.96$). Furthermore, a single variable—the child's likelihood of aversive behavior given his interaction with the mother—was used in a DFA to correctly classify 70% of a sample of normal and clinical families. In a treated sample, this same variable correlated .40 ($p = .001$) with the mother's daily telephone report of child deviancy at termination. The more likely the child was to be aversive in his observed interactions at termination, the more likely she was to perceive him as having been deviant during the last 16 hours.

In passing, it should be noted that these hypotheses do not preclude the possibility of constitutional differences between problem child and siblings. Many of these parents describe the problem child as having been irritable and difficult since birth. It may be that the longevity of difficulty with a particular child plays an important part in the labeling process. See, for example, the discussion of temperament by Olweus (Chapter 4, this volume).

It is also assumed within coercion theory that some important part of the mother's perception of deviancy is determined by variables other than the child's actual behavior (e.g., her mood, stress and support factors, etc.). The correlation between caretaker depression and perception of deviancy was established in the studies by Griest, Wells, and Forehand (1979) and Chamberlain (1985). The recent analyses of a sample of normal families suggested that observed rates of target child deviant behavior correlated in the .20 range with caretaker depression, as did the care-taker's observed difficulties in disciplining the target child (r_{xy}.30). It should be noted that the Griest, Wells, and Forehand (1979) study failed to find a positive correlation between observed rates of child deviancy and the mother's perception of deviancy.

The coercion formulation would have it that it is not the overall likeli-hood per se but the disposition to engage in extended exchanges that is critical in the development of a problem child. Presumably, it is during these exchanges that the problem child acquires high-amplitude behav-iors.

The next analysis was designed to provide a more direct test of this hypothesis. The metaphor for the study was to view a child's aversive initiation to the mother as analogous to a pebble cast into a pool; the mother's reactions over time describe the ripple effect. It was expected that her reaction to the problem child would differ from her reaction to siblings and from the reactions of mothers to normal children the same age and sex. The data were based upon a sample of 37 families of social aggressors and a matched sample of 37 families of normal children (matched for age of target child, father presence, occupational level of parent). When the target child made an aversive initiation to the mother, her reactions were tabulated over the next six consecutive time frames (6 seconds each). For each time frame, the likelihood of the mother being aversive to the child was calculated. As shown in Figure 11.3, the average trend was for a steady reduction in the likelihood of mothers being aver-sive. It should be kept in mind that in many instances a nonaversive reaction could mean that the mother was no longer interacting with the child (e.g., a prior study showed that the likelihood of a mother's con-tinuing to interact with a child for 16 seconds was only .10 [Patterson, 1982]).

It can be seen that the likelihood of the normal mother's initial reaction being aversive was only about half that for the mothers in the clinical sample. The negative slope for the normals' reaction seemed to reach asymptote at around 24 seconds. The ripple effect seemed to be of a larger magnitude and of a longer duration for the clinical sample than for the normal.

These reactions for the mothers in the clinical sample could reflect a generalized disposition to be irritable; they may be as irritable with the siblings as with the problem child. To test this possibility, siblings were selected who matched as closely as possible for sex and age with the problem child. The probability values for the mother–sibling dyads from the clinical sample are represented in Figure 11.3. In keeping with the

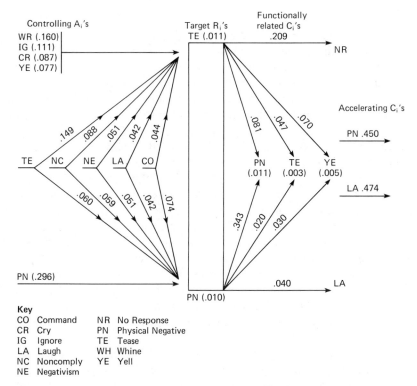

Figure 11.3. The ripple effect.

selective status hypothesis, the mother's reactions to the sibling fell almost exactly along the slope that characterized the normal sample. It seems reasonable to conclude that the mother's reactions to the problem child were more irritable than her reactions to the siblings. Her reactions to the siblings were more analogous to the reactions of normal mothers to their children than were her reactions to her identified problem child.

The question remains unanswered as to what determines this selective status. Does it require a certain level of coerciveness before a child is reassigned to status as a problem child, or is it a shift in the attributions that the mother makes about why the child behaves in such a way? The descriptive data now available attest to the fact that problem children are indeed different in a quantitative sense from their siblings; also that mothers react to them differently. It remains an open and terribly important question as to what the nature of the process might be that brings this about.

IMPLICATIONS

The process model described here details two related phenomena. The first describes the disrupted family-management practices that have permitted the target child to learn antisocial behaviors. The second describes the sibling who becomes caught up in the process and contributes to it.

A disruption in family-management (Discipline) practices creates a situation in which the mother and the problem child become more frequently involved in (extended) coercive exchanges. Presumably, during these exchanges both the mother and the problem child are at risk to escalate the amplitude of their coercive behaviors. This was thought to define the basic or first step in training for fighting. The children "win" enough of these interchanges to be in a position to effectively control the family through pain. As part of this control, they now are permitted to more frequently attack their siblings. Only the problem child is permitted to be out-of-control in interacting with the parents; but in these families, all children are permitted to be out-of-control when interacting with each other. The disruption in Discipline was implicated as a variable that relates to increases in sibling–target child coercive exchanges. It might also be added that the Discipline score correlated .45 (p less than .01) with mothers' reports of how much unsupervised time the target child and siblings were together.

The second stage, the emphasis upon the sibling contribution, is very much in keeping with findings reported by the Cambridge studies of aggression in children described by Dunn, who reported data that suggested the mother's irritable (and depressed) reactions were the prime determinants of aggression for preschool boys. But by ages 7 and 8 years, sibling irritable reactions became the prime determinants. Our own analyses showed that, for school-aged samples, the mean level of irritable exchanges between target children and their siblings were significantly greater than comparable reactions for siblings from normal families (Patterson, 1982, 1984). Furthermore, as shown in the present essay, the level of hitting between problem child and siblings tended to be significantly higher in clinical than in normal families. Finally, it was also the case that the disposition to engage in irritable exchanges with siblings significantly correlated with reports of fighting.

Some effort was also made to explore the differential labeling of siblings and problem child. The hypotheses presented were that the identified problem children were significantly more coercive in their overall reaction to other family members. It was also the case that the target children were differentially coercive to their mothers whereas the siblings were not. Siblings of problem children were no more coercive with their mothers than were siblings from normal families. Siblings from the clinical samples were, however, significantly more coercive than were normals in their coercive exchanges among each other.

It can be concluded that mothers and siblings of identified problem children are caught up in—indeed, they contribute directly to—the coercive process that provides the training for the socially aggressive individual.

ACKNOWLEDGMENT

This report is based upon research funded by the National Institute of Mental Health, Section on Crime and Delinquency, Grant No. MH 32857. The author gratefully acknowledges the contributions made by colleagues Drs J. B. Reid, R. Loeber, T. Dishion, M. Stouthamer-Loeber, M. Weinrott, P. Chamberlain, and M. Forgatch.

REFERENCES

Ageton, S. S., & Elliott, D. S. The incidence of delinquent behavior in a national probability sample of adolescents. In, *The dynamics of delinquent behavior.* Boulder, CO: Behavioral Research Institute, 1982.

Anderson, L. M. Personality characteristics of parents of neurotic, aggressive, and normal preadolescent boys. *Journal of Consulting and Clinical Psychology,* 1969, *33,* 575–581.

Arnold, J., Levine, A., & Patterson, G. R. Changes in sibling behavior following family intervention. *Journal of Consulting and Clinical Psychology,* 1975, *43,* 683–688.

Burgess, R. L., & Conger, R. D. *Family interaction patterns related to child abuse and neglect: Some preliminary findings.* Paper presented at the International Congress on Child Abuse and Neglect, Geneva, Switzerland, September, 1976.

Burgess, J. M., Kimball, W. H., & Burgess, R. L. *Family interaction as a function of family size.* Paper presented at the Southeastern Conference on Human Development Atlanta, Georgia, 1978.

Chamberlain, P. *Determinants for parent reports of child deviant behavior.* 1985. (in prep.)

Church, R. M. Response suppression. In B. A. Campbell & R. M. Church (Eds.), *Punishment and aversive behavior.* New York: Appleton-Century-Crofts, 1969.

Dengerink, H. A., & Covey, M. K. Implications of an escape-avoidance theory of aggressive responses to attack. In R. Geen & D. Stern (Eds.), *Aggression: Theoretical and empirical reviews.* New York: Academic Press, 1981.

Dunn, J., & Kendrick, C. Social behavior of young siblings in the family context: Differences between same sex and different sex dyads. *Child Development,* 1981, *52,* 1265–1273.

Frank, G. H. The role of the family in the development of psychotherapy. *Psychology Bulletin,* 1965, *64,* 191–205.

Gottman, J. M. *Marital interaction: Experimental investigations.* New York: Academic Press, 1979.

Griest, D., Wells, K., & Forehand, R. An examination of predictors of maternal perceptions of maladjustment in clinic referred children. *Journal of Abnormal Psychology,* 1979, *88*(3), 277–281.

260 G. R. PATTERSON

Grotevant, H., Sears, S., & Weinberg, R. Patterns of intrasimilarity in adoptive and biological families. *Journal of Personality and Social Psychology*, 1977, *35*, 667–676.

Hautzinger, M., Linden, & Hoffmann, N. Distressed couples with and without a depressed partner: An analysis of their verbal interaction. *Journal of Behavior Therapy and Experimental Psychiatry*, 1984.

Knutson, J., Fordyce, D., & Anderson, D. The escalation of irritable aggression: Control by consequences antecedent. *Aggressive Behavior*, 1982, *6*, 347–359.

Knutson, J. F., & Viken, R. J. Animal analogs of human aggression: Studies of social experience at escalation. In K. J. Flannelly, R. J. Blanchard, and D. C. Blanchard (Eds.), *Biological perspectives on aggression*. New York: Alan R. Liss, pp. 75–94, 1984.

Larson, D. *The socially aggressive family: An observational multivariate approach*. Unpublished doctoral dissertation, University of Oregon, Eugene, Oregon, 1983.

Loeber, R., & Weissman, W., & Reid, J. B. Family interactions of assaultive adolescents, stealers, and nondelinquents. *Journal of Abnormal Child Psychology*, 1983, *11*, 1–14.

Lurie, O. R. The emotional health of children in the family setting. *Community Mental Health Journal*, 1970, *6*, 229–235.

McCord, J. *A longitudinal view of the relationship between parent absence and crime*. Paper presented at the American Society of Criminology, Dallas, Texas, November, 1978.

Mednick, S. A., & Christiansen, K. O. (Eds.). *Biosocial bases of criminal behavior*. New York: Gardner Press, 1977.

Neilsen, A., & Gerber, D. Psycholosocial aspects of truancy in early adolescence. *Adolescence*, 1979, *14*, 312–326.

Olson, W. *The incidence of nervous habits in normal children. Monograph of the Institute of Child Welfare of the University of Minnesota*, 1929.

Patterson, G. R. The aggressive child: Victim and architect of a coercive system. In E. Mash, L. Hamerlynck, & L. Handy (Eds.), *Behavior modification and families*. New York: Brunner/Mazel, 1976.

Patterson, G. R. Accelerating stimuli for two classes of coercive behaviors. *Journal of Abnormal Child Psychology*, 1977, *5*, 334–350.

Patterson, G. R. Mothers: The unacknowledged victims. *Monographs of the Society for Research in Child Development*, *45* (5, Serial No. 186), 1–64, 1980.

Patterson, G. R. *Coercive family process. A social learning approach*, (Vol. 3). Eugene, OR: Castalia Publ., 1982.

Patterson, G. R. A microsocial process: A view from the boundary. In J. C. Masters & K. L. Yarkin (Eds.), *Boundary areas in psychology: Social and developmental psychology*. New York: Academic Press, 1984.

Patterson, G. R. Siblings: Fellow travelers in coercive family processes. In R. J. Blanchard (Ed.), *Advances in the study of aggression*. New York: Academic Press, pp. 174–213, 1984.

Patterson, G. R. A microsocial analysis of anger. In M. Chesney, S. Goldston, & R. Rosemman (Eds.), *Anger and hostility in cardiovascular and behavioral disorders* New York: Hemisphere-McGraw Hill, pp. 83–98, 1985.

Patterson, G. R., & Cobb, J. A. Stimulus control for classes of noxious behaviors. In J. F. Knutson (Ed.), *The control of aggression: Implications from basic research*. Chicago: Aldine, 1973.

Patterson, G. R., & Dishion, T. J. *A process model for families of antisocial children*. Unpublished manuscript, 1984.

Patterson, G. R., & Stouthamer-Loeber, M. The correlation of family management practices and delinquency. *Child Development*, 1984, *55*, 1299–1307.

Pepler, D. J., Abramovitch, R., & Corter, C. Sibling interaction in the home: A longitudinal study. *Child Development,* 1981, *52,* 1344–1347.

Pulkkinen, L. Search for alternatives to aggression in Finland. In A. P. Goldstein and M. Segall (Eds.), *Aggression in global perspective.* New York: Pergamon Press, 1982.

Rachlin, H., & Herrnstein, R. J. Hedonism revisited: On the negative law of effect. In B. A. Campbell & R. M. Church (Eds.), *Punishment and aversive behavior.* New York: Appleton-Century-Crofts, 1969.

Reid, J. B. (Ed.). *A social learning approach to family intervention, Vol. 2: Observation in home settings.* Eugene, OR: Castalia Publ., 1978.

Reid, J. B. *Final report: Child abuse: Developmental factors and treatment.* Grant No. 7 RO1 MH 37938, National Institute of Mental Health, Washington, DC, 1983. (a)

Reid, J. B. *Final report: Investigation of boys' aggression toward women and girls.* Grant No. MH 25548-03, National Institute of Mental Health, Washington, DC, 1983. (b)

Reid, J. B., Patterson, G. R., & Weinrott, M. *A comparison of social learning and traditional methods of treating families of chronic offenders: Three year follow-up.* Manuscript in preparation, 1984.

Reid, J. B., Taplin, P. S., & Lorber, R. A social interactional approach to the treatment of abusive families. In R. B. Stuart (Ed.), *Social learning approaches to prediction management and treatment.* New York: Brunner/Mazel, 1981.

Reid, J. B., Patterson, G. R., & Loeber, R. The abused child: Victim, instigator, or innocent bystander? In D. Bernstein (Ed.), *Response structure and organization.* Lincoln, NE: University of Nebraska Press, 1982.

Robins, L. N., & Ratcliff, K. S. Risk factors in the continuation of childhood antisocial behavior into adulthood. *International Journal of Mental Health,* 1978, *7,* 96–116.

Rutter, M., Tizard, J., & Whitmore, K. *Education, health, and behavior.* New York: John Wiley & Sons, 1970.

Sells, S. B., & Roff, M. *Peer acceptance-rejection and personal development.* Final Report OE5-0417 and OE2-10-051, Washington, DC, 1967.

Snyder, J. J. Reinforcement analysis of interaction in problem and nonproblem families. *Journal of Abnormal Psychology,* 1977, *86,* 528–535.

Snyder, J. J., & Patterson, G. R. *The identification of reinforcers in social interaction.* Unpublished manuscript, 1985.

Speer, D. Behavior Problem Checklist (Peterson & Quay). *Journal of Consulting and Clinical Psychology,* 1971, *36,* 221–228.

Steinmetz, S. K. Sibling violence. In J. M. Eckelaar & S. N. Kantz (Eds.), *Family violence.* Toronto: Butterworths, 1978.

Sullivan, J. L. Multiple indicators: Some criteria of selection. In A. M. Blalock (Ed.), *Measurement in the social sciences.* Chicago: Aldine, 1974.

Taplin, P. S., & Reid, J. B. Changes in parental consequation as a function of family intervention. *Journal of Consulting and Clinical Psychology,* 1977, *4,* 973–981.

Toch, H. *Violent men.* New York: Aldine Publ., 1969.

Wadsworth, M. E. J. *Roots of delinquency, infancy, adolesence and crime.* Oxford: Robertson, 1979.

West, D. J., & Farrington, D. P. *Who becomes delinquent?* London: Heinemann, 1973.

12

Social Groupings in Childhood: Their Relationship to Prosocial and Antisocial Behavior in Boys and Girls

ELEANOR E. MACCOBY

To a remarkable degree, male and female children grow up in different social environments. From an early age, when children are in situations in which their social groupings are not dictated by adult decisions, they gather predominantly into same-sex clusters. The theme of this essay is that the characteristic of the groups in which children participate may have as much bearing on their prosocial and antisocial behavior as their individual personality dispositions; or at least, that group characteristics may make an independent contribution, over and above the predictions that can be made from individual characteristics. Of course, individual characteristics may play a role in children's selection of the particular groups they will join. But there may be some fairly general constraints on the nature of the group process that occur in male as distinct from female groups, such that the socialization that occurs within the two kinds of groups has a differential impact regardless of the selection factor that led to the entry of individuals into the group.

First, in this essay, some documentation is provided for the fact that spontaneous segregation by sex occurs, with brief comments on possible factors underlying this segregation. Next follows a listing of some of the

DEVELOPMENT OF ANTISOCIAL
AND PROSOCIAL BEHAVIOR

characteristics of the distinctive male and female childhood cultures in naturally occuring groups. Finally, questions are raised about the implications of growing up in these separate cultures for the occurrence and meaning of prosocial and antisocial behavior, with some discussion of the possible ways in which the family environment may interact with the peer environment to generate prosocial or antisocial behavior in different ways for male and female children.

SEX SEGREGATION IN CHILDHOOD

Schofield (1981) studied the social interaction patterns found among sixth and seventh-graders in their classrooms, lunchroom, halls, and playgrounds, in a school where the children were approximately equally divided by sex and race. She reports that although children grouped themselves along both racial and gender lines, sex was the more powerful factor. On a typical day in the cafeteria, where on the average about 200 children were present, almost no cross-sex "adjacencies" were to be seen. Even in the classrooms, whenever teachers did not assign specific seats, students grouped themselves by sex, and resisted being assigned to mixed-sex working groups. In an experimentally contrived situation in which children were brought together in either same-sex or mixed-sex triads, Leimbach and Hartup (1981) report that in same-sex pairs coalition formation usually occurred on the basis of social power, but that in mixed-sex triads, gender emerged as highly important. The two same-sex members of a triad tended to form a coalition, especially if they shared a low-power status.

High degrees of self-segregation are reported for school-aged children by many other investigators. Same-sex preferences are reflected in both sociometric choices and observed behavior (Duck, 1975; Kandel, 1978b; Krenkel, 1972; Singleton & Asher, 1979; St. John & Lewis, 1975; Thorne, 1982). Lockheed and Klein (1985) review a large number of studies of children in school settings, revealing very strong patterns of segregation in children's groupings from preschool through grade school. Lockheed (in press) summarizes the research in this area as showing that students choose same-sex classmates as friends, choose to work with same-sex rather than cross-sex classmates, sit or work in same-sex rather than cross-sex groups, and engage in many more same-sex than cross-sex verbal interchanges. Lockheed also reports that segregation tends to be greater in settings where adults have not structured the children's activities. Certain activities (e.g., doll play) are clearly understood by both sexes to be appropriate for one sex only, and there are strong attitudinal underpinnings for the avoidance of sex-inappropriate play. Damon (1977), in interviews with children ranging in age from 4 to 10 years, documents the strong moral indignation among boys, especially after about the age of 6 years, toward a boy who plays with "girls' stuff." Crossing gender lines is somewhat easier for girls than boys. That is, a girl who is known to have good athletic skills is sometimes accepted into predominantly male activities. Boys receive more criticism for cross-sex play (Fagot, 1977a; Langlois & Downs, 1979). Thorne (1982), and Luria (1985), report that in school playgrounds, there are usually several girls who can be labeled as tomboys in that they like male activities and join male groups for at least part of their playtime. A boy is almost never seen to join a girl's group on a school playground. Gottman (In press), in a study of the conversations between same-sex and cross-sex pairs of close friends, found that it was very difficult to locate such pairs among grade-school–aged children. The few cross-sex friendships that they did identify among children in the first few grades of school had been formed much earlier—during the preschool period—and had gone "underground" in the sense that the children did not acknowledge each other at school but played together after school in the privacy of their homes.

Although sex segregation has been observed in widely different cultures, it varies in degree. Harkness and Super (1985) report that in an East African village, where children spend much of their early lives in compounds comprised of a few families (mainly co-wives with their children), children play with any child or children near their own age, without regard to gender. When they are old enough to move out of the compound, however, same-sex groupings appear. We do not have formal reports on the play patterns of kibbutz-reared children who have lived together in children's houses from infancy, but informal observations are that cross-sex friendships and joint play are quite frequent, although "best friends" tend to be of the same sex. Sex segregation in play becomes more noticeable when the children are old enough to go to consolidated schools, where they have a larger choice of playmates and where more of their age mates are not same-house "siblings." Also, when games turn into more formal competitive sports, separate girls' and boys' teams are formed. These observations suggest that intimate, life-long sibling-type associations with a relatively small same-age cohort can serve to break down some of the barriers against cross-sex association that are commonly found. However, few societies provide these conditions.

How early does segregation of the sexes begin? Preference for same-sex playmates in preschool settings has been reported in many studies done in the last 50 years (see Abel & Sahinkaya, 1962; Charlesworth & Hartup, 1967; Clark, Wyon, & Richards, 1969; McCandless & Hoyt, 1961; Parten, 1932. See also review by Lockheed & Klien, 1985, for additional references.). Serbin, Tonik, and Sternglanz (1977) report that when cooperative interaction occurs among preschoolers, the likelihood is nearly four times greater that it will involve a same-sex than an opposite-sex pair. In their detailed observations of agonistic and affiliative contacts among children in several preschools, Strayer and colleagues (Strayer, 1980) have identified affiliative groupings of children who select one another for play over a considerable period of time. Such groupings are usually made up of a "focal pair" who initiate and reciprocate social behaviors toward one another at a high rate, with several other children who are more marginal for the group, relating themselves (sometimes nonreciprocally) with one or the other of the focal pair. The groups are primarily unisex. Cross-sex relationships take the form of a single boy attaching himself peripherally to a member of a girls' group, or a single girl doing likewise in relation to a boys' group. The focal pair are always a same-sex pair in Strayer's observations to date. In our own observations of children in the Stanford Longitudinal Study, we have found that although segregation is much more marked in the first grade than it is in nursery school, it is nevertheless well advanced in nursery school. At age $4\frac{1}{2}$ years, the ratio of same-sex to opposite-sex play was between $2\frac{1}{2}:1$ and $3:1$ (Maccoby & Jacklin, 1985). Because these figures are consistent with the findings of Luria and Herzog (1985), it seems clearly established that segregation is well under way during the preschool period, for children aged 3–5 years.

There is evidence of self-segregating tendencies at an even earlier age. LaFrenier and colleagues (LaFrenier, Strayer, & Cauthier, 1984) observed 200 children ranging in age from 1 to 6 years, enrolled in a daycare center. They recorded the gender of the child toward whom target children directed their affiliative behaviors at successive ages. They found no tendency for very young children (under age 2) to direct such behaviors toward same-sex others; by 28 months, however, the girls were directing two-thirds of their positive social behaviors toward other girls, while the boys were still not discriminating on the basis of gender. The boys did increase steadily in their same-sex preferences as they grew older, however, so that by the age of $5\frac{1}{2}$, they were significantly more oriented toward same-sex partners than were girls, although preferential orientation was marked in both sexes by this age. This work indicates, then, that girls may be the ones who start the segregation process, but that boys soon come to play an active role in it.

FACTORS AFFECTING SEX SEGREGATION

Serbin et al. (1977) have investigated how easily preschool children's preference for same-sex playmate can be changed by behavior-modification procedures. They trained teachers in two nursery school class rooms to provide positive reinforcement when they saw children playing in cross-sex pairs. Over a 2-week period while this reinforcement schedule was in effect, the frequency of cross-sex play increased monotonically over its initially low baseline level. When the reinforcement was discontinued, however, play quickly returned to its initial bias toward same-sex partners. It should be noted that neither teachers nor observers were able to detect differential reinforcement for same-sex play during the pre- and post-experimental periods when no explicit schedules had been put into effect. From this experiment we learn that the same-sex play pattern can indeed be changed by external contingencies, a fact that might be taken to mean that it was through this means that they had been established in the first place. The fact that the preferences return quickly to baseline when reinforcement is discontinued could mean either that there are factors other than reinforcement that lead children into same-sex play, or that there are reinforcing processes occurring outside the nursery school setting that are maintaining the behavior, or both.

In a similar vein, Lockheed finds (personal communication) that when a year-long program for increasing cross-sex interaction is put in place in school classrooms (by forming mixed-sex work groups that meet regularly throughout the year), there is some increase in the amount of cross-sex interaction occurring outside the work-group setting but no weakening of children's strong *preference* for same-sex work and play partners, and that preferences are strongly correlated with behavior. We thus see that patterns of segregation in childhood are both widespread and resistant to change.

A popular hypothesis to explain the prevalence of same-sex preference is that children first develop sex-typed preferences for certain activities and certain play materials. Having developed these, children prefer to play with others who have similar activity preferences. A further step in the argument sometimes is that the preference for sex-typed activities and toys is the result of early sex-differentiated socialization pressures.

There is no question that many children have already developed sex-typed activity preferences by the time they enter nursery school. And sometimes, pairs of children may be drawn together by their mutual interests in a given set of play materials. Thus, if girls individually gravitate toward the doll corner in a preschool, they will find themselves playing with other girls. Is this the primary factor that underlies same-sex preferences? In a study designed to explore some possible antecedents of same-sex partner choices, Jacklin and Maccoby (1978) observed 46 pairs of previously unacquainted children, all aged 33 months. Most of these children had not yet been enrolled in preschool or daycare settings. The children were brought to an experimental playroom in sex-neutral clothing, and experimenters were instructed not to address the children by name when in each other's presence. Thus, clues to the sex identity of a child's partner were minimized. Some of the pairs were same sex, others mixed sex. Over the whole sample, there were few behavioral differences attributable to the sex of individual children. Girls and boys on the average engaged in similar levels of social initiation toward their partners. However, there were striking effects of the sex composition of the pair: both boys and girls played more actively, and entered into more social interaction, when with a same-sex partner. Girls tended to become "passive"—that is, to stand and watch the partner playing rather than to join in—when with a male partner, in striking contrast to their behavior with a female partner. The toys provided in this study were sex neutral, and there was no indication that children of either sex were more interested in any of them. These findings suggest that there are forces already in place, before children enter nursery school, and independent of their activity and toy preferences, that predispose children to select same-sex playmates.[1]

Current analyses of the data from the Stanford Longitudinal study also indicate that the prior development of sex-typed characteristics may not be the primary factor leading children to prefer same-sex playmates when they enter nursery school. In this study, no relation has been found between the degree of children's sex-typing in earlier childhood and their tendency to choose same-sex playmates at age $4\frac{1}{2}$ years in nursery school. (Maccoby & Jacklin, 1985).

A second hypothesis to explain same-sex preference is a more cognitive one: Children recognize the sex of other children, know their own sex, and make their choice either on the basis of similarity or because of beliefs concerning how children of a given sex ought to act. We still do not know precisely how early clear recognition of the sex of self and other occurs. Presumably it is a gradual process, with important steps being taken by many children toward the end of the third year. However, "recognition" of another's sex is a process that has complex meanings. When a male territorial animal sees an unfamiliar conspecific animal approaching, it

---

[1] The findings of the Jacklin-Maccoby study have been essentially replicated in an unpublished Honors Thesis by Buder and Sutton-Simon, Oberlin College.

reacts differently depending on whether the approaching animal is a male or female. Thus, clearly, it recognizes the sex of the other. In the same sense, a young child may react differently to male and female other persons, without needing to use sex-categorical labels. There is evidence for example that infants, in the first year, may show somewhat more fear of male adults (Morgan & Ricciuti, 1969; Shaffran & Decarie, 1973) and that toddlers show at least rudimentary differential reactions to same- and other-sex peers (Hutt & Hutt, 1970). It is a far cry from these kinds of reactions to the cognitions having to do with sex, e.g., "I am a boy, that other child is a girl, and I am not supposed to play with girls"; or to even more sophisticated cognitions: "I am a girl. That other child is a girl. We are similar." The cognitions that explicitly involve shared sex identify probably come fairly late in the developmental process. Simple labeling of the other comes earlier, and such labeling may carry affective connotations, as in, "That child is a boy. Boys are rough and noisy. I don't want to play with him." Sex-differentiated reactions to others that do not involve explicit sex labeling undoubtedly also occur and may begin still earlier developmentally.

It is difficult to know, at any given age, what is the mix between these types of sex-linked reactions. Certain kinds of warnings and demands emanating from parents—for example, to a boy, "You mustn't hit girls,"—can only be effective if the child has learned to code the sex of other children with reasonable accuracy. Other things that parents can do to build mutuality between same-sex pairs do not necessarily depend on such cognitions. Establishing preferences for frilly or floral patterns of clothing in girls, or engaging in rough physical play with boys, may build certain action or preference patterns that will cause children to find same-sex partners more compatible. However, I wish to suggest that there are probably some elements in the reactions of the two sexes to one another that do not depend on cognitions about the sex of self and others, or upon differential socialization. Here I am taking an ethological perspective. We know that a considerable degree of behavioral sex differentiation and sex segregation occurs in the play of young subhuman primates. Evidently there are compatibilities in the mutual reactions of same-sex pairs that function to sustain interaction—compatibilities that do not emanate from socialization efforts by the parent generation or presumably from cognitive labeling concerning similarity of others to the self. I suggest that probably there are similar reaction patterns in young human children, and that these reactions supplement and interact with the behavioral tendencies that stem from differential treatment by adults. An implication of this point of view is that societies may differ in how strongly they support or oppose the sex segragation of childhood, but that there is an initial bias toward such segregation, so that any society would find it difficult to eliminate it altogether.

HOW THE MALE AND FEMALE CHILDHOOD CULTURES DIFFER

If the spontaneous segregation of the sexes in childhood is a stubborn fact of life, it becomes a matter of some importance for us to understand the nature of the behavior patterns that develop in the male and female cultures of childhood, and to consider how these different cultures affect the development of prosocial and antisocial behavior. How do male and female play groups differ? Some of the characteristics that have been identified in observational studies are the following:

1. Boys tend to play in more public places. For preschool children and early school-aged children, this means that boys are more likely to play outdoors, girls indoors, when the two kinds of play space are available (Lever, 1976; Thorne, in press). For older children, it means that boys are more likely to be found playing in public parks, playgrounds, or streets. Girls, if they are outdoors, are more likely to be on the premises of a private dwelling, and to spend a good deal of their after-school time at one another's houses. It is reasonable to suppose that adult pressures have something to do with these distinctive locations for the play of the two sexes, at least after about the age of 5 or 6 years. Newson and Newson (1976) report that when their longitudinal sample of British children had reached the age of 7 years, the "chaperonage" of girls was significantly greater than that of boys. That is, girls were more likely to be accompanied to or from school by an adult, or required to come directly home after school without stopping to play. Differences in the amount of surveillance were not found at age 4 years.

2. Boys play in larger groups, girls more often cluster in two's or three's (Brooks-Gunn & Mathews, 1979; Eder & Hallinan, 1978; Lever, 1976; Omark, Omark, & Edelman, 1973; Waldrop & Halverson, 1975).

3. Play in boys' groups is rougher than in girls' groups (DePietro, 1979; Omark, Omark, & Edelman, 1973). There is more body contact. Data from the Stanford Longitudinal Study show that in trios of boys of preschool age, there is more rough-and-tumble play (DiPietro, 1981). This kind of interaction among boys has sometimes been classified in the child development literature as a form of aggression; in fact, it usually occurs in a spirit of fun.

4. There is more fighting in boys' groups. There have been large numbers of studies on "agonistic" encounters among children of various ages.

Male preponderance is consistently found, between as well as within a variety of cultures (see Maccoby & Jacklin, 1980, for a summary), although the absolute frequency is not high for either sex. Recent confirmations of this difference in the social interaction of boys' and girls' groups is provided by Thorne (in press) and Luria & Herzog (1985). It should be noted that boys predominate as both the initiators and the targets of aggressive activity, a finding that underlines the fact that fighting is something that characterizes interactive behavior in boys's groups, rather than being entirely a quality that ineres in individual male children regardless of social context.

5. Social encounters among boys tend to be oriented around issues of dominance and the formation of a pecking order (Goodwin, 1980; Omark, Omark & Edelman, 1973; Savin-Williams, 1979; Thorne, 1982; Whiting & Whiting, 1973). Leadership styles reflect these group characteristics. In boys' groups there is more likely to be a specifically designated leader or "captain." Influence attempts tend to take the form of direct commands.

The reader will note that in the five points listed above, the emphasis is on something that characterizes boys' groups that is "missing" from girls' groups. That is, we have a clearer picture of what girls' groups do *not* do than what they *do* do. (This is reminiscent of the oft-noted Freudian penchant for characterizing the two sexes primarily in terms of males having something that females lack!). Recently, scholars are beginning to correct this disbalance by furnishing a more clearly delineated account of interaction in female social groups. The analysis that follows draws from two summary papers (Thorne, in press; Maltz & Borker, (1982) as well as from a number of recent individual studies.

6. In the activities of groups of school-aged girls, there is a strong convention of turn-taking. There may be one girl who is more directive than the others in the sense that she takes a strong role in initiating and organizing the group's activities, but the influence attempts are likely to take the form of suggestions, "Let's . . . ," "Why don't we . . . ," or "We gotta . . ." (Goodwin, 1980). An early manifestation of this style of interaction among girls was seen in the study of preschool triads previously referred to (DiPietro, 1981), in which the establishment and maintenance of turn-taking convention was more common in the girls' groups. Savin-Williams (1979) reports that among young adolescents in a camp setting, both sexes use ridicule fairly often in trying to establish dominance (exert influence) over a cabin mate. However, for girls, dominant girls also exercise influence by complimenting other girls, asking advice, asking favors, or imitating. In contrast, among boys, dominance encounters often take the physical forms of hitting, pushing or displacing.

7. There appear to be some qualitative differences between the sexes in the nature and significance of friendships. Girls' friendships have been labeled "intensive," boys' "extensive." These terms mean more than the above-noted fact that boys tend to congregate in larger groups. Girls are more likely to have one or two specific "best friends" who play an important role in their lives (Waldrop & Halverson, 1975), whereas boys' orientation toward peers stems more from group activities and group games. Girls' friendships tend to be more exclusive (Eder & Hallinan, 1978). Self-disclosure (telling secrets) is an important aspect of girls' "best" friendships (Brooks-Gunn & Schempp, 1979; Lever, 1976; Maltz & Borker, 1982), and the break-up of friendships tends to be emotional, partly because secrets have been shared. New friendships tend to be formed at the expense of old ones. Shifting alliances are common in girls' groups. Pairs of female friends show considerable concordance (similarity) with respect of their psychological characteristics, whereas pairs of male friends do not. The latter tend to be similar with respect to their activity interests and physical skills (Duck, 1975).

8. It is not clear whether boys' or girls' groups are easier for a stranger to enter. Unger (1979) suggests that entry is easier with boys' groups, because boys' activities often involve roles that are well understood by everyone (e.g., second baseman). Anyone who knows the skills associated with a role can participate even with minimally acquainted peers. However, observing younger children, McLoyd (1983) notes that domestic scripts are popular among preschool girls. The stereotyped versions of the "mommy," "daddy," and "baby" roles can be acted out fairly smoothly by trios of girls regardless of how well acquainted they are. Among the preschool boys, who use the domestic scripts less frequently, interaction tends to be briefer and to disintegrate into solitary or parallel play with toys (such as trucks) onto which more individual fantasy scripts can be projected. There may be no general bias toward either sex in terms of the permeability of group boundaries as long as group activities involve generally understood roles. However, a best friend female triad or pair may be more difficult for a new child to enter with fully accepted intimacy than pairs or trios of male friends.

9. Social speech usually has a different content in male and female groups (Schofield, 1981). Also, it appears to serve different functions for groups of the two sexes. Maltz and Borker (1982) interpret the research on speech in girls' groups as showing that girls learn to do three things with words: (1) to create and maintain relationships of closeness and equality; (2) to criticize others in acceptable ways, and (3) to interpret accurately the speech of other girls. Symptomatic of these functions are the facts that girls frequently express agreement with others' ideas, let

others have a turn to talk, and acknowledge what others have said when they speak; in other words, girls use speech as a means of cooperations. Maltz and Borker suggest that girls' strong emphasis on using speech to maintain friendly interaction means that they have difficulty dealing with conflict. They express criticism guardedly or indirectly, and if a quarrel starts, the group tends to break up (Lever, 1976). Boys, on the other hand, according to Maltz and Borker, use speech in three major ways: (1) to assert one's position or dominance, (2) to attract and maintain an audience, and (3) to assert oneself when other speakers have the floor. Thus, verbal interchanges among boys are more likely to involve commands, refusals to comply, threats, boasts of authority, giving of information, heckling a speaker, telling of jokes or suspenseful stories, and topping someone else's story (Goodwin, 1980; Sacks, 1974; Savin-Williams, 1976).

Although boys and girls remain essentially segregated in their respective peer groups, at least at school, there are forms of contact between the two kinds of groups. Thorne (in press) refers to *borderwork,* a term that includes raids by one sex group into the other's territory (mainly raids by boys into girls' territory), sexual taunting, and accusations of contamination (e.g., boys are thought to get "cooties" from girls). Schofield (1981) also notes the mixed sexual and aggressive connotations of encounters between preteen boys and girls in the presence of their peers. What appears to be missing from these encounters at this age is the qualities of friendship that are present within same-sex groupings.

IMPLICATIONS FOR PROSOCIAL AND ANTISOCIAL BEHAVIOR

We have seen that when children are in settings outside the classroom and outside their family homes, they spend much of their time in social groups that are highly sex segregated and in which the cultures maintained by the two sexes are different in important ways. What are the implications of these facts for the incidence and nature of prosocial and antisocial behavior in the two sexes?

Let us begin with antisocial behavior. The fact that rates of antisocial behavior (violent crime, vandalisms, theft, drunk driving, etc.) are considerably higher among adolescent and young-adult males than females is sufficiently well established to need no further documentation here. To what extent do these differential rates represent extensions or elaborations of behavior patterns seen earlier in play groups? In approaching this question, it must be stressed that both male and female play groups operate to control antisocial behavior, although they appear to do so in somewhat different ways. In the girls' groups, a girl risks ostracism and the breaking off of highly valued friendships if she shows hostility or even disagreement too openly. The controls on aggressive behavior appear to be stronger in girls' groups than boys'. At least, in boys' groups, disagreement and heated arguments do not appear to carry such high risk of exclusion from the group. Fighting—perhaps especially retaliatory fighting—is often part of the process of gaining and maintaining a high position in the male-dominance hierarchy, although it must be accompanied by positive leadership qualities for high status to be maintained. High-status males will sometimes come to the aid of lower-status group members if they are unfairly attacked. It is widely alleged that dominance hierarchies, once established, function to place constraints on the amount of fighting in the group as a whole. One piece of evidence that this does occur is the fact that the number of agonistic encounters among boys in a school playground decreases over the year, suggesting that boys settle into their dominance structure with fewer and fewer challenges as they become more familiar with one another.

The fact that controlled fighting has an acceptable place in the boys' culture means that boys socialized into this culture are closer to the borderline between acceptable and unacceptable aggression. The same situation applies to competitive and risk-taking behavior. Boys' games are more competitive than girls' (Thorne, in press; Lever, 1976), and boys enjoy winning in competitive situations more than girls do (Crockenburg, Bryant, & Wilce, 1976). The element of "showing off," either by winning in competition or via acts of daring, is strong in the interactions among boys. Normally, this element is balanced by a simultaneous requirement for cooperation. Frequently, competition is channeled into group activities in which the effort to beat another group, team, or gang calls for highly organized cooperative behavior within a group. For example, Shapira and Madsen (1974) have shown that, in four-person same-sex groups of Israeli children, boys greatly increased their effective within-group cooperation when competing against another team, whereas girls did not. Once again, the fact that competitive and risk-taking behavior are both encouraged and controlled means that boys are at greater risk of an imbalance that will feed into antisocial behavior than are girls, whose groups discourage aggressive or risk-taking forms of self-display, and also discourage open striving for gains that are made at the expense of others.

The fact that boys tend to play in larger groups and on streets and playgrounds rather than indoors, entails another form of risk. In formal after-school athletics, there are likely to be parents or other adults who help to organize, coach, and supervise the activity. But much of the boys' out-of-school activity is not of this formal sort, and it is more difficult for adults to monitor street play than the play of a pair of trio of girls who are at one of the girls' houses. The difference in closeness of supervision may be diminishing as increasing numbers of families have both parents employed, and the girls, though in less open settings, are presumably less closely supervised than was previously the case.

We see, then, that although both boys' and girls' groups function to socialize their members, the influence of boys' groups is probably more mixed than that of girls'. And of course, not all peer groups of a given sex have the same balance between their regulating and stimulating processes. In DiPietro's report of rough-and-tumble play, for example, it was found that approximately 30% of the trios of preschool boys engaged in wrestling and playful attacks at a very high rate—a rate higher than was seen in any of the girls' groups. The majority of boys' groups, however, showed lower levels of this behavior, in the same range as many of the girls' groups. Individual temperament may lead certain boys, who like rough play, to seek out other like-minded boys. Once they have clustered together, it is reasonable to suppose that it is mainly in these mutually chosen groups—which constitute only a minority of boys' groups—that the conditions exist for the mutual arousal and support of "wild," risk-taking behavior. Of course, some of the groups that engage in rough play will develop means of social control to keep the group's activity within acceptable bounds, but others may not.

Not only do groups of a given sex vary in how much they encourage the display or inhibition of borderline antisocial behaviors, but individual children vary with respect to how much they are exposed to the socializing (or counter-socializing) influence of groups. In his review chapter, Hartup (1983) points out that impulsive, hyperactive children with low frustration tolerance and children who initiate fights in inappropriate situations (e.g., teasing or bullying younger children) are unpopular and tend to be excluded from groups of peers. Though self-confident, the bullies studied by Olweus (1978), also were not popular, and the hyperaggressive children in the studies by Patterson and colleagues (1982) tended to be social isolates. In a sense, then, it is not participation in the boys' culture, but failure to participate in it, that is associated with certain kinds of predelinquent activity.

In the history of work on delinquency and criminality, it has proved difficult to "type" antisocial persons. That is, researchers seldom can identify meaningful syndromes based on specializing in certain types of crimes or having distinct social histories. Nevertheless, the Patterson group (Patterson, 1982) is working on the hypothesis that it is meaningful to distinguish between "overtly" and "covertly" antisocial children. The overt cluster involves aggression (particularly unprovoked aggression), temper tantrums, disobedience, and hyperactivity. The covert cluster includes stealing, lying, firesetting, vandalism, truancy, and "wandering" (unsupervised staying away from home). They find, in pilot work, that some boys "specialize" in one or the other of these types of behavior, whereas others display both, and still others (the majority) display neither. According to Patterson, it is the boys who specialize in the covert cluster who are more likely to drift into delinquent peer groups toward the end of the gradeschool years.

We suggest that there are both individual and group factors that contribute to the greater incidence of antisocial behavior among male children. The incidence of low frustration tolerance and other forms of impulsivity appears to be higher in boys. That is, there are more boys at the high end of distributions of these characteristics, though most boys are in the same lower range where most of the girls are found. When impulsivity reaches high enough levels to be identified as hyperactivity, or when it includes many unprovoked attacks on other children, the child's entry into stable peer groups will be delayed, and in the cases of extreme aggressiveness, may not occur at all. One can only suspect that in such cases, the child's future career as a delinquent will take a solitary form.

Most impulsive boys, however, will be able to find other children who enjoy the same kinds of activities they do. They may have more difficulty forming stable dominance hierarchies than will groups of more controlled boys, and hence more fighting is likely to occur within their groups. Gangs of delinquent boys tend not to be cohesive; the friendship bonds within such groups tend to be less close, and individual boys commonly spend less time with their fellow group members than is the case for nondelinquent groups. We suspect that the same point applies to groups that engage in wild and risk-taking behavior that is not explicitly delinquent. However, in most cases there is enough gratification stemming from the group's activities to keep groups of impulsive boys together at least loosely and for some activities. For such groups, the fact that boys tend to congregate in larger groups than girls may have special significance. Given a finite probability that an individual child will think of a bold, antisocial act and be willing to initiate it at any given time, the larger the group the greater the chance that at least one member will do so. And among older children in larger groups there is greater likelihood that at least one of the children will have access to drugs or alcohol. If one member initiates an antisocial behavior, there is a good chance that others in the group will follow suit. It has been alleged that children find it easier to follow bad examples than good ones (Hoffman, 1970). The claim was that when a model carries out an antisocial action, this helps to disinhibit viewers, who now feel that they have, in a sense, been given a license to do the same thing. Hoffman's review suggested that exposures to a model who exhibits self-restraint does not have so powerful an effect.

More recent work has shown that although exposure to antisocial (aggressive) models increases antisocial behavior in preschool children, prosocial models can also have an effect in both increasing the level of prosocial behavior and strengthening self-regulation (Friedrich & Stein, 1973). There is probably no general tendency for modeling to serve more easily to disinhibit than to inhibit the behavior of viewers. However, there is reason to believe that modeling is especially effective in activating behaviors that are in a high state of readiness for performance either because they are intrinsically interesting and gratifying or because they are linked to already-established personality patterns. Thus, aggressive children are more likely to imitate aggression seen on TV than are nonaggressive children (Friedrich & Stein, 1973). It is likely that, especially in impulsive groups, antisocial behaviors are close to the threshold for performance in a number of members of the group, and contagion from initiators to followers is therefore always a likely event.

Hartup (1983), in his review of peer groups and their effects, reports that there is considerable similarity among members of groups in their activities and values. He provides evidence for two sources for the similarity: (1) self-selection, whereby children choose groups of similar others, and (2) mutual influence as group membership continues. It is not the function of this chapter to consider the role that delinquent peer groups play in the etiology of delinquency. However, I wish to point out in summary that there are two basic reasons why more delinquency can be expected in boys' groups. The first is that because of the higher base rates among boys of individual characteristics that predispose children to antisocial behavior (impulsivity, hyperactivity, risk-taking, aggression) and the fact that like-minded children seek one another out, there is greater probability that among males some of the groups that are formed will be made up of members who share antisocial tendencies. The second is that there are a number of aspects of the social interaction that tend to occur within all boys' groups—as distinct from girls' groups—that may have a bearing on the incidence of delinquency once groups are formed. The larger size of boys' groups increases the chances of contagion. The fact that boys' play is less closely monitored (partly because they more often play outdoors, on the streets) not only means that a given boy is less likely to be caught and disciplined in his early explorations of antisocial behavior, but also that he has many opportunities to observe other boys who manage to evade negative consequences when they engage in such activities. Furthermore, even though many boys' groups socialize their members in prosocial ways, certain forms of aggression, risk-taking, noise-making, and showing off are both tolerated and even encouraged more than they are in girls' groups.

We must be careful not to exaggerate the sex difference. Girls, of course, are not free of group pressure toward deviance. There are girls' gangs in some environments. Pairs of best friends can shoplift together, and in adolescence, when cross-sex interactions increase, girls sometimes become accomplices in boys' gang activities. Nevertheless, the conditions of the childhood male and female cultures do not predispose girls to delinquent gang activities to the same extent.

So far, the discussion has focused entirely on group processes predisposing children toward antisocial behavior. What about prosocial behavior? In a sense, there is less here that calls for explanation, at least where sex differences are concerned. Although the male and female rates of a variety of antisocial behaviors are clearly different, the sexes appear to be much more alike when it comes to a prosocial behavior. In their recent review of the developmental research in this field, Radke-Yarrow, Zahn-Waxler, and Chapman (1983) conclude that although there is a slight difference in favor of girls in empathic reactions, studies generally find no sex difference in cooperation, sharing, or offering help and sympathy. However, it should be noted that the very large majority of studies included in the review were done in laboratory settings involving contrived situations and activities. Also, they tended to involve either simulated unfamiliar partners or artificially composed groups of children who either were not previously acquainted or who normally did not play together. In naturalistic settings, individual children often do not show a generalized "trait" of altruism. Rather, their altruistic behavior tends to be target specific, shown toward children who are frequent playmates, as part of the whole pattern of their social interaction (Strayer, 1980). Thus, the more impersonal laboratory studies in which children are asked to donate money, candy, or prizes to anonymous needy persons might easily fail to reflect the amount of altruism that goes on among friends. Hartup (1983) summarized the work in which comparisons are made between the interactions of friends and those of unacquainted children, and finds, not surprisingly, that rates of cooperation, sharing, and other forms of mutual support are higher among friends for children of both sexes. It is possible, then, that the interaction in girls' groups—groupings that tend to involve close friendship ties—really is more cooperative, more mutually supportive, than that which occurs in boys' groups, even though a sex difference does not emerge in artificially composed groups.

We must be cautious when it comes to the distinction between cooperative and competitive behavior, however. The study by Shapira and Madsen (1974), described earlier, showed that boys' groups increased their within-group cooperation when put into competition with other groups. We are reminded that high levels of cooperation are called for in boys' competitive sports (see Maccoby & Jacklin, 1974, for further discussion of this issue), and team sports may represent a sphere in which cooperation is not only great in boys' groups, but qualitatively different from the cooperation found among girls in most settings.

Radke-Yarrow et al. (1983) make the point that girls may have a better reputation for being prosocial than they deserve. They show that there are studies in which teachers' or peers' ratings of prosocial behavior give girls higher scores, whereas observational studies of the same groups of children do not reveal significant sex differences. Once again it should be noted that the observational work in these studies involved contrived, rather than naturalistic, situations (Hartshorne & May, 1928; Shigetomi, Hartmann & Gelfand, 1981). But it may also be true that certain behaviors that girls display frequently during interaction (e.g., smiling, agreeing) cause others to believe that they have benign intent, even when they do not, and this augments their reputation for altruism unrealistically. In addition, of course, a girl may be seen as more altruistic because her efforts to help, comfort, or share are less often accompanied by self-display, teasing, roughness, or the other "male" behaviors that may make the meaning of a given altruistic act more ambiguous.

Assuming for the moment, however, that girls' reputation for altruism is truly undeserved, it nevertheless ought to set in motion circular processes that would augment the girls' actual prosocial behavior. Snyder, Tanke, and Berscheid (1977) have shown that if persons are treated by others as though they had a certain characteristic (e.g., physical attractiveness), they begin to show more of the behaviors called for by their attributed trait. Dodge (1980) has shown that children who have a reputation for being aggressive are reacted to in more irritable ways by other children, even when their actual behavior at the moment does not justify these reactions. Girls' benign reputations, therefore, may create a social environment in which it is easier for them to carry out into action whatever prosocial impulses they may have.

In the discussion of antisocial behavior, the point was made that there is a higher incidence among boys of individual characteristics that predispose them to antisocial behavior in groups. Is there any history in girls' development that feeds into the intimate friendship patterns seen in girls' groups? Evidence is beginning to accumulate that boys are at somewhat greater risk for conflict with their parents, and that, in some respects, girls establish closer familial ties in early childhood period. There appears to be no sex differences in the security of attachment, but Gunnar and Donahue (1980) reported that a group of female infants aged 6–12 months initiated more interaction with their mothers and were more responsive to maternal vocalizations than a group of like-aged infants, and this was true despite the fact that maternal responsiveness was not related to the infant's sex. Bates (1980), reports that in his sample male and female infants up to age 18 months did not differ in their level of "difficultness" (fussyness and resistance to caretaking routines). By age 2 years, however, most of the difficult girl infants had moderated their behavior and settled into a reasonably comfortable relationship with their caretakers, whereas many of the "difficult" boys remained so. This is consistent with the studies of frustration reactions, which show a marked decline between the ages of 18 months and 2 years in girls' tendency to have a flare-up of temper when their ongoing activity is blocked, whereas for boys the frequency and intensity of such reactions remains high (Goodenough, 1931; Van Lieshout, 1975). In our own observations (Snow, Maccoby, & Jacklin, 1983), we have found that in a waiting room situation with their fathers, girls as young as 12 months of age are more likely to refrain from handling "forbidden" objects (tippable vases, filled ashtrays), even though in other respects they are as exploratory as the boys. Based on home observations of children in their second year, higher rates of touching forbidden objects and otherwise getting into mischief have been found for boys' than for girls (Minton, Kagan, & Levine, 1971; Smith & Daglish, 1977).

With somewhat older children, Hetherington, Cox, and Cox (1982) have reported more compliance to the requests of both mothers and fathers on the part of girls than of boys. This is true both in intact and recently divorced families. Block (1979) finds from interview studies that both parents and children report more mutual affection, and more enjoyable joint activities, involving parents and daughters than parents and sons. In our own work (Maccoby & Jacklin, 1983) the interactive play of both mothers and fathers with their 45-month-old children has been observed. In free play with toys brought to the homes by our observers, there were higher levels of thematic play (i.e., play in which the partners act from a shared fantasy script) in the mother–daughter pairs than in any other dyad. Whiting and Whiting (1973) in their cross-cultural study of parents and children in six cultures, reported that girls were often seen joining in, in a friendly way, with their mothers' activities, or trying to get their mothers to join in theirs, whereas boys were more demanding and appeared to be attempting to control or dominate their mothers' activity in the interests of their individual goals.

Not only is it the case that girls appear to develop a closer cooperative relationship with their mothers in "normal" families, but girls also appear to be less vulnerable to familial stress (Hetherington, Cox, & Cox, 1982;

Rutter, 1970; Wallerstein & Kelly, 1980). Even in the face of high levels of mother–father discord, and even during a period following divorce, parent–daughter pairs maintain a closer relationship than parent–son pairs. With boys, there is notable deterioration in the relationship: Boys become defiant and aggressive, and mothers become more coercive.

In all the studies cited above, there is considerable overlap in the distributions of scores for the two sexes. Nevertheless, the body of work does suggest that by the time children are old enough to enter peer groups, girls have had more experience than boys in cooperative interaction with intimate others. This may influence the nature of the peer relations that they characteristically establish, and create a support network made up of both family and close friends. By high school age, girls name twice as many people to whom they could go for support as do boys (Ford, 1982).

The primary theme emerging from the analyses in this chapter is that sex differences in children's characteristics in early childhood may contribute somewhat both to the segregation of the sexes in middle childhood and to the characteristics of the groups that are formed by male and female children, but once the groups are formed, they develop their own dynamics that are powerful in shaping the children's prosocial and antisocial behavior. Although the distributions of the two sexes on individual characteristics overlap greatly, it appears that the distributions of group behaviors may be considerably more differentiated by sex. This is partly a reflection of the different kinds of activities in which boys' and girls' groups normally engage, but the differences in interaction style probably transcend specific activities. Within families, children normally interact with persons of both sexes. It is only in their sex-segregated peer groups that they have an opportunity to develop a highly sex-typed interaction style. It has become clear that sex-differentiated styles do develop and that children monitor one another's behavior and impose pressures for conformity to the group standards. Thus, sex-segregated peer groups add to sex differentiation by contributing new distinctive experiences to the socialization that individual boys and girls have undergone at earlier periods in their lives.

REFERENCES

Abel, H., & Sahinkaya, R. Emergence of sex and race friendship preferences. *Child Development, 1962, 33,* 939–943.

Bates, J. E. *Difficult infants and their mothers.* Unpublished report, *Indiana University,* 1980.

Block, J. H. Another look at sex differentiation in the socialization behavior of mothers and fathers. In J. Sherman and F. L. Denmark (Eds.), *Psychology of women: Future directions of research.* New York: Psychological Dimensions, 1979.

Brooks-Gunn, J., & Schempp, W. *He and she: How children develop their sex role identity.* Englewood Cliffs, NJ: Prentice Hall, 1979.

Charlesworth, R., & Hartup, W. W. Positive social reinforcement in the nursery school peer group. *Child Development,* 1967, *38,* 993–1002.

Clark, A. H., Wyon, S. M., & Richards, M. P. M. Free play in nursery school children. *Journal of Child Psychology and Psychiatry,* 1969, *10,* 205–216.

Crockenberg, S. B., Bryant, B. K., & Wilce, L. S. The effects of cooperatively and competitively structured learning environments on inter- and intrapersonal behavior. *Child Development,* 1976, *47,* 386–396.

Damon, W. *The social world of the child.* San Francisco: Jossey-Bass, 1977.

DePietro, J. Rough and tumble play: A function of gender. *Developmental Psychology,* 1981, *17,* 50–58.

Dodge, K. Social competition and children's aggressive behavior, *Child Development,* 1980, *51,* 162–170.

Duck, S. W. Personality similarity and friendship choices by adolescents. *European Journal of Social Psychology,* 1975, *5,* 351–265.

Eder, D., & Hallinan, M. T. Sex differences in children's friendships. *American Sociological Review,* 1978, *43,* 237–250.

Fagot, B. I. Consequences of moderate cross-gender behavior in preschool children. *Child Development,* 1977, *48,* 902–907.

Friedrich, L. K., & Stein, A. H. Aggressive and prosocial television programs and the natural behavior of preschool children. *Monographs of the Society for Research in Child Development,* 38, No. 4, 1973.

Ford, M. E. Social cognition and social competence in adolescence. *Developmental Psychology,* 1982, *18,* 323–340.

Goodenough, F. L. *Anger in young children.* University of Minnesota Press: Minneapolis, 1931.

Goodwin, M. H. Directive-response speech sequences in girls and boys task activities. In S. McConnel-Ginet, R. Barker, and N. Furman (Eds.), *Women and language in literature and society.* New York: Praeger, 1980.

Gottman, J. *Conversations of friends: Speculations in affective development.* New York: Cambridge University Presss. (in press)

Gunnar, M. R., & Donahue, M. Sex differences in social responsiveness between six months and twelve months. *Child Development,* 1980, *51,* 262–265.

Harkness, S., & Super, C. The cultural content of gender segregation in children's peer groups. *Child Development,* 1985, *56,* 219–224.

Hartshorne, H., & May, M. A. *Studies in the nature of character. Vo. I: Studies in deceit.* New York: MacMillan, 1928.

Hartup, W. W. Peer relations. In P. H. Mussen (Ed.), *Handbook of child psychology,* 4th Ed., Vol. 4. New York: Wiley, 1983.

Hetherington, E. M., Cox, M., & Cox, R. Effects of divorce on parents and children. In M. Lamb (Ed.), *Non-traditional families.* Hillsdale, NJ: Lawrence Erlbaum Associates, 1981.

Hoffman, M. L. Moral development. In P. H. Mussen (Ed.), *Manual of child psychology.* New York: Wiley, 1970.

Hutt, S. J., & Hutt, C. *Direct observation and measurement of behavior.* Springfield, IL: Thomas, 1970.

Jacklin, C. N., & Maccoby, E. E. Social behavior at thrity-three months in same-sex and mixed-sex dyads. *Child Development,* 1978, *49,* 557–569.

Kandel, D. B. Similarity in real-life adolescent friendship pairs. *Journal of Personality and Social Psychology,* 1978, *36,* 306–312.

Krenkel, N. *Self-concept and interaction patterns of children in a desegregated school.* Master's thesis, California State University, San Francisco, 1972.

LaFreniere, P., Strayer, F. F., & Gauthier, R. The emergence of same-sex preferences among preschool peers: A developmental ethological perspective. *Child Development,* 1984, *55,* 1958–1965.

Langlois, J. H., & Downs, A. C. Peer relations as a function of physical attractiveness: The eye of the beholder or behavioral reality? *Child Development,* 1979, *50,* 409–418.

Leimbach, M., & Hartup, W. Forming cooperative coalitions during a competitive game in same-sex and mixed-sex triad. *Journal of Genetic Psychology,* 1981.

Lever, J. Sex differences in the games children play. *Social Problems,* 1976, *23,* 478–487.

Lockheed, M. E. Some determinants and consequences of sex segregation in the classroom. In L. C. Wilkinson & C. B. Marrett (Eds.), *Gender influences in classroom interaction.* San Diego, CA: Academic Press. (in press)

Lockheed, M., & Klein, S. *Sex equity in classroom organization and climate.* In S. Klein (Ed.), *Handbook for achieving Sex equity through education.* Johns Hopkins University Press, 1985.

Luria, Z., & Herzog, E. *Gender segregation across and within settings.* Paper presented at the biennial meetings of the Society for Research in Child Development, Toronto, Canada, 1985.

Maccoby, E. E., & Jacklin, C. N. *The psychology of sex differences.* Stanford: Stanford University Press, 1974.

Maccoby, E. E., & Jacklin, C. N. Six difference in aggression: A rejoinder and reprise. *Child Development,* 1980, *51,* 964–980.

Maccoby, E. E., & Jacklin, C. N. The "person" characteristics of children and the family as environment. In D. Magnussen & V. Allen (Eds.), *Human development: A developmental perspective.* Academic Press, 1983.

Maccoby, E. E., & Jacklin, C. N. *Gender segregation in nursery school: Predictors and outcomes.* Paper presented at the biennial meetings of the Society for Research in Child Development, Toronto, Canada, 1985.

Maltz, D. N., & Borker, R. A. A cultural approach to male-female miscommunication. In John A. Gumperz (Ed.), *Language and Social Identity,* 1982.

McCandless, B. R., & Hoyt, J. M. Sex, ethnicity and play preferences of preschool children. *Journal of Abnormal and Social Psychology,* 1961, *62,* 683–685.

McLoyd, V. The effects of structure of play objects on the pretend play of low-income preschool children. *Child Development,* 1983, *54,* 626–635.

Minton, C., Kagan, J., & Levine, J. A. Maternal control and obedience in the 2-year-old. *Child Development,* 1971, *42,* 1873–1894.

Morgan, G. A., & Ricciuti, H. N. Infant's response to strangers during their first year. In B. M. Foss (Ed.), *Determinants of infant behavior,* Vol. 4. New York: Wiley, 1969.

Newson, J., & Newson, E. *Perspectives on school at seven years old.* Winchester, MD: Allen and Unwin, 1977.

Olweus, D. Aggression and peer acceptance in adolescent boys: Two short-term longitudinal studies of ratings. *Child Development,* 1977, *48,* 1301–1313.

Olweus, D. *Aggression in the schools.* New York: John Wiley & Sons, 1978.

Omark, D. R., Omark, M., & Edelman, M. S. *Formation of dominance hierarchies in young children.* Paper presented at the IXth International Congress of Anthropological and Ethological Sciences, Chicago, 1973.

Parten, M. B. Social participation among preschool children. *Journal of Abnormal and Social Psychology,* 1932, *27,* 243–269.

Patterson, C. R. *Coercive family processes.* Eugene, OR: Castalia Press, 1982.

Radke-Yarrow, M., Zahn-Waxler, C., & Chapman, M. Children's prosocial dispositions and behavior. In P. H. Mussen (Ed.), *Handbook of child psychology*, 4th Ed., Vol. 4, 1983.

Rutter, M. Sex differences in children's responses to family stress. In E. J. Anthony and C. M. Koupernik (Eds.), *The child and his family*. New York: John Wiley & Sons, 1970.

Sacks, H. An analysis of the course of a joke's telling in conversation. In R. Bauman and J. Sherzer (Eds.), *Explorations in the ethnography of speaking*. New York: Cambridge University Press, 1974.

Savin-Williams, R. c. An ethological study of dominance formation and maintenance in a group of human adolescents. *Child Development*, 1976, *47*, 972–979.

Schofield, J. W. Complimentary and conflicting identities: Images of interaction in an inter-racial school. In S. A. Asher and J. M. Gottman (Eds.), *The development of children's friendship*. New York: Cambridge University Press, 1981.

Serbin, L. A., Tonick, I. J., & Sternglanz, S. H. Shaping cooperative cross-sex play. *Child Development*, 1977, *48*, 924–929.

Shaffran, R., & Decarie, T. G. *Short-term stability of infants' responses to strangers*. Paper presented at the Society for Research in Child Devlopment meetings, Philadelphia, April, 1973.

Shapira, A., & Madsen, M. C. Between- and within-group cooperation and competition among kibbutz and non-kibbutz children. *Developmental Psychology*, 1974, *10*, 140–245.

Shigetomi, C. C., Hartmann, D. P., & Gelfand, D. M. Sex differences in children's altruistic behavior and reputations for helpfulness. *Developmental Psychology*, 1981, *17*, 434–437.

Singleton, L. C., & Asher, S. R. Racial integration and children's peer preferences: An investigation of developmental and cohort differences. *Child Development*, 1979, *50*, 936–941.

Smith, P. K., & Daglish, L. Sex differences in parent and infant behavior. *Child Development*, 1977, *48*, 1250–1254.

Snow, M. E., Jacklin, C. N., & Maccoby, E. E. Sex-of-child differences in father-child interaction at 12 months of age. *Child Development*, 1983, *54*, 227–232.

Snyder, M., Tanke, E. D., & Berscheid, E. Social perception and interpersonal behavior: On the self-fulfilling nature of social stereotypes. *Journal of Personality and social Psychology*, 1977, *35*, 655–666.

St. John, N., & Lewis, R. Race and the social structure of the elementary classroom. *Sociology of Education*, 1975, *48*, 346–268.

Strayer, F. F. Social ecology of the preschool peer group. In W. Andrew Collins (Ed.), *Development of cognition, affect, and social relations, the Minnesota Symposium on Child Psychology*, Vol. 13. Hillsdale, NJ: Lawrence Erlbaum Associates, 1980.

Thorne, B. Girls and boys together; but mostly apart: Gender arrangements in elementary schools. In W. W. Hartup & Z. Rubin (Eds.), *Relationships and development*. Hillsdale, NJ: Lawrence Erlbaum Publishers. (in press)

Unger, R. *Female and male: Psychological perspectives*. New York: Harper & Row, 1979.

Van Lieshout, C. F. M. *Reactions of young children to barriers placed by their mothers*. Unpublished manuscript, Stanford University, CA, 1974.

Waldrop, M. F., & Halverson, C. F. Intensive and extensive peer behavior: Longitudinal and cross-sectional analyses. *Child Development*, 1975, *46*, 19–26.

Wallerstein, J. S., & Kelly, J. R. *Surviving the breakup: How children and parents cope with divorce*. New York: Basic Books, 1980.

Whiting, J. W. M., & Whiting, B. B. Altruistic and egoistic behavior in six cultures. In L. Nader & T. W. Maretzk (Eds.), *Cultural illness and health: Essays in human adaptation*. Washington, DC: American Anthropological Association, 1973.

13

The Role of Television in the Development of Prosocial and Antisocial Behavior

LEONARD D. ERON and L. ROWELL HUESMANN

In the past 10 years, there have been over a thousand articles in psychological journals regarding the effects of the media on behavior. Most of these have been concerned with television (TV) and its effect on aggressive behavior, especially the aggressive behavior of children. However, there have also been a number of articles that have dealt with the effect of TV on prosocial behavior. To be precise, we would have to say that the latter research has been mostly concerned with the potential effect of TV on prosocial behavior: What could happen if TV programming were changed to emphasize socially desirable, constructive, cooperative, empathic, altruistic, helpful, sharing and other behaviors defined as prosocial? This is to say that the studies on prosocial behavior, with a few exceptions mentioned below, have emanated largely from the laboratory, whereas the aggression studies have come both from the laboratory and the field where violent programs are common.

In both the laboratory and field investigation of aggression and TV, the emphasis has been on demonstrating a causal effect without much regard for investigating how the effect is produced. On the other hand, the studies of prosocial behavior and TV have been somewhat more concerned with process models. Thus, even though these latter studies have not been nearly so numerous, they have been more convincing in demonstrating how the media, especially TV, have been influential in the socialization of children in our culture. It is very likely, of course, that the same processes explain the effect of TV on the development of both kinds of behaviors.

That there is a consistent relation between TV violence viewing and subsequent aggressive behavior on the part of the viewer is no longer disputed; it has been demonstrated many times both in the laboratory and in field investigations (Lefkowitz & Huesmann, 1981; Huesmann, 1982). Also, there is little doubt that this relation is primarily one of cause and effect. True, the relation is not a powerful one that explains a major portion of the variance. However, the correlations usually obtained are certainly as high as those found in any other research with personality variables, and the fact that the association holds up under a wide variety of experimental conditions and measurement operations increases confidence in the validity of the findings. The same is true for prosocial television and its relation to subsequent behaviors that we label as positive in society. There is little doubt that TV is an influential socializing agent and that viewing of TV affects all kinds of behavior on the part of the viewer. Those who developed TV for commercial purposes could have told us this a long time ago. Television executives, manufacturers, and merchandisers did not need our research to convince them. However, for some reason, these same individuals have consistently denied that there is any proved effect of programming on antisocial behavior, although they have never denied an effect on prosocial behavior.

Although one can never demonstrate cause and effect with certainty from nonmanipulative field studies, the integration of field studies with laboratory experiments leads to the conclusion that TV viewing and subsequent behavior are causally related. Most probably, however, the relation is bidirectional and derives from multiple psychological processes. Laboratory studies have shown conclusively that aggression and prosocial behavior can be induced by TV viewing. The results from field studies are naturally less clear because of methodological complexities. However, causal effects in longitudinal studies have been reported over 10 years (Eron, Huesmann, Lefkowitz, & Walder, 1972), over 1 year (Singer & Singer, 1981) and over 3 years in two countries (Huesmann, Lagerspetz, & Eron, 1984). In the latter study, described in more detail below, we found evidence of weak bidirectional causal effects even when controlling for initial levels of aggression and violence viewing. Milavsky, Kessler, Stipp, and Rubens (1982), in a multi-year longitudinal study, funded by the National Broadcasting Company (NBC), found remarkably similar results using the same analysis techniques. Although their conclusion was that a "causal effect was not proven," their results are actually consistent with a cumulative causal process that produces only small changes over a few years. For example, their causal coefficients increased as the longitudinal period increased.

Obviously, TV violence does not have the same effect on everybody. Some high-violence viewers are unaggressive, and some low-violence viewers are aggressive. What remains to be done is to explicate the boundary conditions within which the cause and effect relation obtains and to delineate the crucial intervening variables in the relation. To accomplish these goals, we conducted a 3-year longitudinal study with children in middle childhood that has now been replicated in five other countries. In this chapter, we refer to these studies as well as to others that have tried to determine under what conditions, and by what processes, the effect of TV on aggressive behavior becomes manifest, and how the effect is exacerbated and/or mitigated. In the area of prosocial behavior, we have relied to a great extent on research already summarized in two review articles by Rushton (1979, 1982).

The subject variables thus far investigated that might mark the boundary conditions of the relation between TV violence viewing and aggression are age, gender, IQ, social status, and sociocultural environment. Additional mediating and/or potentiating variables that might affect the relation are the amount of time spent viewing TV (frequency of viewing), the child's popularity among his or her peers, identification of viewer with TV characters, and how realistic the viewer believes TV programs are. We briefly summarize the evidence for how each of these variables influences the relation and then conclude with an attempt to trace the process by which continued observation of either antisocial or prosocial TV content can influence the behavior of children. The processes that might explain the effect are observational learning, attitude change, and arousal. Rushton, in his 1979 review of prosocial behavior, refers to norms of appropriate behavior and direct emotional response to stimuli as explanatory constructs for understanding television effects. Observational learning and attitude change could easily be interpreted as setting of norms. What is referred to as arousal here has some similarities to emotional response to stimuli as explicated by Rushton.

THE VARIABLES

Age

From results of our earlier studies (Eron, Huesmann, Lefkowitz, & Walder, 1972; Lefkowitz, Eron, Walder, & Huesmann, 1977) in which we followed a large group of subjects from age 8 to 19 years, we surmised that there must be a sensitive period in a child's development, probably around ages 8 to 12 years, when youngsters are especially susceptible to the influence of violent TV. This surmise was based on our finding that there was no relation between the violence of programs these subjects watched at age 19 years and their aggressive behavior at that time, although there had been a significant contemporaneous relation for the same subjects at age 8 years. Further, the correlation over time was larger than the early contemporaneous one. This suggested there might be a cumulative effect at least into late childhood or the early adolescent years.

To check on these suppositions and to determine the boundaries of this sensitive period, we undertook a new 3-year longitudinal study in which we investigated the TV habits and aggressive behaviors of a group of 672 youngsters in Oak Park, Illinois, a socially and economically heterogeneous suburb of Chicago, and 86 children from two inner-city parochial schools in Chicago (Eron, Huesmann, Brice, Fischer, & Mermelstein, 1983; Huesmann, Eron, Klein, Brice, & Fischer, 1983). Half of the subjects were in the first grade (age 6 years) and half in the third grade (age 8 years) at the beginning of the data collection. During the first year of the study, the youngsters were tested in their classrooms with a variety of paper-and-pencil procedures, and their parents were interviewed individually. The children were subsequently tested again in both the second and third years of the study with the same procedures.

With this overlapping, longitudinal design, it was possible to separate age effects from cohort effects and to trace the development of both TV habits and aggressive behavior as well as the relation between them from ages 6 to 10 years. This study has been or is now being replicated in five other countries: Finland, Poland, Australia, the Netherlands, and Israel (Huesmann, Lagerspetz, & Eron, 1984).

In general, as Table 13.1 illustrates, we found that indeed the relation between TV violence viewing and aggression is already emerging at age 6 years, but the relation is not as substantial and consistent across samples of that age as in samples of 9- to 11-year-olds. Such a finding is consistent with the theory that the effect of violence is cumulative (Eron, Huesmann, Brice, Fischer, & Mermelstein, 1983). Other investigators have also demonstrated that violence viewing can affect behavior at even earlier ages. Singer and Singer (1981) followed a sample of 3- and 4-year-olds over the course of a year, measuring a number of variables at four different times and concluded that TV violence is a cause of increased aggressiveness even in children at that age. The Singers state,

> our data reflecting a third or fourth of the life span of preschoolers seem to point to
> . . . (a) causal link between watching TV, especially programs with violent content

and subsequent aggression. Certainly, our results seem to argue against attributing the later watching of violent TV fare to an aggressive trend in personality or to some third underlying factor. (Singer & Singer, 1981, p. 115)

Although not specifically concerned with aggression and TV violence, McCall, Parke, and Kavanaugh (1977) demonstrated that children as young as 2 years old were facile at imitating televised behaviors and some imitation was observed in even younger children. Indeed some children are already attentive to television as early as 6 to 9 months of age (Hollenbeck & Slaby, 1979).

Table 13.1

Correlations between Television Violence Viewing and Peer Nominated Aggression

Grade	Males	Females
United States[b]		
1st	.160*	.215**
2nd	.204*	.245***
3rd[a]	.191*	.205*
4th	.184*	.260***
5th	.199**	.294***
Finland[c]		
1st	—	.139
2nd	.266*	—
3rd[a]	—	.192
4th	.381***	−.158
5th	.278*	—
Poland[d]		
1st	.296**	—
2nd	.170	.179
3rd[a]	.259**	.236*
4th	.185	.127
5th	—	.277**
Australia[e]		
1st	—	—
2nd	—	.223*
3rd[a]	.175	.244*
4th	.329***	.213*
5th	.207**	.236*

[a] The correlations for the two cohorts have been averaged for the third grade.
[b] N = 758.
[c] N = 220.
[d] N = 237.
[e] N = 290.
* $p \} .05$
** $p \} .01$
*** $p \} .005$.

As for the upper end of this susceptibility age range, we had argued (Eron et al., 1972) that once an individual has reached adolescence, behavioral predispositions and inhibitory controls would have become so crystallized that it would be difficult for TV to influence patterns of characteristic behavior such as aggression. However, more recently, Belson (1978) collected data on 1650 teenage boys in London and concluded that "the evidence is very strongly supportive of the hypothesis that high exposure to television violence increases the degree to which boys engage in serious violence" (p. 15). Also, in a study of adolescents in the United States, Hartnagel, Teevan, and McIntyre (1975) found a significant, though low, correlation between violence viewing and aggressive behavior. Thus, it seems likely that TV violence is a cause of aggressive behavior over a wider age spectrum than previously suspected.

However, because of a number of converging developmental trends,

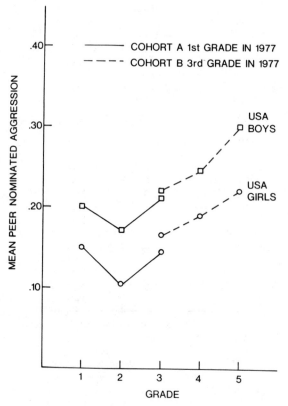

Figure 13.1.   Increase in peer-rated aggression from first to fifth grade.

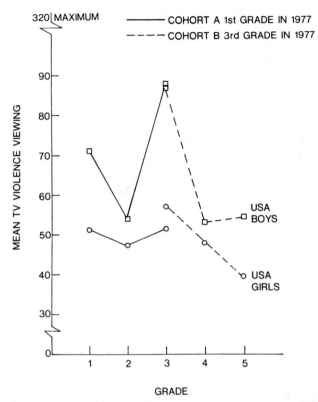

Figure 13.2. Extent of TV violence viewing from first to fifth grade.

such as those demonstrated in our recent developmental study (Eron, Huesmann, Brice, Fischer, & Mermelstein, 1983), it is likely that children around age 8 years in the United States are especially susceptible to the influence of violent TV. From grades 1–5, children are becoming increasingly aggressive; also during that period, the amount of TV violence viewed increases from grade 1 to 3 and then starts to decline. However, the child's perception of televised violence as realistic declines from grades 1 to grade 5. Thus, in the United States, the third grade may be the center of an especially sensitive period when the factors are just right for TV violence to have an effect. (Figures 13.1, 13.2, and 13.3 depict the data.) Some of the strongest relations between television violence and both simultaneous and later aggression have been reported for children about this age (Chaffee, 1972; Lefkowitz et al., 1977). Interestingly, however, the developmental trends for aggression, violence viewing and realism are somewhat different in some of the other countries investigated.

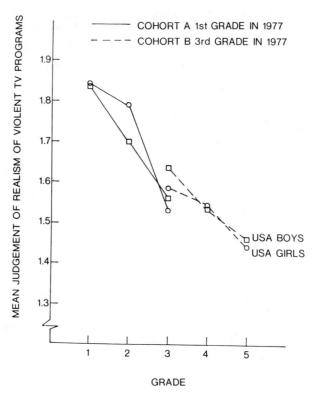

Figure 13.3. Decrease in judgement of TV realism from first to fifth grade.

Thus, one effect of the specific socialization processes employed in a culture may be to alter the time of the sensitive period when TV can have its greatest effects.

The studies concerned with TV and *prosocial* behavior have been conducted almost exclusively with young children from preschool age to 10 years old, and there have been no longitudinal studies to trace the development of prosocial behavior or its relation to TV viewing over the years. Most of the studies have been done in the laboratory. For example, Pitkanen-Pulkkinen (1979) showed that the aggressive behavior of 8-year-old aggressive boys could be reduced by watching films depicting constructive solutions to conflicts that occur frequently in children's everyday life. Even those studies termed *naturalistic* are not really field studies, that is, they do not take measures of the subjects' normal TV-viewing habits and relate them to behavior in real-life settings. A typical naturalistic study is one by Stein and Friedrich (1972) in which approximately 100 nursery school children were randomly assigned to one of three groups to watch selected TV programs for 4 weeks. One group watched aggressive TV programs such as "Batman" cartoons; a second group watched neutral films such as children working on a farm; and a third group watched "Mr. Roger's Neighborhood," a prosocial program in which cooperative, friendly, and calm behavior is modeled. During this 4-week period, the children's free-play behavior was recorded by blind observers, coded into categories such as "aggressive" and "prosocial" compared to the frequency of such behaviors recorded in a baseline period prior to the TV exposure. The results demonstrated the effect of the programs on the subjects' behavior. Exposure to prosocial content led to increased prosocial behavior, whereas exposure to aggressive content led to increased aggressive behavior. However, on a retest 2 weeks after final exposure, the effect both for prosocial and antisocial behavior disappeared although an effect for self-control favoring the Mr. Rogers' group persisted. However, other studies with children of this age have demonstrated the effect over a longer period (Coates, Pusser, & Goodman, 1976).

Wiegman, Baarda, and Seydel (1982) report a study done in the Netherlands with children aged 4–6 years, comparing the effectiveness of prosocial and aggressive films in encouraging corresponding behaviors. The prosocial, aggressive, and neutral films used in the study were carefully matched in terms of duration of explicit content. The researchers found that the prosocial film was more effective in eliciting subsequent prosocial behavior than the aggressive film was in encouraging aggressive behavior. This is contrary to Rosenhan and White's statement (1967) that aggressive behavior is more easily modeled than altruistic behavior. The difference in findings may be the result of lack of control for the salience of the two types of behavior in both studies.

Gender

What are the limits on the relation between TV violence and aggression set by gender? In our 1960–1970 longitudinal study, we found a significant effect for boys but not for girls. During this same period, Schuck (1971) found similar differences between boys and girls in aggressive behavior after listening to a violent radio broadcast. One explanation for this difference in effects on boys and girls was that in 1960, when the measures were taken originally, there were no female aggressive models for girls to imitate. From an observational learning point of view, all other things being equal, the most effective models would be those most similar to the observer. And, in 1960, females on television served only as objects of violence or passive observers. A more complex social learning point of view would implicate the kinds of behavior that are reinforced in young girls as they grow up to become adolescents and adults. In the United States, at least during the period that these girls were growing up and learning their social roles—in the middle or late 1950s—girls were discouraged from being aggressive and participating in masculine-like, large-muscle activities. Thus, aggressive behavior was not relevant for them and would not easily be incorporated into their repertoire of problem-solving behaviors. Also, girls who, as has been known, learn to speak and read earlier than boys are more apt to engage in fantasy-type activities and imaginative play. As Singer and Singer have demonstrated (1981), prosocial imaginative play is related to reduced aggression. Also, the increased use of fantasy may lead to a greater application of the distinction between fantasy and reality. In 1960 and 1970, girls believed TV was less realistic than did boys (Lefkowitz et al., 1978). Further, those girls who believed TV was realistic were more aggressive than girls who did not believe TV was realistic, and they were more like boys in other ways as well (e.g., they preferred boys' games to girls' games and liked to watch contact sports on TV). Thus, it would seem that gender is a limiting factor in the relation between TV and aggression to the extent that girls adopt traditional roles and eschew masculine-type activities.

In our more recent 3-year longitudinal study, we included measurements to evaluate the relative merits of the observational learning and gender-role learning explanations for the discrepancy between the boys and girls in the TV violence–aggression relation. However, we found that now there is an overall significant positive relation between the violence of the TV programs a young girl watches and how aggressive she is judged to be by her peers. Even though boys in general obtain higher aggression scores than girls and also watch significantly more violent TV, the correlation between the two variables is now actually higher for girls than for boys, indicating they are now even more affected by TV violence than are boys. Further, a multiple regression analysis indicates that no matter what the initial level of aggression of girls, those who watch more TV violence are likely to become more aggressive than those who watch less. However, as mentioned above, these more recent data do not support a conclusion of unidirectional casuality. Regressions predicting TV violence viewing from aggressive behavior revealed that those girls who are more aggressive also are more likely to become more frequent violence viewers regardless of their initial level of viewing. The bidirectionality of the effect suggests that a simple observational learning model is not sufficient to explain the correlation between violence viewing and aggression for girls. It should be noted that although there were similar findings of a positive correlation for girls in Poland and the Netherlands, the finding was not replicated in Finland, and Israel in all grades, although it was in some grades.

It does not seem likely that the current relation between a girl's aggression and her violence viewing is due to the presence of more aggressive female models on TV programs now than when the previous longitudinal study was done, although there are indeed many more such models. To test the influence of gender of TV characters on the obtained relation, TV programs were scored for the amount of violence perpetrated by males and females. We found that regardless of the child's gender there were higher correlations between the child's aggressiveness and the child's viewing of a male character's violence than between aggressiveness and the child's viewing of a female character's violence. This apparently greater influence of male models on children has been detected in the data from other countries as well. Thus, it does not seem reasonable to attribute the emergence of a relation between the viewing of violence and aggression in girls to the more recent appearance of aggressive female models on TV.

One of the problems with using gender as a measure of identification with a TV model is that aggression is highly correlated with sex-role orientation (Eron, 1980; Lefkowitz, et al., 1977). Girls who are aggressive may in fact identify more with male actors than with most female actors. It may be that more important than the sex of the model are the behaviors the model is performing and that, if masculine activities are intrinsically more apppealing to subjects of either sex, then all subjects would be more likely to attend to male characters and be influenced most by their behaviors. Along these lines, it has been demonstrated that the more powerful the model, the more likely are the model's behaviors to be copied, regardless of sex (Bandura, et al., 1963). Also as girls get older, they tend to prefer masculine activities more (Eron, 1980).

In our current cross-national study, we measured sex-role orientation by having children select the activities they prefered most from six pictures representing two sterotypic male, two sterotypic female, and two neutral activities. They repeated this task for four sets of pictures, and they received three scores representing the number of masculine, feminine, and neutral activities chosen. The pictures had been selected for use on the basis of 67 college students' ratings of their stereotypicality, and the measure was demonstrated to have good reliability. Table 13.2 shows the correlations between neutral sex-role orientation and peer-nominated aggression for boys and girls over the course of our 3-year study. Although the relations between aggression and either a male or female orientation varied greatly with sex and grade, the relation between aggression and neutral orientation was consistently negative. Children who scored

Table 13.2

Correlations between Preference for Neutral
Sex-Typed Activities and Peer-Nominated
Aggression

	Correlations	
Grade	Girls	Boys
1st	−.197*	−.175*
2nd	−.294**	−.086
3rd[a]	−.135	−.151
4th	−.149	−.200*
5th	−.140	−.117

[a] The correlations for the two cohorts have been
averaged for the third grade.
    * $p \} .05$.
    ** $p \} .01$.

high on neutral sex role apparently were ones who were flexible in their choice of games and activities and not bound by societal stereotypes. Perhaps such children are also more flexible in their choice of behaviors in frustrating situations and therefore less aggressive.

For boys the preference for masculine activities remained relatively constant with age; for girls it increased significantly with age ($r = .284$, $p < .01$). At the same time, as Table 13.1 reveals, the relation between TV violence and aggressiveness was increasing somewhat with age for girls. Also, masculinity in girls was correlated significantly with aggressiveness. The hypothesis is that the recent greater emphasis on the need and desirability for females to be assertive and physically active has resulted in girls having fewer inhibitions about modeling the aggressive behaviors they observe on TV. Thus, many girls now use the actors they observe on TV as models for their behavior. But why should the correlations between TV viewing and aggressive behavior now be even higher for girls than for boys? One possibility is that girls, who have a much lower average level of aggressiveness and are exposed less often to aggressive models in their everyday interactions, have a greater potential for TV violence to change their behavior.

In the literature on prosocial behavior, there is less emphasis on differential effects of prosocial television programming on boys and girls. Prosocial behavior is universally approved for all persons, regardless of gender; therefore, it must be presumed that televised models of prosocial behavior are equally effective for all persons. This lack of difference between genders was indeed found by Collins and Getz (1976). There are a few exceptions to this generalization, however. Friedrich and Stein (1975) analyzed results for boys and girls separately in an investigation of the efficacy of prosocial TV alone and in combination with two kinds of training (verbal labeling and role-playing) in encouraging helping behavior in 73 kindergarten children who were assigned to one of five conditions. All groups except the control group watched "Mr. Roger's Neighborhood." Mr. Rogers is a very cooperative model who verbalizes feelings, copes positively with frustration, and gives high amounts of positive reinforcement. In one group, verbal labels were attached to the program's content; another group engaged in role-playing of the program's content; a third group received both verbal labeling and role-playing; a fourth group received irrelevant training; and the control group viewed a neutral program and received irrelevant training. Effects of the treatments were assessed by a behavioral helping measure (frequency, duration, and latency to help repair another child's destroyed collage). Results showed that children in the role-playing condition displayed the highest levels of helping, especially boys. For girls, helping was greatest in the combined verbal labeling/role-playing condition. There were no differences between the other experimental groups and the control group. These results held for at least 2–3 days after the training. Ahammer and Murray (1979) report similar findings: groups of children (4–5 years old) who viewed prosocial programs such as "Lassie" and "Father Knows Best," $1\frac{1}{2}$ hours per day, 5 days a week for 4 weeks showed more altruistic behaviors 1 week after the end of the training period than children who viewed a neutral program. The altruistic behaviors were helping and cooperating. Helping had been measured by the child's willingness to forego playing with some attractive toys in order to help another absent child complete a task that consisted of placing marbles in a box one at a time. The prosocial increase in this task held for boys only. Cooperation was indicated by the number of candies the child won in contrast to his or her partner while playing a cooperation–competition game. Here, both boys and girls increased cooperation subsequent to watching the prosocial program. Thus, observation of standard TV programs in which the main characters displayed concern for others could be effective in facilitating altruism in specific situational tests quite dissimilar from the situations seen on the programs. However, the effect for boys seemed more pervasive than for girls. Further, altruism was significantly enhanced in three role-playing conditions beyond the prosocial TV viewing condition. These findings as well as those of Friedrich and Stein (1975), suggest that role-playing may be a more important factor than prosocial viewing in fostering imitation of altruistic behaviors, although prosocial television by itself had an independent effect.

In one area of prosocial behavior, displaying affection, the effect on boys of televised models was more limited. Fryear and Thelen (1969) found that boys were likely to become affectionate only if they had observed an adult male behave that way, not if the same behavior had been demonstrated by an adult female.

Intelligence

Intelligence is often invoked as a third variable that might explain the relation between TV violence viewing and aggression. Certainly, intelligence correlates with both these variables. However, in most observational studies, the researchers have measured and partialed out the effect of intelligence and still detected a significant relation between violence viewing and aggression (Belson, 1978; Lefkowitz et al., 1977; Singer and Singer, 1981). In our 10-year longitudinal study, evidence was uncovered that suggested that low achievement led a child to watch more and more TV. Since low achievement and low IQ can be frustrators that may engender aggression, it is not surprising that low achievement and low IQ were also correlated with aggression in that study. However, these correlations could not explain away the relation between violence viewing and aggression. In our later 3-year longitudinal study, low achievement, as measured by the California Achievement Test, was again one of the highest correlates of aggressive behavior. Measured with a standardized test administered by the school system personnel, these reading achievement scores also correlated significantly negatively both with frequency of viewing and with the violence ratings of the favorite programs. When achievement was partialed out, there was no significant change in the relation between TV violence viewing and aggression for girls. However, for boys, the partial correlation between violence viewing and aggression, controlling for achievement, was substantially lower than the raw correlation, although it was still significantly positive. Essentially similar results were obtained in Finland, Poland, and the Netherlands.

It appears that the lower-achieving boys watch their favorite programs more regularly, prefer more violent programs and behave more aggressively. A number of different hypotheses would be consistent with this result, but they are very difficult to distinguish on the basis of observational data. Perhaps the most plausible hypothesis is that the child reacts to poor achievement by turning to TV violence for vicarious gratification, and this increased involvement in TV in turn hampers school achievement. At the same time, the frustration of low achievement coupled with the exposure to TV violence leads the child to more aggressive behaviors. A somewhat different way (admittedly speculative) in which IQ might affect the relation between TV viewing and social behavior would be through the learning process. High-IQ subjects might be more prone to recognize the inappropriateness of portrayed aggressive behaviors and not to change their attitudes or imitate the behavior. Very low-IQ subjects might not learn at all from TV. Thus, IQ might affect the relation between prosocial viewing and behavior as well as between violence viewing and behavior.

However, there has been no systematic investigation of or control for IQ level in research on the effect of TV on prosocial behavior. Most of the studies have been done with normal preschool and primary school subjects. However, at least two studies have been conducted with mentally retarded subjects. Baran and Meyer (1975) presented their subjects, 45 males and 25 female trainable retardates aged 5–20 years, with various hypothetical situations and asked them what they would do in those situations, what was the right thing to do, what their parents would want them to do, and what their favorite TV characters would do. There was a stronger relation between what they said they would do and their favorite TV characters would do than what they would do and their parents would do or what was the right thing to do. Fechter (1971) carried out a study with mental retardates (mean age, 11 years; mean IQ, 36). One group watched a 5-minute film of a 12-year-old child beating up a large inflatable Donald Duck doll. Another group viewed a 5-minute film of the 12-year-old child playing in a friendly manner with the same doll. The behavior of the retardates was then observed for 5 minutes in the experimental room and for 30 minutes on the ward and coded either as friendly (e.g., talking) or aggressive (e.g., fighting) by observers who were not aware of which films the patients had seen. In the ward, the number of aggressive responses increased slightly (but significantly) after the aggressive film and decreased following the friendly film. The change in the number of friendly responses in the ward was not significant, however. From the latter study, it would appear that for intellectually retarded individuals, prosocial programs are not as effective in influencing subsequent prosocial behavior as they are for individuals of average or better intelligence. However, this has not been systematically investigated.

Social Status

Like intelligence, social class is a third variable that is often invoked to explain the relation between two other variables. However, in our 10-year-longitudinal study, partial correlations holding social class constant did not alter the relation between TV violence viewing and aggressive behavior. On the other hand, in the recent 3-year-longitudinal study, although the correlation between TV violence and aggressive behavior is not diminished when social class is controlled, there are some consistent, if weak, effects of father's occupation and education on both the child's aggression and TV viewing. The effects are not significant in Finland or Poland, perhaps because of the greater socioeconomic homogeneity of the population in those countries. In the United States, though, the lower the parents' education and socioeconomic status, the more aggressive was the child, the more the child watched TV and TV violence, the more the child believed the violent shows "tell about life like it is," and the more tha child identified with TV characters. Similarly, the lower the parents' education and social status, the more aggressive were the parents, the more the parents watched TV, and the more the parents believed TV was realistic. Unexpectedly, however, the more poorly educated and lower status parents watched less TV violence and watched more of the same programs that their children watched than the better-educated and higher-status parents. Higher-status parents seem to watch less TV, but more of what they watch is violent. This finding may be a result of the fact that the alternative to violent shows in the United States is most often unsophisticated situation comedies and popular music shows with little appeal to individuals of higher educational attainment.

Socioeconomic status of the family was defined by father's occupation in our 3-year study. However, we also collected data on the mother's occupation and found that in the United States, mothers who were not working had significantly less aggressive children than did working mothers. Yet there were few differences in the TV habits of the children of working and non-working mothers. One possibility is that children of working mothers in the United States are exposed to more frustration and react with more aggressive behavior. Another is that working mothers do not assert as much daily control over their children. Still, another possibility is that working mothers provide a more aggressive role model.

Social status has not often been considered an important variable to be controlled in studies of TV and prosocial behavior. However, in the early study of Stein and Friedrich (1972), discussed earlier in this chapter, the effect they obtained of exposure to prosocial TV content on free-play behaviors was limited to children from the lower half of the socioeconomic status distribution. In a later study, these researchers (Friedrich-Cofer, Huston-Stein, Kipnis, Sussman, & Clewett, 1979) found that 8 weeks of prosocial TV by itself had no influence on the behavior of urban poor children. However, if the prosocial TV was augmented by role-playing of the themes in class, then significant effects were obtained. In other studies, it has also been found necessary to use role-playing and other techniques to reinforce the effect of the prosocial television (Friedrich & Stein, 1975; Ahammer & Murray, 1979). Contrastingly, such techniques have been found useful to mitigate the effects of violence viewing on behavior rather than to exacerbate the effect (Huesmann, Eron, Brice, Fisher, & Klein, 1983; Singer & Singer, 1981). It may be that prosocial behavior is just not as salient as aggressive behavior and its presentation must be enhanced if it is to have mcuh of an effect.

Sociocultural Environment

The last variable to be considered in our survey of the boundary conditions for establishing the relation between TV viewing and behavior is locale. What is the effect of the area of the country or part of the world where the study is done? Our 10-year longitudinal study was conducted in a semirural county in upstate New York from 1960 to 1970. Our recent 3-year study was done in a major urban area of the United States (Chicago) and was replicated in other countries in order to obtain wider variation of sociocultural factors and test the generalizability of the results. Although a number of researchers have reported results from other countries comparable to those reported above for the United States (e.g., Belson, 1978; Gransberg & Steinbring, 1980; Krebs & Groebel, 1977; Murray & Kippax, 1977; Williams, 1978), only a few have studied the effects of TV violence with comparable methodologies in more than one country (e.g., Parke, Berkowitz, Leyens, West, & Sebastian, 1977).

The countries from which we have collected data in the cross-national 3-year longitudinal study (Australia, Finland, Israel, Netherlands, Poland, and the United States) lie in widely separated areas of the world, have different political and economic systems, and vary in degree of governmental control over television programming. Although there are a number of substantial differences in the findings from one country to another, it can be concluded that in general, the relation between the viewing of TV violence and subsequent aggressive behavior on the part of the observer is not limited by sociocultural environment. In each of the countries, a positive relation between the two is obtained.

As for prosocial behavior, although there have been no studies replicated exactly across areas of the United States, or across other countries, studies of the effect of TV on prosocial behaviors have been done in such widely separated areas as the United States (Stein & Friedrich, 1972) England (Rushton & Owen, 1975), Australia (Ahammer & Murray, 1979), New Zealand (Yates, 1974), Canada (Gorn, Goldberg, & Kanungo, 1976), the Netherlands (Wiegman et al., 1982), and Finland (Pitkanen-Pulkinnen, 1979), and the effect holds in all these countries.

So far we have considered some relatively stable variables (e.g., IQ, social class, gender, age) as potential limiters of the relation between television viewing and behavior. However, certain other variables, that are at least in principle modifiable, may also mediate the relations. For example, the child's attitudes about TV, the child's social skills, the child's use of fantasy, and the child's intensity of viewing any type of TV may exacerbate or mitigate a relation. The variables discussed earlier represent defining characteristics of a population to which any generalizations about a specified relation are limited. The mediating variables we now consider also limit a relation, but they refer to more or less ongoing, developing processes that can be understood to intensify, deflect, or inhibit a relation whose possibility or likelihood has already been established.

Intensity of Viewing

One important mediating variable obviously would be the intensity with which a child watches TV in general and particularly the intensity with which he or she watches violent programs. A violent program that is viewed only once in a while would not be expected to have as much effect as a violent program viewed regularly. Although older studies (Eron, 1963; Eron et al., 1972; Robinson & Bachman, 1972) found no relation between total amount of viewing and aggression, McCarthy, Langner, Gerstein, Eisenberg, & Orzeck (1975) reported that frequency of viewing was related to aggression. Similarly, two studies that were done in areas where TV was recently introduced (Granzberg & Steinbring, 1980; Williams, 1978), both suggested that frequency of viewing was a crucial variable. In these and the McCarthy, Langner, Gerstein, Eisenberg, and Orzeck (1975) study, the amount of TV viewed appeared to be a critical potentiating variable in eliciting the relation between violent TV and aggressive behavior.

In our more recent 3-year longitudinal study, the results support this interpretation of frequency as a potentiating variable. The correlations between intensity of viewing and peer-nominated aggression were positive and significant. Intensity of viewing in this context means the frequency with which children watched their favorite programs, not the total numbers of hours TV was watched per week. As a matter of fact, the childrens' report of the intensity with which their eight favorite programs were watched correlated only .20 ($N = 540$, $p < .001$) with the mother's report of the total number of hours the child watched each week, and the mother's report did not correlate with the child's aggression. The correlations in Table 13.1 between TV violence viewing and aggression are based on violence ratings for the child's favorite programs weighted by the intensity with which the child reported watching them. A multiple regression analysis predicting aggression from the product of the frequency and the violence rating indicated that the strongest relation could be obtained if violence ratings, scaled from 4 for "most violent" to 0 for "non-violent," were multiplied by intensity, scaled from 10 for watching "every time it's on" to 0 for watching "only once in a while." This was the method used to compute the violence viewing scores when entering the correlations in Table 13.1. In other words, a program that is only viewed once in a while does not have a significant effect on a child's aggressiveness, no matter how violent the program is. In fact, a violence viewing score unweighted for frequency did not correlate at all with aggressiveness in the United States though it did in other countries. On the other hand, a pure self-reported intensity score correlated as highly as the violence score for some grade–gender combinations. It may be, as some arousal theorists have argued, that excessive viewing, regardless of content stimulates aggressive behavior. Studies cited by Dorr (1982) indicate that aggressive behavior may result as much from arousal produced by hectic sequences in both the commercials and the programs as from specific imitation of aggressive acts. Singer and Singer (1981) demonstrated that children who were consistently heavy viewers of the more frenetic type of programming such as the "Gong Show" and even "Sesame Street" showed increased aggressive behavior in the nursery school 3 months or more later. These results suggest why the movies, on which older generations were raised, did not have the same deleterious effect on young moviegoers as did TV. The serial movies, and the Saturday matinees were certainly violent. The "shoot 'em up Westerns,' and "The Three Stooges," which in their reruns are still among the most aggressive programs on TV, were with us then, but the children were not exposed as often as youngsters are today. It is the incessant, inexorable, ubiquitous nature of day-to-day TV exposure that appears to have a profound effect on the socialization of children, at least in the United States.

Popularity

Individual differences in popularity among one's peers may also play a role as a mediating variable in the aggression–violence viewing relation. Previous studies (Schramm, Lyle, & Parker, 1961) have shown that youngsters with poor social relations spend more time watching TV. Thus, it would be expected that children who are not popular among their peers watch more TV. In our 10-year longitudinal study we indeed found that the less popular child turned to watching more and more TV. At the same time, the less popular child tended to be a more aggressive child. In the current cross-national study, we found significant negative correlations between popularity and aggression in almost all countries and grades in both genders. One may hypothesize that the less-popular child, lacking social reinforcements, watches TV to obtain vicariously the gratifications denied in social interactions. Longitudinal regression analysis indicated that for both genders, unpopularity indeed led to an increase in television violence viewing.

Identification with TV Characters

Although the weight of evidence seems to indicate that all viewers are most likely to imitate a heroic, white male actor, individual differences should not be ignored. It may be that some children identify much more with some actors and this identification mediates the relation between violence viewing and aggressiveness. Such an identification would be important not just in an observational learning model but also in a model that emphasizes norms or standards of behavior. The more the child identifies with the actors who are aggressors or victims, the more likely is the child to be influenced by the scene, believing that the behaviors are appropriate and to be expected.

To test this theory in our 3-year study, we asked the children how much they were like several characters on TV. The characters included two aggressive males, two aggressive females, two unaggressive males, and two unaggressive females. From their responses reliable identification scores were derived.

Not surprisingly, the identification with aggressive characters score correlated significantly with aggressiveness, particulary for boys. More interesting was the discovery that identification with aggressive TV characters interacted with violence viewing to establish an even stronger relation with aggression. Table 13.3 shows a multiple regression predicting later aggression from the product of violence viewing and identification with aggressive characters after earlier aggression was partialed out. The effect is significant for boys. Those boys who watch violent TV and identify with aggressive TV characters are predictably more aggressive 2 years later regardless of their initial level of aggressiveness. Identification with aggressive characters seems to be a catalyst substantially increasing the effect of TV violence on boys. Identification with aggressive TV characters by itself is a good predictor of aggression, but not as significant a predictor as the viewing of television violence.

The relation is illustrated by the means for boys in Table 13.4. Regardless of his initial level of aggressiveness, the boy who watches more violence, perceives it as realistic, and identifies with the violent character,

Table 13.3

Multiple Regressions Relating Boys' Aggression to a Multiplicative Composite of TV Violence Viewing and Identification with Aggressive TV Characters Controlling for Initial Level of the Dependent Variable[a]

Dependent variable	Predictors	Standarized regression coefficients
Aggression in third year		
	Grade	.151**
	Aggression in first year	.679***
	Product of TV violence viewing and identification with aggressive characters for first 2 years	.152**
		$R^2 = .563$, $F (3,187) = 80.3$, $p < .001$
Product of TV violence viewing and identification with aggressive TV characters in third year		
	Grade	−.236***
	Product of TV violence viewing and identification with aggressive characters in first year	.384***
	Aggression in first 2 years	.102
		$R^2 = .232$, $F (3,187) = 18.9$, $p < .001$

[a] N = 191.
* $p \} .05$
** $p \} .01$
*** $p \{ .001$.

is more likely to increase in aggression over 3 years. Furthermore, as Table 13.3 illustrates, this effect is mostly unidirectional from the TV variables to aggression. Aggression is not nearly as good a predictor of the TV variables as the TV variables are of aggression.

It is particularly interesting that this effect is equally strong when one uses the variable "identification with all characters" instead of identification with aggressive characters. Of course, the two variables are correlated. Still, the results show that the child who even believes he is like nonviolent TV characters is more likely to increase in aggressiveness

Table 13.4

Mean Peer-Nominated Aggression in Third Year as a Function of Earlier TV Viewing and
Aggression

| | Girls | | Boys | |
| | TV violence viewing for first 2 years | | Product of TV violence viewing and identification with aggressive TV characters for first 2 years | |
Initial peer-nominated aggression	Low	High	Low	High
High	.284	.334	.419	.427
	(N = 21)	(N = 42)	(N = 25)	(N = 49)
Medium	.131	.167	.195	.214
	(N = 63)	(N = 56)	(N = 38)	(N = 35)
Low	.096	.115	.098	.148
	(N = 37)	(N = 24)	(N = 46)	(N = 27)
Total	.147	.214	.206	.292
	(N = 121)	(N = 122)	(N = 109)	(N = 111)

after regular violence viewing. However, this effect only obtains for boys.
For girls, there is a slight correlation between aggressive behavior and
identification with aggressive TV characters, but the latter variable does
not add to the power of the violence viewing variable in predicting a girl's
aggression. However, the increased predictive power of this combination
for boys is not anomalous. The same result was obtained in Finland.
Although TV violence alone was not a very good predictor of later aggression, the product of violence viewing and identification with aggressive
characters was a highly significant predictor for Finnish boys, regardless
of the child's initial level of aggression. But, as in the United States,
earlier aggression was not a significant predictor of later scores on the
composite TV-viewing variable.

Fantasy–Reality Discriminations

Another potential mediating variable in the relation between television
violence and aggressive behavior might be a child's ability to discriminate
between fantasy and reality as portrayed on TV. Violent scenes perceived
as unrealistic by the child should be less likely to affect the child's behavior. Some evidence for this effect has been provided by Feshbach (1976).

As a result, one might expect that individual differences on this variable could be very important in determining who would be most affected by television violence.

In the 3-year longitudinal study, we measured children's perception of TV violence as fantasy or reality by asking them, "How much do you think "program x" tells about life like it really is? Just like it really is? A little like it is? Not at all like it is?" They were asked this question about 10 violent programs, and their scores were the sum of their responses for the shows they had watched.

In the earlier 10-year longitudinal study (Lefkowitz, et al., 1977) it had been found that girls thought TV was significantly less realistic than boys. It was hypothesized that this might be one of the reasons for the lack of a significant longitudinal relation between violence viewing and aggression for girls at that time. In support of this hypothesis were data indicating that the more aggressive a girl was at both ages 8 and 19 years, the more realistic she thought TV was. In our current study, however, we have found that girls and boys now perceive TV violence to be equally realistic (Huesmann & Eron, 1983). These positive correlations ranged from .11 to .25 depending on the gender and grade of the subjects, and there were no systematic differences though, as indicated previously, the child's perception of TV violence as realistic declines dramatically with age. This adds validity to the theory that fantasy–reality discriminations also mediate the effect of TV violence on aggression since, as pointed out above, girls and boys now display an equally strong relation between violence viewing and aggression. Thus, frequency of this viewing, identification with TV characters, and the tendency to interpret TV as realistic would seem to be significant mediating variables in the relation between TV violence and aggressive behavior in boys.

There has been no report of research in the TV–prosocial behavior relation that has tested directly the effect of any of the intervening variables we have been considering: frequency of viewing, identification with TV characters, or judged realism of programs. However, the study by Fryear and Thelen (1969), discussed above, indicates the importance of identification with someone of the same gender as the observer when the behavior that is to be copied is deemed to be somewhat inappropriate to the observer's gender, i.e., display of affection was only imitated by boys when an adult male demonstrated the behavior. Indirectly, this could be an indication of the potentiating effect of identification with TV characters on subsequent prosocial behavior. There have been no studies of the effect of frequency of exposure or judged realism of the target behaviors on subsequent prosocial behavior.

Fantasy

One final mediating variable that should be considered is the child's use of fantasy. Some theorists have argued that a child who reacts to television violence by fantasizing about aggressive acts might actually become less aggressive (Feshbach, 1964). Although no research has ever reported finding such negative correlation in a field study, this variation of a catharsis theory still raises its head from time to time. A more compelling argument exists that fantasizing about aggressive acts observed on TV through daydreaming or imaginative play should increase the probability that the aggressive acts will be performed. In support of this theory, Singer and Singer (1981) report that children who engage in more prosocial imaginative play and fantasy are less aggressive. The hypothesis is that these children have rehearsed prosocial behaviors sufficiently for them to become dominant responses.

In the current 3-year cross-national study, aggressive and active–heroic fantasy were measured with the Children's Fantasy Inventory (Rosenfeld, Huesmann, Eron, & Torney-Purta, 1982). On this 45-item questionnaire, children report how often they engage in different types of fantasy activity. In the Chicago sample, we found significant positive correlations between peer-nominated aggression and both fantasy variables for boys and girls. The correlation between aggression and active–heroic fantasy was the highest for girls ($r = .17, p < .001$) and the correlation between aggression and aggressive fantasy was highest for boys ($r = .20, p < .001$) (Huesmann & Eron, 1983). These results are consonant with the hypothesis that aggressive fantasizing serves as a cognitive rehearsal of aggressive acts and increases the likelihood of their emission. From the Singers' findings, (1981) it would appear likely that the same is true for prosocial behavior.

A Process Model

We have been considering a number of boundary and mediating variables that define the limits within which the effect of viewing television on the subsequent social behavior of children is operative. We turn now to a consideration of a likely model to explain how this effect comes about.

One aspect of the model has to do with arousal effects. Researchers both in the areas of prosocial and antisocial behaviors have alluded to this process as important in activating the relevant behaviors. However, although the same term is used, authors in the two areas are referring to somewhat different processes, both of which are probably operating. Aggression research has focused on the heightened state of tension, including a strong physiological component, which results from frequent observation of high-action sequences. Arousal here is seen as both a precursor and consequence of aggression (Huesmann, 1982). For prosocial researchers, arousal refers to the acquisition of vicarious emotional responses resulting from observation of models who are displaying strong emotional reactions in the presence of specific stimuli. The emotion presumed to be implicated in such prosocial behaviors as altruism or helping is empathy. The way empathy has been studied in the laboratory bears a close resemblance to observational learning, and the process by which empathy is acquired can probably be subsumed under the rubric of observational learning. Rushton says (1979), "it is likely that seeing a salient model expressing deep concern and distress at the distress cues of another would lead viewers to similar empathic responses" (p. 327). Thus, observational learning would be another part of this model. However, there is more to observational learning than the acquisition of specific emotions. What other aspects of observing a prosocial or antisocial actor and what related behaviors are critical in order for the viewer to behave like the actor? What appears to be important is that the youngster sees his or her favorite TV character acting to solve problems in an aggressive, or on the other hand, cooperative or sympathetic way. Children emulate that behavior when the need arises for solving what appear to be similar problems in their own lives. The evidence for imitation of specific behaviors from field studies of violent TV is only indirect, although confidence in this conclusion is increased to the extent that the effect is exacerbated when the subject identifies with the aggressive TV characters. However, the evidence for imitation is usually more direct in the prosocial studies in which copying of very specific behaviors in the laboratory is the result. It has of course, not been possible to demonstrate a modeling effect in laboratory studies of aggression because of ethical considerations. Thus, such studies are limited to artificial situations in which the direct translation to interpersonal aggression is doubtful (e.g., hitting a BoBo doll). Modeling of prosocial behaviors, however, is generally considered commendable, and thus we have been able to cite a number of studies in which the effect of modeling on prosocial behaviors has been demonstrated unequivocally.

However, whether it is an antisocial or prosocial sequence, the more frequently the child rehearses the sequence by continued viewing, the more likely is it to be remembered and reenacted when the youngster is in a situation perceived to be similar. The fact that role-playing of the model's behavior by the subjects in the prosocial studies increases the relation and that active or aggressive fantasy on the part of the subject in the violence studies exacerbates the effect emphasizes the importance of behavioral rehearsal that results from repeated exposure. Further, by consistently observing either aggressive or prosocial behavior, the younster comes to believe these are expected, appropriate ways of behaving, and that most people solve problems that way. Norms for appropriate behavior are established, and attitudes are formed or changed by observations of other persons' frequent behavior, especially if that behavior is sanctioned by authority figures (Tower, Singer, Singer, & Biggs, 1979). The child who has been watching programs with primarily aggressive content comes away with the impression that the world is a jungle fraught with dangerous threats, and the only way to survive is to be on the attack. The child who has been watching programs with primarily prosocial content will learn that the way to solve problems is through deference, consideration, cooperation, and kindness and that the world is a place where problems can be worked through without unnecessary and irreparable harm done to the self or other persons. These alternatives are, of course, here drawn in the extreme; but the more a youngster is exposed to one or the other type of television content, the more apt he or she is to respond to life situations in a corresponding manner.

However, TV's influence cannot be explained solely in terms of observational learning and the setting of norms of behavior. As results that we have reported earlier indicate, there is a bidirectional effect, at least as far as aggression of girls is concerned, with TV violence causing aggression and aggressive children seeking out TV violence. One possibility is that the aggressive or prosocial child seeks out programs that display behaviors consistent with their own attitudes so these behaviors can be viewed as justified. Another possibility is that aggressive children turn to TV to receive vicariously the social reinforcements that their own aggressive behavior denies them in society. However, there is no evidence that TV violence affects only those children who are already highly aggressive. In both the 10-year and 3-year longitudinal studies, and in both the United States and five other countries in which the study was replicated, the strength of the longitudinal relation varied little as a function of the child's preexisting level of aggression.

As we have said before, aggressive behavior is overdetermined, and the mediating and boundary variables we have discussed all contribute their effects. The process, however, seems to be circular: The viewing of TV violence leads to heightened aggressiveness, which in turn leads to an increase in TV violence viewing. Two mediating variables that appear to play a role in this cycle are the child's academic achievement and social popularity. Children who behave aggressively are less popular and, perhaps because their relations with their peers tend to be unsatisfying, watch more TV and view more violence. The violence they see on TV may reassure them that their own behavior is appropriate or teach them new coercive techniques that they then attempt to use in their interactions with others. Thus, they behave more aggressively, which in turn makes them even less popular and drives them back to TV. The evidence supports a similar role for academic failure. Those children who fail in school watch more TV, perhaps because they find it more satisfying than schoolwork. Thus, they are exposed to more violence and have more opportunity to learn aggressive behavior. Because their intellectual capacities are more limited, the easy aggressive solutions they observe may be incorporated more readily into their behavioral repertoire. In any case, the high frequency of violence viewing isolates them from their peers and gives them less time to work toward academic success. And, of course, any resulting increase in aggression itself diminishes the child's popularity. Thus, the cycle continues with aggression, academic failure, social failure, and TV violence viewing reinforcing each other.

ACKNOWLEDGEMENT

Thanks are due to the National Institute of Mental Health, which has supported much of the research reported here by Grants M1726 and 34410 to Eron and Grants M28280 and 31866 to Huesmann.

REFERENCES

Ahammer, I., & Murray, J. Kindness in the kindergarten: The relative influence of role-playing and prosocial television in facilitating altruism. *International Journal of Behavioral Development,* 1979, *2*(2), 133–157.

Bandura, A., Ross, D., & Ross, S. A. Imitation of film-mediated aggressive models. *Journal of Abnormal and Social Psychology,* 1963, *66,* 3–11.

Baran, S., & Meyer, T. Retarded children's perceptions of favorite television characters as behavioral models. *Mental Retardation,* 1975, *13*(4), 28–31.

Belson, W. *Television violence and the adolescent boy.* Hempshire, England: Saxon House, 1978.

Chaffee, S. H. Television adolescent aggressiveness (overview). In G. A. Comstock and E. A. Rubinstein (Eds.), *Television and social behavior (Vol. 3). Television and adolescent aggressiveness.* Washington, DC: U.S. Government Printing Office, 1972.

Coates, B., Pusser, H. E., & Goodman, I. The influence of "Sesame Street" and "Mister Rogers' Neighborhood" on children's social behavior in the preschool. *Child Development,* 1976, *47,* 138–144.

Collins, W. A., & Getz, S. K. Children's social responses following modeled reactions to provocation: Pro-social effects of a television drama. *Journal of Personality,* 1976, *44,* 488–500.

Dorr, A. L. Television and affective development and functioning. In D. Pearl, L. Bouthilet,

& J. Lazar (Eds.), *Television and behavior: Ten years of scientific progress and implications for the 80's.* Washington, DC: U.S. Government Printing Office, 1982, 68–77.

Eron, L. D. Relationship of TV viewing habits and aggressive behavior in children. *Journal of Abnormal and Social Psychology,* 1963, *67,* 193–196.

Eron, L. D. Prescription for reduction of aggression. *American Psychologist,* 1980, *35,* 244–252.

Eron, L. D., Huesmann, L. R., Brice, P., Fischer, P., & Mermelstein, R. Age trends in the development of aggression, sex typing, and related television habits. *Developmental Psychology,* 1983, *19,* 71–77.

Eron, L. D., Huesmann, L. R., Lefkowitz, M. M., & Walder, L. O. Does television violence cause aggression? *American Psychologist,* 1972, *27,* 253–263.

Fechter, J. V. Modeling and environmental generalization by mentally retarded subjects of televised aggressive or friendly behavior. *American Journal of Mental Deficiency,* 1971, *76,* 266–267.

Feshbach, S. The function of aggression and the regulation of aggressive drive. *Psychological Review,* 1964, *71,* 252–272.

Feshbach, S. The role of fantasy in the response to television. *Journal of Social Issues,* 1976, *32*(4), 71–85.

Friedrich, L. K., & Stein, A. H. Pro-social television and young children. The effects of verbal labelling and role playing on learning and behavior. *Child Development,* 1975, *46,* 27–38.

Friedrich-Cofer, L. K., Huston-Stein, A., Kipnis, D. M., Sussman, E. J., & Clewett, A. S. Environmental enhancement of prosocial television content: Effects on interpersonal behavior, imaginative play, and self-regulation in a natural setting. *Developmental Psychology,* 1979, *15,* 637–646.

Fryear, J. L., & Thelen, M. H. Effect of sex of model and sex of observer on the imitation of affectionate behavior. *Developmental Psychology,* 1969, *1,* 298.

Gorn, G. J., Goldberg, M. E., & Kanungo, R. N. The role of educational television in changing the intergroup attitudes of children. *Child Development,* 1976, *47,* 277–280.

Granzberg, G., & Steinbring, J. *Television and the Canadian Indian.* Technical Report, Department of Anthropology, University of Winipeg, Winnipeg, Manitoba, 1980.

Hartnagel, T. F., Teevan, J. J., & McIntyre, J. J. Television violence and violent behavior. *Social Forces,* 1975, *54,* 341–351.

Hollenbeck, A. R., & Slaby, R. G. Infant visual and vocal responses to television. *Child Development,* 1979, *50,* 41–45.

Huesmann, L. R. Television violence and aggressive behavior. In D. Pearl, L. Bouthilet, and J. Lazar (Eds.), *Television and Behavior: Ten years of scientific progress and implications for the 80's.* Washington, DC: U.S. Government Printing Office, 1982.

Huesmann, L. R., & Bachrach, R. *Aggression and television violence viewing in Israeli kibbutz and city children.* Paper presented at Fifth Biennial Meeting of International Society for Research on Aggression. Mexico City, August, 1982.

Huesmann, L. R., & Eron, L. D. Factors influencing the effect of television violence on children. In M. J. A. Howe (Ed.), Learning from television. New York; Academic Press, 1983.

Huesmann, L. R., Eron, L. D., Klein, R., Brice, P., & Fischer, P. Mitigating the imitation of aggressive behaviors by changing children's attitudes about media violence. *Journal of Personality and Social Psychology.* 1983, *44,* 899–910.

Huesmann, L. R., Fischer, P., Eron, L. D., Mermelstein, R., Kaplan-Shain, E., & Morikawa, S. *Children's sex role preference, sex of television model, and imitation of aggressive behaviors.* Paper presented at Third Biennial Meeting of International Society for Research on Aggression. Washington, DC, September, 1978.

Huesmann, L. R., Lagerspetz, K., & Eron, L. D. *Intervening variables in the television violence-aggression relation;* Evidence from two countries. *Developmental Psychology,* 1984, *20,* 746–775.

Krebs, D., & Groebel, J. *The effects of television violence on children.* Technical report. The Rheinish-Westfalischen Technischen Hochschule, Aachen, West Germany, 1977.

Lefkowitz, M. M., Eron, L. D., Walder, L. O., & Huesmann, L. R. *Growing up to be violent: A longitudinal study of the development of aggression.* New York: Pergamon, 1977.

Lefkowitz, M. M., & Huesmann, L. R. Concomitants of television violence viewing in children. In E. L. Palmer and A. Dorr (Eds.), *Children and the Faces of Television: Teaching, Violence, Selling.* New York: Academic Press, 1981.

McCall, R. B., Parke, R. D., & Kavanaugh, R. D. Imitation of live and televised models by children one to three years of age. *Monographs of the Society for Research in Child Development,* 1977, *42*(5), 95.

McCarthy, E. D., Langer, T. S., Gersten, J. C., Eisenberg, J. G., & Orzeck, L. Violence and behavior disorders. *Journal of Communication,* 1975, *25,* 71–85.

Milavsky, J. R., Kessler, R., Stipp, H., & Rubens, W. S. Television and aggression: Results of a panel study. In D. Pearl, L. Bouthilet, and J. Lazar (Eds.), *Television and behavior: Ten years of scientific progress and implications for the 80's.* Washington, DC: U.S. Government Printing Office, 1982.

Moriarty, D., & McCabe, A. E. Studies of television and youth sport. In *Ontario Royal Commission on Violence in the Communications Industry. Report.,* (Vol. 5). Toronto: Queen's Printer for Ontario, 1977.

Murray, J. P., & Kippax, S. Television diffusion and social behavior in three communities: A field experiment. *Australian Journal of Psychology,* 1977, *39,* 31–43.

Parke, R. D., Berkowitz, L., Leyens, J. P., West, S., & Sebastian, R. J. Some effects of violent and nonviolent movies on the behavior of juvenile delinquents. In L. Berkowitz (Ed.), *Advances in experimental social psychology,* Vol. 10. New York: Academic Press, 1977.

Pitkanen-Pulkkinen, L. Self-control as a prerequisite for constructive behavior, In S. Feshbach and A. Fraczek, (Eds.), *Aggression and Behavior Change.* New York: Preager, 1979.

Robinson, J. P., & Bachman, J. G. Television viewing habits and aggression. In G. A. Comstock & E. A. Rubinstein (Eds.), *Television and social behavior, Vol. 3. Television and adolescent aggressiveness.* Washington, DC: U.S. Government Printing Office, 1972.

Rosenfeld, E., Huesmann, L. R., Eron, L. D., & Torney-Purta, J. V. Measuring patterns of fantasy behavior in children. *Journal of Personality and Social Psychology,* 1982, *42,* 347–366.

Rosenhan, D., & White, G. M. Observation and rehearsal as determinants of prosocial behavior. *Journal of Personality and Social Psychology,* 1967, *5,* 424–431.

Rushton, J. P. Effects of television and film material on the prosocial behavior of children. In L. Berkowitz (Ed.), *Advances in experimental social psychology.* New York: Academic Press, 1979.

Rushton, J. P. Television and pro-social behavior. In D. Pearl, L. Bouthilet, & J. Lazar (Eds.), *Television and behavior: Ten years of scientific progress and implications for the 80's.* Washington, DC: U.S. Government Printing Office, 1982.

Rushton, J. R., & Owen, D. Immediate and delayed effects of TV modelling and preaching on children's generosity. *British Journal of Social and Clinical Psychology*, 1975, *14*, 309–310.

Schramm, W., Lyle, J., & Parker, E. B. *Television in the lives of our children*. Stanford, CA: Stanford University, 1961.

Schuck, S. Z., Schuck, A., Hallan, E., Mancini, F., & Wells, R. Sex differences in aggressive behavior subsequent to listening to a radio broadcast of violence. *Psychological Reports*, 1971, *28*, 931–936.

Singer, J. L., & Singer, D. G. *Television, imagination, and aggression: A study of preschoolers play*. Hillsdale, NJ: Erlbaum, 1981.

Sprafkin, J. M., Liebert, R. M., & Poulos, R. W. Effects of a pro-social example on children's helping. *Journal of Experimental Child Psychology*, 1975, *20*, 119–126.

Stein, A. H., & Friedrich, L. K. Television content and young children's behavior. In J. P. Murray, E. A. Rubinstein, & G. A. Comstock (Eds.), *Television and social behavior, (Vol. 2). Television and Social Learning*. Washington, DC: U.S. Government Printing Office, 1972.

Tower, R. B., Singer, D. G., Singer, J. L., & Biggs, A. Differential effects of television programming on preschoolers' cognition, imagination, and social play. *American Journal of Orthopsychiatry*, 1979, *49*, 265–281.

Wiegman, O., Baarda, B., & Seydel, E. R. Aggression, a Dutch contribution. In A. Goldstein and M. Segall. *Global Perspectives on Aggression*. New York: Pergamon, 1982.

Williams, T. M. *Differential impact of TV on children: A natural experiment in communities with and without TV*. Paper presented at the meeting of the International Society for Research on Aggression. Washington, DC, September, 1978.

Yates, G. C. R. Influence of televised modelling and verbalization on children's delay of gratification. *Journal of Experimental Child Psychology*, 1974, *18*, 333–339.

14

The Developmental–Interactional View of Social Behavior: Four Issues of Adolescent Aggression

ROBERT B. CAIRNS and BEVERLEY D. CAIRNS

One of the central issues for modern child psychology is the problem of how social interactions become established and changed over the course of development. Shortfalls in this study limit progress in diverse areas of psychological application, from clinical interpretation and prediction to theoretical analysis and integration. Our aim in this chapter is to examine some implications of a developmental analysis of continuity and change in social interactions. In keeping with one theme of this volume, we focus on those social patterns that are associated with unhappy, hurtful, or violent consequences.

Before proceeding to the main business of this chapter, some comments are in order on the expression employed in our title, *developmental–interactional*. The ideas and techniques associated with the two root terms of this invention are not interchangeable, nor are they necessarily in conflict. But they differ at some basic levels, including the units of time ordinarily employed and the theoretical concepts they support. For interactions we use seconds and minutes; for development, months and years. As the time units of investigation diverge, so do ways of gathering and combining information, and so do variables and constructs that are perceived to be of greatest importance. In this regard, short-term studies (whether experimental or naturalistic observation) are biased toward identifying changes in behavior that are mediated by adaptational mechanisms of learning or elicitation. Similarly, brief intervention or observational studies are unlikely to be concerned with changes in behavior that reflect the operation of structural changes in morphology or cognitive stage. To the extent that interactional theories are constructed from the results of such short-term, highly controlled experimental and observational studies, they should be expected to emphasize processes of a social learning or social elicitation sort. It is not surprising that statements of interactional theory in the recent past have reflected this methodological bias (e.g., Bandura, 1977; Patterson, 1982).

Developmental theories suffer a similar bias, but in the opposite direction. As larger chunks of time are covered in the course of an investigation, sources of behavioral variation other than elicitation or learning are permitted to become dominant. On this score, major changes in morphological structure and cognitive stage require time intervals measured by calendars rather than by stopwatches. Moreover, it would be unusual—and probably pathological—if significant morphological and cognitive changes *failed* to appear as prominent effects in year-to-year observations. And to the extent that structural changes in the child over a span of years present new conditions for action and reaction, they can enhance, qualify, or reverse earlier short-term experiential modifications. This is because the seemingly stable and unchanging conditions of organismic background in moment-by-moment observations become, in year-to-year assessments, dynamic and controlling features of social adaptation. And the variables that capture empirical variance usually have an impact theoretically. Hence, developmental accounts have tended to emphasize the role played by cognitive and biological changes in children to explain their distinctive social accommodations (e.g., Youniss, 1980).

The idea that we wish to convey by the term *developmental–interactional* can be stated succinctly. We propose that an understanding of social behavior continuity and change—whether the behavior is antisocial or prosocial—requires information about processes in both time frames. The omission of information from short-term interactional studies can skew or invalidate conclusions drawn from long-term developmental ones, and vice versa. Hence, a central methodological problem for the area is the pragmatic one of how to integrate developmental and interactional research designs. Similarly, a central theoretical problem is to establish a framework for synthesizing the information obtained in the two domains.

We begin with some comments on the history and emergence of the developmental–interactional perspective. We then outline certain implications of the perspective for four issues of aggressive behavior in adolescence: (1) gender similarities and differences, (2) individual difference prediction, (3) the problem of reciprocity and escalation, and (4) what to measure and why. In the last section, we summarize the results of some recent empirical work on these issues, including studies in our laboratory.

HISTORICAL BACKGROUND AND CURRENT STATUS

Baldwin deserves major credit for proposing that interactional phenomena are fundamental to understanding the nature and direction of social development. The title of Baldwin's seminal volume, *Social and Ethical Interpretations of Mental Development: A Study in Social Psychology* (1897), signals his belief in the necessary fusion of "mental development," social behavior, and ethics. A direct line of influence may be drawn between Baldwin and much work on these issues today. This includes the investigations of Kohlberg (1969) in ethical development, Selman (1980) and Youniss (1980) in social–cognitive development, and Piaget (1928) in language and thought (see, for instance, Broughton & Freeman-Moir, 1982). Baldwin's view of social–cognitive development also helped inaugurate symbolic interactionism in sociology (see Cottrell, 1969).

It is debatable whether Baldwin's theory should be labeled a theory of the origins of the self or a theory of social organization. In his view, it was both: "the 'self-thought' theory of social organization" (1906, p. xviii). For our purposes, we can abstract two ideas that have special importance for contemporary concepts. One concerns the embeddedness of one's concepts of oneself, and presumably one's behavior, in the social matrix in which the child develops. On this matter, Baldwin (1906) wrote:

> The development of the child's personality could not go on at all without the constant modification of his sense of himself by suggestions from others. So he himself, at every stage, is really in part someone else, even in his own thought of himself. (p. 30)

Within the Baldwinian perspective, social actions—including "thoughts of oneself"—are dynamic and adaptive, responsive to the special demands of the social context in which development occurs. This emphasis on the dynamic nature of development led Baldwin immediately to a second implication concerning the continuity and predictability of behavior, "The only thing that remains more or less stable is a growing sense of the self which includes both terms, the ego and alter" (p. 30). More generally, "personality remains after all a progressive, developing, never-to-be-exhausted thing" (1906, p. 338). This stance on the developing nature of social interchanges and personality was taken before Freud's alternative view on the early infantile determination of personality.

There have been several points of entry and re-entry of interactional concepts into developmental theory over the past century. For our present purposes it should suffice to observe that no single discipline can claim exclusive guardianship of the ideas, because they have been expressed in sociology, psychiatry, and social and developmental psychology. Views as diverse as Sullivan's "Conceptions of Modern Psychiatry" (1940), Mead's *Mind, Self and Society* (1934), and Gesell's *Infancy and Human Growth* (1928) capture significant aspects of the developmental–interactional perspective.

Sears (1951) provided a thoughtful and influential statement of interactional concepts for "personality and social psychology." Following the lead of Cottrell (1942), Sears outlined the ideas of social interdependence and challenged the field to transcend "monadic" views of social behavior and personality. Although the proposal seems not to have had an immediate effect on social psychology or on developmental concepts of personality organization, it did provide direction for theoretical developments over the next three decades. Nonetheless, the theoretical framework outlined by Sears was incomplete on two major counts. First, there were few guides on empirical methods of interactional analysis, a problem that has hindered the incorporation of interactional ideas in personality theory from Baldwin's era to the present. Second, only modest attention was given to the problem of development and how non-learning factors might contribute to age-related and/or individual differences in social behavior.

Over the past 30 years, significant advances have been made in the refinement of interactional methods. Work on the interactional contingency analyses began to appear in the early 1950s in Bales' (1951) studies of human small-group interactions, in clinical process studies, and in Tinbergen's (1951) ethological–animal behavior work. Subsequent attempts to deal with aggressive interchanges owe much to the behavioral interactional studies of Raush (1965), Patterson and Cobb (1971), and Toch (1969), among others. This work demonstrated that interactional processes could be studied under natural conditions as well as in controlled settings.

Despite the progress, some problems of interactional method remain unresolved. A key one is the choice of measure. For instance, Toch (1969), Youniss (1980), and Damon and Hart (1982) rely primarily upon interviews to obtain information about interactional processes. Others, including Patterson (1982) and Raush (1965), employ direct microanalytic observations. A third set of investigators has relied upon sociometric devices (e.g., Coie & Dodge, 1983). What is the relation between interactional measures of the self, from behavioral observations and from the evaluations of others? The question presupposes both theoretical analysis and empirical data to evaluate the analysis. Although some data are now becoming available, there have been few attempts to address directly the theoretical reasons for method outcome similarities and differences. Less progress may be claimed toward resolving the theoretical issues in the developmental perspective.

The commonsense proposition that cognitive and biological changes contribute mightily to social development in adolescence has rarely been disputed. Perhaps it has seemed too obvious to argue. Nonetheless, the problem of how biological changes at puberty are melded with changes in social understanding and interactional behavior remains fundamental. Even seemingly simple questions about the course of development of aggressive behavior cannot be answered without equivocation. Consider, for example, the question "Does aggressive behavior increase with age?" Depending on which set of studies or reviews one cites, the empirical findings have been interpreted to show that the pattern increases, decreases, or remains the same over development (compare, for example, Ferguson & Rule, 1980; Feshbach, 1970; Hartup, 1974; Holmberg, 1980; Loeber, 1982; Parke & Slaby, 1983; White, 1983). The problem of interpretation is directly linked to issues of measurement, including the twin questions of what information sources to employ and how to scale the information given.

To illustrate one aspect of the problem, Bigelow (1977) and others have found that with age, there is a reliable shift in children's descriptions of relationships and friendships from concrete and functional terms to abstract and empathetic expressions. On the basis of these findings one might reasonably expect a concomitant shift in the kinds of strategies of conflict resolution adopted as a function of the age of the children. Accordingly, it would be expected that adolescents would increasingly prefer cognitive, nonviolent strategies as they grow older. Surprisingly, just the opposite has been reported. Independent investigations by Connor, Serbin, and Ender (1978), Ferguson and Rule (1980), and Rule and Duker (1973) have identified what has been labeled a "brutalizing" trend in adolescent development. According to these reports, the judgments of both male and female adolescents (compared to younger children) show increasing acceptance of physically hurtful actions toward others.

Social Development: For Better or for Worse?

Such findings on the increasing acceptance of "aggressive" solutions may be an aberration of our times, or they may reflect an inevitable feature of social development. In either case, the empirical outcomes provide complication for contemporary interpretations of social–cognitive development. In this regard, the field seems to be undergoing a generational shift in what is accepted as the primary direction of development. In contrast with the historical focus of social learning and psychoanalytic theories on aggression and on sexual conflicts, contemporary social developmental theory emphasizes the charitable, assimilative features of social growth.

Why the shift from the past? Three possibilities can be mentioned. One is reality, and the feeling that 20th century psychological theory has been unbalanced by its preoccupation with the conflicts and stresses of life. After all, negative interactions constitute only a modest portion of one's total relationships with others. Simply because negative acts are highly salient and produce immediate distress does not mean that they should be allowed to dominate theoretical considerations. A second possibility is that the shift reflects a broad movement within scientific thought. Sociobiology, for instance, arose primarily as an evolutionary solution to problems of why social organization, sharing, and genetic altruism were so pervasive across invertebrate and vertebrate species (Maynard Smith, 1974; Wilson, 1975).

A third possibility has even deeper roots in our discipline. On this matter, it was assumed by early theorists as disparate as Spencer (1856), Hall (1904), and Piaget (1936) that developmental changes lead to increasingly higher levels of organismic adaptation and competence (see Cairns, 1983; Reinert, 1979). Hence, development has become synonymous with progress and advance. The implicit assumption is made explicit in Kohlberg's (1969) moral dilemmas: The more cognitively advanced children become, the "higher" the level of their moral judgments. Similarly, in social–cognitive theory, it appears that the more advanced the children are in development, the more empathetic they become, the better they understand the qualities of friendship, and the more likely they are to view relationships in benign, sensitive terms (Asher & Gottman, 1981).

Although we agree there is a need for a more balanced focus to the nature of social development, we harbor doubts about equating development with goodness and progress. Whether the gains in interpersonal competence and complexity that occur during childhood and adolescence are used to help or to hurt others should be open to empirical and theoretical inquiry. It is our view that the ontogenetic changes in adolescence serve to enhance one's capacity for both good and evil. Although our contribution to this volume focuses on negative interactions, they are clearly only part of the total picture. Analyses of aggressive patterns are inexorably linked to prosocial and positive ones.

FOUR ISSUES OF ADOLESCENT AGGRESSION

No elaborate theory seems required to predict that the size and strength of a person should covary, over age, with the intensity of his or her acts and the physical damage they might produce. Some contributions are so obvious from a commonsense perspective that they tend to be ignored in scientific formulations. That is a pity, because our job is not necessarily to transcend commonsense; it may be just as important to explain it.

With this objective in mind, it is useful to examine four problems of aggressive expression from a developmental account of interactions. These problems concern (1) developmental differentiation and gender variation, (2) individual difference continuity and change, (3) reciprocity and escalation in aggressive interactions, and (4) the matters of assessment, what to measure and why. The last issue is fundamental to the empirical analysis of the preceding three; hence, it merits extended attention.

Gender Differences and Sexual Dimorphism in Adolescence

One area where the developmental–interactional perspective might extend commonsense concerns gender differences and how they develop. No doubt, one of the more important and vigorously debated areas of gender difference concerns the expression of aggressive patterns. In studies of sexual stereotypy, one of the first areas of gender difference to be identified by young children is the perceived difference between boys and girls in aggressive acts (Best et al., 1977). Further, this area of difference is considered by Maccoby and Jacklin (1974) to be one of the two most reliable areas of gender personality difference. On the other hand, Frodi, Macaulay, and Thome (1977) raise questions about the reliability of the difference in men and women, and Block (1976) questions the nature of the difference in children. In a recent summary of gender differences in aggressive behavior, White (1983) has identified some of the contexts and relationships where gender differences are likely to be observed, and where they are not.

Central to a developmental analysis of gender differences in interactions are two observations. First, both boys and girls pass through successive and predictable cognitive and morphological stages in the course of development. Although there is some debate as to whether the cognitive stage progression is parallel for boys and girls, it cannot be gainsaid that there are gender differences in psychobiological–morphological conditions, both in timing and in outcome. Prior to puberty, boys and girls are nearly identical in terms of biological machinery and presumed potential for vigorous action (see Tanner, 1962). There are some gender-related morphological differences in the prepubertal stages, in length of forearm and in height, but the 1–3% average differences are trival compared to the similarities across sexes and the within-sex differences (Plomin & Foch, 1981). The slight edge favoring boys in terms of height and mass is not useful for determinations of individual differences. In this regard, Tanner (1962) has indicated that it is about as helpful to flip a coin as to use physical morphological measures to guess the gender of a 7-year-old child. This state of affairs shifts drastically at puberty. The 1–3% difference becomes a 7–13% one in most measures of mass, muscle-to-fat ratio, and bodily configuration. By age 17 years, information about the gender of an individual based on muscle mass and morphological information permits an accuracy rate of 95%. All this is to say that, in humans, sexual dimorphism arises at puberty. Prior to puberty, children are quite similar in most morphological measures and might properly be regarded as ''monomorphic.''

The second observation concerns information, both demographic and comparative, which shows dramatic age-by-sex differences in violence and in victims. Although boys and girls up to age 10 years show virtually no differences in either victim or victimizer, a sharp difference in the trajectory of aggressive crimes may be observed near the onset of puberty. The incidence of violent offenders begins to rise in both genders, but the rise for boys is abrupt over the 7-year period from 11 to 18 years (Table 14.1). Young men of 18 years of age are described in the Uniform Crime Report (*Crime in the United States, 1982*) as the most violent persons in the United States. For girls, the rise in the rate of violent crime is rather modest by comparison, so at age 18 years there is a 10:1 difference in the male:female rate of being arrested for murder. Is this an aberration of the 1980s? Probably not, because the same sex differential in homicide was observed in thirteenth century England (Given, 1977). Nor is the effect limited to a given segment of the present century; virtually identical trajectories may be described in each of the past 20 years, when adequate age/sex offense records have been kept by the FBI. Further, the effect is not limited to inner cities or to rural states; parallel curves have been found in all of the major regions of the United States.

To the extent that social exchanges among persons are supported by morphological, cognitive, and social factors, it seems reasonable to expect that robust gender differences in behavioral and attitudinal patterns should either emerge at puberty or become magnified at that developmental stage. Precisely what kinds of differences? In light of the earlier onset in girls than in boys of hormonal states that support sexual development, it seems reasonable to expect girls to show an earlier onset in sexually

Table 14.1

Rate of Arrest[a] for Violent Crimes as a Function of
Sex and Age of the Offender[b]

Age group (years)	Sex of Offender	
	Male	Female
10	15	4
11–12	72	18
13–14	350	71
15–16	760	99
17–18	1053	103
19–20	1024	110
21–22	962	109
32–33	470	74
42–43	281	38
52–53	115	17
62–63	77	6

[a] Per 100,000 persons.
[b] From *Crime in the United States*. Washington,
DC: U.S. Government Printing Office, 1982. These
data include crimes of homicide, assault, and rob-
bery but exclude rape.

relevant behaviors, attitudes, and concerns. Further, the sexual dimorphism might be expected, on the average, to support in boys interpersonal
solutions that emphasize force or physical coercion. Given the advance in
cognitive capabilities at adolescence, these trends must be seen as super-
imposed on a cognitive structure that promotes more employment of
symbolic solutions and abstractions. All this is to say that there should be
an integration of morphological, cognitive, and attitudinal factors in behavior. Gender differences should reflect distinctive features of that integration.

One strong expectation arises from these developmental–interactional
considerations: The magnitude of gender differences in interactions and
attitudes should be age relative. In particular, gender differences in social
behavior should appear more prominent in adolescence and early maturity than in earlier stages of childhood and infancy or in later maturity.
Support for this difference in social behavior should arise as much from
within as without. There should be, as well, differences in early childhood
that are mediated by anticipatory social norms (e.g., Cairns, 1979; Whiting & Edwards, 1974). To the extent that pubertal maturity differences are
anticipated by societal expectations, one should find significant gender
differences in values, behaviors, and judgments in childhood.

Individual Difference Prediction

A developmental–interactional perspective demands as much attention to the factors that mediate stability as to those that mediate change. Indeed, within a developmental framework, change is accepted as inevitable, and it is continuity/stability that requires explanation. Virtually all aspects of interactions shift in form and function from birth to maturity. Given the changes in circumstances and goals of interchanges, it would not be surprising to find that individual differences in the type and quality of interchanges also undergo marked change. From this perspective, five factors contribute to individual difference stability (Cairns, 1979; Cairns & Hood, 1983; Kagan, 1980; Moss & Susman, 1980; Sackett, Sameroff, Cairns, & Suomi, 1981). These factors include the social network in which the person is observed, stability in the person's evocations, biological biases and constraints, actions and choices of the person, and prior experiences that have consolidated particular action patterns. The shorter the interval between observations, the higher the likelihood that there will be some stability in each of the five domains. Further, certain periods/stages of life are likely to yield higher individual difference stabilities in aggressive expression than others because of the relatively stable internal states and external constraints. By the same measure, puberty should be a period of relatively less stability.

Then there is the interaction between the measurement procedures and the levels of individual difference predictability that might be claimed. Since one's cohort over time undergoes change as a function of age, stability must be reflected in the relative rate of change (i.e., whether the change itself occurs at the same rate as obtained in the sample of persons with whom one is compared). Such individual difference predictions, then, must be viewed in terms of variations in changes in the disposition to be predicted.

The question of whether there are differences in the predictability of boys and girls in aggressive behavior is a matter of special interest (e.g., Kagan & Moss, 1962). As Kagan and Moss proposed, one might expect lower levels of individual difference predictability for girls from childhood to maturity than for boys because of the social disapproval of overt aggressive expression in girls. But there are other possible reasons for gender difference in aggressive expression beyond social sanctions. At least part of the difference might reflect emergent sexual dimorphic differences, including actual differences in structure and likelihood of success in physical combat. Similarly, differences in the prediction of girls in general, as opposed to boys in general, might reflect differences in the distribution of girls versus boys on the presumably critical variables. For example, if the aggressive measure is less relevant for girls than for boys (i.e., because more girls get minimum scores than boys), predictions for girls would be attenuated relative to those for boys.

It does not follow, however, that individual difference predictions obtained in one part of the range of aggressive expression are the same as those obtained in other parts of the range. For instance, we have proposed elsewhere (Cairns & Cairns, 1984) that extremely aggressive girls may be more—not less—readily predicted in future behavior than are their male counterparts. Why? The equal (or higher) levels of predictability would be obtained for highly aggressive girls because they, as a group, would be relatively more selected than highly aggressive boys (i.e., would show higher levels of deviation from their respective gender means). This expectation, if supported, could be of special clinical importance in the early identification of children, particularly girls, whose problems would not be likely merely to "go away" in time.

Aggressive Reciprocity and Escalation

In working with teachers, counselors, and parents, we find their special concern to be with the "here and now"; namely, with the events that produce aggressive, violent outbursts in adolescents and how they might be prevented or terminated. Although gender differences and predictions over time are informative, the adults are most concerned with specific children in particular settings. They seek concrete directions and answers. Perhaps the major strength of the interactional method is that it is designed to provide such answers. The procedures require attention to individual children and their relationships; and the more attention, the better.

In the empirical studies that have been completed over the past decade, two concepts—reciprocity and escalation—have been particularly useful in organizing interactional data. The emphasis on reciprocity is not a new one. Interactional researchers from Bott (1933) to Anderson (1939) and Raush (1965) have reported a high mutuality in both positive and negative interactions. Hence, acts are reciprocal to the extent that the behaviors of one child in an interchange toward another are characterized by acts of the same type in return. In this empirical framework, escalation is a special type of reciprocity. It is said to occur when the reciprocity goes beyond "tit-for-tat" and involves a perceived or actual increase in intensity of the action. Accordingly, interactional escalation occurs when (1) negative acts elicit counternegative acts of a similar type, and (2) the intensity of the counter-responses matches or exceeds the intensity of the acts that elicited them. The escalation might arise from faulty perception or from intention. In either case, escalation has been used to describe the entrapment of two or more persons in an interchange that has increasingly severe consequences for one or all persons involved (see Cairns, 1972; Patterson, 1982; Toch, 1969).

There have been various descriptions of aggressive escalation published over the past 15 years. These include accounts of police brutality (Toch, 1969), coercive families (Patterson & Cobb, 1971), peer relations (Hall & Cairns, 1984), and violent mice (Cairns & Nakelski, 1971). Patterson (1982) has described various short-term interventions designed to modulate aggressive escalation in parent–child interactions. In an experimental study of the phenomenon in animals, the probability of escalation was controlled by manipulating the intensity of the counter-responses of the "victim" through tranquillizers (Cairns & Scholz, 1973).

Direct study of interchange processes in children and adolescents suggests, however, that most potential conflicts do not escalate. Moreover, the most violent interchanges typically cannot be reduced to instances of immediate mutual entrapment. Such observations point to the need to amend the escalation hypothesis and its corollary, that virtually any insult or attack would set off an interpersonal chain reaction. What sort of amendments are called for? Among other things, attention should be given to the alternatives to escalation and to the constraints of the social structure. In addition, the notion of mutuality implies attention not only to the onset of negative interchanges, but to their offset—or termination—and the conditions that give rise to recurrence. Further, if escalation is presumed to be an always-present threat for relationship explosion, it seems likely that social mechanisms would come into play during development that might protect persons from bitter conflicts or "fight-to-death" entrapments. Such social mechanisms might take the form of interactional strategies which permit hurtful actions but simultaneously diminish the likelihood of escalation by concealment of the act or the actor by deception. The more cognitively advanced the persons in the relationship, the greater should be the likelihood of such concealment, deception, and indirection.

Accordingly, the "mature" strategies for interpersonal control and coercion observed in adolescence should be expanded beyond childhood to include deception and concealment. For instance, defamation of another person's reputation by rumor and gossip should be a particularly useful aggressive strategy for adolescents in the short-run. The long-term danger is that precisely the same strategy will be employed in return. "Loyalty" and "trust" thus become especially salient qualities of friendship and relationships, assuming greater importance as socially mediated and "hidden" forms of personal attack become extensively employed. Additional interpersonal strategies that diminish the likelihood of aggressive escalation might be expected to emerge in adolescence. These would include the explicit definition of roles within the social structure so that the dominance or priority of persons and actions becomes mutually recognized and accepted. In addition, appreciation of the dangers of reciprocity should be associated with the adoption of nonreciprocal responses to perceived or real injury. Even if one doesn't want to turn the other cheek, one can still pretend to ignore the blow. Such "inattention" to insult or attack, if persistent, presumably should diminish the likelihood of escalation over time.

The Measurement of Aggression: The Self, the Other, and Observed Behavior

One of the more perplexing matters confronting investigators who aspire to study aggressive patterns is the choice of measures. Should the assessments be behavioral, or should they reflect the perceptions of others (teachers, peers, parents)? Should the child's own self-attributions be considered; and if so, what weight should they be given? Should the measures be sociometric, and which of the several forms of sociometry should be given priority? Such questions are not merely matters of procedure or pragmatics; they speak to basic issues of operational definition, construct validation, and interactional theory.

In a thoughtful consideration of the problem of multi-method measurement in young children, Yarrow, Campbell, and Burton (1968) found that measures of aggressive patterns rarely clustered in a single unit. That is so say, the interview reports from mothers did not correlate highly with observed behaviors, and the relations between both of these measures and the reports of teachers were modest. The failure to identify a coherent unitary factor in the several measures points to issues of method and, ultimately, to matters of theory.

As Yarrow et al. (1968) observed, the various measurements of aggressive behavior seem to be directed toward different goals. Cairns and Green (1979) elaborate on this point with the observation that behavioral measures and rating devices typically serve different aims for the investigator. In behavioral observations, the goal is typically to obtain an accurate, veridical, and objective account of the person's actions and reactions, irrespective of his or her comparisons to other persons of the same sex or age. These behavioral records, if taken carefully and reliably, provide the stuff for a precise analysis of action–interaction chains and the controls that are operative. In dispositional ratings or summary evaluations, on the other hand, the goal is usually to identify stable differences among persons so that reliable individual difference predictions are permitted over time and space. Hence, most ratings or rankings identify the child's standing on some behavioral or attitudinal disposition relative to a reference group of children in the same sex–age range and circumstances. But if age–sex group standards are employed—implicitly or explicitly—the effects of gender and development are likely to be reduced or eliminated. Nonetheless, at least two advantages follow from "zooming in" on individual differences and removing the effects of sex–age–circumstance variance. Relative to direct observations, dispositional ratings are (1) cheaper to obtain, and (2) able to provide more stable predictions over time and space. Why the difference in predictive power? According to Cairns and Green (1979), it reflects the different sources of variance captured by the two measurement procedures. Olweus (1979) has arrived at a similar conclusion.

To the extent that the above analysis is correct, the gap between behavioral and rating measures can be reduced—or eliminated—under specified conditions. First, one can produce observational outcomes that are similar to ratings. When observations are extensive and capture information from multiple relationships over time, a summary behavioral observation measure should tend to converge with dispositional ratings. That is, multiple observations should, when summed, cancel out relationship–specific and context–specific sources of variance, thereby increasing the proportion of variance distinctive to the person being observed. Second, one can produce ratings that are similar to observation. Accordingly, one could successively narrow the phenomenon to be rated (in terms of time covered and actions rated) so that the rating judgment approximates the activity of a behavioral observer. Both strategies for achieving convergence can be shown to work, but the convergence can be costly. The cost, for the behavioral analysis, is a risk in the precision in interpersonal process analysis. Idiosyncratic, but stable, relational patterns may be blurred by summing over disparate relationships. There is also a risk in producing dispositional ratings that approximate behavioral observations. If the disposition to be rated is narrowly restricted to a particular relationship, the unique advantage of ratings to identify stable individual differences may be compromised.

Self-assessments, which may be viewed as a special form of dispositional ratings, present special measurement possibilities and problems. Consider, for example, when children are asked to judge the extent to which they themselves "argue" with peers. The task is distinctively different from the one confronting the same persons when they are asked to judge the same disposition in another child. Why? When the task is "outside" the self, there are multiple grounds for between-person agreement. These include shared observations of the person, consensual judgments about the child's reputation for arguing, and shared demographic stereotypes of which the "other" is an exemplar (e.g., stereotypes about the likelihood for arguing by persons of different ages, genders, socioeconomic classes, or ethnic groups). But when the task is to judge one's own disposition, one has both more "private" information about one's dispositions and less "public" information. The lens through which we observe our own actions has different filters from that through which we observe others. Nor are we always privy to the most damaging information about our social reputations. Moreover, in the case of self-assessments, it is often unclear which reference standard is being employed. For self-assessments, it may be *normative* (as in ratings compared to one's sex–age group), *ipsative* (compared to one's own experience or intrapsychic balance), or some combination of the two referential standards.

It should be noted that not all self-reports are self-ratings of dispositions. To the contrary, most of the information obtained directly from children in questionnaires or interviews does not require reference to internal or normative standards. For instance, questions about the child's age, home address, or number of brothers or sisters do not require reference standards. Similarly, the names of the persons with whom the children affiliate and their reports of prior conflicts or arguments do not require within or between individual comparisons. Because of the quasi-objective and public properties of such information, it may be expected to show high levels of correspondence with the reports of other persons.

To the extent that the above analysis is correct, there should be certain conditions under which discrepancies are minimized between the self-assessments, on the one hand, and those of the "self" obtained from other persons and from behavioral observations, on the other hand. Elsewhere (Cairns & Cairns, 1981, 1984) we have proposed that the three measurement domains—the self, the other, and observations—would converge to the extent that one's standing relative to other persons is explicit and public. Under such public conditions, the child would share directly in information about his or her reputation, group standing, and ranking with respect to others. Conversely, the more private the information available to the self, the less likely it should be that high agreement would be obtained between dispositional ratings of the self and dispositional ratings made by others. On the other hand, children should be in reasonable agreement among themselves in providing accounts of the social groups in their immediate environment, including the composition of groups in which they themselves participate. Similarly, there should be substantial agreement between self-reports and the objective accuracy of phenomena and events that do not require evaluation (e.g., birthdates, family composition, time spent in particular activities).

In summary, three proposals may be offered on the properties of ratings, self-evaluations, and behavioral measurements of aggressive behavior in adolescence:

1. It is expected that the highest levels of individual difference predictive correlations will be obtained with rating scales (peer, adult, parent) and other devices that capture distinctive between-individual sources of variation. To the extent that behavioral observations are extensive, over multiple settings and relationships, they should converge with judgments obtained from rating scales.

2. Behavioral observations are invaluable for two major tasks of developmental–interactional study. First, direct observation and objective recording in behaviorally explicit categories should be sensitive to mean levels of developmental change in particular forms and types of aggressive behavior. Such information is typically obscured in ratings that implicitly call for age- and gender-relativity of the score. Hence, real or absolute changes over time require objective quantification of acts and functions. Second, behavioral observations are necessary to capture the processes of interactional transition and change, as well as the accommodations that occur over time. Such process information typically is beyond the limits of everyday life ratings and reporting. The key events may pass unnoticed, they may become obscured by faulty interpretation at the first level of cognitive input, or they may be overshadowed by subsequent happenings and forgotten.

3. Self-assessments of aggressive behavior should yield outcomes that are relatively independent of other measurement methods save under special conditions. These conditions include those where the acts to be evaluated are highly public and/or individuals are privy to the communication network where their relative placements are discussed. Nonetheless, self-assessments should be reasonably consistent in predicting subsequent self-assessments, in that they presumably will assess common sources of within-person variance. In addition, children's reports of their social structures and interactions, and objective personal information that is nonevaluative and independent of reference group comparisons, should be more in accord with social consensus than with self-assessments.

EMPIRICAL FINDINGS

The task of commenting upon some empirical findings on the four developmental–interactional issues outlined above is eased by the availability of recent comprehensive reviews, including those by Geen and Donnerstein (1983), Patterson (1982), Parke and Slaby (1983), and Cairns (1979). Our comments here are necessarily selective, sampling work that has appeared since those reviews and ongoing studies in our own laboratory.

Our recent work on these four issues has concentrated on aggressive behavior in adolescence. It grew out of our longstanding concern with aggressive problems and how they might be dealt with in school and clinical settings (e.g., Bandura & Walters, 1959; Cairns, 1961). Recent work in our laboratory has involved primarily three different samples of subjects: 220 elementary school boys and girls (fourth and fifth grades) who were studied for 1 year (Cairns & Cairns, 1984); 479 boys and girls (7th grade) in public middle schools (Cairns, Cairns, & Ferguson, 1984); and 43 boys and girls (seventh–ninth grades) in a private school, with a 1-year followup (Cairns, Perrin, & Cairns, 1985). Beyond our concern with normal development, special focus was given in this work to children who were deemed at risk for future violent, aggressive behavior. Accordingly, we identified in each investigation subsets of male and female subjects who, by virtue of prior and current behavior, might be expected to show heightened aggressive behaviors. These special subgroups and their matched controls could be contrasted with a parallel study of 40 adolescents who were incarcerated for delinquent behavior (Perrin, 1981; Perrin & Cairns, 1980).

Characteristics of the samples and procedures have been published (see Cairns & Cairns, 1984). The children, 9–17 years of age, were drawn from suburban, small town, and rural areas of North Carolina. Their socioeconomic and ethnic status represented persons living in that region of the country. Parallel measures were used across all age groups and across all investigations. Accordingly, each of the studies involved (1) extensive behavioral observations, (2) teachers' ratings of the subjects' social dispositions on a 7-factor scale consisting of 15 items, (3) self-assessments by subjects on the same scale, (4) peer nominations for conflicts, and (5) self-reports by subjects of the social structure in the classroom and concrete examples of prior conflicts with peers. It was thus possible to determine within each study the configuration of relationships across measures and their correspondence to the primary dependent variables. These patterns could be replicated or disconfirmed by the successive investigations.

Because of the centrality of measurement, we first comment upon the patterns of correspondence across measurement domains. Then we consider the issues of gender difference, prediction, and interactional dynamics.

Multiple Methods: Multiple Outcomes or Underlying Organization?

Given the concerns that we had expressed about measurement prior to beginning this study (e.g., Cairns & Cairns, 1981; Cairns & Green, 1979), we first determined whether the expected interrelation among measures would be confirmed in the organization of the several data sets. It was. The patterns of intercorrelation were robust and extended across the separate investigations. Specifically, individual difference measures of aggression from sources "outside" the subject were consistently interrelated. Hence, the median correlations among direct observations of aggressive behavior in school, teachers' ratings of the aggressive factor, and peer nominations of persons who "bothered them" or observed conflicts ranged from $r = +.37$ through $r = +.75$.

Relations between these outside measures of aggressiveness and inside measures (i.e., self-assessments) of the same variable are less impressive. Across the investigations, the correlations have been modestly negative or negligible, or modestly positive. Such self-other inconsistency was obtained regardless of the risk status and gender of the subjects. One of the component self-assessment scales (embedded in the aggressive factor) has, nonetheless, shown a consistent relationship to teachers' ratings across studies. This is the scale where the rater is asked to judge whether the subject has "gotten into trouble at school." Teachers and subjects consistently show levels of agreement on the "trouble" item that range from $r = +.40$ to $r = +.60$.

Information obtained from the self about the self is not necessarily unreliable. To the contrary, one of our most robust findings involved the high consensus among persons in their perceptions of the social structures that exist among peers. In one investigation (Cairns, Perrin, & Cairns, 1985), we found greater than 90% accuracy in agreement among individuals on the composition of social groups in their classes. The information was obtained by asking, in individual interviews, questions such as "Are there any people in your class who hang around together? Who are they?" Even when subjects were isolated from the groups themselves, their reports about the social groupings of "others" and themselves were in high agreement with independent reports from peers.

One lesson we have learned from this multi-method analysis is that the relations among methods are not invariant. To identify their underlying organization requires attention to the sources of variance tapped by the operations as well as to methods of scaling and analysis. Focus upon simply one feature of measurement—such as reliability or interrater agreement—can be misleading to the extent that other critical features of assessment are ignored or forgotten. When such features were taken into account, reasonably clear patterns of individual difference assessment of aggressive patterns emerged.

Gender Differences in Development

Consideration of the scaling properties of the different measures proved to be of special importance in our attempts to clarify the developmental trajectory of aggressive patterns for male and female adolescents. Depending on whether the measures reflected individual differences from implicit age group norms or from an absolute scale, aggressiveness could be shown to decrease or increase with age.

Consider the outcomes of the direct behavioral observations. Comparisons between the 4th and 7th grade high-risk subjects showed a highly significant age-related increase in the rate of hostile–aggressive acts per hour. Parallel findings were obtained for boys and girls, and no gender differences were obtained at either age-grade level in the high-risk groups (Cairns, Cairns, & Ferguson, 1984). Similar findings were obtained for the matched control sample (individually paired to high-risk subjects in terms of sex, grade, classroom attended, size, race), with two qualifications. One was that significant differences were obtained in aggressive behavior between the high-risk and control groups in both grades and both genders. The second qualification is that the "normal" or control girls did not show a reliable behavioral increase as a function of age, whereas the boys did. Accordingly, a strong gender difference in aggressive behavior was observed in the seventh grade but not in the fourth grade, with classroom observations of "normal" children taken as the basis for comparison. Hence, gender differences appeared in the control groups, but not in the high-risk groups, and there was a general increase in hostile–aggressive expression as a function of age.

Parallel results were obtained when "absolute" measures of aggressive expression were employed, regardless of whether they were behavioral or obtained from interviews. For instance, boys (regardless of risk status) reported an age-related increase in the acceptance of physical aggression as a preferred technique for settling disputes with other boys. Unselected girls, however, showed only a modest age-related increase in interview reports of physically aggressive acts in same-sex conflicts. Instead, the girls reported that they tended to ignore the offense and/or ostracize the offender. This "indirect" attack involved telling their friends about the offense and recruiting the friends' assistance in ostracizing the other girls or talking about her (see also Feshbach & Sones, 1971). Such social alienation was rarely reported by boys in either age group. For girls, however, there was a sharp increase in the use of this strategy as a function of the girls' age-grade level.

Just the opposite age-developmental function was obtained when the criterion aggressive measures were teachers' and self-ratings. The teachers' ratings, for instance, indicated that the adolescents (seventh grade) were reliably *less* aggressive than were the younger children (fourth grade). Similarly, the self-ratings for both boys and girls indicated that they thought they were getting better and better (i.e., less aggressive) as they grew older.

Why the discrepancy between the developmental trends found in ratings (either teacher or self) and behavioral observations? The answer seems to lie in how the information was originally scaled by the respondents and whether the information was expressed in terms of age group norms (implicit or explicit) or in some absolute age-independent units. On this score, it should be recalled that the subjects' concrete descriptions of how they handled conflicts were directly in line with behavioral observations. But when either the teachers or the adolescents were requested to rate/evaluate behavior, the ratings/evaluations were in terms of some reference norms. In the case of the teachers, this reference group consisted of children who occupied the same age status. In the case of subjects who rated themselves, the reference group appeared to be a combination of intrapsychic factors as well as the normative standard of same-age peers. In both cases, absolute differences in terms of age (and many gender differences) were "controlled" or eliminated at the first step of assessment.

To sum up, changes in direct aggressive expression from late childhood to early adolescence were strong and reliable when age-independent assessment procedures were employed. The major exception appeared in unselected girls (i.e., non-risk), whose rate of increase was less than in males. (Nonetheless, Ferguson and Rule, 1980, observed an increase in "brutalizing" norms among both boys and girls in this age range.) Our finding that negative or negligible developmental functions were obtained with teachers' ratings and self-evaluations points to the age relativity of the measuring devices, not the behaviors of the adolescents. This interpretation is happily parsimonious and accounts for otherwise curious discrepancies between the forms of self-report.

Predicting Boys and Girls

Our findings have indicated moderate to high levels of predictive correlations over a 1-year period, whether assessed in elementary or junior high school or in boys or girls. Hence, the findings are well within the range specified by Olweus (1978) in his work with boys in the same age groups. Examination of the patterns of longitudinal correlation—to determine which measures predict which outcomes, and how well—suggests one reason why previous summaries of the empirical issues have been clouded. Not all predictors were effective in predicting all criteria. In general, we found that the highest levels of prediction were obtained when the two measures (predictor and criterion) were in the same domain. For example, teachers' ratings in the fourth grade were the best predictors of teachers' ratings in the fifth grade, even though different teachers were involved in producing the assessments in the 2 years (Cairns & Cairns, 1984). A similar within-domain consistency held for the self-ratings and the peer nominations. Further, for certain predictors, there were few linkages with outcomes obtained by other methods a year later. The failures of prediction centered around the self-report measures, which in themselves were predictable but that had only modest contact with the other assessments of aggressive expression.

Multiple regression and multiple correlational procedures were employed to determine whether combinations of predictors would improve single measures. Overall, there was scant gain in employing combinations of variables. Both stepwise and simultaneous regression analyses indicated that most if not all of the predictable variance was captured by the same-dimension measures taken 1 year earlier. (Included in the multiple regression equations were sex of subject, teachers' ratings, two measures of peer nominations, self-assessments, risk assignment, and behavioral summary score.) Again, the patterns of relationship obtained in boys replicated, for the most part, the patterns obtained in girls.

Beyond similarities in pattern, one might ask about similarities in magnitude, and whether the predictive relations obtained with boys exceeded those obtained with girls. Over all measurement domains, there was one predictor/criterion relationship where the levels of prediction were higher for boys than for girls. Teachers' ratings of boys in the fourth grade showed reliably higher correlations with those obtained on boys in the fifth grade than did the corresponding correlations for girls. Both the two-variable product–moment correlations and multiple correlations showed this pattern of difference (although both male and female longitudinal correlations were highly reliable, considered by themselves). Other measures—including peer nominations and self-reports—were approximately equal for boys and girls in the predictive relationship. Why did the teachers' ratings work differently for boys and girls? A clue to the answer is provided by reference to the distribution of scores. Teachers, as a group, see aggressive outcomes as being more relevant to boys than to girls. This differential relevance, and the associated differences in distribution of summary rating scores (e.g., the "floor" effect for a large proportion of the girls), could have contributed to the difference in levels of predictive correlations.

It should be noted that these relationships are for the entire sample of preadolescent children, what we have grandly called "boys in general" and "girls in general." It does not follow, however, that the differences obtained in the sample as a whole are necessarily representative of the differences obtained in the groups for which prediction would be most clinically and theoretically relevant. On this score, we might ask whether "at-risk" aggressive boys were more stable in their orientation than were at-risk aggressive girls. For children in late childhood, assessed over a 1-year period regardless of measure, the answer is no. Indeed, our data suggested the reverse effect: that high-risk girls may sometimes be more predictable than high-risk boys.

In the work reported in Cairns and Cairns (1984), teachers and principals nominated a subset of subjects in the fourth grade as being particularly aggressive and troublesome to peers. Surprisingly, almost as many girls were nominated at this age level for this dubious honor as were boys. In the fourth grade, at least, aggressive girls have not been difficult to identify in the school setting. (This state of affairs shifted by the seventh grade, when the ratio of boy:girl high-risk nominees was approximately 2:1, a reliable difference.) These at-risk girls differed from girls in general more than the at-risk boys differed from boys in general on most measures. Given the greater relative deviance of the high-risk girls, it seemed reasonable to expect that they would be at least as distinguishable from their peers one year later as high-risk boys. This expectation was confirmed. The differential assessment of the predictability of at-risk boys and girls was evaluated by a series of conditional probability analyses of the predictive error and accuracy rate. Girls identified as being at-risk in the fourth grade were more likely to be nominated by peers in the fifth grade than were girls in general, whereas the parallel relationship was less strong among the boys. Similarly, as high a level of accuracy of prediction was obtained for highly aggressive girls in the fifth grade as for highly aggressive boys (Cairns & Cairns, 1984).

To sum up, the individual prediction results in elementary school children demonstrated moderate to strong levels of prediction over a period of one year. Further, the findings obtained for both boys and girls. On the other hand, there was a reliable "method" effect in that the highest levels of prediction were obtained when the measures were in the same domain. The "public" measures (including peer nominations, teachers' ratings, and actual behavior) clustered together, whereas the "private" measures were predictive mostly of future "private" assessments. On the matter of a gender differential in prediction, we found there was some basis for expecting boys to be more predictable than girls in the general population. But in the groups that count most for clinical prediction, girls were at least as readily identified and as stable as boys, if not more stable, over a 1-year period. Does this equal-to-higher level of prediction hold beyond one year? It should be noted in this regard that fewer girls appear at-risk in adolescence than do boys. Given the distributional shift of risk as a function of gender across development, more errors of a false–positive sort might be expected among girls than among boys as they enter adolescence.

Interactional Dynamics: A New Look at Escalation and Termination

The last issue concerns interactional dynamics, namely, the problem of escalation and how it occurs. Although the general proposition that aggression occurs when negative interactions become entrained toward increasingly higher levels of mutual hurtfulness seems to describe some conflicts, our observations indicated there are many serious aggressive episodes that do not fit the escalation account. For instance, Perrin (1981) found in her work with incaracerated youth that approximately 50% of the aggressive conflicts occurred with explosive abruptness. Equally important, Perrin (1981) obtained scant evidence in these incarcerated adolescents for remediation in their termination of conflicts. When they ended, 95% of the conflicts stopped abruptly and without efforts by either combatant to remedy or otherwise ameliorate the interpersonal rift.

Are explosive patterns of conflict onset and termination restricted to highly aggressive youth? Apparently not, if our observations of conflicts among normal junior high students are generalizable. In one sample of normal middle-class adolescents, virtually the same proportion of abrupt, explosive onset and abrupt, unremediated termination of conflicts was observed as among the incarcerated youth of the same age (Cairns, Perrin, & Cairns, 1984).

Such observations do not mean that there is not a build-up of hostile feelings or an escalation toward increasing levels of violence so much as they suggest that the concept of escalation may have been too narrowly defined to the immediately present episode. In this regard, the Cairns, Perrin, and Cairns (1984) work found that there was an escalation across aggressive episodes in any given observation session, such that the probability of new conflicts arising was greatest in the brief period immediately following a previous conflict. In that particular study, concerned with conflicts observed in physical education classes, the duration of the "zone of danger" was 5 minutes, with the likelihood of a new conflict emerging diminishing to baseline levels after that interval. There was, in effect, a form of temporal catharsis in that the greater the distance in time since the last conflict, the less likely it was that the subject was "primed" to become involved in a new one. (Approximately two thirds of the "new" conflicts involved a different interactional partner than the immediately preceding conflict. Those "new" instances thus were not merely a continuation of the old fight.)

Interview reports indicate that the conditions for abrupt conflict renewal may be met, in large measure, by the failure to resolve previous ones. That is, most of the "serious" conflicts reported by adolescents in their interviews were ones that were ongoing and recurrent, not single episodes. In other words, escalation seemed to occur across time and across episodes as much as within episodes. Furthermore, the typical failure to resolve the conflict seemed to set the stage for the abrupt recurrence at a later time. The signs of escalation are thus not available when the behavioral observations are made. Hence, it appears that the episodes are abrupt in onset when, in fact, they may have been the product of previous unobserved and unrecorded interchanges.

One additional refinement of the escalation hypothesis seems called for in light of the present observations. It is that fewer instances of overt anger episodes are observed among girls as they enter mid- and late adolescence than are seen among boys. Analyses of the interview information about the social network suggests that adolescent girls, relative to boys, tend to employ more socially mediated and less readily escalated techniques of hurtful actions. These techniques include the use of social cliques to ostracize other girls, spreading malicious rumors (i.e., embarrassing or humiliating information), and performing other socially mediated forms of personal abuse. Such "hidden" aggressive expressions, although deadly effective in producing discomfort and distress, are not readily traced or detected. Moreover, such covert actions are unlikely to elicit immediate or direct reciprocation. It is perhaps for this reason that, with the onset of adolescence and into maturity, the characteristics most valued by subjects in personal relationships are "loyalty," "honesty," and worthiness of "trust." They presumably detect what must be the most critical hazards of relationships.

To sum up, direct observations of conflicts and aggressive episodes confirm that, in some settings, approximately 50% of the aggressive interchanges may be described in terms of an escalation of reciprocated negative acts; the remainder seem explosive and abrupt. Interview findings and direct observations indicate that escalation may occur across episodes as well as within episodes. And it appears that the across-episode build-up is associated with the most serious aggressive exchanges. Such across-episode escalation could possibly be averted by more effective forms of termination/remediation.

A CONCLUDING COMMENT

Even if one prefers to soar with the eagles in theoretical speculations, it is useful on occasion to slog through the muddy empirical issues of scaling and measurement. As it turns out, the technical aspects of the scientific enterprise can be rewarding, whether or not the outcomes were expected. In the present case, *expected* meant additional support was secured for the view that gender differences in aggressive behavior are appropriately viewed as dynamic and development–emergent phenomena. Additionally, our results on longitudinal prediction concur with those of Olweus (1979), Pulkkinen (1982), Loeber (1982), and Magnusson and Duner (1981). Nowadays, psychologists should no longer be embarrassed by the magnitude and meaningfulness of their longitudinal predictions of aggressive behavior. The present work also produced its share of surprises. These include the finding that some girls (i.e., high risk) are as predictable as high-risk boys over a 1-year period. It is also informative to learn that relationships escalate, not merely acts. But possibly the most intriguing set of outcomes are those on the nature and development of the child's self-constructions. The more carefully one examines these concepts, the more likely it seems that their functions differ from those of other social concepts, and of behavior. All this suggests that J. M. Baldwin (1906) may have been correct in emphasizing that personality is a developing, adapting, "never-to-be-exhausted thing."

REFERENCES

Anderson, H. H. Domination and integration in the social behavior of young children in an experimental play situation. *Genetic Psychology Monographs,* 1939, *21,* 287–385.

Asher, S. R., & Gottman, J. M. (Eds.). *The development of children's friendships.* London: The Cambridge University Press, 1981.

Baldwin, J. M. *Social and ethical interpretations of mental development: A study in social psychology,* (3rd ed.). New York: Macmillan, 1906. [Original work published 1897]

Bales, R. F. *Interaction process analysis: A method for the study of small groups.* Cambridge, MA: Addison-Wesley, 1950.

Bandura, A. *Social learning theory.* Englewood Cliffs, NJ: Prentice-Hall, 1977.

Bandura, A., & Walters, R. H. *Adolescent aggression.* New York: Ronald Press, 1959.

Best, D., Williams, J. E., Cloud, J. M., Davis, S. W., Robertson, L. S., Edwards, J. R., Giles, H., & Fowles, J. Development of sex-trait stereotypes among young children in the United States, England, and Ireland. *Child Development,* 1977, *48,* 1375–1384.

Bigelow, B. J. Children's friendship expectations: A cognitive-developmental study. *Child Development*, 1977, *48*, 246–253.

Block, J. H. Debatable conclusions about sex differences. *Contemporary Psychology*, 1976, *21*, 517–522.

Bott, H. *Personality development in young children*. Toronto: University of Toronto Press, 1934.

Broughton, J. M., & Freeman-Moir, D. J. *The cognitive developmental psychology of James Mark Baldwin: Current theory and research in genetic epistemology*. Norwood, NJ: Ablex, 1982.

Cairns, R. B. The influence of dependency inhibition on the effectiveness of social approval. *Journal of Personality*, 1961, *29*, 466–488.

Cairns, R. B. Fighting and punishment from a developmental perspective. In J. K. Cole and D. D. Jensen (Eds.), *Nebraska Symposium on Motivation*, (Vol. 20). Lincoln: University of Nebraska Press, 1973.

Cairns, R. B. *Social development: The origins and plasticity of interchanges*. San Francisco: Freeman, 1979.

Cairns, R. B. The emergence of developmental psychology. In P. H. Mussen (Gen. Ed.) & W. Kessen (Vol. Ed.), *Handbook of child psychology*, (Vol. 1). New York: Wiley, 1983.

Cairns, R. B., & Cairns, B. D. Self-reflections: An essay and commentary on "Social cognition and the acquisition of self." *Developmental Review*, 1981, *1*, 171–180.

Cairns, R. B., & Cairns, B. D. Predicting aggressive patterns in girls and boys: A developmental study. *Aggressive Behavior*, 1984, *10*, 227–242.

Cairns, R. B., Cairns, B. D., & Ferguson, L. L. *Aggressive behavior in elementary school children: Gender similarities, differences, and developmental continuities*. Paper presented at the Eighth Biennial Meeting of the Southeastern Conference on Human Development, Athens, GA, April, 1984.

Cairns, R. B., & Green, J. A. How to assess personality and social patterns: Ratings or observations? In R. B. Cairns (Ed.), *The analysis of social interaction: Methods, issues, and illustrations*. Hillsdale, NJ: Erlbaum, 1979.

Cairns, R. B., & Hood, K. E. Continuity in social development: A comparative perspective on individual difference prediction. In P. B. Baltes & O. G. Brim, Jr. (Eds.), *Life-span developmental psychology*, Vol. 5. New York: Academic Press, 1983.

Cairns, R. B., & Nakelski, J. S. On fighting in mice: Ontogenetic and experiential determinants. *Journal of Comparative and Physiological Psychology*, 1971, *71*, 354–364.

Cairns, R. B., Perrin, J. E., & Cairns, B. D. Social structure and social cognition in early adolescence: Affiliative patterns. *Journal of Early Adolescence*, 1985, (in press).

Cairns, R. B., Perrin, J. E., & Cairns, B. D. Social cognition and social behavior in adolescence: Aggressive patterns, 1984 (in editorial review).

Cairns, R. B., & Scholz, S. D. On fighting in mice: Dyadic escalation and what is learned. *Journal of Comparative and Physiological Psychology*, 1973, *85*, 540–555.

Coie, J., & Dodge, K. A. Continuities and changes in children's social status: A five-year longitudinal study. *Merrill-Palmer Quarterly*, 1983, *29*, 261–282.

Connor, J. M., Serbin, L. A., & Ender, R. A. Responses of boys and girls to aggressive, assertive, and passive behaviors of male and female character. *Journal of Genetic Psychology*, 1978, *133*, 59–69.

Cottrell, L. S. The analysis of situational fields in social psychology. *American Sociological Review*, 1942, *7*, 370–382.

Cottrell, L. S., Jr. Interpersonal interaction and the development of the self. In D. A. Goslin (Ed.), *Handbook of socialization theory and research*. Chicago: Rand McNally, 1969.

Crime in the United States. Washington, DC: U.S. Government Printing Office, 1982.

Damon, W., & Hart, D. The development of self-understanding from infancy through adolescence. *Child Development*, 1982, *53*, 841–864.

Ferguson, T. J., & Rule, B. G. Effects of inferential set, outcome severity, and basis of responsibility on children's evaluation of aggressive acts. *Developmental Psychology*, 1980, *16*, 141–146.

Feshbach, S., Aggression. In P. H. Mussen (Ed.), *Carmichael's manual of child psychology*, Vol. 2 (3rd ed.). New York: Wiley, 1970.

Feshbach, S., & Sones, G. Sex differences in adolescent reactions toward newcomers. *Developmental Psychology*, 1971, *4*, 381–386.

Frodi, A., Macaulay, J., & Thome, P. R. Are women always less aggressive than men? A review of the experimental literature. *Psychological Bulletin*, 1977, *84*, 634–660.

Geen, R. G., & Donnerstein, E. I. *Aggression: Theoretical and empirical reviews*. New York: Academic Press, 1983.

Gesell, A. L. *Infancy and human growth*. New York: Macmillan, 1928.

Given, J. B. *Society and homicide in thirteenth-century England*. Stanford: Stanford University Press, 1977.

Hall, G. S. *Adolescence: Its psychology and its relations to physiology, anthropology, sociology, sex, crime, religion, and education*. New York: Appleton, 1904.

Hall, W. M., & Cairns, R. B. Aggressive behavior in children: An outcome of modeling or reciprocity? *Developmental Psychology*, 1984, *20*, 739–745.

Hartup, W. W. Aggression in childhood developmental perspectives. *American Psychologist*, 1974, *29*, 336–341.

Holmberg, M. C. The development of social interchange patterns from 12 to 42 months. *Child Development*, 1980, *51*, 448–456.

Kagan, J. Perspectives on continuity. In O. G. Brim, Jr., & J. Kagan (Eds.), *Constancy and change in human development*. Cambridge, MA: Harvard University Press, 1980.

Kagan, J., & Moss, H. A. *Birth to maturity: A study in psychological development*. New York: Wiley, 1962.

Kohlberg, L. Stage and sequence: The cognitive-developmental approach to socialization. In D. A. Goslin (Ed.), *Handbook of socialization theory and research*. Chicago: Rand McNally, 1969.

Loeber, R. The stability of antisocial and delinquent child behavior: A review. *Child Development*, 1982, *53*, 1432–1446.

Maccoby, E. E., & Jacklin, C. N. *The psychology of sex differences*. Stanford: Stanford University Press, 1974.

Magnusson, D., & Duner, A. Individual development and environment: A longitudinal study in Sweden. In S. E. Mednick & A. E. Baert (Eds.), *Prospective longitudinal research*. Oxford: Oxford University Press, 1981.

Maynard Smith, J. The theory of games and the evolution of animal conflict. *Journal of Theoretical Biology*, 1974, *47*, 523–527.

Moss, H. A., & Susman, E. J. Longitudinal study of personality development. In O. G. Brim, Jr., & Kagan, J. (Eds.), *Constancy and change in human development*. Cambridge, MA: Harvard University Press, 1980.

Mead, G. H. *Mind, self, and society*. Chicago: University of Chicago Press, 1934.

Olweus, D. *Aggression in the schools: Bullies and whipping boys*. Washington, DC: Hemisphere, 1978.

Olweus, D. Stability of aggressive reaction patterns in males: A review. *Psychological Bulletin*, 1979, *86*, 852–875.

Parke, R. D., & Slaby, R. G. The development of aggression. In P. H. Mussen (Ed.), *Handbook of child psychology*, Vol. 4 (4th ed.). New York: Wiley, 1983.

Patterson, G. R. *Coercive family process*. Eugene, OR: Castalia, 1982.

Patterson, G. R., & Cobb, J. A. A dyadic analysis of "aggressive" behaviors. In J. P. Hill (Ed.), *Minnesota Symposium on Child Psychology,* Vol. 5. Minneapolis: University of Minnesota Press, 1971.

Perrin, J. *Reciprocity of aggression in youthful offenders.* Paper presented at the annual meeting of the American Psychological Association, Los Angeles, 1981.

Perrin, J. E., & Cairns, R. B. *Aggressive patterns in adolescent offenders.* Paper presented at the Southeastern Conference on Human Development, Alexandria, VA, 1980.

Piaget, J. *Judgment and reasoning in the child.* New York: Harcourt, Brace, 1928.

Piaget, J. *The origins of intelligence in children.* New York: International Universities Press, 1952. (Originally published, 1936)

Plomin, R., & Foch, T. T. Sex differences and individual differences. *Child Development,* 1981, *52,* 383–385.

Pulkkinen, L. Self-control and continuity from childhood to late adolescence. In P. B. Baltes & O. G. Brim, Jr. (Eds.), *Life-span development and behavior,* Vol. 4. New York: Academic Press, 1982.

Raush, H. L. Interaction sequences. *Journal of Personality and Social Psychology,* 1965, *2,* 487–499.

Reinert, G. Prolegomena to a history of life-span developmental psychology. In P. B. Baltes & O. G. Brim (Eds.). *Life-span development and behavior,* (Vol. 2). New York: Academic Press, 1979.

Rule, B. G., & Duker, P. Effects of intentions and consequences on children's evaluations of aggressors. *Journal of Personality and Social Psychology,* 1973, *27,* 184–189.

Sackett, G. P., Sameroff, A. J., Cairns, R. B., & Suomi, S. J. Continuity in behavioral development: Theoretical and empirical issues. In K. Immelmann, G. W. Barlow, L. Petrinovich, & M. Main (Eds.), *Behavioral development.* Cambridge: Cambridge University Press, 1981.

Sears, R. R. A theoretical framework for personality and social behavior. *American Psychologist,* 1951, *6,* 476–483.

Selman, R. *The growth of interpersonal understanding.* New York: Academic Press, 1980.

Spencer, H. *Principles of psychology.* New York: Appleton, 1855.

Sullivan, H. S. Conceptions of modern psychiatry. *Psychiatry,* 1940, *3,* 1–117.

Tanner, J. M. *Growth at adolescence.* Oxford: Blackwell, 1962.

Tinbergen, N. *The study of instinct.* Oxford: Clarendon Press, 1951.

Toch, H. *Violent men: An inquiry into the psychology of violence.* Chicago: Aldine, 1969.

White, J. W. Sex and gender issues in aggression research. In R. G. Geen & E. I. Donnerstein (Eds.), *Aggression: Theoretical and empirical reviews,* (Vol. 2). New York: Academic Press, 1983.

Whiting, B. B., & Edwards, C. P. A cross-cultural analysis of sex differences in the behavior of children three through eleven. *Journal of Social Psychology,* 1973, *91,* 171–188.

Wilson, E. O. *Sociobiology: The new synthesis.* Cambridge, MA: Harvard University Press, 1975.

Yarrow, M. R., Campbell, J. D., & Burton, R. V. *Child rearing: An inquiry in research and methods.* San Francisco: Jossey-Bass, 1968.

Youniss, J. *Parents and peers in social development.* Chicago: University of Chicago Press, 1980.

15

Instigation and Insulation: How Families Affect Antisocial Aggression*

JOAN MCCORD

Despite intermittent skepticism by pundits, popular opinion and professional judgment typically agree that parents contribute importantly to the etiology of crime. Healy and Bronner (1926), for example, found the evidence about parental impact so powerful that they recommended removing children from "bad" homes in order to prevent delinquency. Their study of two thousand juvenile delinquents led them to conclude, "Where to place a large measure of responsibility, where to direct a strong attack in treatment for prevention of delinquency stands out with

* This study was supported by U.S. Public Health Service Research Grant No. R01 MH26779, National Institute of Mental Health (Center for Studies of Crime and Delinquency). It was conducted jointly with the Department of Probation of the Commonwealth of Massachusetts. The author wishes to express appreciation to the Division of Criminal Justice Services of the State of New York, to the Maine State Bureau of Identification, and to the states of California, Florida, Michigan, New Jersey, Pennsylvania, Virginia, and Washington for supplemental data about the men, though only the author is responsible for the statistical analyses and for the conclusions drawn from this research. The author would also like to thank Richard Parente, Robert Staib, Ellen Myers, and Ann Cronin for their work in tracing the men and their records and to thank Joan Immel, Tom Smedile, Harriet Sayre, Mary Duell, Elise Goldman, Abby Brodkin, and Laura Otton for their careful and thoughtful coding. Special thanks to Geoffrey Sayre McCord for his cogent editorial criticisms.

striking clearness" (p. 129). In a similar vein, Monahan (1957) remonstrated,

> the place of the home in the genesis of normal or delinquent patterns of behavior
> . . . is so strong that, if ways could be found to do it, a strengthening and preserving of family life . . . could probably accomplish more in the amelioration and prevention of delinquency and other problems than any other single program yet devised. (p. 258)

Perhaps most convincingly, in a longitudinal study of character development, Block (1971) found "an unequivocal relationship between the family atmosphere in which a child grew up and his later character structure" (p. 258).

Apparent consensus camouflages the fact that links between family characteristics and crime have not been well specified. High rates of crime among the same groups who have high rates of broken homes have led some observers to assume that parental absence provides a paradigm instance of inadequate conditions for child rearing (Bacon, Child, & Barry, 1963; Monahan, 1957; Toby, 1957; Wadsworth, 1979; Willie, 1967). Yet Gibson (1969) found no higher incidence of delinquency among London school boys from low-income broken homes than among boys from low-income intact homes. In the United States, too, studies controlling social class do not confirm a causal relationship between broken homes and crime (Grinnell & Chambers, 1979; Hennessy, Richards, & Berk, 1978; McCord, 1982). In fact, Craig and Glick (1963) improved their accuracy in predicting which boys living in New York slums would become delinquent when they started to count some broken homes as cohesive and therefore not criminogenic. Several studies of lower-class blacks have found crime rates no higher among broken homes than among united homes (Austin, 1978; Chilton & Markle, 1972; Robins & Hill, 1966). A broken home, therefore, appears to be a proxy for other potent variables.

Because homes broken by death of a parent are less criminogenic than those broken by divorce or separation, parental conflict, rather than parental absence, may be responsible for the delinquency commonly associated with broken homes. Studying children whose parents were patients in a London psychiatric clinic, Rutter (1971) found conduct disorders prevalent only among those whose parents were in conflict. Children separated from their parents for reasons other than parental conflict developed few signs of disturbance, and those removed from conflictful homes improved when placed in tranquil environments.

Power et al., (1974) studied children aged 10–16 years living in London between 1958 and 1968. Delinquents overrepresented children from both broken homes and conflictful, intact families. Among the 246 delinquents, those exposed to parental conflict were most likely to reappear in court.

In longitudinal studies of 411 boys from six school districts in London, West and Farrington (1973, 1977) found elevated criminal rates related to broken homes only if parental separation was not due to parental death. Further analysis (Farrington, 1978) traced aggression that developed initially at age 14 years to concurrent parental discord.

Relationships between family life and subsequent delinquency among children of a 1955 birth cohort in Hawaii echo those reported for the urban studies in England. Werner and Smith (1982) identified a significant association between behavior problems and parental discord for boys. Werner and Smith observed that some children from poor families who had experienced at least four conditions leading to psychological problems among a majority of their peers were nevertheless psychologically healthy. They considered these children "resilient." Compared with those who developed problems, the 42 resilient girls were more likely to live in single-parent homes but less likely to have been subjected to parental conflict. Broken homes were no more common in the backgrounds of nonresilient boys than they were in the backgrounds of resilient boys. The nonresilient boys were, however, more likely to have lived through exposure to chronic parental conflict.

In London and on the Hawaiian island of Kauai, parental affection apparently protected children against otherwise stressful conditions (Farrington & West, 1980; Werner & Smith, 1982). A study of the impact of paternal absence on males reared in Massachusetts during the pre-war depression yielded similar results (McCord, 1982). Traced 40 years after they had participated in a youth study, slightly over half those reared by two parents in discordant homes had been convicted for serious crimes. This proportion was twice that found among men reared by affectionate mothers in broken homes. Criminality was not more common among those raised by affectionate, solo mothers than among those raised by two parents in tranquil homes.

Farrington and West (1980) summarized their study of London boys by noting that "delinquents tend to come from families characterized by parental disharmony, cold, harsh parental attitudes, and erratic discipline" (p. 145). Similarly, longitudinal studies in Sweden and in Finland suggest that parental affect and discipline influence antisocial aggression in varied cultural contexts. Olweus (1980) found that descriptions of family life obtained through interviews with parents of sixth grade Swedish boys predicted aggression of the boys as reported by their peers 3 years later. Maternal rejection, parental punitiveness, and parental permissiveness presaged aggressiveness. In her study of Finnish youths, Pulkkinen (1983) discovered that aggressiveness at age 8 years predicted antisocial behavior at age 20 years. Parents who lacked interest in their children's activities, who used physical punishments, and whose discipline was inconsistent when the children were 14 years old were most likely to have 20-year-olds who committed crimes known to the police. These conclusions from longitudinal research tend to confirm conclusions based on retrospective and concurrent studies.

Cross-sectional studies also tie delinquency to parental conflict, rejection, and unfair disciplinary practices. For example, Glueck and Glueck (1950) compared 500 male delinquents incarcerated in Massachusetts with 500 nondelinquent boys of similar age, domicile, ethnic origin, and intelligence. They found that the former were more likely to have been reared by rejecting parents and less likely to have been guided by firm but kindly discipline, to have received supervision, and to have been part of a cohesive family. Nye (1958) asked high school pupils to report the frequency of their delinquencies and also to describe their family relationships. Those students who perceived mutual rejection between either their mothers and themselves or their fathers and themselves reported more delinquencies than did their classmates. Furthermore, the students who thought their fathers unfair tended to commit more offenses than those who judged their fathers to be fair (perceived fairness of the mother was not related to reported delinquencies). In a more extensive study, Hirschi (1969) asked over 4000 students in Richmond, California, to describe their families and report on their own delinquent behavior. His data suggested that parental attachments help prevent delinquency and that attachment to one parent had as much beneficial influence as attachment to both.

Crime tends to run in families, as shown by studies in England (Farrington & West, 1980), the United States (Glueck & Glueck, 1950; McCord, 1982; Robins, 1966; Robins & Ratcliff, 1979), and Denmark (Hutchings & Mednick, 1977). Yet, as Rutter and Madge (1977) remarked, "the exceptions are many and a surprisingly large proportion of people reared in conditions of privation and suffering do *not* reproduce that pattern in the next generation" (p. 6).

Responding to the inconsistent findings and methodological inadequacies, such researchers as Yarrow, Campbell, and Burton (1968), Clinard (1974), and the Clarks (1976) suggested that parental behavior may be irrelevant to adult personality. Few attempts have been made to identify conditions that account for normal development following a disadvantaged childhood. Cass and Thomas (1979) retraced 200 cases from a university child-guidance clinic in St. Louis. Like Robins (1966), Robins and Ratcliff (1979), and Werner and Smith (1982), Cass and Thomas found that exposure to fewer stressful conditions in childhood forecast better adjustment as an adult. In their review of research on delinquency, Rutter and Giller (1983) suggest that a single good relationship seems to serve as an insulating factor.

The present study utilizes a longitudinal design to identify conditions in the family that seem to generate or to retard development of serious antisocial behavior. The interaction of these conditions and their relationship to subsequent crime provides a framework for considering instigating and insulating effects of families on antisocial aggression.

METHOD

Data for the longitudinal analysis have been drawn from a study of men who had been part of a counseling program aimed at preventing delinquency. That program, known as the Cambridge–Somerville Youth Study, included both "difficult" and "average" youngsters living in deteriorated areas of eastern Massachusetts.

Once selected and chosen by random process for the treatment program, a boy was assigned a counselor. Between 1939 and 1945, counselors visited the homes of 253 boys approximately twice a month. Counselors assisted the boys and their families in a variety of ways, aiding them both inside and outside the home.

After each encounter with one of the boys or with a member of his family, the staff would file a report. Counselors recorded conversations, described behavior in detail, and attempted to convey a verbal picture of life in the families they assisted. Covering a span of more than 5 years, these running records reveal the texture of interactions that escapes most case histories.

To prepare for a longitudinal study, in 1957 coders read each case record thoroughly, transcribing information into categorical scales. The scales described the parents, the boys, and family interaction. Coders had no access to criminal histories or to information about the families other than that contained in the case records. To estimate reliability, a second coder read and rated 25 randomly selected cases. Uncontaminated by retrospective bias, these scales contain the descriptions of family life used in the present study.

Counselors described many interactions between each boy and his parents. When the interactions indicated that a parent generally seemed pleased with the boy and was concerned for the welfare of the child, that parent was considered to be affectionate. Two raters reading the same records agreed on affection ratings for 84% of the mothers and for 80% of the fathers.

If generally, when frustrated or annoyed, a parent yelled, threw things, or attempted to injure someone, that parent was coded as showing unrestrained aggression. In rating parental aggression, independent coders agreed on 92% of the mothers and on 84% of the fathers. A boy was classified as having or not having at least one unrestrained, aggressive parent.

Several dimensions qualified the types of discipline to which the boy was exposed. A mother was classified as permissive if she exerted little control over her son's behavior. Ratings on permissiveness were in agreement for 84% of the cases read to assess reliability. A parent was coded as consistent and nonpunitive if the standards of the parent were reasonably constant and predictable and if the parent enforced them without recourse to physical punishments. Two independent readings were in agreement for 84% of the ratings of mothers, but for only 60% of ratings of fathers on this categorization. Therefore, only the mother's rating was used for evaluating effects of consistent, nonpunitive discipline. Supervision of the boy was rated on the basis of whether or not the child's activities outside of school were governed by an adult. Two raters agreed on 88% of the cases regarding this classification. A measure of the level of parental expectations for the boy's behavior was gleaned from the records by looking to see whether the boy was expected to care for younger siblings, assist in preparations for meals, contribute to the financial support of the family, or do "extremely well" in school. Evidence for any of these expectations was sufficient to classify a boy as exposed to high expectations. Independent codings yielded agreement on 76% of the classifications.

Raters had been instructed to look for disagreements between the parents about the child, values, money, alcohol, or religion. For the present research, cases were divided into those whose parents evidenced considerable conflict and those in alternatative categories (no indication, apparently no conflict, or some conflict). Independent readers agreed on 80% of the cases used to estimate reliability of this variable.

A more subtle measure of parental interaction was revealed through a rating of the father's esteem for the mother. Agreement regarding whether a father showed at least moderate esteem for the mother occurred in 84% of the cases read to check reliability of coding.

The 1957 codes included a measure of the mother's self-confidence, based on whether or not she appeared to have confidence in her abilities to overcome difficulties. With alternative categories to indicate inadequate information or acceptance with resignation, independent raters agreed in 84% of the cases used to estimate reliability.

A father was considered to be a deviant role model if he was either alcoholic or criminal. Coders rated a father as alcoholic if the case record indicated that he had lost jobs because of drinking, if marital problems were attributed primarily to his excessive drinking, if welfare agencies had repeatedly pointed to the father's drinking as ground for family problems, or if the father had received treatment specifically for alcoholism. Independent coders agreed in 96% of the ratings on this variable. In 1948, after termination of the counseling program, criminal records for the family members of subjects were collected; these records were locked in a file separate from the case histories. An assistant unfamiliar with the subjects' case records coded these criminal histories. If a father had been convicted at least three times for public drunkenness, he was classified as being alcoholic. If he had been convicted for theft, burglary, assault, rape, attempted murder, or murder, he was considered criminal.

Cluster analysis of the variables describing family backgrounds revealed three principle, unidimensional components (SAS, 1981). Each cluster had only a single eigenvalue greater than one. Mother's affection, self-confidence, and consistency were the three variables forming the first cluster. This cluster represented a dimension of maternal leadership. The second cluster included the father's esteem for the mother and his affection for the son, weighted negatively, with parental conflict, parental aggressiveness, and paternal deviance given positive weights. This cluster appears to be a parental interaction dimension. The third cluster included the mother's permissiveness, weighted negatively, with supervision and high expectations for the boy given positive weights. Thus, the third cluster appears to represent parental control.

Scoring coefficients for the variables in each cluster have an interpretation similar to factor loadings. Squared correlations of each variable with its own cluster and with the next best cluster indicate the degree of separation among the dimensions. These coefficients, percents of variance accounted for, and the intercorrelations among the clusters describing family interaction are shown in Table 15.1.

In addition to information about family interaction, the case records provided data about family structure and social class. If, for at least 6 months, the boy's domicile was not with both parents, he was classified as having lived in a broken home. Interrater agreement on this variable was 96%. In 1938 and 1939, each boy's neighborhood was given a rating based on delinquency rates of the area, availability of recreational facilities, and proximity to bars, railroads, and junkyards. These ratings were coded on a 4-point scale from better to worse neighborhoods. The case records also reported the father's occupation. Boys whose fathers were unskilled or semiskilled and who lived in the worst neighborhoods were classified as in the lowest social class. A second rating of social class was based on the

Table 15.1

Cluster Analysis and Correlations

Group variable	R-square Highest	Second	Scoring coefficient
1. Mother's self-confidence	.517	.087	.431
Mother's affection	.485	.084	.418
Mother's consistency	.666	.104	.489
2. Father's esteem for mother	.596	.053	−.354
Parental conflict	.540	.049	.337
Parental aggressiveness	.400	.074	.290
Paternal deviance	.321	.044	.260
Father's affection	.325	.058	−.261
3. Mother's permissiveness	.710	.079	−.478
Supervision	.692	.130	.472
Expectations for boy	.360	.088	.341

Correlations

Groups:	1	2
2	−.312	—
3	.406	−.323

boy's residence in 1942. This rating classified the area as being transitional or residential. Two coders agreed for 88% of the ratings on neighborhood and for 96% of the ratings of father's occupation.

The present follow-up began in 1975, when the boys (now men) were middle-aged. By 1978, 248 (98%) had been located. About four out of five were living in Massachusetts, where complete court records were available. These records were supplemented by information on criminal histories from states to which the men had migrated. Men convicted for larceny, auto theft, burglary, assault, attempted rape, rape, attempted murder, kidnapping, or murder were considered criminals.

To justify treating the men as independent when testing hypothesized relationships, only one man from a family was used in the analyses. From the pool of 232 men, each from a different family, 77 had been convicted for serious crimes and 155 had not. To uncover conditions that differentiated the criminals from their more law-abiding peers, home backgrounds of the criminals were compared with home backgrounds of men who had no convictions for index crimes. Both dichotomous scales and unidimensional clusters of these scales were used to identify criminogenic families. To discover insulating factors, crime rates among various types of homes were compared; in each comparison, a set of descriptions was held constant in order to estimate effects of other variables on crime rates.

RESULTS

With the exception of social class and family structure, each dichoto-mous variable distinguished between criminals and noncriminals. Fami-lies that produced criminals proved less likely to provide supervision or high expectations for the boy's behavior. The parents were less likely to be affectionate and more likely to be aggressive. Parental conflict, pater-nal deviance, and inconsistent discipline appeared more frequently among families that produced delinquent sons. Mothers in criminogenic families were less likely to exhibit self-confidence, and fathers in such families were less likely to show esteem for their wives. Differences on these variables appear in Table 15.2.

The clusters that identified a three-dimensional space (described above) provide a simplified means for considering the relationship between fam-ily background and crime. A discriminant function analysis using the clusters (SAS, 1979) showed that, together, the three clusters account for approximately 19% of the variance in distinguishing between criminals and noncriminals. The parental interaction cluster accounted for 13% of the variance, $F = 34.40$ and $p = .0001$. The maternal leadership cluster accounted for an additional 5% of the variance, $F = 11.93$ and $p = .0007$. And the parental control dimension accounted for 2.8% of the remaining

Table 15.2

Family Background and Crime[a]

	Criminals[b]	Noncriminals[c]	p
Lowest social class	47	53	>.05
Transitional neighborhood	33	44	>.05
Broken home	51	59	>.05
Parental conflict	49	24	.0001
Parental aggressiveness	42	16	.0001
Father deviant	55	35	.0041
Father affectionate	14	31	.0060
Mother affectionate	31	55	.0005
Mother consistent	17	37	.0019
High expectations for boy	13	31	.0029
Boy supervised	40	65	.0003
Mother permissive	52	28	.0003
Mother self-confident	12	37	.0001
Father respects mother	26	55	.0001

[a] Percentage of families for which description is applicable.
[b] N = 77.
[c] N = 155.

variance, $F = 4.10$ and $p = .0440$. Based on data collected in childhood, the discriminant function correctly identified 66% of the noncriminals and 65% of the criminals identified more than three decades later.

The discriminant analysis showed that criminogenic families tend to be located in a three-dimensional space that can be characterized as one in which deviant, aggressive parents show little respect for other members of the family; mothers are insecure, inconsistent, and not affectionate; and no one provides supervision or attempts to direct the children's behavior. Within that space, some types of families seem to be more criminogenic than others.

Each dimension identified in the cluster analysis ranges from a "bad" or criminogenic end to a "good" or anticriminogenic end. Ninety-one boys had been reared by unaffectionate mothers who lacked self-confidence and whose discipline was erratic or punitive. Among them, 46 (51%) became criminals. However, despite the absense of a mother's affection, the presence of maternal self-confidence or consistency appeared to reduce the risk of subsequent criminality from 51 to 23%, $p = .0068$. The criminogenic risk among boys reared by mothers who lacked self-confidence and failed to use consistent discipline was reduced from 51 to 32% by maternal affection, $p = .0401$. Thirty boys had been described as having affectionate, self-confident mothers who provided consistent and nonpunitive discipline. Among them, only 3 (10%) became criminals. Discipline appeared to have little effect on the low rates of crime among boys reared by affectionate, self-confident mothers. Only 1 (8%) of the 13 boys who had inconsistent discipline and were raised by self-confident, loving mothers became a criminal.

Twenty-three boys were reared by aggressive, quarreling parents and were exposed to alcoholic or criminal, unaffectionate fathers who seemed not to respect the boy's mother. Among them, 17 (74%) became criminals. Paternal deviance was associated with parental conflict and aggressiveness. Conflict or aggressiveness was evident among 64% of the families in which the father was alcoholic or criminal but among only 28% of the families in which the father was not deviant, $p = .0001$.

Parental conflict or aggressiveness appeared to increase the criminogenic effect from 29 to 52% among boys whose fathers were deviant, $p = .0232$. Among boys whose fathers were not deviant, criminogenic effects increased from 19 to 42% if they were exposed to parental conflict or aggressiveness, $p = .0065$. Paternal affection and esteem by the father for the mother reduced the criminogenic effect of having a deviant father. Among boys whose fathers were deviant, 53% of those whose fathers had low esteem for the mothers had become criminals, but only 23% of those whose fathers had high esteem for the boy's mother had become criminals, $p = .0066$. And whereas 49% of the boys whose fathers were deviant and not affectionate became criminals, only 22% of the boys with affectionate deviant fathers became criminals, $p = .0411$. The latter proportion is not reliably higher than the 17% criminal rate among sons whose fathers were not deviant, $p > .05$.

At the other end of the scale, boys whose fathers were nondeviant, affectionate, respected the boy's mother, and whose parents got along reasonably well and were not aggressive had low rates of criminality. Among the 30 boys whose families appeared at the anticriminal end of the parental interaction dimension, 4 (13%) became criminals. Lacking paternal affection or having a deviant father had little criminogenic impact in the absence of conflict or aggression, so long as the father seemed to respect the mother. Among the 46 boys raised in such families, 7 (15%) became criminals. A combination of deviance, absence of affection, or low paternal esteem for the mother raised the criminogenic liability to 36%, $p = .0276$.

At the criminogenic end of the parental control dimension, 62 families had combined maternal permissiveness with low expectations for the boy and little supervision of his activities. Among these families, 33 (53%) of the boys had become criminals. Supervision without high expectations for the boy appears to have little impact. Among the 98 families in which the mother was not unusually permissive and in which expectations were not high, 72 boys were supervised and 26 were not. The crime rate for each group was 31%. High expectations appear to reduce criminogenic risk. From the 44 families in which the mother had high expectations and was not permissive and in which the boys were supervised, 4 (9%) of the boys became criminals. This proportion was less than a third that found among 72 boys raised by mothers without high expectations for them, though these mothers provided supervision and were not permissive, $p = .0071$.

The intracluster analyses suggest that some types of parenting have greater impact on criminality than others. Consideration of particular descriptions or categories of families can shed additional light on the ways in which child-rearing affects subsequent criminal behavior.

The 11 variables used in the cluster analysis were used in a stepwise discriminant function analysis (SAS, 1981). Five contributed reliably (using $p = .10$ to enter and to stay) to the discrimination between criminals and noncriminals. In order of their importance to the discrimination, these identified fathers who showed high esteem for the mothers, self-confident mothers, permissive mothers, aggressive parents, and affectionate mothers. Together, the five variables accounted for approximately 19% of the variance in subsequent criminal behavior. Thus, the 5 variables performed as well as the 3 clusters built on 11 variables. Two of the variables had been part of the cluster that described maternal leadership: maternal affection and self-confidence. Two had been part of the parental interaction cluster: father's esteem for the mother and parental aggressiveness. And one, mother's permissiveness, had been part of the parental control cluster. These five variables provided a discriminant function that successfully identified 67% of the noncriminals and 69% of the criminals. Overall, the discriminant function based on 3 clusters using 11 variables had correctly identified 152 (65.5%) of the men; the discriminant function based on 5 variables correctly identified 157 (67.7%). The five variables, then, appear to capture most of the information relevant to predicting criminality in terms of the three-dimensional space identified by maternal leadership, parental interaction, and parental control.

Three variables appeared to insulate at-risk boys from criminogenic conditions: maternal affection, maternal self-confidence, and paternal esteem for the mother. Maternal affection apparently reduces the criminogenic impact of permissiveness and parental aggressiveness. Among the 57 boys whose mothers were permissive and not affectionate, 32 (56%) became criminals; of the 26 boys whose mothers were permissive and affectionate, 8 (31%) became criminals, $p = .0319$. Among the 38 boys reared by aggressive parents in the absence of maternal affection, 25 (66%) became criminals; of the 19 reared by aggressive parents but with maternal affection, 7 (37%) became criminals, $p = .0379$.

Maternal self-confidence seemed to provide effective insulation against criminogenic conditions whether or not the mother was affectionate. Among the 67 boys reared by affectionate mothers who lacked self-confidence, 20 (30%) became criminals; of the 43 raised by self-confident, affectionate mothers, 4 (9%) became criminals, $p = .0109$. Among the 99 boys reared by unaffectionate mothers who lacked self-confidence, 48 (48%) became criminals; of the 23 raised by unaffectionate but self-confident mothers, 5 (22%) became criminals, $p = .0198$.

A father's respect for the mother appeared to reduce the criminogenic effect of being reared by a mother who was neither affectionate nor self-confident. Ninety-nine boys were reared by mothers who lacked self-confidence and were not affectionate. The fathers of 62 seemed to have little respect for the mothers and 39 (63%) became criminals. A significantly lower proportion of the 37 whose fathers showed esteem for their mothers, 9 (24%), became criminals, $p = .0002$.

SUMMARY AND DISCUSSION

This essay reports results of comparisons between the families of two groups of teenage youngsters. Families whose sons later became criminals constituted the first; families from similar urban neighborhoods whose sons had not been convicted for serious crimes constituted the second. Descriptions of family life had been drawn from case records in files of the Cambridge–Somerville Youth Study. These records had been written between 1936 and 1945. They were coded in 1957. Criminal histories were collected between 1975 and 1978. Thus, retrospective bias could not have influenced analyses.

Comparisons indicated that families of the criminals differed in many ways from those of the noncriminals. These differences appeared to reflect three dimensions: maternal leadership, parental interaction, and parental control.

A stepwise discriminant function identified five variables as maximally distinguishing families of criminals from families of noncriminals. Parental aggressiveness and maternal permissiveness appeared to be particularly criminogenic, whereas a father's esteem for the mother, a mother's self-confidence, and maternal affection seemed to help insulate a boy against criminogenic stresses. Paternal deviance appeared to have an indirect, rather than a direct, effect on criminality.

These results tend to falsify the argument that child rearing has only a temporary effect. Supported by similar findings among British, Swedish, Finnish, and Hawaiian youths, these results show that child rearing does indeed have a long-term impact on antisocial aggression. Yet the analyses also suggest that some of the conditions of family life believed to be most pernicious may be rendered innocuous by certain insulating conditions. Paternal deviance, for example, has often been held responsible for crime. Yet the risk for criminality from paternal deviance tends to disappear if the parents give the child affection.

The analyses also suggest that maternal affection reduces the impact of criminogenic conditions. Parental aggression, permissiveness, and disciplinary inconsistency had less damaging effects for boys whose mothers were affectionate than for boys whose mothers were not.

Two frequently ignored variables turned out to be particulary potent. Both seemed to meliorate conditions that tend to produce criminality. A mother's self-confidence, if coupled with consistent discipline, seemed to overcome effects from absence of affection. And a father's respect for the mother reduced the criminogenic impact of affectional deprivation and permissiveness.

In some respects, instigation and insulation are different ways of describing the same phenomena. Yet a focus on conditions that reduce the harmful consequences from adverse conditions can be advantageous. Such a focus can lead to insights about how to decrease crime when faced with conditions that may be unchangeable. Thus, the approach may elucidate "the less identifiable processes which enable people to break out of cycles of disadvantage" (Rutter & Madge, 1977, p. 6).

The study of men reared during the depression era preceding World War II has shown criminogenic factors similar to those found in other cultures and at other times. Going beyond this discovery, the present research also suggests that maternal leadership may be an insulator against some of the pressures toward crime.

REFERENCES

Austin, R. L. Race, father-absence, and female delinquency. *Criminology,* 1978, *15,* 4, 487–504.

Bacon, M. K., Child, I. L., & Barry, H. A cross-cultural study of correlates of crime. *Journal of Abnormal and Social Psychology,* 1963, *66,* 4, 291–300.

Block, J. *Lives through time.* Berkeley: Bancroft Books, 1963.

Cass, L. K., & Thomas, C. B. *Childhood pathology and later adjustment.* New York: Wiley, 1979.

Chilton, R. J., & Markle, G. E. Family disruption, delinquent conduct and the effect of subclassification. *American Sociological Review,* 1972, *37,* 93–99.

Clarke, A. M., & Clarke, A. D. B. *Early experience: Myth and evidence.* New York: The Free Press, 1976.

Clinard, M. B. *Sociology of deviant behavior,* (4th ed.). New York: Holt, Rinehart & Winston, 1974.

Craig, M. M., & Glick, S. J. Ten years experience with the Glueck Social Prediction Table. *Crime and Delinquency,* 1963, *9,* 240–261.

Ewing, J. A., & Rouse, B. A. *Identifying the hidden alcoholic.* Paper presented at the 29th International Congress on Alcohol and Drug Dependence, Sydney, Australia, February, 1970.

Farrington, D. P. The family backgrounds of aggressive youths. In L. A. Hersov and M. Berger (Eds.), *Aggression and antisocial behaviour in childhood and adolescence.* Oxford: Pergamon, 1978.

Farrington, D. P., & West, D. J. The Cambridge study in delinquent development (United Kingdom). In S. A. Mednick & A. E. Baert, (Eds.), *Prospective longitudinal research: An empirical basis for primary prevention.* Oxford: Oxford University Press, 1980.

Gibson, H. B. Early delinquency in relation to broken homes. *Journal of Child Psychology and Psychiatry,* 1969, *10,* 195–204.

Glueck, S., & Glueck, E. T. *Unraveling juvenile delinquency.* Cambridge, MA: Harvard University Press. 1950.

Grinnell, R. M., & Chambers, C. A. Broken homes and middle-class delinquency: A comparison. *Criminology,* 1979, *3,* 395–400.

Healy, W., & Bronner, A. F. *Delinquents and criminals: Their making and unmaking.* New York: Macmillan, 1926 (Republished by Patterson Smith, 1969).

Hennessy, M., Richards, P. J., & Berk, R. A. Broken homes and middle class delinquency: A reassessment. *Criminology,* 1978, *15,* 4, 505–528.

Hirschi, T. *Causes of delinquency.* Berkeley: University of California Press, 1969.

Hutchings, B., & Mednick, S. A. Criminality in adoptees and their adoptive and biological parents: A pilot study. In S. A. Mednick & K. O. Christiansen, (Eds.), *Biosocial bases of criminal behavior.* New York: Gardner Press, 1977.

McCord, J. A longitudinal view of the relationship between paternal absence and crime. In J. Gunn, & D. Farrington, (Eds.), *Abnormal Offenders, Delinquency and the criminal justice system.* London: Wiley, 1982.

Monahan, T. Family status and the delinquent child: A reappraisal and some new findings. *Social Forces,* 1957, *35,* 251–258.

Nye, F. I. *Family relationships and delinquent behavior.* New York: Wiley, 1958.

Olweus, D. Familial and temperamental determinants of aggressive behavior in adolescent boys: A causal analysis. *Developmental Psychology,* 1980, *16,* 644–660.

Power, M. J., Ash, P. M., Shoenberg, E., & Sirey, E. C. Delinquency and the family. *British Journal of Social Work,* 1974, *4,* 13–38.

Pulkkinen, L. Search for alternatives to aggression in Finland. In A. P. Goldstein & M. Segall, (Eds.), *Aggression in global perspective.* New York: Pergamon, 1983.

Robins, L. N. *Deviant children grown up.* Baltimore: Williams & Wilkins, 1966.

Robins, L. N. & Hill, S. Y. Assessing the contribution of family structure, class and peer groups to juvenile delinquency. *Journal of Criminal Law, Criminology, and Police Science,* 1966, *57,* 325–334.

Robins, L. N., & Ratcliff, K. S. Risk factors in the continuation of childhood antisocial behavior into adulthood. *International Journal of Mental Health,* 1979, *7,* 96–116.

Rutter, M. Parent-child separation: Psychological effects on the children. *Journal of Child Psychology and Psychiatry,* 1971, *12,* 233–260.

Rutter, M., & Giller, H. *Juvenile delinquency: Trends and perspectives.* Middlesex: Penguin, 1983.

Rutter, M., & Madge, N. *Cycles of disadvantage.* London: Heinemann, 1976.

SAS Institute. *SAS user's guide: 1982 edition.* Raleigh, NC: SAS Institute, 1979.

SAS Institute. *SAS 79.5: Changes and enhancements.* Raleigh, NC: SAS Institute, 1981.

Toby, J. The differential impact of family disorganization. *American Sociological Review,* 1957, *22,* 5, 505–512.

Wadsworth, M. *Roots of delinquency.* New York: Barnes & Noble, 1979.

Werner, E. E., & Smith, R. S. *Vulnerable but invincible.* New York: McGraw Hill, 1982.

West, D. J., & Farrington, D. P. *Who becomes delinquent?* London, Heinemann, 1973.

West, D. J., & Farrington, D. P. *The delinquent way of life.* London, Heinemann, 1977.

Willie, C. V. The relative contribution of family status and economic status to juvenile delinquency. *Social Problems,* 1967, *14,* 3, 326–335.

Yarrow, M. R., Campbell, J. D., & Burton, R. V. *Child Rearing.* San Francisco: Jossey-Bass, 1968.

16

Stepping Stones to Adult Criminal Careers*

DAVID P. FARRINGTON

INTRODUCTION

In general, adult criminal careers do not emerge without prior warning. They are usually preceded by juvenile delinquency and by other kinds of childhood deviance. One of the most interesting demonstrations of this has been provided in the United States by Robins (e.g., Robins & Ratcliff, 1980). For a sample of black men born in St. Louis, she related the number of adult (nontraffic) arrests up to age 30–35 years and the number of childhood deviant behaviors, such as truancy, school failure, early sexual intercourse, illicit drug use, alcohol problems, leaving home, and juvenile arrests. She found that both the number and variety of adult arrests increased with the variety of childhood deviance. For example, of those with 5 or more out of 9 aspects of childhood deviance, 69% had 3 or more adult arrests, 63% had been arrested for theft, 29% for a drug offense, and 27% for violence. In comparison, of those with no childhood deviance, only 12% had 3 or more adult arrests, only 10% had been arrested for theft, and none had been arrested for drugs or violence.

Using a British sample, the aim of the present essay is to investigate stepping stones along the road to adult criminal careers, or the determi-

* The analyses on which this essay is based were completed while the author was a Visiting Fellow at the National Institute of Justice, Washington, DC.

nants of deviant, delinquent, and criminal behavior at different ages from 8 to 25 years.

THE PRESENT RESEARCH

The present analyses use data from the Cambridge Study in Delinquent Development, which is a prospective longitudinal survey of 411 males. Data collection began in 1961–1962, when most of the boys were aged 8 years, and ended in 1980, when the youngest person was aged 25 years 6 months.[1] The major results of the survey can be found in four books (West, 1969, 1982; West & Farrington, 1973, 1977), and a concise summary is also available (Farrington & West, 1981).

At the time they were first contacted in 1961–1962, the boys were all living in a working-class area of London. The vast majority of the sample was chosen by taking all the boys aged 8–9 years who were on the registers of six state primary schools that were within a 1-mile radius of a research office that had been established. There were other schools in this area, including a Roman Catholic school, but these were the ones that were approached and agreed to cooperate. In addition to 399 boys from these 6 schools, 12 boys from a local school for the educationally subnormal were included in the sample, in an attempt to make it more representative of the population of boys living in the area.

The boys were almost all caucasian in appearance. Only 12, most of whom had at least one parent of West Indian origin, were black. The vast majority (371) were being brought up by parents who had themselves been reared in the United Kingdom or Ireland. On the basis of their fathers' occupations, 93.7% could be described as working class (categories III, IV, and V on the Registrar General's scale), in comparison with the national figure of 78.3% at that time. This was, therefore, overwhelmingly a white, urban, working-class sample of British origin.

The boys were interviewed and tested in their schools when they were aged about 8, 10, and 14 years, by male or female psychologists. They were interviewed in the research office at about 16, 18, 21, and 24 years, by young male social science graduates. Up to and including age 18 years, the aim was to interview the whole sample on each occasion, and it was always possible to trace and interview a high proportion. For example, at age 18 years, 389 of the original 411 (94.6%) were interviewed. Of the 22 youths missing at this age, one had died, one could not be traced, 6 were

---

[1] Since this essay was written, a further round of interviews with the whole sample, at age 31–32, has begun.

abroad, 10 refused to be interviewed, and in the other 4 cases the parent refused on behalf of the youth.

At age 21 years, the aim was to interview only the convicted delinquents and a similarly sized, randomly chosen sample of unconvicted youths. At this age, 218 of the target group of 241 were interviewed (90.5%). At age 24 years, the aim was to interview four subgroups of youths: persisting recidivists (those with two or more convictions up to age 19 years and at least one more in the next 5 years), temporary recidivists (those with two or more convictions up to age 19 years and no more in the next 5 years), unconvicted youths from seriously deprived backgrounds (from large families, in poor housing, with convicted parents, and with families supported by state welfare), and a random sample of unconvicted youths. At this age, only 85 of the target group of 113 (75.2%) were successfully interviewed, primarily because so many of these youths had left home and were difficult to trace.

In addition to interviews and tests with the boys, interviews with their parents were carried out by female social workers who visited their homes. These took place about once a year from when the boy was about 8 years old until he was aged 14–15 years and was in his last year of compulsory schooling. The primary informant was the mother, although the father was also seen in the majority of cases. Most of the parents were cooperative. At the time of the final interview, when the boy was 14–15 years old, information was obtained from the parents of 399 boys (97.1%). The boys' teachers also filled in questionnaires about their behavior in school when the boys were aged about 8, 10, 12, and 14 years. Again, the teachers were very cooperative, and at least 94% of questionnaires were completed at each age.

It was also possible to make repeated searches in the central Criminal Record Office in London to try to locate findings of guilt sustained by the boys, by their parents, by their brothers and sisters, and (in recent years) by their wives. These searches were assisted by the large numbers of birth and marriage certificates obtained to supplement the information from the interviews. The searches continued until March 1980, when the youngest sample member was aged 25 years 6 months. The criminal records of the boys who have not died or emigrated are believed to be complete from the 10th birthday (the minimum age of criminal responsibility in England and Wales) to the 25th birthday.

MEASURES OF CRIME AND DEVIANCE

Detailed information about the rates of offending of this sample at different ages can be found in Farrington (1983). The period from the 10th to the 25th birthday spans four legal categories in England and Wales: children (10th to just before 14th birthday), young persons (14th to just before 17th birthday), young adults (17th to just before 21st birthday), and older adults (21st birthday onward). In this sample, 35 boys (8.5%) were convicted as children, 74 (18.0%) as young persons, 95 (23.6%) as young adults, and 46 (11.6%) as older adults.

Convictions were only included if they were for offenses normally recorded in the Criminal Record Office. This category is more or less synonymous with "serious" or "criminal" offenses. For example, no convictions for traffic offenses were included, nor convictions for offenses regarded as minor (e.g., public drunkenness or common assault). The most common offenses included were thefts, burglaries, and unauthorized takings of motor vehicles. For young adults and older adults, the percentages convicted refer to the populations at risk, that is the number of boys who had not died or emigrated (402 and 395, respectively at the different ages). The percentages for children and young persons refer to all 411 boys. No boy died before age 17 years, and enquiries were made abroad in regard to the six youths who spent at least a year of their juvenile period outside England and Wales.

The number of boys convicted in the different age ranges overlaps, of course. For example, 25 of the 35 convicted as children were among the 74 convicted as young persons. Over one-fifth of the boys (84) were convicted as juveniles (children or young persons), and over one-quarter (110) as adults. Overall, just over one third of those at risk up to the 25th birthday were convicted at some stage (136 out of 395, or 33.9%).

In addition to the information about convictions, self-reports of offending were also obtained at different ages. At age 14 years, the boys were asked to say whether they had committed each of 38 delinquent or fringe-delinquent acts (West & Farrington, 1973). The 108 boys (out of 405 interviewed) who admitted 13 or more different acts were referred to as the "self-reported delinquents" at 14 years. For the purposes of the present analysis, each variable was dichotomized into the "worst" quarter and the remaining three quarters, wherever possible. There were various reasons for this. First of all, in order to compare variables, it was desirable that each should be measured equally sensitively (or insensitively). Secondly, in order to carry out loglinear or logit analyses, it was desirable to have as few categories as possible for each variable. Thirdly, the one quarter/three quarters split had been used from the beginning of this study, because of the prior expectation that about one quarter of the sample would be convicted, and the desirability of equating the proportion of those identified who were convicted and the proportion of those convicted who were identified.

At age 18 years, the youths were asked about the commission of 7 specified acts in the previous 3 years (West & Farrington, 1977; further information about all the variables included in this essay can be obtained in the four books referred to above). The scoring system at this age reflected the frequency as well as the variety of offenses committed, and 97 youths out of 389 interviewed were categorized as self-reported delinquents, on the basis of their relatively high scores.

Two other measures of crime and deviance were used in the present essay. One was the rating of the troublesomeness of the boys at age 8–10 years, made by their peers and teachers. This proved to be the best predictor of juvenile convictions. It might therefore be suggested that the understanding of why boys get convicted might be increased if it was understood why they behaved badly at an early age. The other measure was of "antisocial tendency" at age 18 years. Generally, at this age, the convicted youths were leading more deviant life styles than the remainder. The aim of the antisocial tendency index was to measure the extent of this deviant life style, excluding the kinds of deviance that usually led to convictions (i.e., property offenses such as thefts and burglaries). Therefore, antisociality reflects deviant behavior that is rarely, or in some cases never, dealt with by the police and courts. The antisocial tendency score was based on 11 factors that were interrelated (heavy gambling, heavy smoking, driving after drinking, use of prohibited drugs, sexual promiscuity, unstable job record, spending time hanging about, involvement in antisocial groups, most aggressive in behavior, anti-establishment attitudes, and tattoos). The 110 youths scoring 4 or more were identified as the most antisocial at age 18 years. Antisociality was the variable that was most closely related to convictions at any age (i.e. the best discriminator of the 136 convicted up to the 25th birthday from the remainder).

PREDICTORS OF CRIME AND DEVIANCE

The aim in this study was to measure as many factors as possible that were alleged to cause or contribute to delinquency. One of the major reasons for this was to investigate the interrelationships between variables, and the extent to which one variable was related to delinquency independently of others. In any nonexperimental study, it is desirable to achieve statistical control of as many variables as possible. In this research, the major problem was that almost every measured variable was significantly related to official delinquency. The key issue was to establish which underlying theoretical variables acted to produce delinquent behavior. In a study in which only a limited range of variables was measured, or in a study designed narrowly to test only one theory, misleading conclusions might be reached because of the failure to control for important, but unmeasured, variables.

The disadvantage with casting the net wide was that the large number of measured variables (over 200 at age 8–10 years alone) made the analyses almost unmanageable. It was essential to reduce the number of measured variables, and the primary aim in doing this was to have each distinct theoretical variable measured by only one empirical variable. Reduction was, of course, a subjective procedure. Clusters of measured variables were identified that were related empirically and theoretically, and then either one variable was chosen as the best representative of a cluster or several variables in a cluster were combined into a single composite measure. In addition, for the purposes of the present analysis, variables on which less than 350 boys were known were eliminated. On most variables included, the number of missing cases was 5% or less, and there were no missing cases on many variables measured at age 8–10 years.

Some of the variables were derived from records, such as convictions of parents and delinquency of older siblings (both up to the boy's 10th birthday). Some were provided by the boys' classmates, for example the peer ratings of dishonesty and unpopularity at age 8–10 years. Some came from the boys' teachers, for example, the ratings of aggressiveness and truancy at age 12–14 years. Many variables were derived from interviews with the boys' parents, such as family income, family size, poor housing, social class of the family breadwinner, Roman Catholic affiliation, parental supervision, parental uncooperativeness, and parental behavior (which was a composite variable reflecting attitude, discipline, and parental agreement). Some measures were obtained in tests and questionnaires given to the boys, for example, IQ, vocabulary, psychomotor clumsiness, neurotic extravert personality, hostile attitude to the police at 14 years of age, anti-establishment attitudes at 18 years of age, and reported delinquent acts of the boy's friends at 14 years of age. Others were obtained in personal interviews with the boys, such as most of the elements of the antisocial tendency score mentioned above. Finally, in some instances measures from different sources were combined, for example troublesomeness (rated by peers and teachers) and daring (rated by peers and parents). It was thought that errors and biases in variables might cancel out to some extent when they were combined.

Many other variables were included in the analysis other than those mentioned above. Apart from the 8 measures of crime and deviance specified in the previous section, there were 26 variables measured at age 8–10 years, 20 at age 12–16 years (mostly at age 14 years), and 25 at age 18 years. The same variable was often measured at different ages, for example, height, weight, IQ, vocabulary, neurotic extraversion, income, family size, social class, and poor housing.

RELATIONSHIPS WITH CONVICTIONS AT
10–13 YEARS

Table 16.1 shows which independent variables were related to each dependent measure of crime or deviance. With the exception of the analysis of troublesomeness, only independent variables prior in time to each dependent measure were included in each analysis. Thus, family income

Table 16.1

Relationships with Crime and Deviance at Different Ages[a]

Dependent measure age (N)	Independent variables age (N)	Corrected X^2	Partial correlation	Multiple regression	Loglinear/ logit	Logistic regression
Troublesomeness 8–10 (92)	Psychomotor clumsiness 8–10 (104)	24.60	**	***	—	—
	Poor supervision 8 (74)	25.90	**	***	**	***
	Convicted parent 10 (104)	17.16	*	*	**	**
	Low vocabulary 10 (124)	18.64	*	**	**	***
	Low family income 8 (93)	25.01	*	—	*	*
Convictions 10–13 (35)	Troublesomeness 8–10 (92)	33.57	***	***	***	***
	Uncooperative family 8 (43)	15.59	***	**	—	—
	Poor housing 8–10 (151)	12.49	**	**	**	*
	Poor parental behavior 8 (96)	13.29	*	*	*	—
	Low IQ 8–10 (103)	12.67	*	*	*	**
	Catholic family 8 (73)	7.19	*	—	*	*
Self-reported delinquency 14 (108)	Convictions 10–13 (35)	29.63	***	***	***	***
	Daring 8–10 (121)	20.35	***	***	***	***
	Convicted parent 10 (104)	13.70	**	**	**	**

Table 16.1 (*Continued*)

Dependent measure age (N)	Independent variables age (N)	Corrected X²	Partial correlation	Multiple regression	Loglinear/ logit	Logistic regression
Convictions 14–16 (74)	Convictions 10–13 (35)	70.06	***	***	***	***
	Daring 8–10 (121)	36.76	***	***	***	***
	Convicted parent 10 (104)	21.70	***	***	***	***
	Dishonest 10 (88)	18.75	**	*	**	*
	Delinquent sibling 10 (46)	14.09	*	*	—	—
Convictions 17–20 (95)	Convictions 14–16 (74)	76.07	***	***	***	***
	Delinquent friends 14 (101)	38.79	***	***	**	***
	Low social class 14 (58)	8.18	**	**	**	**
	Truancy 12–14 (73)	41.88	**	***	***	***
	Convicted parent 10 (104)	28.53	**	*	*	*
	Teacher rating aggressive 12–14 (134)	29.12	*	*	—	—
	Delinquent sibling 10 (46)	22.95	*	*	*	—
	Neurotic extraversion 16 (118)	6.30	—	*	—	—
Self-reported delinquency 18 (97)	Convictions 14–16 (74)	46.29	***	***	***	***
	Self-Reported delinquency 14 (108)	28.34	**	**	*	**
	Teacher rating aggressive 12–14 (134)	19.86	*	*	*	*
	Neurotic extraversion 16 (118)	8.20	*	*	*	*

(*Continued*)

Table 16.1 (*Continued*)

Dependent measure age (N)	Independent variables age (N)	Corrected X^2	Partial correlation	Multiple regression	Loglinear/ logit	Logistic regression
Antisocial tendency 18 (110)	Convictions 14–16 (74)	71.36	***	***	***	***
	Self-reported delinquency 14 (108)	60.37	***	***	***	***
	Teacher rating aggressive 12–14 (134)	34.85	**	**	*	*
	Convicted parent 10 (104)	31.09	**	**	**	*
	Truancy 12–14 (73)	40.47	*	***	**	***
	Large family size 10 (99)	20.62	*	*	**	**
Convictions 21–24 (46)	Convictions 17–20 (95)	53.91	***	***	***	***
	Convictions 14–16 (74)	53.36	***	***	**	***
	Unstable job record 18 (92)	26.57	**	*	*	*
	Low family income 14 (79)	7.64	*	*	*	*
	Anti-establishment attitude 18 (98)	18.01	*	**	—	—
	Hostile attitude to police 14 (90)	23.38	*	—	*	**
	Convictions 10–13 (35)	29.97	—	*	*	—

* p < .05; ** p < .01; *** p < .001; — not significant.
[a] Number in parentheses = number in extreme category (e.g., 92 most troublesome). Corrected X^2 derived from 2 × 2 table relating each independent and dependent measure (3.84 significant at .05, 6.63 at .01, 10.83 at .001).

at 8 years was investigated as a predictor of self-reported delinquency at 14 years, but family income at 14 years was not. Dependent measures at one time were included as independent variables in the analysis of a later dependent measure. Thus, convictions at 10–13 years of age were investigated as predictors of self-reported delinquency at 14 years. The derivation and meaning of Table 16.1 is explained in detail in this section for convictions at 10–13 years as a dependent measure. The results obtained with other measures of crime and deviance are summarized in the next section.

For each dependent measure, the aim of the analyses was to specify which independent variables were related to it independently of all other independent variables. Since all variables were categorical, the most defensible methods statistically of doing this were logistic regression and loglinear analysis (Fienberg, 1980). However, both were difficult to use. Logistic regression was carried out using the GLIM (Generalised Linear Interactive Modelling: Baker & Nelder, 1978) program package, but this was a laborious process. After entering in the equation the independent variable that was most closely related to the dependent variable, it was then necessary to enter all the other independent variables one by one to establish which one produced the greatest decrease in G^2 (the likelihood ratio goodness-of-fit statistic). Having established the first two variables in the equation, it was then necessary to repeat the whole process to select the third, and so on. This took a great deal of time.

This stepwise selection process is done automatically in the SPSS (Statistical Package for the Social Sciences: Nie, Hull, Jenkins, Steinbrenner, & Bent, 1975) multiple regression program. However, the dichotomous data involved here (like most social science data) do not conform to the underlying statistical assumptions of multiple regression (which require interval scales and normal distributions, for example). My previous comparisons of multiple regression and logistic regression suggest that the two procedures produce very similar results with these dichotomous data. Therefore, it was decided to use multiple regression initially with all the variables to identify those that appeared to be independent predictors. The more defensible logistic regression was then carried out to investigate the independent contributions of the variables identified by the multiple regression. It was thought unlikely that any important relationships would be missed in this two-stage method.

The results obtained with convictions at 10–13 years of age are shown in Table 16.1. In the multiple regression, the variables entering the equation were as follows, with the significance of the change in F given in parentheses: troublesomeness at 8–10 years ($p < .001$), uncooperative family at 8 years (p = .001), poor housing at 8–10 years (p = .006), poor parental behavior at 8 years (p = .021), low IQ at 8–10 years (p = .039), and Catholic family at 8 years of age (p = .056). Variables that were not quite significant at p = .05 in the multiple regression analysis were included in the logistic regression analysis. The following variables produced a significant decrease in G^2 when they entered the equation in the logistic regression analysis: troublesomeness at 8–10 years (p < .001), low IQ at 8–10 years (p < .01), poor housing at 8–10 years (p < .05), and Catholic family at 8 years of age (p < .05).

The differences between the multiple regression and logistic regression results may be a function of the way missing data were treated in the two analyses. Boys who were not known on any one variable were eliminated completely in the logistic regression, but they were only eliminated from correlations involving that particular variable in the multiple regression. It is likely that an uncooperative family did not appear to be important in the logistic regression because boys whose parents were rated as uncooperative towards the social workers tended to be rated as not known on other variables and hence excluded from the analysis. For example, all 15 rated as not known on parental behavior were among the 43 rated as having uncooperative parents. Therefore, the importance of uncooperative parents could not be apparent in the logistic regression.

It was also difficult to carry out the loglinear analysis. Since this is based on a multidimensional contingency table, it cannot be used to investigate many variables at a time, given the present sample size. With all variables dichotomous and a sample size of about 400, the maximum number of variables that can safely be included in a loglinear analysis is 6 (5 independent and 1 dependent), totaling 64 cells and an average cell size of about 6. It would not be safe to carry out a loglinear analysis with an average cell size of less than 5. If the variables had not all been dichotomized, the number that could have been included in a loglinear analysis would have been less.

Because each investigation of the prediction of crime or deviance had to include many more than five independent variables, it was decided to use partial correlations to identify a small number of variables that were independently important, and then to carry out a loglinear analysis with these. The partial correlation method is less defensible statistically, but it seemed unlikely that it would produce misleading results. Zero order (phi) correlations derived from 2 × 2 tables are simply related to χ^2 without the correction for continuity ($phi^2 = \chi^2/N$), and first-order partial phi correlations produce results almost identical to those obtained in comparable loglinear analyses (Farrington, Biron, & LeBlanc, 1982).

Concentrating on convictions at 10–13 years of age, the first step was to investigate which of 27 variables measured at 8–10 years (including troublesomeness) predicted these convictions significantly. The criterion used to select variables was whether the phi correlation was .100 or greater, because this value of phi almost always corresponded to a significant χ^2 value (corrected for continuity). It should perhaps be pointed out that phi^2 should not be interpreted as the percentage of the variance explained. The maximum value of phi^2 depends on the marginal frequencies of the 2×2 table, and may be considerably less than 1. For example, in the table relating troublesomeness (marginals 92 and 319) to convictions at 10–13 years (marginals 35 and 376), the maximum value of phi^2, if all convicted boys were troublesome, is .323 (319×35 divided by 376×92). The actual value of phi in this case was about half the maximum (.296 as opposed to .568).

Eighteen of the 27 variables investigated in the first stage of the analysis significantly predicted convictions at 10–13 years of age, that is all except convicted parents at 10 years, peer rating unpopular at 8–10 years, nervousness of the boy at 8 years, nervousness of this mother at 8–10 years, nervousness of his father at 8 years, neurotic extraversion of the boy at 10 years, social class of the family at 8–10 years, whether the mother had a job at 8–10 years, and the weight of the boy at 8–10 years of age. The best predictor was troublesomeness at 8–10 years of age. Twenty-two of the 92 troublesome boys were among the 35 convicted, in comparison with 13 of the remaining 319 ($\chi^2 = 33.57$, 1 df, $p < .001$, phi = .296; see Table 16.1).

The next stage of the analysis was to investigate first-order partials, to see if each variable predicted convictions at 10–13 years of age independently of each other variable. The criterion for retention in the analysis at each stage was a partial phi of .100 or greater. In the case of convictions at 10–13 years old, 6 variables were not related independently of troublesomeness: delinquent siblings at 10 years, daring at 8–10 years, dishonesty at 10 years, parental supervision at 8 years, separations from parents up to 10 years, and an unstable paternal job record at 8–10 years of age. The advantage of this successive partialing technique is that it is possible to explain why each variable with a high zero-order correlation was dropped from the analysis.

Second-order partials were then calculated for 12 variables, and 4 were not significantly related to convictions at age 10–13 years independently of troublesomeness and low family income taken together (the two variables with the highest zero-order correlations): large family size at age 10 years, psychomotor clumsiness at 8–10 years, low vocabulary at 10 years, and poor junior school leaving results at 10 years of age. Third-order partials were then calculated for the remaining eight variables, but all seemed to be related independently of the most obvious combinations of three other variables.

Fourth-order partials were then calculated for these eight variables, and all partials were scrutinized systematically. Low family income fell below .100 on 10 occasions, low height on 7 occasions, and poor housing once. Since the lowest partial correlation was achieved by low family income, it was decided to drop this variable from the analysis. This eliminated the low partial for poor housing, because that occurred when controlling for troublesomeness, low family income, low IQ, and low height. It also eliminated six of the seven low partials for low height, but one was left (controlling for troublesomeness, low IQ, a Catholic family, and poor housing). Therefore, low height was eliminated from the analysis. Fifth-order partials were then calculated for the remaining 6 variables (troublesomeness at age 8–10 years, uncooperative family at age 8 years, poor housing at age 8–10 years, poor parental behavior at age 8 years, low IQ at age 8–10 years, and a Catholic family at age 8 years), and each proved to be significantly related to convictions at 10–13 years of age independently of the other 5. These significant partials are shown in Table 16.1.

The final stage was to carry out a loglinear analysis. Actually, a logit analysis was used since, in investigating relationships with a clear dependent variable, this gives exactly the same results as a loglinear analysis. The great advantage of the logit analysis is that it takes far less computer time (about 2 seconds on the Cambridge IBM 370/165, as opposed to over 40 seconds for the comparable loglinear analysis). The point of each logit analysis was to investigate if each independent variable had a main effect on each dependent variable over and above the main effects of all other independent variables. Thus, the contributions of all other independent variables were investigated first, and then the additional contribution of the independent variable under investigation (measured by G^2, with 1 df, distributed as χ^2). It was always true that the model containing main effects only was not significantly different from the data, suggesting that it was not necessary to investigate interactions.

As mentioned above, a maximum of five independent variables can be investigated in these logit analyses. When more than five survived the partial correlation analyses (as in the case of convictions at 10–13 years of age), more than one logit analysis was carried out. The first logit analysis investigated the separate contributions of the five independent variables with the highest partial correlations. Each other logit analysis investigated the separate contribution of each other independent variable over and above the four with the highest partial correlations. In the case of convictions at 10–13 years of age, the first logit analysis investigated the separate contributions of the first 5 independent variables listed in Table 16.1.

The second logit analysis investigated the contribution of a Catholic family over and above troublesomeness, an uncooperative family, poor housing, and poor parental behavior.

The results of the logit analyses confirmed the results of the partial correlation analyses in showing that troublesomeness, poor housing, poor parental behavior, low IQ, and a Catholic family were all independently predictive of convictions at age 10–13 years. However, an uncooperative family, which was significantly related according to partial correlations, was not significantly related according to the logit analysis. This was almost certainly because the logit analysis, like the logistic regression, only included boys known on all variables (see above).

With categorical data commonly obtained in the social sciences, there is no ideal way of handling a large multivariate problem. However, there are considerable advantages in using a variety of methods. If both the partial correlation/multiple regression and logit/logistic methods indicate that a variable makes an independent contribution to a measure of crime or deviance, it is reasonable to accept this conclusion. When a variable is identified by only one method, its contribution is less certain. Only variables identified by both methods will be discussed below.

PREDICTING CRIME AND DEVIANCE

Table 16.1 shows that the boys who were rated troublesome at age 8–10 years tended to be those from low-income families; those having poorly supervising, convicted parents; and those having a low vocabulary. Troublesomeness was the most significant determinant of whether a boy was convicted at 10–13 years of age. However, in addition to troublesomeness, these convictions were predicted by poor housing, poor parental behavior, low IQ, and coming from a Catholic family. The absence of any of the predictors of troublesomeness from this list suggests that they may have had their effect in producing troublesomeness at 8–10 years of age, and that they may not have any effect on convictions over and above their effect on troublesomeness.

Self-reported delinquency at 14 years of age and convictions at 14–16 years of age were predicted best by convictions at 10–13 years of age. However, being rated as daring, having convicted parents, and being rated as dishonest (for convictions at 14–16 years of age only) all had additional independent effects. Convictions at age 17–20 years, self-reported delinquency at 18 years, and being antisocial at 18 years were all predicted best by convictions at 14–16 years. However, whereas self-reported delinquency at 14 years of age added to the prediction in the cases of self-reported delinquency at 18 years and antisociality, it was a boy's reported delinquency of his friends at age 14 that added to the prediction of convictions at age 17–20. (Self-reported delinquency and reported delinquency of friends were highly correlated, no doubt because most delinquent acts were committed with friends.) Teachers' ratings of aggressiveness, convicted parents, and truancy were other factors that appeared more than once in predicting these three measures. In contrast, low social class and having a delinquent sibling predicted only convictions at age 17–20 years, neurotic extraversion predicted only self-reported delinquency at age 18, and large family size predicted only antisociality.

Finally, adult criminal convictions at 21–24 years of age were predicted best by convictions at age 17–20 and by convictions at age 14–16. However, if the boy himself had an unstable job record at 18 years of age, came from a low income family at age 14, had a hostile attitude to the police at age 14, and if he had been convicted at age 10–13, all of these made additional contributions to his likelihood of sustaining adult criminal convictions. An anti-establishment attitude at age 18 years was highly correlated with a hostile attitude to the police at age 14, and if one of these factors remained in an analysis the other did not, in general.

CONTINUITY IN BEHAVIOR?

It seems clear that the causes of adult criminal convictions can be traced back to childhood. The best predictors of convictions at age 21–24 years were convictions at age 17–20 and convictions at age 14–16. The best predictors of convictions at age 17–20 years were convictions at age 14–16. The best predictors of convictions at age 14–16 years were convictions at age 10–13 and daring behavior at age 8–10. And the best predictor of convictions at age 10–13 years was troublesome behavior at age 8–10. The same is true of other measures of deviance. The best predictors of self-reported delinquency at 18 years of age and antisocial tendency at age 18 were convictions at age 14–16 and self-reported delinquency at age 14, and the best predictors of self-reported delinquency at age 14 were convictions at age 10–13 and daring behavior at age 8–10. As with aggression (Olweus, 1979), the continuity of troublesome, delinquent, deviant, and criminal behavior from childhood to adulthood seems striking.

Alternatively, it could be argued that the continuity of behavior is illusory. Convictions at one age may predict convictions at a later age because of continuity in police and court bias, and self-reports at one age may predict self-reports at a later age because of continuity in willingness to admit delinquent acts. However, it is interesting that the two self-

reported delinquency measures (at ages 14 and 18 years) were best predicted by earlier convictions, and the same was true of antisocial tendency. It might be expected that convictions and self-reports would be
subject to different biases, and that similar results obtained with the two
measures might reflect offending behavior rather than bias. The continuity between convictions and self-reports supports the hypothesis that
there is continuity in behavior rather than in biasing factors.

Against this, it could be argued that convictions predict self-reports
because convicted youths are more likely to admit delinquent acts than
unconvicted youths. Continuity in delinquent behavior is best demonstrated by the prediction of convictions by self-reports, which did happen
but is not shown in Table 16.1. Nearly half of those high on self-reported
delinquency at 14 years of age (42.9%) were convicted at age 17–20, in
comparison with only 16.7% of the remainder ($\chi^2 = 28.03$, 1 df, $p < .001$,
phi $= .271$). However, self-reported delinquency at age 14 years was
dropped from the partial correlation analysis of convictions at age 17–20
because it did not predict independently of reported delinquency of
friends at age 14 and convictions at age 14–16 years. Similarly, self-
reported delinquency at ages 14 and 18 years significantly predicted convictions at age 21–24, but neither prediction held independently of antisociality and earlier convictions. In turn, antisociality at age 18, which had
been expected to be one of the most important predictors of convictions
at age 21–24 years, did not predict independently of earlier convictions
and an unstable job record at age 18.

Of course, if self-reported delinquency, convictions, and antisociality
are all measures of the same underlying theoretical construct (deviant
behavior?), it is not surprising that they do not predict independently.
Perhaps the best evidence in favor of the argument that there is continuity
in deviant behavior rather than in biasing factors is the earlier demonstration that self-reported delinquency predicts convictions among unconvicted youths (Farrington, 1973). Taking into account other evidence
about the validity of self-reported delinquency measures (see, e.g., Hindelang, Hirschi, & Weis, 1981), the most plausible conclusion is that the
continuity of troublesome, delinquent, deviant, and criminal behavior
from childhood to adulthood is real rather than artifactual.

The above discussion should not be taken to assert that there were no
differences between results obtained with convictions and those obtained
by self-report. There were many similarities. In particular, at age 14–16
years the best predictors of both were convictions at age 10–13, daring at
age 8–10, and convicted parents at age 10. However, there were some
differences that may reflect bias. For example, low social class at 14 years
of age was one of the independent predictors of convictions at age 17–20

but was unrelated to self-reported delinquency at age 18. One possible explanation for this difference is that the police were biased against lower-class youths (see also Farrington, 1979).

INFLUENCES ON CRIME AND DELINQUENCY

The independent predictors of crime and delinquency at different ages are shown diagrammatically in Figure 16.1. In this, low family income at age 8 years and poor housing at age 8–10 are grouped under the heading of economic deprivation at age 8–10; poor supervision at age 8 and poor parental behavior at age 8 are grouped as parental mishandling; convicted parents and delinquent siblings as family criminality; low vocabulary at age 10 and low IQ at age 8–10 as school failure at age 8–10; and low family income at age 14 and low social class at age 14 as economic deprivation at age 14 years. These groups could be justified on theoretical and empirical (correlational) grounds. Converting the results shown in Table 16.1 to Figure 16.1 was a subjective process to some extent, but it is believed that Figure 16.1 summarizes the major influences.

The continuity from troublesome behavior at 8–10 years of age to criminal behavior at 21–24 years is shown in the middle of Figure 16.1. The troublesome boys, and the juvenile delinquents, were those who had experienced economic deprivation, parental mishandling, family criminality, and school failure at an early age. Later measures of economic deprivation (at age 14 years) and of school failure (truancy at age 12–14 years) predicted delinquency at the young adult and adult ages. There were no later measures of family criminality, and so the measures up to age 10 years continued to predict adult crime. There were later measures of parental mishandling, but they did not appear to be important in relation to later criminal behavior.

Parental mishandling, therefore, seemed important only in relation to troublesome and delinquent behavior at an early age. Economic deprivation, family criminality, and school failure, on the other hand, seemed to have continuing and longer-lasting effects. In addition, adult criminal behavior seemed to be influenced by delinquent friends at age 14 years, an unstable job record at age 18 years, and anti-establishment attitudes at age 18 years.

These kinds of predictive factors have been identified in other projects in Great Britain and North America. For example, in a study with 10- to 11-year-old boys in England, Wilson (1980) identified three factors that were related to delinquency: poor parental supervision, convicted parents, and "social handicap," which included low social class, large family

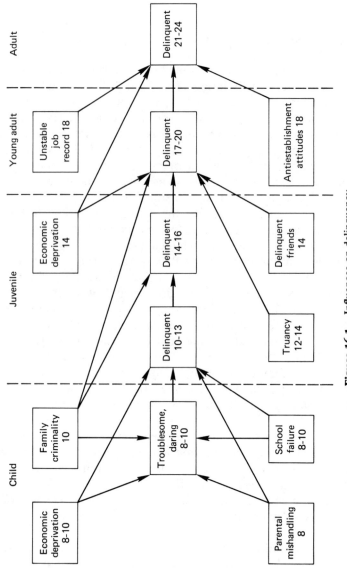

Figure 16.1. Influences on delinquency.

size, parental neglect, and truancy. In an impressive American longitudinal survey, McCord (1979) found that criminal behavior was predicted by maternal affection, parental conflict, paternal deviance (alcoholism or convictions), parental supervision, and parental aggressiveness (especially in disciplining children).

Of course, the independent variables tended to be interrelated, and Figure 16.2 shows the strongest of these relationships. The broken lines indicate relationships that were significant at $p = .001$ (phi greater than .160) and the solid lines indicate phi values greater than .220. The relationship between economic deprivation at age 8–10 years of age and economic deprivation of age 14 probably reflects two measures of the same underlying theoretical construct, but some of the other relationships may be causal.

Some of the more important speculative interpretations of Figure 16.2 are as follows:

1. boys from poor families tend to fail in school at age 8–10 years;
2. school failure at age 8–10 years tends to be followed by truancy at 12–14 years and, in turn, by an unstable job record at 18 years;
3. parents who are poor and/or criminal tend to exercise poor supervision over their children and to bring them up harshly and erratically;
4. poor parental supervision leads to truancy and in turn to an association with delinquent friends;
5. boys from criminal families tend to have delinquent friends and anti-establishment attitudes; and
6. anti-establishment attitudes lead to an unstable job record.

A SPECULATIVE THEORY

In trying to put forward one theory to explain the results of this research, a combination of suggestions made in five existing theories seems most plausible. These are Cohen's (1955) delinquent subculture theory, Cloward and Ohlin's (1960) opportunity theory, Trasler's (1962) social learning theory, Hirschi's (1969) control theory, and Sutherland and Cressey's (1974) differential association theory. Before outlining a speculative theory of my own, the five existing theories are summarized briefly. The emphasis in the delinquent subculture, opportunity, and differential association theories was on explaining why people committed delinquent acts, whereas the emphasis in the social learning and control theories was on explaining why people did not commit delinquent acts.

Cohen (1955) suggested that boys committed delinquent acts because they were conforming to the standards of a delinquent subculture. Work-

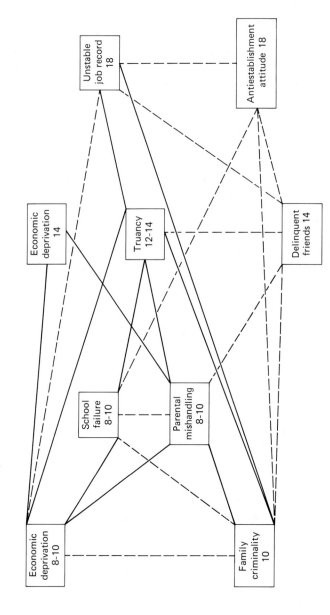

Figure 16.2. Relationships among independent variables.

ing-class boys competed with middle-class boys in school according to middle-class standards. Working-class boys were handicapped in this competition, because their parents were less likely to have taught them reasoning, middle-class manners, the avoidance of aggression, and the postponement of immediate gratification in favor of long-term goals. Consequently, they were likely to antagonize their teachers and perform badly in school. Faced with the problem that they could not achieve status according to the middle-class standards of the school, these boys solved this problem by joining a delinquent subculture, with standards in opposition to those of the larger society, in which they could achieve status. Cohen's theory explains why there is an association between delinquency and a lower-class environment, school failure, and certain methods of child rearing.

Cloward and Ohlin (1960) argued that Western society encouraged everyone to strive for material wealth but made it very difficult for lower class youths who had failed within the educational system to achieve wealth by legitimate methods. These youths were therefore driven to use illegitimate methods and to commit delinquent acts in order to achieve their goals. However, they could only adopt illegitimate methods, and join delinquent subcultures, if they had successful adult criminals in their neighborhood, Just as legitimate opportunities were necessary for success by legitimate methods, illegitimate opportunities were necessary for success by illegitimate means.

Trasler (1962) suggested that children were naturally selfish and hedonistic, trying to maximize their pleasure and minimize their pain. Delinquency arose naturally in the pursuit of hedonism, so the problem was to explain why people refrained from it. According to this social learning theory, people refrained because the hedonistic tendency to commit delinquent acts was blocked by the conscience. The crucial factor in building up the conscience was punishment imposed by the parents. After the child committed an act that the parent considered to be socially undesirable and for which the child was punished, the child had an anxiety reaction. After the behavior was followed by the punishment a number of times, the contemplation of the act by the child led to an involuntary resurgence of this anxiety, which tended to block the commission of the act. In this theory, the punishment did not have to be physical punishment, and in fact Trasler thought that "love-oriented" discipline, characterized by withdrawal of love, warm consistent treatment, and reasoned explanations, was especially effective. It was argued that delinquency was more common among lower-class children because lower-class parents used less-effective child-rearing techniques.

Hirschi (1969) suggested that people did not commit delinquent acts if they had a strong bond to society. In discussing the elements of this bond, Hirschi emphasized four theoretical constructs. *Attachment* referred to the extent to which people cared about and internalized the wishes and expectations of others, such as parents. *Commitment* referred to the rational element in crime, suggesting that people weighed the benefits against the costs, and did not commit crimes if the costs outweighed the benefits. *Involvement* drew attention to the fact that many people were so busy doing conventional activities that they had little time or opportunity for delinquency, and *belief* referred to the extent to which people believed in the rules of society. This theory is quite similar in many ways to Trasler's, for example, in predicting that parental affection and close supervision should be negatively related to delinquency.

Finally, Sutherland and Cressey (1974) suggested that delinquent attitudes and techniques of committing crimes were learned during interaction with other people in small groups. Whether a person committed many or a few delinquent acts depended on whether he or she came into contact more with delinquent than with law-abiding attitudes. This theory fits in well with the facts that criminal parents tend to have delinquent children and that the more delinquent boys tend to have delinquent friends.

Based on our research findings, and inspired by the above five theories, the speculative theory that I put forward to explain the most common varieties of male delinquency (crimes of dishonesty such as thefts and burglaries) can be summarized as follows:

1. Delinquent acts are the end product of a four-stage process.

2. In the first stage, motivation arises. It is suggested that the main desires that ultimately produce delinquent acts are desires for material goods, status among intimates, and excitement. (In our survey, when the youths were asked why they committed delinquent acts, the most common reasons stressed the desire for the material goods obtained and for excitement.) No attempt will be made to explain why these desires exist. They may be culturally induced in general, or a response to a specific situation (e.g., a desire for excitement arising from a feeling of boredom). How they vary with other factors is not clear. For example, it may be that the desire for excitement is greater among children from poorer families, because excitement is more highly valued by lower-class people than by middle-class people, because poorer children lead more boring lives, or because poorer children are less able to postpone immediate gratification in favor of long-term goals (which may be linked to the emphasis in lower-class culture on the concrete and present as opposed to the abstract and future).

3. In the second stage, a legal or illegal method of satisfying the desire is chosen. It is suggested that some people (e.g., children from poorer

families) are less able to satisfy their desires for material goods, excitement, and social status by legal or socially approved methods, and so they tend to choose illegal or socially disapproved methods. The relative inability of poorer children to achieve goals by legitimate methods may be partly because they tend to fail in school and hence tend to have erratic, low-status employment histories. School failure in turn is often a consequence of the unstimulating intellectual environment that lower-class parents tend to provide for their children, and the lack of emphasis on abstract concepts.

4. In the third stage, a motivation to commit a delinquent act is magnified or opposed by internalized beliefs and attitudes about law-breaking that have been built up in a learning process as a result of a history of rewards and punishments. The belief that delinquency is wrong, or a 'strong conscience', tends to be built up if parents are in favor of legal norms, if they exercise close supervision over their children, and if they punish socially disapproved behavior using love-oriented discipline. The belief that delinquency is legitimate, and anti-establishment attitudes generally, tend to be build up if children have been exposed to attitudes and behavior favoring delinquency, especially by members of their family and by their friends.

5. The fourth stage is a decision process in a particular situation, and is affected by immediate situational factors. If any resulting motivation to commit a delinquent act survives the third stage, whether the tendency becomes the actuality in any given situation depends on the costs, benefits, and probabilities of the possible outcomes (e.g., the material goods that can be stolen, peer approval, being caught by the police). In general, people are hedonistic, and make rational decisions.

This theory is very speculative, and it can only be sketched out roughly within the limitations of this chapter. Applying it more explicitly to the results of this project, children from poorer families are especially likely to commit delinquent acts because they are unable to achieve their goals legally (partly because they tend to fail in school) and possibly because they value some goals (e.g., excitement) especially highly. Children who receive parental mishandling are especially likely to commit delinquent acts because they fail to build up internal controls over socially disapproved behavior, whereas children from criminal families and those with delinquent friends tend to build up anti-establishment attitudes and the belief that delinquency is justifiable. The whole process is self-perpetuating in that early school failure may lead to truancy and to a lack of educational qualifications, which in turn leads to low-status jobs and periods of unemployment, all of which make it even harder to achieve goals legitimately. Similarly, delinquent acts themselves may have causal effects, since they may lead to official processing and hence to anti-establishment attitudes (Farrington, 1977), delinquent friends, and unstable job histories.

Delinquency may peak between ages 14 and 20 years because boys (especially lower-class school failures) have high desires for excitement, material goods, and status between these ages, little chance of achieving these desires legally, and little to lose (since legal penalties are lenient and their intimates—male peers—approve of delinquency). In contrast, after age 20 years, desires become attenuated or more realistic, there is more possibility of achieving these more limited goals legally, and the costs of delinquency are greater (since legal penalties are harsher and their intimates—wives or girlfriends—disapprove of delinquency).

Ideally, the theoretical constructs in this theory, and their causal relationships, should be specified more explicitly. A mathematical model should be constructed, and attempts made to estimate the value of parameters so as to provide the best fit to the data. Up to the present, this has only been done with very simple theories and simple data (see, e.g., Blumstein & Moitra, 1980).

Both the theory and the data have obvious limitations. The theory is only intended to apply to property crimes by males. No hereditary or biological factors are included in it, because the research was not specifically designed to investigate these. Also, no individual difference factors are included in it (e.g., pre-existing differences in daring or aggressiveness). Limitations of the research stem from the fact that it was based on one cohort of white, British working-class, urban males born about 1953. How far the results can be generalized is uncertain.

CONCLUSIONS

These results are consistent with Robins' argument that "there exists a single syndrome made up of a broad variety of antisocial behaviors arising in childhood and continuing into adulthood" (Robins & Ratcliff, 1980, p. 248). The kinds of youths who were convicted or who admitted large numbers of delinquent acts were identified as troublesome, daring, dishonest, and aggressive by their teachers, peers, and parents from an early age. Over and above the continuity in behavior, some factors had persistent effects. The most important of the earliest factors were economic deprivation, family criminality, parental mishandling, and school failure, whereas the most important of the later ones were truancy, delinquent friends, anti-establishment attitudes, and an unstable job record.

A tentative theory was put forward to explain these results, with four elements: (1) the arousal of desires for material goods, status among intimates, and excitement, (2) the choice of illegal methods of achieving these goals, (3) the operation of beliefs that delinquency is right or wrong, built up in a learning process, and (4) the decision to commit delinquent acts, depending on the perceived costs and benefits in the immediate situation. This theory, combining elements of several existing theories, needs to be specified and tested in more detail.

REFERENCES

Baker, R. J., & Nelder, J. A. *The GLIM system, release 3*. Oxford, Numerical Algorithms Group, 1978.

Blumstein, A., & Moitra, S. The identification of "career criminals" from "chronic offenders" in a cohort. *Law and Policy Quarterly*, 1980, *2*, 321–334.

Cloward, R. A., & Ohlin, L. E. *Delinquency and opportunity*. New York: Free Press, 1960.

Cohen, A. K. *Delinquent boys*. Glencoe: Free Press, 1955.

Farrington, D. P. Self-reports of deviant behavior: Predictive and stable? *Journal of Criminal Law and Criminology*, 1973, *64*, 99–110.

Farrington, D. P. The effects of public labelling. *British Journal of Criminology*, 1977, *17*, 112–125.

Farrington, D. P. Environmental stress, delinquent behavior, and convictions. In I. G. Sarason & C. D. Spielberger (Eds.), *Stress and anxiety*, (Vol. 6). Washington, DC: Hemisphere, 1979.

Farrington, D. P. Offending from 10 to 25 years of age. In K. T. Van Dusen & S. A. Mednick (Eds.), *Prospective studies of crime and delinquency*. Boston: Kluwer-Nijhoff, 1983.

Farrington, D. P., Biron, L., & LeBlanc, M. Personality and delinquency in London and Montreal. In J. Gunn & D. P. Farrington (Eds.), *Abnormal offenders, delinquency and the criminal justice system*. Chichester: Wiley, 1982.

Farrington, D. P., & West, D. J. The Cambridge study in delinquent development. In S. A. Mednick & A. E. Baert (Eds.), *Prospective longitudinal research*. Oxford: Oxford University Press, 1981.

Fienberg, S. E. *The analysis of cross-classified categorical data*, (2nd ed.). Cambridge: MIT Press, 1980.

Hindelang, M. J., Hirschi, T., & Weis, J. G. *Measuring delinquency*. Beverly Hills: Sage, 1981.

Hirschi, T. *Causes of delinquency*. Berkeley: University of California Press, 1969.

McCord, J. Some child-rearing antecedents of criminal behavior in adult men. *Journal of Personality and Social Psychology*, 1979, *37*, 1477–1486.

Nie, N. H., Hull, C. H., Jenkins, J. G., Steinbrenner, K., & Bent, D. H. *Statistical package for the social sciences* (2nd ed.). New York: McGraw-Hill, 1975.

Olweus, D. Stability of aggressive reaction patterns in males: A review. *Psychological Bulletin*, 1979, *86*, 852–875.

Robins, L. N., & Ratcliff, K. S. Childhood conduct disorders and later arrest. In Robins, L. N., Clayton, P. J., & Wing, J. K. (Eds.), *The social consequences of psychiatric illness*. New York: Brunner/Mazel, 1980.

Sutherland, E. H., & Cressey, D. R. *Criminology,* (9th ed.). Philadelphia: Lippincott, 1974.
Trasler, G. B. *The explanation of criminality.* London: Routledge & Kegan Paul, 1962.
West, D. J. *Present conduct and future delinquency.* London: Heinemann, 1969.
West, D. J. *Delinquency: Its roots, careers and prospects.* London: Heinemann, 1982.
West, D. J., & Farrington, D. P. *Who becomes delinquent?* London: Heinemann, 1973.
West, D. J., & Farrington, D. P. *The delinquent way of life.* London: Heinemann, 1977.
Wilson, H. Parental supervision: A neglected aspect of delinquency. *British Journal of Criminology,* 1980, *20,* 203–235.

17

The Consequences of Conduct Disorder in Girls*

LEE N. ROBINS

INTRODUCTION

It is well known that conduct disorder is a predominantly male disorder, and that in males it predicts the adult diagnoses of antisocial personality, alcohol abuse and dependence, and drug abuse and dependence—three disorders that are regularly found to be more common in men than women.

Although not unknown in girls, conduct disorder among them is sufficiently rare that studies of later outcomes have generally either concen-

*This research was supported by the Epidemiological Catchment Area program (ECA). The ECA is a series of five epidemiologic research studies performed by independent research teams in collaboration with staff of the Division of Biometry and Epidemiology (DBE) of the National Institute of Mental Health (NIMH). The NIMH Principal Collaborators are Darrel A. Regier, Ben Z. Locke, and William W. Eaton; the NIMH Project Officer is Carl A. Taube. The Principal Investigators and Co-Investigators from the five sites are: Yale University, U01 MH 34224—Jerome K. Myers, Myrna M. Weissman, and Gary Tischler; Johns Hopkins University, U01 MH 33870—Sheppard Kellam, Ernest Gruenberg, and Sam Shapiro; Washington University, St. Louis, U01 MH 33883—Lee N. Robins and John Helzer; Duke University, U01 MH 35386—Dan Blazer and Linda George; University of California, Los Angeles, U01 MH 35865—Marvin Karno, Javier Escobar, and Audrey Burnam. This work acknowledges support of this program as well as Research Scientist Award MH 00334.

DEVELOPMENT OF ANTISOCIAL
AND PROSOCIAL BEHAVIOR

385

Copyright © 1986 by Academic Press, Inc.
All rights of reproduction in any form reserved.

trated exclusively on boys or have treated all children with conduct disorder together without examining girls separately. In the latter case, results are, of course, dominated by the outcomes of the males. As a result, we have very little empirical data about the consequences of conduct disorder in girls. Nor do we have substantial theory to enable us to predict whether the occurrence of a disorder in that part of the population in which it is statistically unlikely has implications for its duration, course, or associated outcomes.

Our own early study (Robins, 1966) was one of the few that did present adult outcomes for girls referred to a child-guidance clinic for antisocial behavior. As adults, these girls were somewhat less likely than boys seen for antisocial behavior in the same clinic to be diagnosed as having antisocial personality, although they shared with the boys an increased risk of this disorder, as well as an increased risk of alcoholism and drug abuse. They were also found to have an increased risk of what was then called *hysteria,* which is approximated by the diagnosis of somatization disorder in DSM-III (1980), although the DSM-III diagnosis omits the affective symptoms (anxiety and depression) included as symptoms of hysteria.

This early study was a long-term follow-up of children from a single cohort, those born just before World War I, and referred to a child-guidance clinic, usually by the juvenile court or a social agency. Although valuable because of the longitudinal design and the rich supplementation of follow-up interviews with childhood and adult records from a great variety of sources, that study was limited in the number of antisocial girls available for follow-up (there were only 75 for whom diagnosis in adult life could be assessed), it was restricted to patients, and it was restricted to a single age cohort, representing only one historical period. Although we went on to replicate results for the male patients of that clinic in two nonpatient samples born in different eras, one a sample of black school boys and the other a national sample of Vietnam veterans (Robins, 1978), we did not attempt to replicate the results for female patients in a nonpatient sample because the rarity of serious conduct problems in girls made identifying a high-risk nonpatient population difficult.

We are thus particularly appreciative of the opportunities offered by a recent study of mental health in the general population, which because of its unprecedented size, makes it possible to rectify this omission. The new study is known as the Epidemiological Catchment Area (ECA) study (Regier, Myers, Kramer, Robins, Blazer, Hough, Eaton, & Locke, 1984). It is being carried out in five sites, each of which provides a stratified random sample of approximately 3500, including both community and institutionalized samples. So far results are available for the community samples in three sites, New Haven, St. Louis, and Baltimore. Respondents in each site have been weighted to make the samples representative of the age, sex, and racial composition of the sampled areas. At the present time, we have information for approximately 5000 women aged 18 years or older.

The general goal of the ECA study is to assess the prevalence and incidence of the major adult psychiatric disorders in the general population according to DSM-III criteria. One of those disorders, antisocial personality, according to DSM-III criteria, requires the occurrence before age 15 years of at least three of 12 childhood behavior problems. Consequently, repondents are asked about these behavior problems and the ages at which they first occurred.

The requirement for having three or more of these 12 behavior problems before the age of 15 years does not precisely correspond with criteria for conduct disorder in DSM-III; however, the overlap is substantial (Table 17.1). The 12 behaviors include the symptoms of fighting, vandalism, stealing, lying, and running away, all of which are symptoms of DSM-III conduct disorder. Another DSM-III conduct disorder symptom is "chronic violations of rules," which is covered in the 12 behavior problems by school discipline problems, truancy, precocious sexual activity,

Table 17.1

Symptoms of Conduct Disorder versus the 12 Childhood Symptoms of Antisocial Personality in DSM-III

Conduct disorder	Childhood symptoms for antisocial personality
Agressive	
1. Physical violence against persons or property	Fighting, vandalism
2. Thefts outside the home involving confrontation with the victim	Stealing
3. Duration of pattern for 6 months	—
Non-Agressive	
1. Chronic violations of rules	School discipline, truancy, substance abuse, sex before 15 years
2. Repeated running away overnight	Runaway
3. Serious lying	Lying
4. Stealing (non confrontive)	Stealing
5. Duration of pattern for 6 months	—
Consequences of Behavior	
None	Expulsion or suspension Arrests Underachieving

and precocious drinking and drug use. The 12 juvenile precursors of anti-social personality problems also include consequences of conduct disorder: poor school success despite adequate capacity, school expulsion, and arrest. To be eligible for a diagnosis of antisocial personality, three of these behaviors must have occurred before age 15 years; for a diagnosis of conduct disorder, only one type of behavior problem need occur, although behavior difficulties must persist over a 6-month period. The maximum age of onset is unspecified for conduct disorder. Despite differences in criteria, in practice these alternative definitions probably select the same children most of the time.

The fact that these 12 behavior problems are inquired about and their age of onset ascertained makes it possible to use the ECA data to look at the consequences of childhood conduct disorder for adult diagnoses and symptoms and for adult life events. Because the female sample is so large, we can compare consequences for women with those for men. Because the same questions were asked in three different sites (with exceptions noted below), we can look upon these sites as replications, to learn whether the patterns detected are stable in large representative samples of the general population. As attractive as these assets are, we must nonetheless recognize that we are missing the advantages of the longitudinal design of our earlier prospective study. That is, we must rely on recall many years after the occurrence of the behaviors because we lack access to records made during the childhoods of these respondents. Not only may memory be faulty, but because the study is not prospective, we cannot take into account differential mortality associated with these behaviors. Thus, we are looking only at survivors, and at survivors who have passed through varying periods of risk of the adult consequences of conduct disorder, depending on their age at interview. Because we are studying three urban locales in the East and Midwest, we must also be concerned that our results may not be representative of the country as a whole, particularly if these behaviors are associated with a tendency to migrate westward.

Despite these limitations, these data do allow us for the first time to ask some questions of great theoretical interest. One such question is whether or not the fact that a behavior is rarer in females than in males implies that it is more serious when it occurs in females. It is often assumed that the less common a symptom is, the greater the likelihood that it indicates a serious underlying disorder, which in turn means a worse prognosis. Previous research has shown know that it takes a worse environment to produce conduct problems in girls. Our own study (Robins, 1966) showed that girls referred to a clinic for antisocial behavior, as compared with the much larger number of boys so referred, came from somewhat more disturbed homes. There was more psychiatric disorder in the parents and more financial dependence. However, the fact that rarity implies that more or stronger predictors are required for a disorder to appear does not necessarily mean that its course will be more malignant.

Indeed, most studies that have looked at the consequences of conduct problems in the two sexes do not suggest a worse prognosis for girls. Lefkowitz and Eron (1977) found that not only was aggression more common in male than in female third-graders, but it was also more predictive of aggression at age 19 years for males than females. Similarly, Kellam, Simon, and Ensminger (1983) found aggression in first grade was more predictive of delinquency before age 17 years for boys than girls. Havighurst (1962), following seventh graders into young adulthood, found that aggressive girls were less likely to have bad outcomes than aggressive boys. Stewart and Livson (1966) found that school conduct problems predicted smoking for both boys and girls, but the effect was visible earlier for boys (in fifth grade versus seventh grade for girls). Richman (1982) assessed 3-year-olds for restlessness, and followed them again at age 8 years. She found that restlessness predicted antisocial behavior at 8 years of age only for boys. Hathaway and Monachesi (1963) predicted 12th grade adjustment on the basis of teachers' predictions in 9th grade. They found the predictions less accurate for girls than for boys. A follow-up of a birth cohort in Britain (Wadsworth, 1979) showed that more delinquent boys than girls became recidivists, again indicating that the same early event is more ominous for boys than girls.

However, there are also studies suggesting no difference by sex. Simcha-Fagan (1979) found that the mother's report of delinquent behavior in a sample of Manhattan children was equally predictive of problems at follow-up 5 years later for girls and boys. Rutter, Tizard, Yule, Graham, and Whitmore (1976) evaluated all the 10-year-olds on the Isle of Wight and then reassessed them at age 14 years. He found behavior problems at age 10 to be equally powerful predictors of continuity of problems for the two sexes.

There are also reports of more continuity of disapproved behaviors for girls than boys. Jessor and Jessor (1977) studied the degree to which one type of precocious behavior in junior high schoolers predicted transition to other types yet untried. They were able to predict the onset of marijuana use better in girls than boys on the basis of non-conforming attitudes and behaviors. Morris, Escoll, and Wexler (1956) found that among hospitalized aggressive children followed into early adulthood, girls had worse outcomes than did boys. The literature, in sum, is not unanimous. The outcome for antisocial girls may be better, the same, or worse than for antisocial boys. Unfortunately, in none of the studies cited can we be sure that the girls and boys were equally severely affected, nor were there always sufficient numbers of affected girls to be reasonably sure that the trends were stable.

A second question of great interest is whether conduct problems in girls predict the same outcomes that they do in boys. Some of the studies cited above that found that girls did better may simply have failed to look at the kinds of outcomes in which antisocial girls do worse. In general, the outcomes on which they were compared were those for which antisocial boys were known to be at high risk: various types of acting out; including smoking, drinking, crime and delinquency; and aggression. We noted in our earlier study (Robins, 1966) that antisocial girls, but not boys, had increased rates of hysteria as adults, a disorder characterized by medically unexplained physical complaints, anxiety, and depression. We also found that men and women who were both diagnosed antisocial personality as adults differed in the particular antisocial symptoms displayed. Although the sexes shared high rates of social isolation and poor job histories, women had more marital problems and were more neglectful of their children than men, and they more often transmitted behavior problems to their offspring. They fell behind men in frequency of arrest and substance abuse. Thus, it is possible that childhood conduct disorder predicts *different* outcomes in women and men, rather than *better* outcomes.

There is little information in the literature to guide our expectations here. However, Pritchard and Graham (1966), in studying adult psychiatric patients who had also been psychiatric patients at the same center as children, found among those seen for behavior problems in childhood that the boys more often became antisocial adult patients than did girls (48% versus 9%), whereas the girls as adults were more often seen for anxiety or depression than boys (36% versus 16%). Of course, the fact that the sample consisted entirely of adult patients guaranteed that all cases studied had to have some adult disorder. Thus, the higher rates of anxiety and depression in women may only have been found by default, that is, because they did not have adult antisocial behavior. We will be able to examine the data from the ECA community sample to determine whether women with a history of conduct disorder develop distinctive problems that men do not.

A third question to be answered is whether among the various behaviors that qualify as symptoms of conduct disorder, it is the case that those that are more distinctively masculine predict the more masculine consequences for women. We have found no previous attempt to answer this question in the literature.

THE ECA SAMPLES

In the three ECA sites that provide the data for this investigation, community samples of approximately 3000 cases were selected by various methods of area sampling. Each site used multistage sampling, which began with the selection of mental health catchment areas. Within these, certain subareas were selected at random, then blocks within those areas, and households within those blocks. In each household, the residents were enumerated and one resident chosen at random. Thus, there were two ways in which to fail to get an interview: first, by failing to complete the enumeration of residents of a dwelling unit, either because none could be found at home or the person contacted refused; and second, once the household was enumerated and a prospective respondent selected, by failing to get the selected respondent's cooperation. This double hazard resulted in completion rates of 75–80% in each site. The ECA sites also each conducted interviews with 500 residents of institutions, and carried out follow-up interviews with each respondent 1 year after the initial interview. Selected respondents were also reinterviewed by clinicians to evaluate the reliability and validity of the first interview. However, the data to be discussed in this paper come exclusively from the first interview with members of the community sample. The results have been weighted to make the respondents' demographic characteristics match census distributions for adult residents of the mental health catchment areas represented.

The interview that provides our data was given by a trained lay interviewer, and took about 90 minutes. It covered all the diagnostic criteria necessary to make 15 DSM-III diagnoses (and also Feighner and RDC diagnoses, but the latter two are not discussed in the present essay) by means of the Diagnostic Interview Schedule (Robins, Helzer, Croughan, Williams, & Spitzer 1981), a highly structured interview written expressly for this study and used in each site. Responses were combined by computer to evaluate the DSM-III criteria for each diagnosis. In addition, there were uniform questions across sites with respect to demographic characteristics and health services utilization. Recent life events and a number of other topics chosen locally were asked about in questions written at the respective sites and not shared.

To evaluate DSM-III diagnostic criteria, it was necessary to ask about drinking, illegal activities, drug taking, sexual behavior, wife beating, and many other topics considered "sensitive." Nonetheless, in all sites refusal to answer any question was rare, and less than 1% of respondents broke off the interview without completing it.

The 12 conduct problems inquired about appear in Appendix A. They vary between simple questions (See Q.15: "Were you ever arrested as a juvenile or sent to juvenile court?") to more complex questions. For example the question about truanting (Q.8) not only asked whether it had happened, but whether it had occurred at least five times in two different school years other than the one in which the respondent left school. This further specification was necessary to meet the severity criteria specified in DSM-III for the more common behaviors.

One of the 12 criterion symptoms for conduct disorder, age of first sexual intercourse (Q.16), was included in the St. Louis interview but not at the two other sites. The New Haven study entered the field prior to the revision of the Diagnostic Interview Schedule, Version III. The version used there differs from that used elsewhere with respect to only one conduct problem, substance abuse. In New Haven, respondents were asked at what age they first drank alcohol frequently or used "drugs of any kind." In the other sites, it was the age the respondent first drank enough to get drunk or first used any drug "on your own."

RESULTS

Frequency of Conduct Problems

Because St. Louis was the only site in which all 12 conduct problems questions were asked, we present frequencies as reported there (Table 17.2). However, results in the other sites were very similar. Rank-order correlations between the frequencies of the 10 conduct problems available in all sites comparing St. Louis with Baltimore and New Haven were .77 and .71, respectively, for males, and .83 and .63, respectively, for females.

We note that the survey data agree with data from previous studies showing that conduct problems are more common for males than females. This was the case for each problem inquired about, although the difference was less than 1% for running away overnight, a rare behavior in both sexes. But it is also noteworthy that the 12 behaviors ranked similarly in frequency for boys and girls ($r = .93$). It appears, therefore, that the low frequency of conduct disorder in girls can best be described as a general depression of conduct problems, rather than as girls' eschewing certain behaviors that might be perceived as specifically masculine.

As you would expect from these results, every site found that fewer girls than boys met the criteria we use for conduct disorder, that is, having three or more of these behaviors before the age of 15 years. (We use this

Table 17.2

Frequency of Conduct Problems Before Age 15
Years by Sex[a]

	Males (%)	Females (%)
Stealing	28	12
Sex	20	6
School discipline	16	6
Fighting	16	6
Lying	15	9
Expelled or suspended	10	5
Truant	10	4
Subtance abuse	8	2
Underachievement	7	3
Vandalism	7	1
Arrest	6	1
Runaway	2	2

[a] St. Louis only.

criterion because it is the minimum with which DSM-III permits a diagnosis of antisocial personality.) This finding also holds for every age group in every site (Figure 17.1). Moreover, all sites found that each successively younger age group reported a higher rate of conduct problems than the one before it for both males and females. Rates for men rise from about 8% in those 65 years or older to an average of 34% in men under age 30 years. Rates for women rise from about 1% in those 65 years or older to approximately 16% in those under age 30 years. It is hard to say whether rates for the two sexes are converging. The male:female *ratio* of the proportions affected has decreased from 16:1 to 4:1, but the *absolute* change in percentages affected shows a greater increase for men then women, 26% versus 15%.

One way of interpreting the progressively higher rates of reported conduct disorder with decreasing age would be to argue that the frequency of conduct disorder has been increasing steadily over the last 50 years. However, as we noted earlier, this interpretation is problematic because we are asking each older group to remember events farther in the past than the younger group, and because each older group has survived the risks of death that might be consequent to conduct problems for longer than younger persons.

Nonetheless, a look at the particular behaviors that have increased the most in frequency encourages the belief that there has been a true historic increase, not simply more forgetting or a longer exposure to risks of

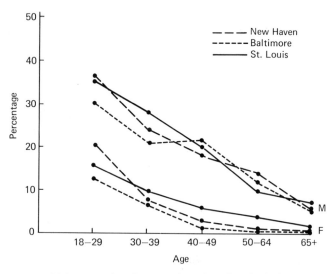

Figure 17.1.   Male versus female rates of conduct disorder in five age cohorts.

mortality on the part of the older respondents. Across all three sites, substance abuse is the behavior that has increased most in those less then 30 years old as compared with those older (Table 17.3). Indeed, it has moved up an average of 4.2 ranks out of 10 for males and 3.2 out of 10 ranks for females. This makes sense given the drug epidemic of the 1960s and 1970s. Also in every site, school expulsion has increased steeply for males, up an average 2.5 ranks, and truancy has increased steeply for females, up an average of 2.0 ranks out of 10. This fits the general observation of a recent increase in school discipline problems that has led to a

Table 17.3

Gains in Rank of Frequency Consistent
across Three Sites[a]

Average Change in Rank		
	Men	Women
Substance abuse	+4.2	+3.2
School expulsion	+2.5	—
Truancy	—	+2.0

[a] Positive change in ranks in all three sites, comparing those under 30 years with those over 50 years.

Table 17.4

Correlations between the Sexes in Each Age
Cohort with Respect to Rank Order of Frequency
of 12 Conduct Problems[a]

Age	r	z^b
18–29	.85	2.82
30–39	.89	2.95
40–49	.81	2.69
50–64	.68	2.26
65+	.84	2.78

[a] St. Louis.
[b] Scores are all highly significant.

national crisis in teacher recruitment. Arrests, fighting, underachievement, and running away show much more modest changes over time.

The sharp rise in drug abuse and school discipline problems in the youngest sample members has not reduced the strong correlation between the sexes in the ranking of conduct problems by frequency. It remains as high in the youngest cohort as it was in the oldest (Table 17.4). Thus, if there has been a real increase in rates of conduct disorder over time, it has occurred because the same behaviors have shown substantial increases for both boys and girls.

Age of Onset of Conduct Problems

Our study of child-guidance clinic patients (Robins, 1966) had shown that girls with conduct problems were referred to care at a somewhat later age than boys, and this seemed to reflect a later age of onset of problems rather than a delay in referral. The later age of onset of conduct problems in girls was confirmed in the ECA survey (Table 17.5). Nine out of the 12 behaviors inquired about were begun by girls at a somewhat older age than by boys, although the average difference was only half a year. The greatest age difference was for sexual experience, which began about $1\frac{1}{4}$ years later for girls than boys.

Thus, one of the reasons that girls have fewer conduct problems before age 15 years than boys is that they start accruing them later. It is noteworthy, however, that behaviors that occur early for males are the same behaviors that occur early for females. The correlation between the sexes for rank order by age is .87. Arrest and substance abuse are the last behaviors to appear for both sexes, whereas lying and school discipline problems tend to occur early for both.

Table 17.5

Age of Initiation before 15 Years[a][b]

Problems in order of occurence	Men	Women
School discipline	9.0	9.8
Underachievement	9.3	10.2
Fighting	9.4	10.0
Lying	9.9	9.6
Stealing	10.0	9.7
Truant	11.0	12.0
Vandalism	11.2	10.7
Drunk	11.2	11.8
Runaway	11.6	12.3
Sex[c]	11.7	13.0
Expelled	11.8	12.1
Arrest	12.4	12.6
Drugs	12.7	13.1

[a] Mean of three ECA sites.

[b] $r = .87; z = 2.01$.

[c] St. Louis only.

Association among Conduct Problems

As a final check on our impression that despite the differences in levels, patterns of conduct problems were very similar for girls and boys, we submitted the 12 conduct problems to a factor analysis for the St. Louis sample (Table 17.6). Three factors were found for each sex. Although they were not identical, three groups of problems clustered on the same factor for both boys and girls. These clusters were (1) sex, substance abuse, and fighting, which clustered on Factor 1 for both boys and girls; (2) the four school behavior problems, discipline, explusion, truancy, and underachievement, which appeared together on Factor 1 for girls and on Factor 2 for boys; and (3) arrest and running away, which appeared together on Factor 3 for both boys and girls. Only vandalism, lying, and stealing assorted differently for the two sexes.

Association of Conduct Problems with Adult Psychiatric Status

Previous prospective studies (Robins et al., 1971) have shown that conduct problems in childhood are frequent forerunners of antisocial personality, alcoholism, and drug abuse. These findings were confirmed in this cross-sectional survey (Figure 17.2). By definition, antisocial person-

Table 17.6

Factor Analyses of 12 Conduct Problems before Age 15 Years as Recalled by ECA Household Respondents[a]

	Boys' factors		
	1	2	3
Girls' factors			
1. Sex (.54/.38) Substance Abuse (.43[d]/.72) Fight (.36[c]/.64)	Discipline (.70/.51[b]) Expelled (.60/.66) Truant (.59/.58) Underachievement (.47/.63)		
2. Vandalism (.74/.60)	Lying (.66/.52)	Stealing (.51/.44)	
3.		Arrest (.84/.72) Runaway (.65[b]/.75)	

[a] Loadings for girls/boys are shown in parentheses.
[b] Also loads on Factor 1.
[c] Also loads on Factor 2.
[d] Also loads on Factor 3.

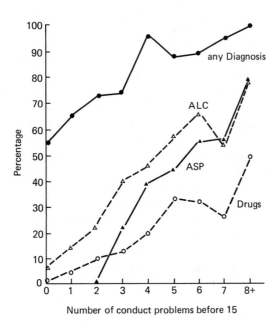

Figure 17.2. Conduct problems before age 15 years and adult diagnoses.

ality cannot occur in the absence of at least three conduct problems. When only the minimum number of childhood conduct problems were reported, about 20% also reported sufficient adult symptoms to merit that diagnosis. However, with each additional childhood behavior problem, the chances of meeting diagnostic criteria as an adult increased, reaching more than 75% when eight or more childhood problems were reported. Previous research had never found a level of behavior problems that predicted this outcome for more than 50%, the level found in this study for persons with seven conduct problems. The higher level found here may be due to the fact that this is the first study large enough to allow looking at a group with eight or more conduct problems, a very small percentage of the population indeed.

There is also a regular increase in the proportion diagnosable as alcohol abuse or dependence as the number of childhood behavior problems increases. Rates increase from less than 8% of those without childhood problems to close to 80% of those with eight or more problems. Except at the very highest levels of childhood problems, the risk of an alcohol diagnosis is consistently higher than the risk of the diagnosis of antisocial personality, even though DSM-III does not require conduct problems for that diagnosis. The association of number of conduct problems in childhood and an adult diagnosis of alcohol abuse or dependence closely resembles its association with antisocial personality disorder, as shown by the similarity in the slopes of their curves. The risk of drug abuse or dependence on the other hand, increases less steeply with an increase in childhood behavior problems, indicating a lesser kinship with conduct disorder, although a clear association exists.

To compare the sexes with respect to the prediction of adult diagnoses by conduct problems in childhood, we will combine the diagnoses of antisocial personality, alcohol abuse or dependence, and drug abuse or dependence into the "externalizing" disorders. Developing at least one of these disorders in adult life is well predicted by the number of conduct problems in childhood for both sexes (Figure 17.3). For men, the average proportion ever having had one of these disorders rises from 14% with a history of no conduct problems to 84% with a history of at least seven conduct problems. For women the relationship is equally strong (as shown by the parallel slopes of the curves), but the risk of developing one of these externalizing disorders is lower than men's risk at every level of childhood behavior problems. It rises from 4% for women with no history of childhood behavior problems to 64% for those with seven or more problems.

In addition to predicting these externalizing disorders, conduct problems were found to predict tobacco use disorder for both sexes in the St.

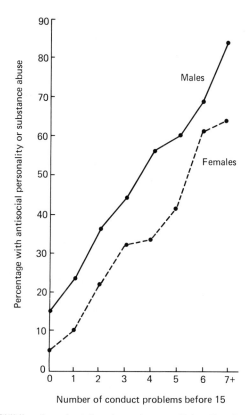

Figure 17.3. Childhood conduct disorder and externalizing disorders after age 18 years. (pooled across three sites).

Louis sample. (This disorder, which first appeared in the official psychiatric nomenclature in 1980, was not investigated in the other two sites.) For tobacco use disorder, the association was even stronger for women than for men. The association between conduct disorder and smoking is consistent with Stewart and Livson's (1966) observation that early aggression predicts smoking, and with the fact that alcoholics and drug abusers are typically heavy smokers, so that any predictor of these substance abuse disorders is likely to predict smoking as well.

A more surprising finding is that an increased rate of almost every disorder was found in women with a history of conduct problems. This association was not found for men, although there was a weak trend in the same direction. As a result of the substantial association between conduct problems and the "internalizing" disorders for women, when we look at the overall diagnostic consequences of conduct problems for the two

Table 17.7

Childhood Conduct Disorder (Three or More Problems) and
Type of Diagnosis for Young and Older Men and Women[a]

| | Percentage of conduct problems | | | |
| | Persons under 30 years | | Persons over 30 years | |
	3+	<3	3+	<3
Men				
Externalizing disorders (drug, alcohol, ASP[b])	73	25	64	25
Other disorders[c]	26	25	19	15
Neither	16	57	31	65
Women				
Externalizing disorders (drug, alcohol, ASP[b])	39	10	55	14
Other disorders[c]	73	35	63	27
Neither	17	56	15	59

[a] St. Louis only.
[b] Antisocial personality.
[c] Affective, anxiety, obsessive compulsive, psychosexual, somatization.

sexes (Table 17.7), we find that women have been as much affected as men. The excess of internalizing disorders has made up for their lower rate of externalizing disorders, so that the proportion with at least one positive diagnosis is as much increased for women as men when both have had significant conduct problems in childhood. It seems probable that the finding in most previous studies of better outcomes for antisocial girls than boys was attributable to the choice of outcomes studied. When the outcome of interest is aggression, delinquency, or substance abuse, that is, externalizing behaviors, girls appear to do better. If these studies had looked at general psychiatric adjustment, the girls' advantage might have disappeared. It is noteworthy, however, that the higher rate of conduct problems in boys than in girls does not entirely explain the different rates of externalizing and internalizing disorders in men and women. With or without conduct disorders in childhood, men are more likely to develop externalizing disorders and women to develop internalizing disorders.

The less-specific impact of conduct disorder on women than on men is further illustrated by looking at the association of childhood conduct problems with psychiatric symptoms rather than diagnoses. A symptom is counted as having psychiatric significance in this diagnostic interview only if it meets criteria for severity and is not always explained by physical causes. Figure 17.4 shows that women report more psychiatric symptoms than men, whether or not they had a history of conduct problems in childhood. However, their overall symptom level is much more affected by a history of conduct problems than is men's. Whereas for men the non-antisocial symptoms (the white space above the dotted areas) are a small part (21%) of the total set of symptoms in men with conduct problems, among women with a history of conduct disorder, more than half (58%) of the total symptoms are of a non-antisocial type. Further, the average number of solely non-antisocial symptoms increases with the number of conduct problems for women (from 3.5 to 5.4), but actually decreases slightly for men (from 2.7 to 1.2). For both sexes, the average number of adult antisocial symptoms goes up with the number of conduct problems, and approaches the minimum of four required for a diagnosis of antisocial

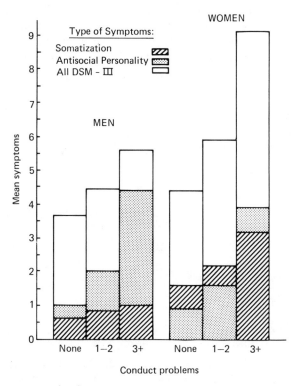

Figure 17.4.   Conduct disorder predicts high symptom levels.

personality only when the criterion for childhood conduct problems—
three or more before age 15 years—is met.

In sum, although we found no striking qualitative differences between
males and females with respect to childhood symptoms of conduct disorder, we have found a major difference in the adult consequences of conduct disorder. For men, conduct problems before age 15 years predict
only the symptoms of the externalizing diagnoses, antisocial personality,
and the various forms of substance abuse. In women, conduct problems
also predict these, but they predict internalizing symptoms as well.

Changes in the Impact of Conduct Disorder as It Becomes More Common

It seems intuitively reasonable that as a form of deviance becomes
more commonplace and is adopted by less pathological persons, it should
lose some of its power as a forecaster of later adverse outcomes. If this
reasoning is correct, then conduct problems of childhood should have
greater predictive power for older cohorts, in whom they were relatively
rare, than for young people, in whom they were common.

To test this hypothesis, we looked at the association of number of
conduct problems with number of antisocial symptoms and number of
positive diagnoses for men and women in three age groups (Table 17.8).

Table 17.8
Has the Meaning of Conduct Problems Changed over Time?

	r			
	Cohort			
	Oldest (50+ years)	Middle (30–49 years)	Youngest (18–29 years)	All ages
Men				
No. conduct problems versus				
No. ASP symptoms[a]	.37	.60	.60	.59
No. positive dx[a]	.28	.46	.55	.49
Women				
No. conduct problems versus				
No. ASP symptoms[a]	.33	.36	.48	.45
No. positive dx	.23	.31	.48	.37

[a] Includes arrest, illegal income, fighting, wife or childbeating, job problems, desertion,
child neglect, frequent lying, transiency, prostitiution, or pimping.

Contrary to the hypothesis proposed, we found associations between number of conduct problems and both number of adult antisocial symptoms and number of positive adult diagnoses to be as strong or stronger in the youngest cohort, where conduct disorder is most common, as in older cohorts. If there has been a true rise in conduct disorder over time, this would indicate that the adult disorders predicted by conduct disorder must be rising at about the same rate. Another possibility is that being young is associated with both excellence of memory and willingness to report problem behavior in both childhood and adult life, and it is this greater reporting ability that explains young people's higher level of problems in both childhood and adulthood and creates a false association between problems in the two periods. This issue is difficult to resolve in a cross-sectional study.

Predicting Life Events

In addition to psychiatric diagnoses, we looked at the extent to which conduct disorder predicted adverse life events in the 6 months prior to the interview (Table 17.9). Those events found to have been predicted by early conduct disorder were getting arrested, losing a job, breaking up

Table 17.9

Conduct Disorder Predicts Recent Events: Odds Ratios Comparing 3+ Behaviors before Age 15 Years versus 0-2

| | Age in years | | | | | |
| | Men | | | Women | | |
	(<30)	(30–49)	(50+)	(<30)	(30–49)	(50+)
N with 3+ conduct problems before 15	124	105	45	84	47	16
N with 0–2 conduct problems before 15	235	285	379	433	544	658
In last 6 months						
Moved	2.1	1.0	1.1	3.4	0.8	1.2
Lost job	1.4	1.9	1.0	2.1	3.1	5.8
Broke up with spouse/lover	2.0	4.2	1.1	2.3	2.3	5.2
Broke up with best friend	1.3	1.7	0.9	4.0	2.5	60.5
Sued or suffered repossession	0.6	3.8	1.7	7.1	5.1	13.7
Arrested	2.1	4.0	24.0	1.8	6.3	193.5
Median	1.7	2.8	1.1	3.0	2.8	9.8
Number of behaviors with Odds ratio of 2 or higher	3	3	1	5	5	5

with a spouse or lover, having something repossessed or being sued for debts, breaking up with one's best friend, and moving. These events were predicted by conduct disorder for both men and women, but women showed the greater effect, particularly among the elderly. Events not related to childhood conduct disorder included being mugged or beaten, having one's car quit running, being the victim of a theft or break-in, getting a serious illness oneself, or having someone in the household get ill or die. Events predicted by conduct disorder seem to be events that people might bring down upon themselves, whereas those unrelated to conduct disorder appear to be events over which people have little control.

"Masculinity" of Childhood Behaviors and "Masculine" Outcomes for Girls

We have found that even when girls had as many childhood behavior problems as boys, they were less likely than boys to develop antisocial personality and alcoholism as adults and more likely to develop disorders more typically feminine, such as depression, psychosexual dysfunction, and phobia. We were curious as to whether those girls with conduct disorder who developed externalizing disorders had had more masculine-like conduct problems in childhood as well. Although we showed earlier that the ranked frequency of behaviors were similar for girls and boys, we could divide girls' conduct problems into those more or less exclusively male to learn whether outcomes varied accordingly.

To divide the girls' behaviors into those that were more and less masculine-like, we compared the frequency ranks among males and females of the 10 symptoms asked about in all three sites. We divided the 10 symptoms into those that had higher ranks for boys, those with higher ranks for girls, and those where ranks were approximately the same in the two sexes (an average difference of less than one in the three sites).

Table 17.10 shows that four behaviors had higher ranks in males than females: vandalism, school discipline problems, fighting, and stealing. The three behaviors that ranked higher for girls were lying, running away, and substance abuse. Although boys exceeded girls with respect to each conduct problem, the difference was greatest for the behaviors called "more masculine," with an average of 9.5% more boys than girls having each of them; among the "least masculine" behaviors, the male excess averaged only 4.7%.

When we looked for differences in the psychiatric disorders in women predicted by the most and least masculine childhood behaviors, we found essentially no difference; all adult diagnoses were predicted by all behav-

Table 17.10

Ten Conduct Problems Inquired about in Three Sites: St. Louis, Baltimore, and New Haven

	Sum of ranks in 3 sites (range = 3–30)		Male–female differences in summed ranks	Male–female differences in 3 sites[a] (%)
	M	F		
"Masculine"				
Vandalism	22.0	28.5	−6.5	7
School discipline	11.0	17.0	−6.0	9
Fighting	17.0	18.0	−1.0	7
Stealing	3.0	4.0	−1.0	15
Average			−3.6	9.5
Least "Masculine"				
Lying	11.0	6.0	+5.0	7
Runaway	30.0	26.0	+4.0	1
Substance abuse	22.0	18.0	+4.0	6
Average			+4.3	4.7
Indeterminate				
Expelled, suspended	11.5	12.0	−0.5	9
Truant	11.5	12.0	−0.5	10
Arrests	26.0	25.5	+0.5	5
Average			−0.1	8.0

[a] Average difference between percentages.

iors (Table 17.11). The choice of behavior problems did not appear to help in understanding why women show the long-term effects of conduct disorder in a greater variety of diagnoses than men or why women with a history of conduct problems have a lower rate of the externalizing diagnoses than men.

DISCUSSION

We have found that women and men reported the same types of conduct problems to have been most and least common before the age of 15 years, and we have found that for both sexes there is a clear quantitative association between the number of such childhood behaviors reported and the variety of adult antisocial behaviors they admit to having committed since age 18 years, as well as their frequency of drinking and drug problems. Conduct problems of childhood are reported more frequently by each successively younger cohort. Since the behavior that has in-

Table 17.11

Diagnoses Predicted for Women with More and Less
Masculine Behavior Problems in Childhood

	Number of adult diagnoses predicted	
	Out of 3 internalizing[a]	Out of 4 externalizing[b]
"Male" behaviors		
Vandalism	3	3
School discipline	3	4
Fighting	2	4
Stealing	3	4
Mean	2.75	3.75
Less "Male"		
Runaway	3	4
Substance abuse	2	4
Lying	3	4
Mean	2.67	4

[a] Phobia, obsessive–compulsive, and depression.
[b] Tobacco, drug, alcohol, and antisocial personality.

creased the most is drug abuse, this increase is probably not entirely an
artifact of the increasing length of recall required with increasing age.
Another piece of evidence that there may have been a true increase rather
than an increase attributable purely to differences in reporting is the finding that conduct disorder predicts events within the last 6 months as well
for older women as for younger women. Since these events were equally
recent for all age cohorts, there should be no greater recall bias for older
than younger persons. If recent events had been accurately recalled by
both young and old, but childhood behaviors recalled accurately only by
the young, one would expect better correlations for younger persons,
assuming true associations remained constant.

Assuming that there has been a true increase in conduct disorder in
younger persons, we find no clear evidence for a convergence of female to
male rates. This parallel increase is, of course, possible only because
rates in boys are not yet so high that there is a ceiling on possible further
increase.

Although both sexes show a strong association between childhood behavior and the externalizing disorders, antisocial personality, and alcohol
and drug abuse, only in women do these childhood behaviors also predict
internalizing disorders, major depression, phobia, dysthymia, and obsessive–compulsive disorder. Women's overall level of non-antisocial symp-

toms is also more affected by conduct problems than are men's. This finding suggests that much female depression and related disorders may be secondary to alcohol and drug abuse. If so, an interesting issue is raised about psychiatric nosology: are the internalizing disorders truly separable from the externalizing disorders for women?

In our early work (Robins, 1966), we noted that there was little correspondence between the precise type of childhood behavior problem and its adult consequences. Rather there seemed to be a constellation of childhood behavior problems that predicted to a constellation of adult behavior problems, and the precise choice of behaviors in both age periods seemed to be largely a function of how deviant age and sex roles were defined at the time. For example, we noted that for girls, both theft and sexual activities in childhood were more likely to predict sexual and marital problems in adult life than theft, since theft was largely reserved to men. This same nonspecificity of particular behaviors was echoed in the current study. Girls' childhood behaviors tended to predict adult diagnoses of both the "masculine" (externalizing) or "feminine" (internalizing) types, regardless of the degree to which they were more or less typically masculine.

Finally, we found that if conduct problems have become more common, their predictive impact has not lessened. To verify this observation based on a retrospective cross-sectional study will require validation in objective records, since it is possible that our associations are inflated by respondents' simultaneous reporting on two distinct eras. That is, respondents with good recall may report high rates for both time periods; reluctant or forgetful respondents may under-report for both periods. However, if the finding is correct, one would predict that the youngest cohort, being still within the ages of risk for developing new adult disorders, will eventually have higher rates of psychiatric disorder of the externalizing type than preceding generations.

REFERENCES

Diagnostic and statistical manual of mental disorders, (3rd ed.). 1980. Washington, DC: American Psychiatric Association.

Hathaway, S., & Monachesi, E. *Adolescent personality and behavior.* Minneapolis: University of Minnesota Press, 1963.

Havighurst, R., Bowman, P., Liddle, G., Mathews, C., & Pierce, J. *Growing up in river city.* New York: John Wiley & Sons, 1962.

Jessor, R., & Jessor, S. *Problem behavior and psychosocial development.* New York: Academic Press, 1977.

Kellam, S., Simon, M., & Ensminger, M. Antecedents in first grade of teenage substance use and psychological well being. In D. Ricks & B. Dohrenwend (Eds.), *Origins of psychopathology*. Cambridge: Cambridge University Press, 1983.

Lefkowitz, M., Eron, L., Waldron, L., & Huesmann, L. *Growing up to be violent*. New York: Pergamon, 1977.

Morris, H., Escoll, P., & Wexler, R. Aggressive behavior disorders of childhood: A follow-up study. *American Journal of Psychiatry*, 1956, *112*, 603–612.

Pritchard, M., & Graham, P. An investigation of a group of children who have attended both the child and adult department of the same psychiatric hospital. *British Journal of Psychiatry*, 1966, *112*, 603–612.

Regier, D., Myers, J., Kramer, M., Robins, L., Blazer, D., Hough, R., Eaton, W., & Locke, B. The NIMH Epidemiologic Catchment Area (ECA) Program: Historical context, major objectives and study population characteristics. *Archives of General Psychiatry*, 1984, *41*, 934–941.

Richman, N., Stevenson, J., & Graham, P. *Pre-school to school: A behavioural study*. London: Academic Press, 1982.

Robins, L. *Deviant children grown up*. Baltimore: Williams & Wilkins, 1966.

Robins, L. Sturdy childhood predictors of adult outcomes: Replications from longitudinal studies. *Psychological Medicine*, 1978, *8*, 611–622.

Robins, L., Helzer, J., Croughan, J., Williams, J., & Spitzer, R. *The NIMH Diagnostic Interview Schedule: Version III*. Washington, DC: Public Health Service (PHS) ADM-T-42-3, 1981.

Rutter, M., Tizard, J., Yule, W., Graham, P., & Whitmore, K. Research report: Isle of Wight studies, 1964–1974. *Psychological Medicine*, 1976, *6*, 313–332.

Simcha-Fagan, O. The prediction of delinquent behavior over time: Sex specific patterns related to official and survey-reported delinquent behavior. In R. Simmons (Ed), *Research in community and mental health*, (Vol. 1). Greenwich, CT: JAI Press, 1979.

Stewart, L., & Livson, N. Smoking and rebelliousness: A longitudinal study. *Journal of Consulting Psychology*, 1966, *30*, 225–339.

Wadsworth, M. *Roots of delinquency*. Oxford: Martin Robertson, 1979.

APPENDIX: CONDUCT DISORDER QUESTIONS FROM THE DIAGNOSTIC INTERVIEW SCHEDULE (DIS)

Substance Abuse

1. Now I am going to ask you some questions about using alcohol. How old were you the *first* time you ever drank enough to get drunk? (NEVER = 00; BABY, INFANT = 02)

    ENTER AGE: ☐☐

INTERVIEWER:	IF 15 OR OLDER, SKIP TO Q. 2.
	IF LESS THAN 15, ASK B.
	IF "DK", ASK A.

A. Do you think it was before or after you were 15?

    Before 15   (RECORD 01 ABOVE & ASK B)
    15 or older   (RECORD 95 ABOVE & SKIP TO Q. 2)
    Still DK   (RECORD 98 ABOVE & SKIP TO Q. 2)

B. Did you get drunk more than once before you were 15?

    No 1
    Yes 5

2. Now I'd like to ask about your experience with drugs. (HAND CARD A*) Have you ever used any drug on this list to get high or without a prescription, or more than was prescribed—that is, on your *own*?

    No ....(ASK A) 1
    Yes ....(SKIP TO Q. 3) 5

A. Have you taken any other drugs on your own either to get high or for other mental effects? IF R SAYS ONLY ALCOHOL, TOBACCO OR COFFEE, CODE 1.

    No ....(SKIP TO Q. 4) 1
    Yes ....(ASK Q. 3) 5

3. How old were you when you first used (this drug/any of these drugs) on your own?

    ENTER AGE: ☐☐

    INTERVIEWER: IF YOUNGER THAN 15, SKIP TO Q. 3B.
                        IF 15 OR OLDER, SKIP TO Q. 4.
                        IF "DK", ASK A.

A. Were you younger or older than 15?

    Younger than 15 ....(RECORD 01 ABOVE AND ASK B)
    15 or more ....(RECORD 95 ABOVE AND ASK Q. 4)
    Still DK ....(RECORD 98 ABOVE AND ASK Q. 4)

B. Had you tried any of these drugs more than once before you were 15?

    No 1
    Yes 5

Underachievement

4. Now I'd like to ask about your life as a child. Let's begin with some questions about school. Did you ever repeat a grade?

    No ....(SKIP TO Q. 5) 1
    Yes ....(ASK A) 5

A. Did you get held back more than once?

    No, only once 2
    Yes, more than once 5

5. How were your grades in school—better than average, average, or not so good?

    Better than average ....(SKIP TO Q. 6) 1
    Average ....(SKIP TO Q. 6) 2
    Not so good ....(ASK A) 5

* See page 414 of this Appendix.

A. Did your teachers think you did about as well as you could or did they think you had the ability to do much better?

    Did as well as could ....(SKIP TO Q. 6) 3
    Could have done much better ....(ASK B) 5

B. How old were you when your teachers first felt that way?

    ENTER AGE &
    GO TO Q. 6 ☐☐

INTERVIEWER: IF R SAYS "DK": ASK C

C. Do you think it was before you were 15 or later than that?

    Under 15 ....(RECORD 01 ABOVE)
    15 or more ....(RECORD 95 ABOVE)
    Still DK ....(RECORD 98 ABOVE)

School Discipline

6. Did you frequently get into trouble with the teacher or principal for misbehaving in school? (ELEMENTARY, JUNIOR HIGH, OR HIGH SCHOOL)

    No ....(SKIP TO Q. 7) 1
    Yes ....(ASK A) 5

A. How old were you when you first got into trouble for misbehaving in school?

    ENTER AGE &
    GO TO Q. 7 ☐☐

INTERVIEWER: IF R SAYS "DK": ASK B

B. Do you think it was before you were 15 or later than that?

    Under 15 ....(RECORD 01 ABOVE)
    15 or more ....(RECORD 95 ABOVE)
    Still DK ....(RECORD 98 ABOVE)

School Expulsion

7. Were you ever expelled or suspended from school? (ELEMENTARY, JUNIOR HIGH OR HIGH SCHOOL)

    No ....(SKIP TO Q. 8) 1
    Yes ....(ASK A) 5

A. How old were you when you were first expelled or suspended?

    ENTER AGE &
    GO TO Q. 8 ☐☐

INTERVIEWER: IF R SAYS "DK": ASK B.

B. Do you think it was before you were 15 or later than that?

    Under 15 ....(RECORD 01 ABOVE)
    15 or more ....(RECORD 95 ABOVE)
    Still DK ....(RECORD 98 ABOVE)

Truancy

8. Did you ever play hooky from school at least twice in one year?

    No ....(SKIP TO Q. 9) 1

    Yes ....(ASK A) 5

    A. Was that only in your last year in school or before that?

        Last year only ....(SKIP TO Q. 9) 2

        Before last year ....(ASK B AND C) 5

    B. Did you play hooky as much as 5 days a year in at least two school years, not counting your last year in school?

        No 1

        Yes 5

    C. How old were you when you first played hooky?

        ENTER AGE &
        GO TO Q. 9. ☐☐

> *INTERVIEWER:*   IF R SAYS "DK": ASK D

    D. Do you think it was before you were 15 or later than that?

        Under 15 ....(RECORD 01 ABOVE)

        15 or more ....(RECORD 95 ABOVE)

        Still DK ....(RECORD 98 ABOVE)

Fighting

9. Did you ever get into trouble at school for fighting?

    No ....(SKIP TO Q. 10) 1

    Yes ....(ASK A) 5

    A. Did that happen more than once?

        No ....(SKIP TO Q. 10) 1

        Yes ....(ASK B AND C) 5

    B. Were you sometimes the one who started the fight?

        No 1

        Yes 5

    C. How old were you when you first got into trouble for fighting at school?

        ENTER AGE &
        GO TO Q. 10. ☐☐

> *INTERVIEWER:*   IF R SAYS "DK": ASK D

    D. Do you think it was before you were 15 or later than that?

        Under 15 ....(RECORD 01 ABOVE)

        15 or more ....(RECORD 95 ABOVE)

        Still DK ....(RECORD 98 ABOVE)

10. Before age 18, did you ever get into trouble with the police, your parents or neighbors because of fighting (other than for fighting at school)?

No .....(SKIP TO INSTRUCTIONS BEFORE Q. 10E) 1
Yes ....(ASK A) 5

A. Did that happen more than once?

    No ....(SKIP TO C) 2
    Yes ....(ASK B) 5

B. Were you sometimes the one who started the fight?

    No 1
    Yes 5

C. At what age did you first get into trouble because of fighting (away from school)?

    ENTER AGE &
    GO TO Q. 11. ☐☐

INTERVIEWER: IF R SAYS "DK": ASK D

D. Do you think it was before you were 15 or later than that?

    Under 15 ....(RECORD 01 ABOVE & SKIP TO Q. 11)
    15 or more ....(RECORD 95 ABOVE & SKIP TO Q. 11)
    Still DK ....(RECORD 98 ABOVE & SKIP TO Q. 11)

INTERVIEWER: ARE BOTH Q. 9 AND 10 CODED 1?
HH
☐ No ....(SKIP TO Q. 11) 1
Yes .... (ASK E) 5

E. Even though you didn't get into trouble for fighting, did you start fights more than once before you were 15?

    No 1
    Yes 5

Runaway

11. When you were a kid, did you ever run away from home overnight?

    No ....(SKIP TO Q. 12) 1
    Yes ....(ASK A) 5

A. Did you run away more than once?

    No, just once 2
    Yes, more than once 5

B. How old were you when you first ran away from home overnight?

    ENTER AGE &
    GO TO Q. 12 ☐☐

INTERVIEWER: IF R SAYS "DK": ASK C

C. Do you think it was before you were 15 or later than that?

    Under 15 ....(RECORD 01 ABOVE)
    15 or more ....(RECORD 95 ABOVE)
    Still DK ....(RECORD 98 ABOVE)

Lying

12. Of course, no one tells the truth *all* the time, but did you tell a lot of lies when you were a child or teenager?

> No ....(SKIP TO Q. 13) 1
> Yes ....(ASK A) 5

A. How old were you when you first told a lot of lies?

> ENTER AGE &
> GO TO Q. 13 ☐☐

> *INTERVIEWER:* IF R SAYS "DK": ASK B

B. Do you think it was before you were 15 or later than that?

> Under 15 ....(RECORD 01 ABOVE)
> 15 or more ....(RECORD 95 ABOVE)
> Still DK ....(RECORD 98 ABOVE)

Stealing

13. When you were a child, did you more than once swipe things from stores or from other children or steal from your parents or from anyone else?

> No ....(SKIP TO Q. 14) 1
> Yes ....(ASK A) 5

A. How old were you when you first stole things?

> ENTER AGE &
> GO TO Q. 14 ☐☐

> *INTERVIEWER: IF R SAYS "DK": ASK B*

B. Do you think it was before you were 15 or later than that?

> Under 15 ....(RECORD 01 ABOVE)
> 15 or more ....(RECORD 95 ABOVE)
> Still DK ....(RECORD 98 ABOVE)

Vandalism

14. When you were a kid, did you ever intentionally damage someone's car or do anything else to destroy or severely damage someone else's property?

> No ....(SKIP TO Q. 15) 1
> Yes ....(ASK A) 5

A. How old were you when you first did that?

> ENTER AGE &
> GO TO Q. 15 ☐☐

> *INTERVIEWER: IF R SAYS "DK": ASK B*

B. Do you think it was before you were 15 or later than that?

> Under 15 ....(RECORD 01 ABOVE)
> 15 or more ....(RECORD 95 ABOVE)
> Still DK ....(RECORD 98 ABOVE)

Arrest

15. Were you ever arrested as a juvenile or sent to juvenile court?

    No ....(SKIP TO Q. 16) 1

    Yes ....(ASK A) 5

    A. How old were you the first time?

        ENTER AGE &
        GO TO Q. 16 ☐☐

INTERVIEWER: IF R SAYS "DK": ASK B

    B. Do you think it was before you were 15 or later than that?

        Under 15 ....(RECORD 01 ABOVE)

        15 or more ....(RECORD 95 ABOVE)

        Still DK ....(RECORD 98 ABOVE)

Sex

16. How old were you when you first had sexual relations?

    ENTER AGE ☐☐

INTERVIEWER: IF R SAYS "NEVER": CODE 00
IF R SAYS "DK": ASK A

    A. Do you think it was before you were 15 or later than that?

        Under 15 ....(RECORD 01 ABOVE)

        15 or more ....(RECORD 95 ABOVE)

        Still DK ....(RECORD 98 ABOVE)

CARD A

Marijuana, hashish, pot, grass

Amphetamines, stimulants, uppers, speed

Barbiturates, sedatives, downers, sleeping pills, Seconal, Quaaludes

Tranquilizers, Valium, Librium

Cocaine, coke

Heroin

Opiates (other than heroin: codeine, Demerol, morphine, Methadone, Darvon, opium)

Psychedelics (LSD, mescaline, peyote, psilocybin, DMT, PCP)

Other

Author Index

Subject Index

A

Active–constructive personality and impulse control, 167, *see also* Impulsivity

Active–destructive personality and impulse control, 167, *see also* Impulsivity

Adaptedness, evolutionary, 14–15

Adler's four lifestyles, 166–168, *see also* Impulsivity

Adolescents
aggression and, developmental interactional view of, *see* Developmental-interactional view of social behavior, adolescent aggression
crime
male, 8
female, 8–9, *see also* Girls, conduct disorder in

Adrenaline level
aggression and
related findings, 70–71
unprovoked, 69–70
determination, 62–63
model, 63–66
study
empirical tests, 67–69
implications, 66–67
procedure, 60–61
results, 61–62

Age and television, 287–293

Age of onset, conduct problems in girls, 395, 396, *see also* Girls, conduct disorder in

Aggression inventory, Olweus
adrenaline and unprovoked, 69–70
testosterone and
physical, 53, 54
provoked, 55–57, 60
unprovoked, 55, 57–59, 60
verbal, 53–54

Ainsworth Strange Situation procedure, 24–25, 106–107, 108, 109

Alcoholism
conduct problems in childhood leading to, 396, 397, 400, *see also* Girls, conduct disorder in
in fathers, 349

Alertness regulating system, 63–69

Altruism
kin selection and, 16–17
reciprocal, 17–18
self-control and, 163

Animals and nurturant acts of very young children, 83–85

Animateness and very young children, 83, 88

Antisocial Personality Disorder, 179

Antisocial *v* prosocial behavior research, 1–2

Ants, kin selection in, 16

Anxiety regulating system, 63, 69

Arrow–Dot test, 150, 168

Arousal effects of TV, 308–309

Attachment to parents, boys *v* girls, 279–280

Attachment theory, *see* Infant–parent attachment